The Political Economy of Poverty, Equity, and Growth

Series editors
Deepak Lal and Hla Myint

A World Bank
Comparative Study

*The Political
Economy of Poverty,
Equity, and Growth*

Sri Lanka
and
Malaysia

Henry J. Bruton

in collaboration with
Gamini Abeysekera
Nimal Sanderatne
and Zainal Aznam Yusof

Published for the World Bank
Oxford University Press

Oxford University Press

OXFORD NEW YORK TORONTO DELHI
BOMBAY CALCUTTA MADRAS KARACHI
KUALA LUMPUR SINGAPORE HONG KONG
TOKYO NAIROBI DAR ES SALAAM
CAPE TOWN MELBOURNE AUCKLAND
in associated companies in
BERLIN IBADAN

Published by Oxford University Press, Inc.
200 Madison Avenue, New York, N.Y. 10016

Oxford is a registered trademark of Oxford University Press.

Manufactured in the United States of America
First printing February 1992

The findings, interpretations, and conclusions expressed in
this study are entirely those of the authors and should not
be attributed in any manner to the World Bank, to its
affiliated organizations, or to members of its Board of
Executive Directors or the countries they represent.

Library of Congress Cataloging-in-Publication Data

Bruton, Henry J.
    Sri Lanka and Malaysia / Henry J. Bruton.
        p.   cm. — (A World Bank comparative study. The Political
economy of poverty, equity, and growth)
    Includes bibliographical references (p.   ) and index.
    ISBN 0-19-520824-2
    1. Sri Lanka—Economic conditions.   2. Sri Lanka—Economic policy.
3. Income distribution—Sri Lanka.   4. Poor—Sri Lanka.
5. Malaysia—Economic conditions.   6. Malaysia—Economic policy.
7. Income distribution—Malaysia.   8. Poor—Malaysia.
I. International Bank for Reconstruction and Development.
II. Title.   III. Series: World Bank comparative study. Political
economy of poverty, equity, and growth.
HC424.B78   1992
330.95493—dc20   92-1243
                                                                CIP

Foreword

This volume is the third of several emerging from the comparative study "The Political Economy of Poverty, Equity, and Growth," sponsored by the World Bank. The study was done to provide a critical evaluation of the economic history of selected developing countries in 1950–85. It explores the *processes* that yielded different levels of growth, poverty, and equity in these countries, depending on each country's initial resource endowment and economic structure, national institutions and forms of economic organization, and economic policies (including those that might have been undertaken).

The Scope of the Comparative Study

The basic building block of the project is a coherent story of the growth and income distribution experiences of each country, based on the methods of what may be termed "analytical economic history" (see Collier and Lal 1986) and "political economy." Each country study provides both a historical narrative and a deeper explanation of how and why things happened. Each study also seeks to identify the role of ideology and interest groups in shaping policy.

Our comparative approach involved pairing countries whose initial conditions or policies seemed to be either significantly similar or significantly different. Although initial impressions of similarity or difference may not have been borne out on closer inspection, this binary approach offered a novel and promising way of reconciling in-depth case studies with broader comparative methods of analysis.

To provide this in-depth study of individual cases, a smaller number of countries was selected than is conventional in comparative *statistical* studies. We have serious doubts about the validity of inferences drawn from such cross-sectional regression studies about historical processes (see Hicks 1979). Therefore this project, by combining qualitative with quantitative analysis, has tried instead to interpret the nature and significance of the usual quantifiable variables for each country in its historical and institutional context.

To provide some unifying elements to the project, we presented the authors of the country studies with several provisional hypotheses to be considered in the course of their work. These concern the determinants of growth, the importance of historical and organizational factors in determining alternative feasible paths of growth to redress poverty, and the relative roles of ideas, interests, and ideology in influencing decisionmaking.

Our synthesis volume in this series discusses the extent to which these hypotheses were or were not substantiated in each of the country studies. The following list of the country studies and their principal authors suggests the range of the overall comparative study:

Malaŵi and Madagascar	Frederic L. Pryor
Egypt and Turkey	Bent Hansen
Sri Lanka and Malaysia	Henry J. Bruton and Associates
Indonesia and Nigeria	David Bevan, Paul Collier, and Jan Gunning
Thailand and Ghana	Oey A. Meesook, Douglas Rimmer, and Gus Edgren
Brazil and Mexico	Angus Maddison and Associates
Costa Rica and Uruguay	Simon Rottenberg, Claudio Gonzales-Vega, and Edgardo Favaro
Colombia and Peru	Antonio Urdinola, Mauricio Carrizosa Serrano, and Richard Webb
Five Small Economies: Hong Kong, Singapore, Malta, Jamaica, and Mauritius	Ronald Findlay and Stanislaw Wellisz

Many of these volumes will be published in this series by Oxford University Press. In addition, a volume of special studies on related topics, edited by George Psacharopoulos, will be published.

This Volume

Henry Bruton's study of Sri Lanka and Malaysia is concerned with two countries that have much in common in terms of size, resource endowments, colonial background, and the coexistence of a large plantation and mining export sector with a peasant rice economy. The expansion of the plantation and mining sector in the past centuries attracted a large number of immigrant Indian and Chinese workers and created "plural societies" consisting of different ethnic groups with different cultures and traditions.

Bruton has cogently argued that in such plural economies and societies the economists' usual notions of "growth" of gross domestic product per capita as an indicator of economic welfare and "equity," defined in terms of income distribution between the rich and the poor, require careful reinterpretation. The indigenous Sri Lankans and Malays are shown to attach a great importance to the continuance of the traditional ways of peasant life and to qualify the objective of maximizing the growth of gross national product as such. Similarly, greater significance is attached to income distribution among different ethnic groups than to the distribution of income between the rich and poor as such.

Starting from this perspective, Bruton has taken an independent view of the prevailing assessments of the economic performance of Sri Lanka and Malaysia. He takes a more tolerant attitude to Sri Lanka's policies of rice subsidies, arguing that while the "distortions" that result from them are highly visible and attracted criticism, they may in aggregate be no worse than the diffused and less visible distortions in resources allocated in other countries. However, he would not go along all the way with those who regard Sri Lanka as a "model" country, which has deliberately and successfully pursued policies of growth and equity. He suggests that Sri Lanka's egalitarian policies have been, so to speak, thrust upon it by historical circumstances and pressures and the constraints of the plural society.

Bruton also takes a rather cool attitude toward Malaysia's rapid growth through expansion of primary exports or maintenance of an open economy, emphasizes the need for capacity to transform through industrialization, and suggests a "protectionist" policy through exchange depreciation. He also carefully appraises Malaysia's New Economic Policy after 1970, which was meant to redistribute economic assets to the indigenous Malays.

In both countries he emphasizes the constraints within which government policies were made and seeks to evaluate the origins and legitimacy of these constraints.

Bruton has written a new, interesting, and sometimes provocative work. Even those who are unable to accept some of his arguments will find his stimulating work a much-needed, full-scale comparative study of Sri Lanka and Malaysia.

Deepak Lal and Hla Myint
Series editors

Contents

Acronyms and Abbreviations

CWC	Ceylon Worker's Congress
DID	Drainage and Irrigation Department (Malaysia)
FEEC	Foreign exchange entitlement certificate (Sri Lanka)
FELDA	Federal Land Development Authority (Malaysia)
f.o.b.	free on board
GDP	Gross domestic product
GMP	Guaranteed minimum price (Malaysia)
GNP	Gross national product
ICOR	Incremental capital output ratio
LPN	National Paddy and Rice Authority (Malaysia)
MARA	Council of Trust for Indigenous People (Malaysia)
MIC	Malaysian Indian Congress
MTR	Mid-term review (Malaysia)
NCC	National Consultative Congress (Malaysia)
NEP	New Economic Policy (Malaysia)
NOC	National Operations Council (Malaysia)
OECD	Organisation for Economic Co-operation and Development
PERNAS	National Corporation (Malaysia)
PES	Post Enumeration Survey (Malaysia)
PLF	People's Liberation Front (Sri Lanka)
RIDA	Rural and Industrial Development Authority (Malaysia)
RRI	Rubber Research Institute (Sri Lanka)
SLFP	Sri Lanka Freedom Party
TULF	Tamil United Liberation Front (Sri Lanka)
UMNO	United Malay National Organization
UNP	United National Party (Sri Lanka)

Preface

Our study of growth, poverty, and equity in Sri Lanka and Malaysia was begun in 1986. The objective was to examine these central aspects of the economic history of the two countries from their independence to 1985. The book was long in writing and even longer in being published, and now 1985 seems long in the past. Much has happened since 1985 that might be studied, but we do feel that our analyses of the pre-1985 decades still hold, and, indeed, that much of what has happened since 1985 supports our main themes.

The general approach and content of the book reflects the outcome of discussions and debates among the four authors. Although continuing discussion is difficult when two of the authors are in Sri Lanka, one in Malaysia, and one in the United States, we did manage a number of meetings and discussions together. Gamini Abeysekera and Nimal Sanderatne prepared a great deal of material on Sri Lanka, as did Zainal Aznam Yusof on Malaysia. This material, plus that emerging from our discussions, provided the basis of the final version of the manuscript. Although each person made contributions at every stage, Dr. Abeysekera and Dr. Sanderatne concentrated their efforts on the years after 1977 in Sri Lanka, and Dr. Yusof on the New Economic Policy and the period after 1980 in Malaysia. Fong Chan Onn was a member of the group in the early stages of the effort, and it is a pleasure to refer to his contributions.

I wrote the final version of the manuscript, but much of the language and many of the arguments were those of my collaborators. It was also unfortunately not possible for them to see the final edited version before publication. For these reasons it seems appropriate for me to assume the responsibility for the published version and to allow each of my collaborators the freedom to disagree with what actually is here. At the same time it is important to make clear that the effort was genuinely collaborative, and the present version is intended to be consistent with everyone's views and arguments.

Substantial parts of the manuscript were discussed at meetings with the editors and other authors of the series of comparative studies on "The Political Economy of Poverty, Equity, and Growth." These meetings were illuminating in a variety of ways and reflected rather sharply the lack of agreement among economists that exists on matters related to poverty, equity, and growth. Still we are grateful for the debates and the opportunity to learn a bit more.

Henry J. Bruton
Williamstown, Massachusetts

I Introduction

1 Purposes, Disclaimers, Cautions, and Definitions

It is easier to say what this book is not than what it is or even is intended to be. So we begin with the easier task. There have been numerous general economic surveys of both Malaysia and Sri Lanka in recent years. Malaysia especially has been the subject of several book-length studies of economic development and income distribution during the past decade. There have been fewer book-length studies of Sri Lanka, but articles abound. Sri Lanka has attracted a great deal of attention because its commitment to social welfare and income distribution has, since independence, impressed many observers as greatly significant, not only for Sri Lanka itself, but also for other countries. Within the World Bank, the project known as Evolution of Living Standards in Sri Lanka has produced several papers that examine various aspects related to growth and social welfare. The present study is not intended to be either a duplication or a summary of these readily available materials, nor is it an effort to update them or to discuss the issues in greater depth.

The principal reason for this book is to tell a story that centers around and illuminates issues identified as political economy, poverty, equity, and growth. The term "story" is used judiciously and purposefully to emphasize the existence of boundaries and a point of view—a theme that is to be explored and developed. A story does not tell everything—only those things that are necessary to inform the plot and develop the characters. The storytellers try to make their theme convincing or, if not convincing, at least relevant and, above all, interesting. Hypotheses are to be suggested and developed, employed and questioned, and occasionally abandoned. Insight and feel are as important as statistical series and formal, detailed analysis. At the conclusion of a section, chapter, or even the entire book, one should not expect to see a QED or even a "Voilà"! Rather it is hoped that one will have an urge to say "Ah, so" or, possibly, if we are especially successful in one or two places, an "Ah, yes."

The story is meant to be nonfiction, although data problems may

3

create a hint of fiction at some points. Data are, of course, a problem in all countries, and rarely do they measure exactly the theoretical concepts whose names they bear. To the extent possible, we have used the data accumulated and published by government agencies of the two countries. In instances in which these data are thought to be misleading or downright wrong, attention is called to that fact, and efforts are made to adjust or correct the problem where possible. In general, we believe that these data are reasonably valid in that they provide a fair general representation of what occurred in the two countries during the period being examined. All data for any country can be improved, and it might be useful to study data for Malaysia and Sri Lanka (and other countries) in detail to determine their shortcomings. This is not the purpose of this book, and we alert the reader that there are questions, especially in particular series at particular times, about the quality of the numbers we use. To repeat, the general picture is, we believe, acceptable.

Data are not the only source of ambiguity. Every term in the title of the study is, to some extent, ambiguous. The rest of this chapter attempts to lessen that ambiguity with brief comments on each of the concepts—poverty, equity, and growth. Political economy is sufficiently complex and so central to the approach that a separate chapter is devoted to it. No specific definition of a complex concept can be completely satisfactory, and throughout the book we will seek to make clear what it is we are talking about. Again, the idea of a story is relevant. No character is very interesting who is not somewhat ambiguous and open-ended, and malleable. So too it is for poverty, equity, growth, and political economy.

Throughout the book, we use the current names for the countries. Sri Lanka was Ceylon before 1973, and Malaysia was Malaya before 1962. As Malaysia, it briefly included Singapore. Most of the data, and essentially all of the analysis, apply to West or Peninsula Malaysia and largely exclude the two states of East Malaysia—Sabah and Sarawak. To include those two states would not modify the story in any significant way and would add greatly to the cost of gathering data. Using the present names seems much more agreeable than using the name that was in effect at the particular date or period that happened to be under discussion.

Now some comments on the other main concepts in our title.

Poverty

The literature distinguishes between poverty and inequality, although the latter is usually necessary for the former to exist. Poverty, sometimes called low-end poverty, refers to a living standard below some more or less arbitrary cutoff point. This poverty line may be based on notions of the physical requirements for continued existence or on some more socially determined considerations. In the latter case, there will always be poverty, unless income is perfectly equally distributed. In the former case, poverty could be eliminated, but rarely has it been in any country. The usual practice is for a government (or other) agency to announce that a given level of income per family member is necessary to prevent a family's being classified below the poverty level. Such a figure is usually higher than some minimum physical requirements would indicate, but is affected by such requirements as well as by social considerations.

Much is wrong with this approach, but it is also useful in a simple way. In instances in which income is so low that a family is deprived of basic necessities or important social conventions, it certainly suffers relative to families that are not so deprived. There are, however, many problems. Measurement problems are obvious, and we know that welfare, especially individual welfare, is not uniquely determined by income. There is ample evidence that many people opt for jobs that pay less than others available, opt for housing that appears to be lower in quality than other housing available, opt for more leisure rather than more work, and so forth. Similarly, people may be poor but have access to help in one form or another in times of difficulty—a common arrangement in many villages in many countries. In this case, poverty is much less of a burden than it would be were such help not available or not known to be available. Many factors determine why people are poor—more accurately, why people have a measured income below the accepted standard or poverty line.

Another point about a poverty line refers to its meaning over time. Those parts of social welfare that depend on accumulated or acquired knowledge are not usually lost when income falls. New information and understanding about health and medical care, sanitation, family planning, school attendance, and the like may have had their beginnings because of a rising income, but their continuation and spread often depend on learning and maintaining routines that are more or less independent of the level of income. Their diffusion among the population is also less related to income than is their creation. Thus, a level of real family income measured in 1980 may well represent significantly higher living standards than the same level did ten years previously. Nonetheless, because "poverty lines" are in part socially determined, new wants may appear before their satisfaction is possible, and unfulfilled wants tend to depress welfare, although physical living standards have improved.

Despite these qualifications and difficulties, poverty is an issue that must be considered. A development story that leaves poverty unexamined is an incomplete and unconvincing story, and a development experience that leaves poverty undisturbed is equally incomplete and unconvincing.

Equity

The notion of poverty is simple compared with that of equity. Economists tend to equate equity with the degree of equality in the distribution of measured income. This measure is of interest, but it is far from an adequate definition. The main difficulty arises from the fact that almost all societies have acceptable and unacceptable inequalities. Acceptable means that the observed inequalities of income are recognized as earned or as consistent with prevailing traditions, culture, and religion. Indeed, in some instances inequality is not even acknowledged by the members of the society, although an outsider—an "objective" observer—would "see" the inequality. All societies, less developed or otherwise, have conventions and practices that may not only allow, but actually insist upon, certain inequalities. These conventions and practices, these rules, are themselves sources of welfare and of tranquility, and their destruction in the name of greater equality of income may well result in reduced welfare, even if the greater equality is actually achieved.

Life-styles, including ideas with respect to employment, affect one's decisions and responses to opportunities. Perceptions of what is right and wrong emerge from prevailing traditions, shared historical experiences, and religious and moral commitments. Such aspects of a society change slowly in response to various stimuli, to learning, and to new and different contacts. The society whose organization and values are, in some sense, consistent and accepted, and, indeed, revered, may understandably resist changes that violate this consistency. Numerous observers in various contexts have referred to these issues. A quote from Alexis de Tocqueville (1856) reflects the general point. In writing of the continuity between earlier views and the ideas that dominated the late eighteenth century, de Tocqueville writes, "The torch which set Europe on fire in the 18th Century was easily quenched in the 15th. Arguments of this kind cannot succeed till certain changes in the conditions, customs, and minds of men have prepared a way for their reception" (p. 27). Later in the same book he writes, "It may be said with perfect truth that the destruction of a part of that system [feudalism] rendered the remainder a hundredfold more odious than the whole ever appeared" (p. 49). It is not, therefore, surprising, or "irrational," for individuals or for societies to reject changes that destroy, or appear to destroy, the consistency and the completeness of a prevailing system. This may well be true even if—as de Tocqueville's quotation suggests—the changes result in improved incomes, reduced income inequality, or increased employment.

A good example of all this is land development and reform. These large-scale projects uproot individual homes and entire villages. Anthropologists and sociologists have found reason to believe that loss of home, or loss of an established environment, imposes trauma—frequently severe trauma—on those affected (see Mair 1984, Scudder 1975, Cernea and Hammond 1980). Even where relocations appear better in some objective sense, there is usually resistance to the moves. There are many examples of peasants (or factory or other workers) complaining strongly that the landowner is not performing the role that tradition dictates he perform. Complaints are not about, for example, sharecropping as such, or even the terms of sharecropping, but rather about a principal person in the traditional arrangement not performing his assigned task. There are also examples of individuals who borrow from neighborhood moneylenders to whom they pay exorbitant interest rates rather than borrow from a government bank that is convenient. To explain such a phenomenon in terms of transactions costs or similar categorizations is simply to give it a name rather than attempt to understand its origins and rationale.

At the same time, it is also abundantly clear that most people react in one way or another to the lure of more money or the prospect of more money. They do so, however, within an existing set of institutions and rules, opinions, and perceptions that strongly and directly affect both the way in which various incentives work and the capacity of the actor to perceive the incentive. Responses that violate accepted equity rules or conditions are rejected or resisted, and policies that force a violation can be expected to reduce equity or at least to offset any apparent improvement in income distribution. These considerations may also affect people's capacity to see, to perceive economic opportunities, and to accept different responsibilities and assignments.

All of these arguments are greatly complicated by the presence of diverse ethnic groups in the society. Their presence means that there exist various histories, traditions, perceptions, and, therefore, different ideas of equity among the groups. And what constitutes equity among such groups is a matter on which understanding and insight are primitive, indeed.

There are no unique answers to all these issues, not even unique or convincing modes of analysis. This is one of the reasons that we tell a story, rather than apply or test a theory; it is also one of the reasons that generalizations are of dubious validity, and the reason that one must be cautious in advancing a particular point of view. What we try to do is discuss and examine, worry with and ponder over, considerations that appear to illuminate the many sides of the equity question.

In most instances, when we begin to discuss equity explicitly, we will begin with a discussion of the inequality and the change in inequality of the distribution of measured national income. From that beginning, an effort will be made to elaborate on other themes, explore other avenues that are relevant to the equity issues in the two countries. At virtually every step, not only in sections marked "equity," attention will be directed to matters that seem helpful to an understanding of these issues. It is in this way that we hope to learn and understand more clearly ourselves and to help readers appreciate these intricate issues with more clarity and depth.

Growth

The literature frequently distinguishes between growth and development. Growth refers to increases in gross domestic product (GDP) per capita, and development is a more general term that is associated with poverty, equity, and structural change. Growth in these pages refers to the growth of GDP or GDP per capita, as conventionally measured. Such a concept and its measurements are important despite the well-known difficulties and ambiguities. Everyone recognizes that GDP is not the same thing as welfare, but it is relevant to welfare. It is preferable to say relevant to, rather than a component of, because welfare does not seem to be decomposable into components (Little 1957).

The production of more goods and services offers new and greater opportunities and creates new potential. The opportunities and potential are, of course, for both good and bad. An important task of development is to ensure, or to try to ensure, that the new potential is realized in a way that results in a positive effect on social welfare. Most of the points made in the preceding discussion of equity are applicable in this context as well. Two additional points may be noted here, as they will be mentioned again in specific situations.

First, individuals often find ingenious ways to elude some of the damaging effects of poverty. They find satisfaction in a variety of "free" things—in sitting, in conversation, in socializing, in participating in the customs and events of the social system. Such people may actually experience few needs. Several observers (for example, Naipul, 1977) have argued that poverty in many societies was not really recognized until Western "objective" analysts pointed it out. For an individual who has low productivity, the cost of leisure is low. Why then not consume a lot of it? This argument does not mean that as income rises—as productivity increases—these same individuals will choose leisure over more income. It means that they find ways to increase welfare, to consume, although their measured income is very low. That people have established such consumption habits also means that new opportunities that impose new demands—that force a reduction of one kind of consumption, such as leisure, to achieve higher incomes and allow other forms of consumption—may be resisted or responded to more slowly than would be the case if no such changes were required. Custom and tradition are extremely adaptable to niceties and subtle distinctions and, therefore, can change when the demands of change are acceptable. How a traditional society changes has not been studied thoroughly by economists, and the temptation to assume that tradition and custom are static (and modernism dynamic) is strong. Colleagues in other disciplines assure us that such temptation must be resisted.

The second point follows directly. A high rate of growth of GDP may or may not lead to rapid increases in social welfare. Rapid growth is not the end; increased social welfare is the objective; and slower growth may well be more efficacious.

A capacity to increase the quantity of available goods and services raises the question of choice to a strategic level. Good choices require searching and learning, and experiencing growth is perhaps the best way, maybe the only way, to learn how to make choices that increase welfare. One may actually define the development objective in terms of creating a flexible, responsive social system in which search, discovery, and choice are inherent characteristics (Bruton 1985). It is the emergence of this kind of society that we seek as we study Malaysia and Sri Lanka.

2 The Policymaking Question

There are three main tasks that we seek to perform: the first is establishing as clearly as possible the way poverty, equity, and growth evolved in each country from its independence to about 1985. The second task is to explain how and why these variables did what they did during this period. In this undertaking, the greatest attention is given to the principal development strategies and policies followed by the two governments. The third task is to seek understanding and insight into the reason that certain policies were implemented. The last two assignments, especially the third, define or help to define the final term in the title—political economy. This chapter elaborates a bit on some of the issues associated with these policymaking matters. Because it is the why and how of policymaking that concerns us, we have identified the chapter as such rather than as political economy, which is a more inclusive term.

Both of the last two tasks have many dimensions. Hence, neither can be undertaken in a comprehensive way. The present discussion is meant to examine a bit more fully our approach to these questions and to set some limits on what is to be undertaken.

One may identify two categories of policies: the first refers to the broad overall development strategy or orientation that a nation follows; the second refers to the specific policies that it chooses to implement the broad strategy at various times over the years.

An example of policy orientation is the common one of "outward looking" in contrast to "inward looking" or export promotion rather than import substitution. Other examples would be a strategy based on industry or agriculture as the sector to set the economy in motion and pull it along, or the choice between a physical planning approach and the use of a market mechanism as the main instrument of policy implementation. Similarly, a government must make a decision about public and private ownership of the means of production. Evidently a country must make several of these choices. The strategy that a country chooses—or drifts into—is the result of a great variety of factors. There are few, if any, examples of a newly independent country carefully examining alternative strategies, and then choosing the one that calculations and deliberations have shown to be the most nearly optimal. Rather, a strategy emerges from historical and political considerations; from the policies and practices of the colonial government (where the country is a former colony); from the attitude and training of the first president or prime minister; from the state of the world economy, or the demand for a major export in the recent past; and, in some cases, from prevailing professional opinion.

In the following three background chapters, we provide some general information on these matters for our two countries. Given the experiences of the Great Depression and World War II and the interpretation of the consequences of colonialism that one found in most countries of Latin America, Asia, and Africa, it seems understandable that these countries would have tried to circumvent the world economy in some way, and to look, as well, for instruments other than the market mechanism to implement their policies. In addition, most economists, including those in international organizations, pushed planning of a very comprehensive sort. Similarly, the view that industrialization was essential to long-run development was widely held by policymaker and academic economist alike. The way to accomplish these objectives was to bar manufactured imports, and either to remove resources from agriculture or to mobilize both the unemployed and underemployed labor assumed to exist in the traditional sector to produce manufactures domestically. The major constraint that was recognized, indeed the only constraint in many instances, was capital, which could be acquired through foreign aid and loans.

This strategy, it is argued, was an understandable outgrowth—an integral part—of the history that produced the complex of circumstances that prevailed in the 1950s. The academic literature reflects basically the same vision of development. It was not until the latter part of the 1960s that attacks on the import substitution approach became common, and only in the late 1970s that lambasting import substitution became the thing for fashionable economists to do (Bruton 1970 and 1989). That is to say, it was not until major problems with the import substitution strategy had appeared and successful exporters emerged that economists began to insist that the outward-looking strategy was the preferred strategy.

The new strategy emerged, as did the old, from the circumstances that evolved in the postwar period in such a way that successful exporting seemed to solve a wide range of problems. Evidently, had other circumstances evolved—for example, had world trade not boomed, but rather, as many expected, returned to the 1930s doldrums—the successful exporters, the outward lookers, would have faired much less well, and the shift in the preferred strategy would surely not have occurred. One may also note that virtually no one in the late 1940s projected the world trade boom that occurred after 1950.

Broad strategy decisions are, therefore, made in a historical context and should be viewed in that light. It is also evident that criticisms of a strategy based on what actually happened are often misguided and unhelpful, and they frequently boil down to saying that because things turned out well the policy was right or because things turned out wrong the policy was wrong. Thus, one must try to re-create the milieu in which the strategy was established and evolved, and try to appreciate the various considerations that produced the decisions. All decisions are necessarily made in the presence of great uncertainty and outright ignorance and are necessarily subject to error. Similarly, so-called objective advisers, (especially from outside the country) are always incompletely informed and inadequately attuned to the many issues that are relevant in a given context. Economics in general, and development economics in particular, offers at best a "Blue Guide" that suggests useful questions, describes the general landscape, possible places to spend the night, and so forth (Solow 1984). The economic theorist can, indeed must, make simplifying (that is, unreal) assumptions, including often the assumption of complete knowledge. The policymaker does not have this luxury and must recognize and appraise the importance of many issues and problems that the economist can assume away. So the design of a broad development strategy is the outcome of a many-sided process, and one must be cautious about either criticism or praise.

The same set of arguments applies to specific policies taken within the context of a broad strategy. Policy changes almost always have implications that harm some groups in the short run or that are ineffectual until other things are accomplished. So to change policy—to devalue, to reduce tariffs, to raise interest rates, and so forth—has ramifications that are relevant to many parts of the economy and the government and, hence, affect the decision. Groups that are hurt by a policy change will oppose it and often can prevent a change from occurring. Governments frequently must accommodate special interests to remain in power, and it is difficult to criticize a government for trying to remain in power.

In democracies, as Sri Lanka and Malaysia are, governments are appropriately responsive to what the electorate wants, and electorates are frequently myopic and otherwise uninformed. Governments, even wise and honest ones, must then convince the electorate that certain policies, with short-run costs, have long-run gains. It is important to recognize that there is nothing necessarily nefarious about this state of affairs, but it is necessary to recognize that it exists. Just as there are various interests in the economy that must be considered, so it must be recognized that governments are not monolithic, and the policies that are implemented result from much compromise within the government. That this is true is in part a consequence of the nature of decisionmaking in any large organization (government or otherwise), and in part a consequence of the absence of complete information. Bargaining among agencies is very much an inherent part of policymaking, and must be considered in appraising policy. Perceptions of the world differ among informed people of good will; the capacity to hear and appreciate arguments differs as well. Advisers, outside and inside, are rarely in complete accord. Policymaking is, therefore, an exceedingly complex process. To criticize a policy without recognizing the role of the decisionmaking process is to omit one of the principal considerations that determine which policies are implemented at what time.

There is relatively little literature explaining the reasons that countries pursue "wrong" policies. Earlier it was suggested that the import substitution strategy of development evolved from both the history and circumstances of the Great Depression and World War II and the interpretations of the nature and consequences of colonialism. Given the widespread view at present that an export-oriented strategy is "right," it is useful to ask why so many countries have found it difficult or impossible to adopt such a strategy. There are many reasons, of course, and any generalization is dangerous, but disputes over narrowly defined economic arguments are frequently less important than other reasons. In particular, it may be emphasized that there is no correct policy, independent of the policymaking process and the ideas that pervade the community at the given time. Thus, the policy must be sought within this context and must be found there. The policy does not emerge from a model or from a theoretical argument, nor is it derived from the experience of other, more successful, countries. A correct policy is a feasible policy, and feasibility depends in part on the policymaking process.

An important aspect of the foregoing considerations is the identification of the objectives of the policymaker. In no government does an "objective function" in any specificity exist before the search for policy, and, as already seen, the notion of social welfare is a genuine can of worms. What national objectives are, and should be, is found during the policy search process, and the outcome is necessarily some unpredictable mixture of the preferences of a great number of officials and pressure groups. This is especially evident in those countries where ethnic, religious, regional, or other divisions in the population complicate the notion of a national policy and, even more so, the notion of equity. There is a conflict situation, but in the best of worlds, there is also a learning situation, out of which emerge new insight and understanding. Therefore, condemning one policy and praising another is a risky undertaking.

Rather, one might best look at the process or mechanism of policy-making and see what it reveals about the factors that determine decisionmaking. One of the most relevant characteristics of effective policymaking is the capacity to adjust—to respond as new data and information and argument appear. If ignorance is necessarily part of the environment and error is equally omnipresent, then the learning and adjusting of policy becomes especially important. If trial and error are inevitable, then it is the correcting of perceived error that is of interest, not the mere fact of its appearance—not the mere fact that results emerged that differed from those that were either anticipated or desired. (Bruton and Clark 1987 develop this argument in more detail.)

The question of society's objectives is relevant in numerous ways to the appraisal of policies and to the growth and equity story in general. Two examples may illuminate the specific content of the present discussion. As noted earlier, the debate between import substitution and outward-looking adherents has been moving in favor of the latter position, and countries whose policies fail to reflect this view are strongly and frequently chastised. Along with the emphasis on export promotion has been an equal emphasis on the use of the market mechanism as an instrument of policy.

But the use of the market mechanism is not independent of normative issues. In the industrial countries, market systems evolved along with other institutions and rules and ideas that have made them seem more acceptable and appear more natural. In the developing countries, many features of market systems were imposed by colonial powers and many more pushed by advisers, aid donors, and so forth on societies that have not experienced this evolutionary process. The policymaker must be sensitive to the fact that moral distaste for market mechanisms has remained widespread in these circumstances. It may help to note, for example, that many people in industrial countries reject proposals to allow firms to "buy" pollution, simply on the grounds that polluting is wrong (Kelman 1981). Buying friends or votes is seen as improper behavior, while sharing food with your neighbor or relative rather than selling it is seen as proper. These considerations are one reason that it is frequently difficult for policymakers in developing countries to understand arguments that depend primarily on the workings of the market.

The second illustration refers to the creation of wants. International contacts are often a source of ideas as to what constitutes the good life, and hence affect the composition of consumption. Wants stimulated in this way can often conflict with either customary behavior or the religious tenets of the importing society. Consumption is learned, as is production. These moral considerations may then affect the way in which a country shapes its trade policies and the way in which it thinks about openness, as well as with nationals' assessments of the welfare created by rising incomes.

Production is not the only thing that a country can protect. Identifying one country as pursuing an outward-looking strategy and another as inward looking is indeed often troublesome and misleading. For example, a very homogeneous society with a great sense of itself can tolerate freer trade without undesirable consequences (on consumption, life styles, culture, production, social and economic organization, and so forth) than can a new society characterized by great heterogeneity and little sense of what it believes to be its own heritage. When viewed from this broad perspective, it is not always clear how open, or closed, a society really is. Thus, to criticize a general strategy or a specific policy requires a feel or understanding of what it is the society really seeks to do, and this, for reasons given above, is a complex task.

Earlier it was noted that policies are often evaluated by what happens: things turn out well, so the policies must have been right. This is, of course, hardly acceptable. There are problems that right policies cannot resolve, and because a country is in trouble, or appears to the outsider to be in trouble, does not mean necessarily that it followed the wrong policies. In part, this is due to ignorance and to the fact that certain right policies—policies that would solve the problems—may simply not be possible or even known at a given moment; in part, it is due to the fact that certain objectives may not be achievable.

Technology is a good example. Malaysia has had considerable success in developing higher yielding strains of rubber. Was its policy unsuccessful because it failed to develop such a high-yielding strain that natural rubber could drive synthetic rubber completely off the market? Few observers would say that it was. Similarly, should one say that policy in Malaysia and Sri Lanka has been unsuccessful because it has failed to prevent ethnic tensions and disturbances? Probably not, although opinions might differ about this. Did population grow too fast because of wrong policies? Few would say it did. And so on. All of these considerations, however, were a major part of the objectives of the government, and of the factors that determine its success.

If it is nonsense to blame all problems on wrong policies, is it also nonsense to blame *any* problem on wrong policies? This is not a simple question. The burden of the preceding pages has been to emphasize that policymaking and policy evaluation are sufficiently complex that the simple categories, success and failure, are often not helpful. In particular, it is necessary to appreciate the great variety of constraints and objectives with which the policymaker must contend. Indeed, one of the most complex tasks is to determine the degrees of freedom that the policymaker has. A policymaker frequently has great difficulty seeing that more than one policy is actually feasible. In some instances there may well have been only one option, and the policymaker had no alternative available but to do what he did. In another instance there may have been numerous options available (available includes understanding the policy option and understanding that it is available) and the policymaker had a genuine choice. Then, of course, one must explain why the choice was made the way it was.

In light of all this, how can one proceed to study policymaking and its consequences in Malaysia and Sri Lanka? The overriding consideration would appear to be to try to view the world from the vantage point of the policymaker, to try to place oneself in the position of the policymaker. This helps the observer to appreciate why the policymaker acted in a certain way and to understand more clearly how the policymaker was constrained or thought to be constrained. Similarly, it helps to understand what the desired objective really is. Finally, it helps the analyst make appraisals that are more legitimate and that rest on firmer empirical grounds than simply saying that because given variables, for example gross domestic product (GDP), and exports grew well, policy was right, or because the country ran into problems, policy was wrong.

This approach has an important danger. The policymaker presumably makes decisions that are thought to be right given particular circumstances. If one understands why a policy was followed, must one also accept that it was right? This is a complex issue. One's final duty is to seek understanding, then to try to identify the options open to the policymaker. The latter is especially difficult. Emphasis is placed on understanding and the idea that from understanding can emerge improved approaches to policymaking. What is rejected is an approach that simply condemns policies that were in fact followed without reference to the context—prevailing and historical—in which policies were made and executed.

As we examine the policies followed in Sri Lanka and Malaysia, an effort is made to explain the reasons that policies were implemented, to evaluate that explanation, and to try to identify ways in which both policy and policymaking could be improved. Some observers believe that they know what the right policy for each country was. We do not. Therefore, we cannot condemn with confidence and so leave such condemnation to those who are more secure in their belief.

II Sri Lanka

3 Background to the Economy of Sri Lanka

This chapter provides a brief survey of those parts of the history of Sri Lanka that appear most important in understanding the policymaking environment at the time of independence and identifies the ideas that seemed to be most prevalent among the country's leaders.[1] As argued in the previous chapter, policymaking and policymakers do not exist in a vacuum, and the latter do not have a clean slate on which to write down a new policy. To understand Sri Lankan policy at independence requires some acquaintance with its history. Several points are noted:

- The origins of the modern plantation economy and its existence alongside a peasant rice culture
- The evolution of the increasingly diverse population
- The rise of religious nationalism
- The origins of the commitment to a large role for government in social welfare activities.

The Plantation Economy

The background most relevant to the story of Sri Lanka is that of the plantation economy. Experimentation with plantation crops began in the 1830s; by 1850 coffee had become the dominant crop, and production expanded rapidly. Demand for coffee in Great Britain and Western Europe was strong, and British tariffs favored Sri Lankan coffee relative to foreign coffee. (Sri Lanka had become a British crown colony in 1801.) This rapid growth of coffee was accompanied by the decline of the cinnamon industry. Cinnamon had long been the principal export commodity and a major source of revenue of the trade monopolies controlled by the state. Tea and coconut also began to appear as important plantation crops by the 1860s. Coffee's domi-

---

[1] The short review of some aspects of Sri Lanka's economic history in this chapter is based on a variety of generally available secondary sources, especially Snodgrass (1966), World Bank (1953), Wilson (1974), De Silva (1977), and Corea (1965).

nance was completely eliminated by a leaf disease that began to appear about 1870. Within a decade or so this disease had essentially eliminated coffee growing in Sri Lanka. Any slack in the development of the plantation economy caused by the collapse of coffee was more than compensated by the development of tea and coconuts, and, beginning at the turn of the century, rubber. The period from 1880 to the outbreak of World War I was generally a buoyant period for Sri Lanka's plantations, and by the end of it they dominated the economy. Virtually all of the tea and rubber was exported, as was much of the coconut. The commercial and financial activities, as well as transportation and other services that developed, were oriented toward facilitating this foreign trade. The government and its machinery were dominated by this sector. The large export sector, heavily concentrated and easily taxed, made it possible to expand and sustain welfare expenditures in both the colonial period and after independence.

The plantations and their related activities were largely controlled by foreign entrepreneurs and capital, and, important for the present story, employment was largely immigrant labor. The only resources that Sri Lanka itself supplied were the land and a climate suitable for these tree crops. Both coffee and tea are quite labor intensive in their cultivation. Tea especially requires regular attention throughout the year, but apparently fewer workers were needed per land unit for tea than for coffee. Rubber was much less labor intensive, and could be cultivated in a more relaxed fashion. Coconuts are even easier to cultivate than rubber, and they demand less regular attention.

Smallholders, rather than plantations, grow most of the coconut, and a much smaller proportion of coconut products are exported than is the case for tea and rubber. The acreage cultivated for coconuts is naturally much larger than that for rubber; the acreage for tea is even less than that for rubber. In any event, the main point of interest here is that the rapid establishment and evolution of the plantation sector in Sri Lanka created a great and continuing demand for labor, which was provided by Indians who migrated into Sri Lanka in substantial numbers. Snodgrass (1966, p. 25) estimates that by the 1880s approximately, 200,000 Indian estate workers and their families were more or less settled in Sri Lanka. There were additional Indians in urban areas. The total population for the entire island at this time was less than three million.

The Indians were Tamils. Though they traveled a relatively short distance to reach the plantation areas of Sri Lanka they brought a different culture, tradition, language, and history from that prevailing among the Sinhalese of Sri Lanka. They lived apart from the Sinhalese and, in time, emerged as a distinct group within the country. Sri Lanka's already multiracial society became more complex, as did the very notion of equity, to say nothing of its achievement. By the 1930s there were perhaps 400,000 Indians working the plantation sector. By independence in 1948, the Tamil Indian population was approximately 800,000—about 11 percent of the total population.

Why was it necessary to import labor in such enormous numbers? Why did the Sinhalese not work on the plantations? These are basic questions that affect numerous issues that in turn affect poverty and equity, as well as the kinds of policies that it has been possible to design and implement. Initially there were very few Sinhalese who worked on the plantations; by the 1930s, only 100,000 Sinhalese were counted among a plantation labor force of half a million. The living standards on the plantations were generally far below those in the villages, and in many instances Indian laborers were indentured so that they could not leave the plantations even had they wished to do so. The fact that Indians were willing to make the journey and to work on the plantations under these conditions suggests, of course, that living standards in India were even lower. Estates were essentially enclaves, cut off from the villages, which imposed significant hardships on Sinhalese who might work there, but much less so on immigrants from abroad. Indeed, for the Sinhalese to have been forced to live on estates—not to have lived in their villages—would have resulted in a major decline in their welfare, irrespective of any possible income effect. The plantation managers doubtless found the Indians more docile and less able to create difficulties over their treatment than the Sinhalese would have been.

Data on the incomes in the villages are apparently not available, but several people (Snodgrass 1966, p. 24) have noted that the incomes in the villages were not bad, given the bounty of nature. It would appear, however, that by the latter part of the nineteenth century the Kandyan Sinhalese may have been sacrificing measured GDP to stay in their villages and honor their traditions. Thus inequality of income, as conventionally measured, probably increased over time. Whether this increase in inequality represents a declining equity is another matter. Snodgrass also mentions another complication—estate per capita income was higher than village per capita income, but income in the estate sector was much more unequally distributed. This measured inequality was surely a result of including all estate personnel—superintendents and managers, as well as workers. Among the workers, mainly Indian Tamils, income was very equally distributed. In any event, the Kandyans opted in large part to stay put, and not join the estates—even as the Sri Lankan economy became increasingly dominated by them.

Peasant agriculture, therefore, continued alongside the estates with very little contact—economic, social, political, or other—between them. The plantations imported virtually everything (including much of their food), and exported virtually their total output. The village farmer raised paddy in quantities sufficient for his own needs. He may have had a coconut tree or two or possibly some rubber trees. His technology had changed only slightly over the years. Paddy yields in particular remained low and unchanged over long periods of time. The peasant economy, indeed their entire society, was dominated by paddy. As Snodgrass (and others) have noted, there was a certain mystique about paddy and a strong compatibility between a paddy culture and the other traditions of the peasant society. Similar situations have been observed elsewhere—for example, the cotton culture of the old South in the United States and the wine culture in areas of France and Italy. Birth and death rates were high and population growth was modest, especially so until around 1920. The estates went their own way, and production and export receipts enjoyed a fairly steady and rapid increase. In the traditional sector, however, there was little change over the decades in output, technology, per capita income, or anything else.

There was one other important feature of Sri Lanka's economy during these years. British interests dominated all commercial activities. As already noted, the British owned most of the plantations, the estate factories that processed the rubber, tea, and coconuts, the import-export trade, banks, and other service activities. There was, therefore, little opportunity for the evolution of genuinely indigenous industrial and commercial sectors. This dominance was partly a consequence of the colonial status of Sri Lanka until 1948, but this was probably not the most important reason. Given the dynamism of the estate economy, the imported nature of that dynamism, and the sharp separation of the indigenous village economy from the estates, the composition of the demand for commercial and industrial activities was such that it could not be met by resources available to the nationals of the country. In addition, a large portion of the profits of the estates were remitted abroad. It is also fair to say that the plantation way of life was considered by most of the Sinhalese to be less desirable and less rewarding than was the paddy culture to which they had long been committed. In a very real sense the following observation holds: during the 100 years or so preceding its independence, a composite of economic activities evolved in Sri Lanka that proved alien to almost everything in the country, except its land and climate. This notion is an essential element of the initial conditions with which Sri Lanka began its independence.

Ethnic Diversity

A brief comment on two other background characteristics is in order. The first refers to the pluralistic nature of the society at independence and the implications of that fact for ideas and policies for equity and growth. The second refers to some aspects of the political economy, especially as it affects views and attitudes toward the role of government in providing food and other basic needs to the population.

Throughout most of its history, Sri Lanka's population has been composed of diverse groups. This history is interesting and important, but only a few observations are relevant in the present context. From the earliest times social pluralism referred to the existence of two groups—the Sinhalese and the Tamils. The Sinhalese were Aryans and Buddhists, whereas Tamils classified themselves as Dravidians and were Hindus. These Tamils had long been in Sri Lanka and were distinct from those who were brought in during the colonial period to work on the plantations. This latter group is identified as Indian Tamils, and the first group as Sri Lankan Tamils. Both were mainly Hindu in their religion, but the two groups have distinct sociocultural backgrounds and histories. In general, the Sinhalese and Sri Lankan Tamils enjoyed peaceful relations in the early centuries, although there was not a great deal of socializing between them. With the coming of the Portuguese and the Dutch with their new religions and new languages, the social pluralism was made more complicated. Both of these European groups intermarried with the Sinhalese to a considerable extent. The descendents of Portuguese and Dutch who did not marry Sinhalese are usually identified as burghers, and their presence adds more complexity. With the beginning of British rule at the end of the eighteenth century, some efforts were made to increase communication among the groups as well as to lessen the isolation of the various geographic regions. These efforts did not succeed, and at least one historian, DeSilva (1977), thinks that they probably worsened relations. He goes on to say (p. 90), "It is as true to say that the social groups were inherently incapable of achieving integration as to say that exogenous forces beyond their control acted as insurmountable obstacles to integration."

As the British gained a dominant position, the Anglican church became the new established church, and this development seemed to create greater conflict among the western religious groups than existed previously. The activities of Western missionaries, not surprisingly, induced resentment and conflict among adherents of traditional religions. These confrontations indeed produced a greater cohesiveness among the Sinhalese than seems to have prevailed prior to the arrival of the British. Coexisting with this greater cohesiveness was an important division between Kandyans and the Sinhalese in the southwest region of the nation. The Hindus also resisted the Christian missionaries, but apparently less sharply, and they gained support from the Dravidian and other Hindu groups in south India. This support in turn raised misgivings among the Sinhalese Buddhists who feared a tight relationship between the Tamil Hindus and those in south India. Thus the presence of the British and their missionaries, in addition to other Protestant groups, generated a religious resurgence among Sri Lanka's traditional ethnic groups, which then induced considerable competitiveness among these groups, especially in education and employment (DeSilva 1977, p. 93).

The strongest resurgence of both Buddhist and Hindu religious groups occurred in the latter part of the nineteenth century and the first years of the twentieth. The Buddhist revival was to some extent supported by American and British Buddhist groups, and was especially important in the development of Buddhist schools to counter those of the Christian missionaries. The better schools of the country were almost all originally established by foreign church groups. The Buddhist resurgence resulted in Buddhism's becoming a major political force and contributed significantly to the emergence and rise of language politics.

Within both the Hindu and Sinhalese societies there existed a caste system. Among the Tamils the caste system was very similar to that in India and was particularly rigid with respect to the highest caste—the Brahmins—and the lowest—the so-called untouchables. The rigidity of the caste system helps account for the fact that many lower-caste Tamils were converted to Christianity. Though the Sinhalese had a caste system, it was much less rigid and was not a major barrier to social mobility. There was no Brahmin caste among the Sinhalese; the Goigama caste (farmers) was considered the highest caste, and it formed a large majority of the Sinhala community. It was the Goigama that appears to have dominated the political life of the country. Members of Parliament and of the cabinet were usually from this majority caste. It is of the utmost importance to appreciate that this group consisted mainly of landholders and farmers committed to agricultural fundamentalism. This commitment affected many aspects of Sri Lanka's development—especially those concerning land and land development and paddy farming. People of another caste, the Karavata, generally among the richest of the Sinhalese, were mainly associated with mercantile activities. No major caste seemed especially linked to manufacturing.

In addition to these groups, there were further sources of plurality created by the distinction between those with command of English and with an English education and those with neither. An English education was, by the beginning of the twentieth century, an absolute requirement for obtaining and holding any professional job or any administrative position in government or commercial activity.

Table 3-1, which shows data on males in five professions from the census for 1921, illustrates the kinds of imbalances that prevailed. The role of the burghers is especially stark, and apparently most of these

Table 3-1. Distribution of Males in the Population and in Five Professions, 1921

Group	Percentage in the population	Percentage in five professions
Sinhalese	76.0	46.0
Low-country	49.0	42.5
Kandyans	27.0	3.5
Tamils	13.3	31.9
Burghers	0.7	17.7
Muslims	7.9	1.8
Other	2.1	2.6

Note: The five professions are doctor, lawyer, engineer, land surveyor, and appraiser.
Source: DeSilva (1977), p. 95.

were Dutch burghers. The sharp contrast within the Sinhalese community is also important to note. The low-country Sinhalese, especially in the western province, had greater access to English education than did the Kandyans, and they also had other routes to profitable economic activities. It was they who led in the development of plantations by indigenous groups and who later became leaders in political activities. The Kandyans were also more directly squeezed by the evolution of the plantation economy and were therefore more acutely aware of the presence of Tamils in increasing numbers. The 13.3 percent of the population in 1921 who were Tamils include the estate workers, none of whom was in the professions. The ratio of professional Tamils to Sri Lankan Tamils was, therefore, well in excess of the 31.9 percent shown in the table.

A further distinction between the low-country and high-country (Kandyan) Sinhalese is relevant to the pluralism issue. The low-country areas—the maritime provinces—were under foreign rule (Dutch and Portuguese) long before the Kandyan kingdom was. The latter kingdom remained free of foreign rule and relatively isolated until 1815 when it was conquered by the British. This difference in status over such a long period (about 300 years) had consequences for differences in attitudes toward trade and toward foreigners in general. It meant, too, some differences in culture and social organization, because the foreigners must have had some impact over the years on the low-country Sinhalese that was not experienced among the Kandyans.

The Commitment to Social Welfare

The final issue in this review of the background of independent Sri Lanka refers to the well-known commitment of Sri Lanka to income equality and to poverty alleviation. What can be said about its origins and early history? Evidently there is no single, simple explanation. The intense commitment observed in Sri Lanka to such a fundamental issue must emerge from deep roots that have long been in place. The role of Buddhism is naturally highly relevant, as is the great hydroculture of ancient history. The long period of colonialism appeared to encourage cooperation and community feelings. At the same time a few recent events are equally crucial, and it is these that will be emphasized. For example, in 1947 at the time of independence approximately 56 percent of government revenues went for social services, whereas twenty years earlier the ratio had been 16 percent. Evidently something happened in that short period that produced a sharp change in the allocation of government revenues to the support of social welfare.

The relation between the ideas of welfare and social justice in Sri Lanka and the teachings and philosophy of Buddhism are of interest. Several observers have noted that what are considered to be basic needs in today's discussion were identified by the Buddha for the Sangha (priest) Society as the Sivu Pasaya (the four main needs), including clothing, food, housing, and health. For the monks, basic needs were not to be exceeded, and, given the idea of the Karma, incomes of lay people were often given less attention. In particular, there appears to have been little concern with increasing incomes or with any reforming zeal in traditional Buddhism. The need for education was not identified separately, since the primary objective of joining the Sangha Society was to learn and to preach. Another related characteristic was the ancient political philosophy of Sri Lankan kings, which directed that they govern the country according to the Dasa-Raja Dharma—the Ten Principles of Government. These principles explicitly and strongly emphasized equality, justice, and welfare. Ancient kings had Buddhist priests as advisers, and these traditions are woven into modern political institutions and principles of government.

The most explicit and directly relevant factor accounting for the commitment to social welfare seems to have been the introduction of universal suffrage in 1931. That universal (except for estate Tamils) suffrage began in Sri Lanka in 1931 is truly remarkable, and would require an explanation if space (and knowledge) were available. DeSilva (1977, pp. 81 and following) argues that universal suffrage, intertwined with the cultural heritage of Buddhism, was a principal force in the upsurge of nationalism. The emergence of this "religious nationalism" (DeSilva's term) and universal suffrage then produced the broad movement toward social welfare. The Great Depression of the 1930s was especially difficult for Sri Lanka, owing to the collapse of exports. For example, between 1929 and 1932, employment on the estates fell sharply. Data in Snodgrass (1966) show that between 1930 and 1933 more than 100,000 immigrant plantation workers returned to India. Workers in other sectors of the economy were equally hard hit. The initial reaction of the British officials was essentially to retrench further and reduce spending. As the depression wore on and the plight of large numbers of the population became increasingly evident, local governments took some ad hoc actions to find ways to help. To add further to the woes of the country, one of the worst outbreaks of malaria in history occurred at this time. By the mid-1930s tea and rubber prices began to rise rather rapidly, unemployment eased, and government revenue rose sharply. Thus the government had more money and faced great social and economic problems at the same time that nationalism was gaining strength. The government then began to move into social welfare activities in a significant way. The role of education and its unequal distribution (already noted) made education an obvious choice for attention, and because of its strategic position in religious and modernization issues, this attention created some controversy. Laws to protect workers and to provide them with other benefits, including a program of maternity benefits, were less controversial, as were land development programs.

More generally the political changes of 1931 allowed for the existence of, indeed created, a competitive political system and greatly increased political participation, reflected not only by the ballot, but in other ways as well. Throughout the developments from 1931 to independence, reflected in the Constitution of 1931, successive governments became increasingly responsive to the wishes of the people. With this responsiveness in full view, it is easy to appreciate that rival political parties would seek to outdo each other in finding ways to accommodate the voters. With the Constitution of 1931, the British granted what amounted to self-government, although the British governor still held veto power. This veto was never used to block policies that affected health, education, or land settlement. The political changes introduced by the Constitution of 1931 were indeed fundamental to understanding policy and the policymaking process after independence.

The majority of those elected to Parliament in 1931 were from the property-owning classes, but there were also several Marxists who were able to make their presence felt. Many of this latter group had been educated in Britain, especially at the London School of Economics, where they were influenced by Harold Laski (Oliver 1957, Kearney 1967). This group was especially active in trade union activities and among the more articulate urban electorate. These socialists were often potent advocates of the emphasis on welfare and in that respect were comfortable with more traditional attitudes and ideas of the role of government.

With the outbreak of World War II, the government assumed additional social welfare obligations, chiefly in the form of price controls and efforts to provide food and medical services at subsidized prices to an increasing proportion of the population. The presence of British military units in Sri Lanka provided ample revenues and made the financial part of these efforts relatively simple, but importing commodities was difficult. Given the widespread poverty, it was virtually impossible to end these activities at the end of the war even though financial resources became a major and continuing problem. The malarial epidemic of the 1930s emphasized for everyone the inadequacy of medical facilities in the country, especially in the rural areas, and the great need for additional expenditures to meet what then appeared to be unending malarial epidemics was evident to all. Finally, there was the memory for many, and written evidence as well, of the chronic destitution and near famine conditions prevalent in rural areas in the decades before World War I. Apparently conditions were more severe in the dry zones, where mostly Sinhalese lived.

Several conditions prevailed as Sri Lanka approached independence. There was universal suffrage that resulted in a nationalism linked closely with Buddhism and other traditions of the society. This nationalism emerged, partly as a result of resistance to the evangelical efforts of the missionaries of the colonial power combined with the importance to many of maintaining Sri Lanka as the great home of Buddhism. The harsh effects of the Great Depression on the country riveted attention on the problems of an economy so heavily dependent on a few exports. These harsh effects were deemed by many to be unnecessary and had been allowed to continue so long because the British were unwilling to act. Added to all this were the malarial epidemic of 1934, the war shortages, and the inequality in educational opportunities. Any group that sought to wrest control of the government from the British, therefore, could hardly expect to gain any popular support without making a strong commitment to an all-out effort to increase significantly social welfare in the society.

From outside the country there was the influence of the British political system on the views of Sri Lankan leaders. Especially important in this respect was the growth of the British Labour Party as well as the more explicit socialist-oriented policies that were advocated. The good relations between Sri Lanka and Britain contributed to the influence of the British example, and, of course, numerous Sri Lankan leaders had attended British schools and universities. The British system in general—and not just the Marxists educated in it—affected the thinking of Sri Lankans.

The government also had an obvious source of revenue from taxing the plantations. An unassailable political and economic strategy, therefore, emerged—tax large (mainly foreign-owned) plantations and use the revenues to subsidize food, health, education, and so forth for the Sinhalese population. The government then emerged as something of a transfer state and, unlike governments in other developing states, was not involved on a large scale in direct economic activities. Such a strategy had great appeal to everyone but, as argued later, did little to equip the Sri Lankans to survive independently when the plantations declined and ownership was changed from foreigners to Sri Lankan nationals.

It should also be noted that in this preindependence period, GDP growth as such was not a specific objective of government policy, although growth in the plantation sector was essential to permit the government to continue as a transfer state. While the plantations were prosperous and foreign owned, growth continued rather well.

4 The Initial Conditions: The Sri Lankan Economy in 1950

The General Picture

Table 4-1 shows the major macroeconomic indicators for Sri Lanka in 1950. Some very rough estimates of GDP in the late 1940s (Snodgrass 1966, p. 240) suggest that total output was increasing well in these years. The estimates made by Summers and Heston (1984) of real gross product per person in international prices give Sri Lanka a figure twice that of India and 80 percent that of Japan in 1950. When Summers and Heston consider the terms of trade, Sri Lanka's position is even stronger. The balance of payments is strong. The merchandise trade balance has a substantial export surplus, as does the overall current account. In both 1948 and 1949 there was a very small (Rs17 million and Rs34 million, respectively) export surplus. Foreign exchange reserves equaled nine months' imports, and the foreign debt was modest—less than 5 percent of exports. There was virtually no inflationary pressure because the government deficit was negligible and money supply growth was well under control.[1]

---

1. There is a debate in the literature on Sri Lanka about the extent to which Sri Lanka sacrificed growth of GDP to achieve low infant mortality and high levels of literacy, longevity, nutrition, and so forth. The argument, as usually stated, is that the levels that these variables reached in Sri Lanka were far more favorable than in other countries with similar levels of per capita income. This result has been achieved by direct action on the part of the Sri Lankan government. Other observers have argued, however, that Sri Lanka in fact inherited from its past favorable values for these "basic needs," and that little improvement has occurred since independence. So the favorable basic needs picture did not compensate for an apparent low rate of growth of GDP. The latter observers usually argue also that in the post-1977 period, when the government became more committed to a market strategy and (somewhat) less committed to direct social welfare outlays, the value of the basic needs variables generally increased. This group is, therefore, generally extremely critical of the policies followed by Sri Lanka from independence to 1977.

This debate has obvious links with the more general question of whether a growth strategy built on widespread reliance on market forces and open international trade is more effective in achieving social welfare than is one that seeks directly to meet social

Table 4-1 also shows the great dependence of Sri Lanka on the export of tea, rubber, and coconut products. In 1950 these three items accounted for more than 90 percent of total exports. The price of tea and rubber rose markedly in 1950 relative to 1949. The f.o.b. (free on board) unit value of tea jumped from Rs2.12 a pound in 1949 to an average of Rs2.56 in 1950, an increase of more than 20 percent. The average unit value of rubber more than doubled in the same period. Rubber production increased by 25 percent as both acreage and yields rose sharply, as did production per employee. Yields were up by 20 percent, and output per employee rose by 25 percent. The increased output of tea was much less spectacular, but there was some supply response to the favorable price. (Increased tea output was limited to some extent by international agreement.) Similarly, coconut prices rose somewhat as output remained fairly constant. The year 1950 and much of 1951 thus were a boom period for Sri Lanka's traditional exports—a boom strongly affected by the war in Korea. Demand for rubber in particular was affected by the Korean War. The central bank's overall export price index was 78 in 1949, 105 in 1950, and 127 in 1951. The terms of trade were, therefore, favorable in 1950 relative to 1948 and 1949 but probably less favorable than they were before the war, mainly because the price of rice was so much higher in 1950 than it was before World War II. The developments of 1950 in the balance of payments represented a sharp change from the years before and immediately after the war, when there was severe balance of payments pressure. There appeared no really basic change in the underlying situation. There was, however, some breathing room.

The suddenness of the balance of payments strength is also revealed in other ways. The national saving rate was almost 17 percent of gross national product (GNP) in 1950. In 1948 and 1949 it was probably less than 10 percent, although the data are extremely rough. This saving rate could not be absorbed by investment outlays, which amounted to less than 10 percent of GNP, approximately the level reached in the immediately preceding years. Imports, in current prices, jumped by about 13 percent but continued to be dominated by consumer goods,

---

welfare objectives and allows growth to take care of itself. Articles by Bhalla and Glewwe (1986), Glewwe and Bhalla (1987), Pyatt (1987), Isenman (1980 and 1987), and Sen (1981) address these issues in some detail.

The approach taken in the present study is much broader and attempts to identify more fundamental factors and to search for the historical forces that produced Sri Lanka's approach to development and to social welfare. Emphasis is, therefore, placed on ethnic issues, language, life-styles, religion, traditions, and similar things as well as on the distribution of measured GDP and the products and services that GDP can buy. Growth affects all of these variables in a way that directly affects social welfare, its perception, and its distribution. The very narrow question studied in the articles referred to in the preceding paragraph is viewed as an incidental in the larger, wider approach taken here.

Table 4-1. Macroeconomic Indicators of the Sri Lankan Economy, 1950

(millions of rupees, unless otherwise noted)

Indicator	Measure
GDP	4,169[a]
GDP per capita (rupees)	545
Merchandise exports	1,563
Tea	752
Rubber	405
Coconut	252
Merchandise imports	1,167
Balance of trade	396
Foreign exchange reserves	911[b]
Foreign currency debt	75
Current account balance	137
Price changes, 1947–50	
Colombo consumer price index (percent)	2.5
Colombo food price index (percent)	6.6
Money supply growth, 1947–50 (percent)	11.7
Government deficit	14
Percentage of GDP	negligible
Percentage of government expenditure	0.02
Demographic features	
Population (millions)	7.6
Population growth, 1945–50 (percent)	2.9
Labor force participation (percent)	36.9
Age distribution, 1953 (percent)	
20 and under	49.0
60 and over	5.0
Land area (square miles)	65,610

a. Rs17.1 billion in 1980 prices.
b. $191 million, the equivalent of nine months' worth of imports.
Source: Central Bank of Ceylon (annual) and other documents prepared in the Research Department of the Central Bank of Ceylon; Snodgrass (1966).

especially food products. Sri Lanka in 1950 was a major food importer—over 60 percent of the rice consumed was imported, as was 90 percent of pulses, currystuffs, dried fish, and so forth. In general about one-half of imports was foodstuff. The main factor explaining the high saving rate and low investment rate is doubtless simply a lag in response. It takes time to gear up for investment and to achieve an increase in consumption. At the same time it also suggests that neither the government nor the private sector was pressing against a saving or foreign exchange constraint. Also it would seem that the government at this time was not trying to undertake development projects and then find resources to implement them. The attitude toward the development question was more passive than it would be later.

Agriculture was the major economic activity. In 1950 it accounted for something less than 40 percent of GDP. The tea and rubber estates were strongly export oriented, were thoroughly modern activities, and were often foreign owned and managed. Over half the tea industry was foreign owned, as was about 40 percent of the rubber industry (Snodgrass 1966, p. 104). There were thousands of smallholders who produced a little tea, usually at yields very much below those of the estates. Some of the estates covered more than 1,000 acres, and the average (in 1951) was 835 acres (World Bank 1953, p. 229). Tea is said to have significant economies of scale, and apparently estates of fewer than 500 acres were generally less efficient than larger ones. The scale effect is discounted by others, but if there is no scale effect, the source of the advantages that the larger estates clearly had is not easily identified. Manufacturing was largely concerned with the processing of tea, rubber, and coconut products. There were numerous (small) tea factories, rubber mills, and coconut oil plants. There were machine shops that produced much of the equipment used on the tea and rubber plantations. There were also a variety of small-scale activities that produced consumer goods—matches, shoes, beer, and so forth. The first textile mill was established in 1883 and the first brewery in 1884. In late 1950 a government-managed cement factory began its operations, as did other manufacturing projects. Thus manufacturing activities were not entirely lacking, although they were far less important than agriculture. More important than their small size, these manufacturing activities seemed to have offered little opportunity for learning and little inducement to search.

A number of new manufacturing activities had been established during World War II. These were mainly government owned and operated, and appeared largely because of the curtailment of imports of manufactured goods owing to the war. The war provided a natural protection behind which manufacturing could take place. Although these activities were principally government owned, that fact seems more or less incidental and did not spring from any philosophical ideas of the role of government in industrialization. It did, however, set a precedent for such a role, and precedents matter in any society. Historical accidents account for many situations in many countries.

The employment data of table 4-2 show that labor productivity was markedly lower in agriculture than in most other activities—for example, the 60 percent of the labor force in agriculture produced 40 percent of the GDP. Labor productivity on the tea and rubber estates was higher than in agriculture elsewhere. Tea growing is an unusually labor-intensive activity, and estimated labor productivity is expected to be

Table 4-2. Other Indicators of the Sri Lankan Economy, 1950

Indicator	Amount (thousands) of rupees	Percent
Composition of GNP		
Private consumption	n.a.	72.7
Government consumption	n.a.	10.6
Gross domestic investment	n.a.	9.6
Exports	n.a.	39.6
Imports	n.a.	−31.3
Net factor payments abroad	n.a.	−1.2
Gross national saving as share of GNP	n.a.	16.6
GDP by industrial origin		
Agriculture	n.a.	38.9
Manufacturing	n.a.	10.6
Construction	n.a.	2.9
Transportation and communication	n.a.	6.3
Trade and finance	n.a.	18.0
Public administration and defense	n.a.	2.7
Employment		
Agriculture	1,484	59.5
Estates	668	26.8
Other	816	32.7
Manufacturing	193	7.7
Construction	50	2.0
Transport and communication	92	3.6
Trade and finance	298	11.9
Other	376	15.3
Total employed	2,493	100.0
Labor force	2,831	n.a.
Unemployed	338	11.9

n.a.   Not applicable.
Source: GDP composition data: World Bank, *World Tables;* employment and unemployment: Snodgrass (1966); composition of GNP: IMF, *International Financial Statistics Yearbook* (1984).

lower than in more capital-intensive activities. Productivity in manufacturing was not much higher than for the economy as a whole; it took 7.7 percent of the labor force to produce 10 percent of GDP. Labor productivity can differ because of difference in capital-labor ratios, in technology, or in the quality of labor. Labor intensity did vary greatly within and among sectors, but so also did technology and labor skills. The technology on the estates was much more advanced than in any other sector of the economy. The trade and finance category occupied a larger role in Sri Lanka in 1950 than in most other developing countries with its level of per capita income, mainly because of the large foreign trade sector.

The largest employment category was traditional agriculture, where the major crop was paddy. In 1950 there were hundreds of thousands of paddy holdings, most of which were extremely small, with land yields (and labor productivity) that were very low compared with estate agriculture and compared with yields in other rice-producing countries. The average size of paddy holdings varied widely among regions, and more than one-quarter of agricultural families possessed no land at all. The technology employed in paddy growing was ancient, and many of the conventional problems—dependence on the landlord for financing, holdings of an uneconomic size, inadequate marketing arrangements, and so forth—were present in abundance. Of the 816,000 people shown in table 4-2 as engaged in "other" (that is, nonestate) agriculture, almost all had some role in paddy production. Perhaps two-thirds or more of the population depended greatly on paddy. Yet Sri Lanka could produce only about one-third of the rice it consumed. This fact, in addition to the primitive nature of paddy cultivation in Sri Lanka, made paddy an obvious area for government action after independence.

Two other points in the employment picture are relevant to our story. One is that the data show a 12 percent unemployment rate. Even in 1950, Sri Lanka experienced a high rate of unemployment—a problem that has never been effectively resolved. The employment and unemployment data are from Snodgrass, who emphasizes that they are especially crude, but the figure seems to be legitimate, even somewhat low. Open unemployment was recognized as a serious problem at independence and has proved to be particularly intractable over the years since. The open unemployment was concentrated among young people, especially those seeking their first job. This fact eased somewhat the welfare consequences of the unemployment, but also added to its political and social implications. Snodgrass's data show a slight drop in unemployment in 1950 compared with 1949, another reason—though a slight one—that 1950 appeared to be a fairly good year. There are apparently no explicit estimates of underemployment for 1950, but there is no doubt that it was significant, especially in the traditional sectors.

The second point refers to the relatively large size of the wage earner category in Sri Lanka. In most developing countries with a large agricultural sector, the self-employed category (farmers) is much the largest sector. Paid employees in Sri Lanka about this time accounted for more than 60 percent of the number identified as employed (Snodgrass 1966, p. 324). The figure for Tanzania was less than 40 percent, for India less than 20, for Indonesia about 30 percent, and so on. Sri Lanka's distinctiveness is of course owing to the presence of the estates, where all workers were paid employees. This fact makes the consequences of unemployment more damaging because the work sharing that characterizes the traditional sector is not feasible on the estates. The predominance of the estates, therefore, made the task of providing for the unemployed more difficult than usual in agricultural societies. At the same time, the Indian Tamils (the estate workers) had essentially no political power nor were they in a position to pressure the plantation owners.

Data that tell us something about the quality of the work force around 1950 are difficult to find, but some bits and pieces are available that provide a clue or two. About 80 percent of men over fifteen years of age were literate as were probably one-half of the women in this age group. These figures mean that most peasants—the members of the great paddy society—were able to read and write. Between 55 and 60 percent of the 5–19 year olds were enrolled in some kind of educational program. So the work force appeared ready and able to undertake new activities and to learn new techniques. There were, of course, relatively few people with postsecondary education, but that fact may well have been an advantage in the Sri Lanka of 1950.

The work force and the population were growing fast. Sri Lanka had long experienced a relatively modest rate of population growth. The birth rate since 1900 had only occasionally exceeded forty per thousand and generally was in the high thirties. The death rate in this period also had been well below that for most developing countries. In 1900, for example, it was 27.6 per thousand and in 1940 it was 20.6 per thousand, while the (natural) population growth rate was 1.5 percent. In 1947 the death rate was 14 per thousand compared with 20 in the previous year; in 1948 it was 12.9, and the natural rate of population growth increased to 2.8 percent per year. In 1950 it was also 2.8 percent. The abrupt fall in the death rate was primarily a result of the increasing eradication of malaria. In the first half of the 1940s the death rate of infants under one year of age was twice the figure it was ten years later, 133 compared with 66. So the newly independent country was in the midst of a sharp spurt in population growth after a long history of very slow growth. This meant that the population was relatively young. Almost half were under twenty years of age in 1950, which meant that the work force was going to expand in the following decades. It would also have some impact on the equity and distribution issue.

Equity

Equity is an enormously complex topic and has many aspects. Perhaps its simplest component is the distribution of measured income, which is a convenient place to begin. There are no data for distribution for 1950, but there are some for 1953. These are summarized in table 4-3.

Table 4-3. Decile Shares of Income, 1953

Income decile	Spending units	Income receivers
Lowest	1.90	1.31
Second	3.30	3.56
Third	4.10	3.56
Fourth	5.20	4.37
Fifth	6.40	5.71
Sixth	6.90	6.31
Seventh	8.30	7.94
Eighth	10.10	10.39
Ninth	13.20	14.16
Highest	40.60	42.49
Gini coefficient	0.46	0.50

Source: Central Bank of Ceylon, *Report on Consumer Finances* (1953).

These data imply considerable inequality.[2] Data for the early 1950s for other countries are rare and rough, but where comparisons are possible, Sri Lanka appears to have had a more unequal distribution than most other countries. This is especially true at the lowest and highest income levels. It seems fairly clear that the share of income received by the lowest decile in Sri Lanka in 1953 was below that for Malaysia and India and probably the Philippines. Similarly, the share of the highest decile was higher for Sri Lanka than for the other countries. In particular the share of the highest 5 percent in Sri Lanka in this period was much larger than for other developing countries for which there is any evidence at all. Evidently there must have been a few people in Sri Lanka who were enormously wealthy compared with the rest of society. The eighth and ninth deciles received only modestly more than their 10 percent share, so income seemed to have been concentrated at the top 10 percent. The distribution among income receivers is somewhat greater than that for spending units. This is generally the case for most countries because of differences in the number of family members who earn some income.

The major source of this income inequality was the inequality in land holdings. In 1950 perhaps one-quarter of the farmers owned

2. These and other data in later tables were calculated from sample surveys. Included in the sample were Indian Tamils, the group with by far the lowest income. Estate workers' income in 1953 was about one-half that of nonestate workers. Distribution data without the Indian Tamils would be more helpful in showing the extent of inequality in the "real" Sri Lankan economy. It seems clear enough that the inclusion of the estate workers is an important factor contributing to the inequality. At the same time, there is no reasons to exclude this group, since they were a part of the Sri Lanka society and work force.

no land and one-half owned less than one acre (Weerawardana and Weerawardana 1956). At the other extreme there were the very large holdings of the estates. Considerable earnings were also made in trade, especially foreign trade, and in finance. There appear to be no data on the breakdown of land ownership by ethnic community. Because a very large proportion of the Sinhalese were peasants engaged primarily in paddy farming (supplemented in some cases by a little coconut, tea, and rubber), it seems safe to conclude that the majority of the Sinhalese owned very little land and were, therefore, in the lower income groups. The nature of the constraint that land constituted is difficult to pin down. Population density per unit of arable land was not especially high by Asian standards, but the existence of the large estates convinced many Sinhalese that they (the Sinhalese) faced a major land constraint. There are additional comments on this issue in later pages.

The other important aspect of the explanation of inequality is the diversity of wages. It is unlikely in any society that very high incomes come simply from high wages, but it is also clear that in most developing countries there is often significant inequality within the wage-earning groups. The large estate sector, with its low and uniform wage rates, is an especially important source of the very low income shares. This tendency was somewhat countered by various wage controls prevalent in Sri Lanka during this period. Minimum wages were set in several industries and these usually were the actual wages that prevailed. Data for 1949 in Snodgrass (1966, pp. 326–28) show that daily rates in tea and rubber growing and manufacturing activities and in copra manufacturing were reasonably similar for young male workers. Wages for female workers were lower than for male, but were also closely bunched. Skilled workers in engineering and most manufacturing activities would earn approximately twice what estate workers received. Printing, for some reason, seemed to be an especially lucrative activity because employees here received more than twice the amount that skilled workers in other activities received. Government employment was relatively well paid, but the main attraction of a job with the government was the prestige, as well as the security, that it bestowed. Most of the government positions required an education in an English language school, and it was primarily the higher income groups that had access to these schools.

Table 4-4 provides more specific estimates of some wage differentials that prevailed in 1953. These estimates indicate that the largest wage differential is that between beginning secondary schoolteachers and the average agricultural wage. The starting pay for a government clerk is also relatively high. Although no data are available that compare wage income for more experienced workers, the presumption is that it would be greater than that shown in table 4-4. It is doubtful,

Table 4-4. Wage Differentials, 1953

Job class	Factor differential over agricultural wage
Agriculture	1.0
Urban unscheduled labor	1.3
Government starting wage	1.7
Government starting clerical	3.2
Starting primary teacher	2.7
Starting secondary teacher	5.3
Engineering skilled labor (average)	2.0
Engineering unskilled labor	1.4
Agricultural wage[a]	52.0

a. Agricultural wage is the average of monthly earnings (in rupees) of the main occupations of unskilled and semiskilled labor in rural and estate areas.
Source: Richards and Gooneratne (1980), p. 45.

for example, that the wage income of secondary schoolteachers would maintain the rank it has in table 4-4 in a comparison with the wages of experienced skilled workers.

It seems plausible to conclude that the inequalities shown in table 4-3 for Sri Lanka in the first five or six deciles are owing primarily to differentials among wage rates, but above that the inequality results principally from differentials in property income. It is also relevant to our story to note that the income of people with an O-level education was on the average about three times that of people with only primary education.

An estimate of the share of national income that takes the form of employee compensation is even more difficult to make. Something in the range of 50 percent may be in the right league, if not the right ballpark. For example, one set of data for 1950 shows domestic factor income to be Rs3,780 million, and wage compensation of Rs1,816 million and an "operating surplus" of Rs1,964 million (Economic Commission for Asia and the Far East 1957). Other data are a bit different—sometimes more than a bit. This percentage will vary widely among sectors, and in some activities (for example, paddy farming) the distinction between wage income and operating surplus is very ambiguous. This ambiguity is especially apparent where the paddy farmers own their land. On the estates, the employee compensation share was, almost certainly, well under one-half. In trade and finance, it was doubtless more. Within the manufacturing sector, wage share would probably be quite high in the more traditional activities such as shoemaking, match production, woodworking, and so forth, but much lower in more modern plants that used imported machinery. There is, however, nothing in these estimates of the share of wages in national income that disputes the evidence of the inequality in the size distribution of income.

The preceeding discussion does not consider the government food—mainly rice—subsidy, which began during the depression and continued during the difficulties of World War II. Once established, a subsidy is difficult to discontinue, and the rice subsidy continued long after World War II ended. In the late 1940s, when the world price of rice fell from the high wartime levels, the government still maintained a subsidy, although the burden was then much less. During the Korean War, the government again tried to protect the consumer from rising prices by continuing the food subsidy. For 1950 the data in Snodgrass (1966, pp. 274–75) show that food subsidies were almost 10 percent of total government receipts; in 1951 they were 20 percent, and in 1952 they were over 25 percent. In 1953 when the government attempted to reduce these subsidies significantly, there was considerable unrest, and a change in prime ministers resulted. Although the particular external historical circumstances in Sri Lanka—the depression, the malarial epidemic, World War II, the Korean War—help to explain the increasing commitment to food subsidies, it is equally important to appreciate the specific characteristics within Sri Lanka that made their elimination so difficult. In 1950 food and other subsidies were well entrenched in the Sri Lankan economy.

Along with food subsidies, the government was heavily committed to providing education and health care to virtually everyone. The emphasis on education is explained in large part by the widely held view that education was the key to respectable jobs—that is, government jobs, and that inequality in access to education was a fundamental source of other important inequalities. Education outlays included funds to provide lunch to students in the vernacular schools—those schools where all classes were held in the Sinhalese and Tamil languages.

The expenditures on food, education, and health subsidies helped then to offset the income inequality. In the early 1950s the distribution of food (rice especially), the incidence of education and literacy, and the access to health care were far more equitable than for most other Asian (or other developing) countries. The greatest declines in the death rate took place in the late 1940s and early 1950s. Malaria eradication was extremely important in this reduction directly and indirectly because the debilitation produced by malaria often made people susceptible to other diseases. Also of great importance were the improved availability of food and medical services (Richards and Gooneratne 1980; United Nations 1976). Given the low level of per capita income and the inequality of its distribution, these achievements were almost entirely dependent on direct government support and organization. The World Bank emphasizes (World Bank 1953, p. 775) that in many cases the quality of instruction in the schools was very poor, especially so in the primary grades of the Sinhalese and Tamil schools. Health care, too, was far from perfect. Even so the results are an important aspect of Sri Lanka at independence. Data do not permit a measure of inequality that considers these numerous government subsidies and benefits, but undoubtedly they played an important role in modifying inequality and, especially, in reducing the costs of poverty. The general picture was that the economic process and the distribution of wealth produced a substantial inequality in the distribution of income, but the inequality and the attendant poverty were partially offset by a widespread use of various subsidies.

It may, however, be true that the inequality in income distribution was not generally perceived to be the most important source of inequity. In terms of accounting for the tensions and the unrest that prevailed, the deeply ingrained differences in the culture, the religious traditions, the mores, and life-styles among Sri Lanka's population were more important. The Sinhalese were generally convinced that the estate system had evolved at their expense. In an important sense, it seems clear that the Sinhalese would have greatly preferred to continue the rural life-styles of their paddy culture and exercise their great commitment to Buddhism and other traditions. The coming of the estates and of many thousands of Indians combined with their own very high natural growth rate made this continuation impossible. The very fact that "other" people were getting rich (or at least richer) was upsetting, even if they themselves were not especially keen on it. To seek more riches imposed, or would impose, changes in life-style that, it may be argued, were not completely compensated by the greater quantity of potentially available goods and services. Yet the presence among them of "others" who were taking advantage of Sri Lanka's natural endowments forced the Sinhalese to make such changes. They were less annoyed because they were poor in the GDP sense than because they felt pushed to act in ways—to begin to pursue a life-style—to which they basically objected.

Thus there was a great feeling of inequity based on extremely fundamental considerations of what a large part of the society wanted. Income inequality was an aspect of this, but its reduction or elimination would not have been sufficient to remove the main source of the perceived inequity. This is a complex issue, but is frequently discussed in the literature of both Sri Lankans and others. Ellsworth (1953) and Hanson (1959) especially emphasize this and similar points. They cite considerable additional literature and several surveys to buttress their position. (See also *The Economist*, August 13, 1983, for a short but clear argument along these lines.) This set of circumstances, in addition to others, such as religion and history, created feelings of antagonism by the Sinhalese toward the Tamils, which made any sort of amicable, secure pluralism exceedingly difficult to achieve.

Simultaneously, it should be noted that neither the Sinhalese nor the Tamils constituted a completely homogeneous group. Long before the British came, many Sinhalese had responded to the commercialism of the Portuguese and the Dutch and cultivated and sold tradable commodities, such as pepper, cinnamon, cloves, cardamom, and so forth. In addition, after the plantations were established, both groups, but mainly the Sinhalese, grew tea, rubber, and coconuts for the market on smallholdings. Fishing was an important activity for both groups. Finally, one should note that Tamils, too, were often reflective and content with a given place, and their caste system was more rigid.

All this means simply that there was considerable diversity, and resulting tension within the two main groups. This diversity, of course, adds to the complexity of policy design and implementation, and to the notion of equity. It also means that there existed the force for dynamism and change, albeit one of modest proportions, that arises from diversity. Indeed, one of the most fundamental changes in Sri Lanka over the years may well be these changes in attitudes and values and ideas of the good life. Such changes, it hardly need be stated, are difficult and contribute to strife and unrest.

Table 4-5 provides a breakdown of the population in 1953 into ethnic communities and religious affiliations. A very large proportion of the Sinhalese were Buddhists, and an equally large proportion of Tamils were Hindus. Available income data (from central bank surveys) show

Table 4-5. Population by Ethnic Community and Religion, 1953

Category	Population (thousands)	Percentage of total
Community		
Low-country Sinhalese	3,470	42.8
Kandyan Sinhalese	2,147	26.5
Sri Lankan Tamils	885	10.9
Indian Tamils	974	12.0
Sri Lankan Moors	464	5.7
Religion		
Buddhists	5,209	64.3
Hindus	1,611	19.8
Christians	724	8.9
Muslims	542	6.7
Others	12	0.3
Total	8,098	100.0

Source: DeSilva (1977), pp. 277–78.

that, except for Moors, burghers, and others, Sri Lankan Tamils had the highest average income per income receiver in 1953. Their average income was about 7 percent higher than that of low-country Sinhalese, 37.5 percent higher than Kandyan Sinhalese, and almost twice that of Indian Tamils. The last group worked mainly on the estates. A rough measure of inequality (the ratio of the median income to the average) suggests that the incomes of Indian Tamils and Kandyan Sinhalese were more equally distributed than were the incomes of Sri Lankan Tamils and low-country Sinhalese. It seems safe to say that in 1953 the most pervasive incidence of poverty was found among the former two groups. The Indian Tamils on the estates especially suffered widespread and severe poverty. It is useful to note that shortly after independence citizenship was defined to exclude this group.

Summary

By 1950 an independent Sri Lanka had moved away from the war-affected economy. The government that had led the country toward independence was heavily influenced by the approach and general orientation of the British. The export, estate-dominated economy was firmly in place, and alongside but definitely outside it was a genuine peasant paddy society and culture. Also present was the memory and appreciation of the trauma that could befall—and had befallen—the economy owing to external circumstances. More specifically there was the recognition that Sri Lanka had to import about twice as much rice as it produced to feed itself. At the same time, largely because of the war in Korea, the export-import, balance of payments situation offered some breathing room. There was also an appreciation of the rapidly growing population and the limitations on the availability of arable land. It was equally evident that there was a major unemployment and underemployment problem, as well as a complex array of job preferences. Income was unequally distributed primarily because of the distribution of property ownership, and large numbers of people were extremely poor. There was significant control of the estate sector by the British and other Europeans. Food subsidies and other welfare programs took an important percentage of the government budget outlays and offered considerable relief to those whose money income was very low. The subsidies were financed largely by taxing the plantations.

The government, therefore, performed as a transfer state, which greatly eased poverty and inequity and helped maintain a familiar lifestyle for the Sinhalese. Meanwhile this arrangement did essentially nothing to prepare the Sinhalese to take over and manage their economy once independence was achieved. Finally, the heterogeneity of the population—with respect to culture, religion, ideas of the good life, and many other things—was recognized, although it is probably correct to say that the depth of feeling on these issues was not fully appreciated by the new government. In such a situation and environment, which economic objectives and which kinds of economic policies made sense; which kinds were politically and administratively feasible?

5 Growth and Equity in Sri Lanka: A General Survey

The purpose of this discussion is to establish the broad outlines of the developments in the period from 1950 to 1985 with respect to the major economic indicators. Sri Lanka was an economy dominated by three major export commodities—tea, rubber, and coconut products. The foreign trade sector, therefore, was a prime mover or source of depression, and much of the discussion will center around developments in this sector, and how they affected the other variables of the system—growth, wages, employment, and especially income distribution. The following chapters will provide greater detail and more explicit consideration of specific policies and change. The present chapter also identifies the main elements in the story, the hypotheses and arguments that underlie later analysis.

Macroeconomic Variables

Figure 5-1 shows a number of changes in the trade sector over the period. From 1950 to 1975 both the trade balance and the current account balance moved relatively modestly around a zero balance. Foreign debt began to increase in the late 1960s, but did not really take off until after 1975. Because exports were unambiguously exogenously determined, they drove (or held back) the system. This meant that imports had to adjust to the availability of foreign exchange earned by the exports. Sri Lanka maintained a fixed exchange rate until 1967. It was not until November 1977 that Sri Lanka shifted to a floating exchange rate, but between 1967 and 1977 the exchange rate rose (the price of domestic currency fell) fairly consistently. From 1967 there was a foreign exchange entitlement scheme that was, in effect, a devaluation that applied to a narrow range of commodities. In these circumstances imports would move to keep the trade account and the current account in balance, and the volume of imports would vary with their world price. The effect on GDP and its rate of growth would depend on the relationship between imports and investment on the one hand

Figure 5-1. International Transactions for Sri Lanka, 1950-85

A. Terms of trade

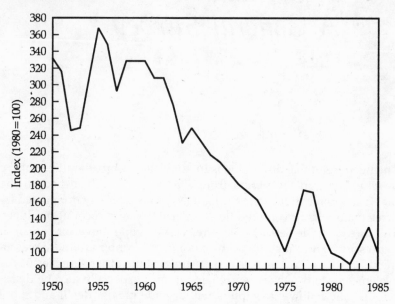

B. Current account balance

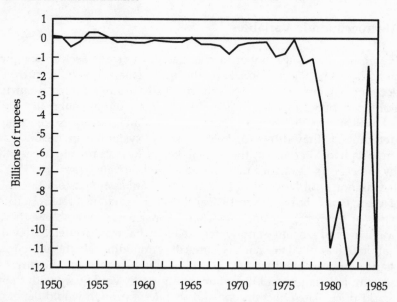

Figure 5-1. (continued)

C. Balance of trade

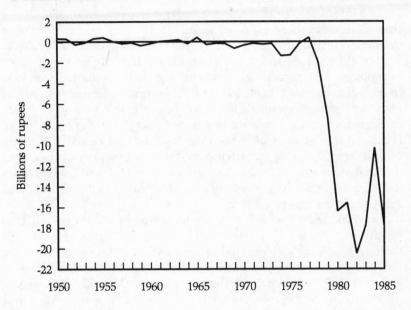

D. External debt

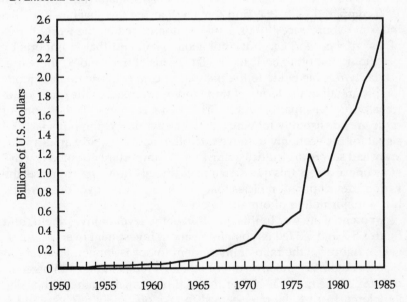

Source: A, B, and C, Statistical Appendix, Table A-4; D, Statistical Appendix, Table A-5.

and GDP on the other. As shown later this relationship appeared quite weak, at least until 1977.

In this situation it is expected that the volume of imports (and possibly GDP in constant prices) will move about sharply. Figure 5-2 shows that there were these expected sharp fluctuations in the volume of imports. The volume of exports, however, experienced relatively modest fluctuations as it was determined essentially by the capacity to produce. This capacity grew slowly, but fairly regularly, from 1950 to 1965 at an average annual rate of 2.3 percent, and then was about constant from 1965 until 1980 when it began to show some evidence of increasing. Such a balance of payments adjustment process is, of course, common to small economies that depend heavily on a few commodity exports as the driving mechanism. It will be argued later that one of the major objectives of successive Sri Lankan governments has been to modify the economy in such a way that this driving and adjusting mechanism is altered.

Part A in Figure 5-1 shows the terms of trade during 1950–85. This picture conveys a rather unambiguous message. From 1955 to 1975 the terms of trade deteriorated virtually without interruption. After 1965 the deterioration was quite sharp. There was a brief recovery in 1976 and 1977, and then the decline began again. In 1950–51 the export prices (mainly rubber) were favorable because of the Korean War, and the fall in the index from 1951 was owing to the ending of that boom. The index of the Singapore price of rubber was 62.7, 136.9, 214.5, 121.5, 85.3 in 1949–53. The price of rice—the major import—fell in 1950 compared with 1949 and remained at the low level in 1951. An index of export prices for Sri Lanka is dominated by the world prices of tea, rubber, and coconut until about 1980, and that of imports by rice, flour, and other basic foods. The terms of trade index, therefore, is a fairly reliable guide to the theoretical concept. The unambiguous long-term fall in the terms of trade index emphasizes the question of transformation capacity within Sri Lanka's economy. If the terms of trade are consistently moving against an economy, then this fact is a signal for the economy to move into other activities. Sri Lanka apparently had severe difficulties doing this. An important question is why? How one answers this question affects directly how one appraises the various development policies followed in Sri Lanka over these years. It is a major notion of our story.

A potential answer to this question is the level of investment, and figures 5-2 and 5-3 tell us something about investment over our interval. In figure 5-3 the ratio of investment to GDP is shown. From about 1956 through 1977 the investment rate hovered just under 15 percent. In 1969–72 the rate was higher, but did not remain at the higher rate very long. In 1978 the rate seemed to take off, and a rate very much above the previous levels was achieved and maintained through the end of the period under review. In the early 1950s the investment rate was—with the exception of one year—below 10 percent. A 12 to 15 percent investment rate is about the average of countries with Sri Lanka's per capita income in the 1960s and 1970s. The rate achieved after 1977 was well above the average for such countries, and, as will be discussed below, was owing mainly to the sudden availability of foreign loans and aid that occurred with the change in government in 1977. A 15 percent investment rate is a satisfactory rate for a country of Sri Lanka's level of per capita income, and one is entitled to assume that, after 1955, the rate of investment was not a bottleneck that restricted the economy. The growth of total investment (in real terms), shown in figure 5-2, is, of course, consistent with the performance of the investment-GDP ratio. It grows fairly constantly from around 1955 to 1970, levels off for several years, and then takes off strongly in 1977.

There are three things to note about the saving and consumption ratios shown in figure 5-3.

- The first refers to the sharp increases in private consumption in the early 1950s, late 1960s, and from 1977 to 1981. The saving rate, of course, moved in the opposite direction.
- Government consumption is of special interest. As a percentage of GNP, it falls more or less consistently from 1960 and never rises above 15 percent. It is the decline in this ratio after 1960 that is especially relevant to the story. In the early 1980s Sri Lanka had a lower public consumption–GNP ratio than almost any other country listed in the *World Tables* of the World Bank. In 1980, for example, the *World Tables* show only three countries—Bangladesh, Paraguay, and Hong Kong—with lower government consumption–GNP ratios. Government consumption expenditures, therefore, did not appear to be absorbing resources at a rate that could have impeded development.
- There appears to be very little relationship between investment and imports until after 1975. The initial impression is that investment was neither limited nor greatly encouraged by the capacity to import. Given the large proportion of imports made up of foodstuff, this result is not surprising. Even so, it is an important component of the investigation into why and how the economy moved.

It is also evident from figure 5-3 that foreign saving became extremely important after 1977. Both private consumption and investment as proportions of GNP rose sharply, so foreign saving also had to rise. The splurge in investment after 1977 offered opportunities and created problems. These general points on investment, combined with the terms of trade picture, point to additional and, in some sense,

Figure 5-2. GDP and Its Components for Sri Lanka, 1950-85

A. Volume of imports

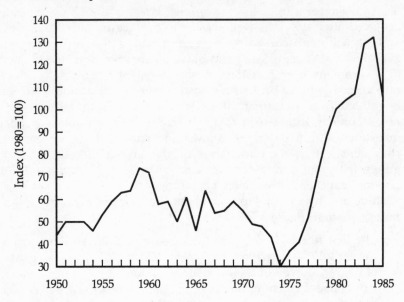

B. Volume of exports

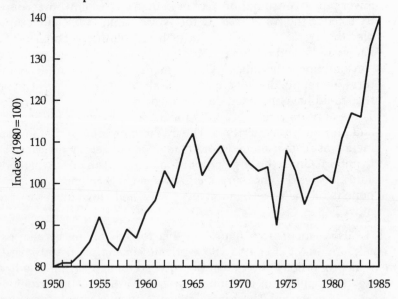

Figure 5-2. (continued)

C. GDP (in 1980 prices)

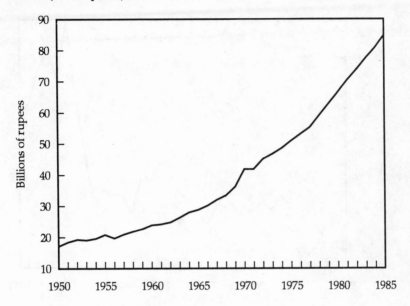

D. Investment (in 1980 prices)

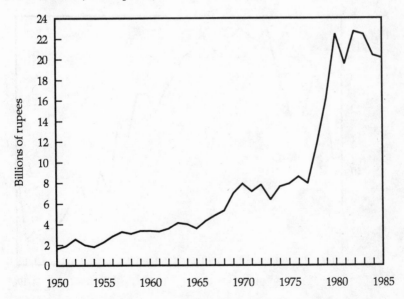

Source: A and B, Statistical Appendix, Table A-4; C and D, Statistical Appendix, Table A-1.

Figure 5-3. Macroeconomic Indicators for Sri Lanka, 1950-85

A. Investment - GDP

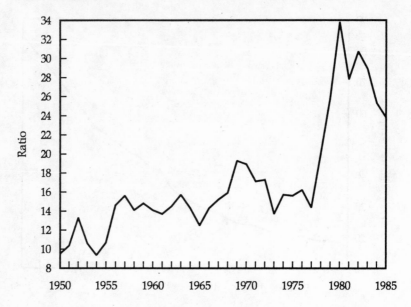

B. Government consumption - GDP

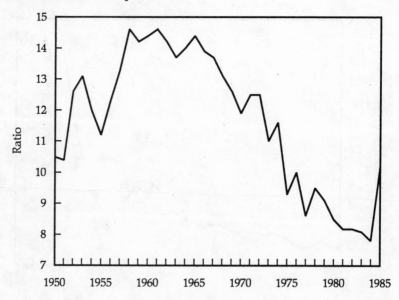

Figure 5-3. (continued)

C. Savings - GDP

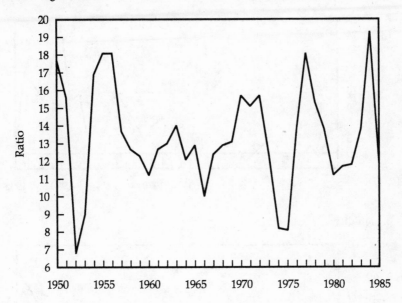

D. Private consumption - GDP

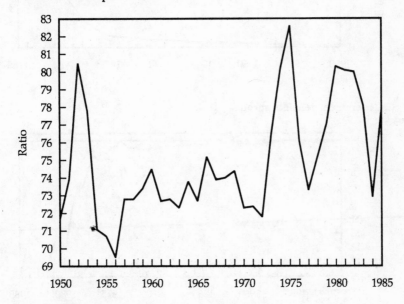

Source: Statistical Appendix, Table A-2.

Figure 5-4. Money and Prices in Sri Lanka, 1950-85

A. Change in the consumer price index

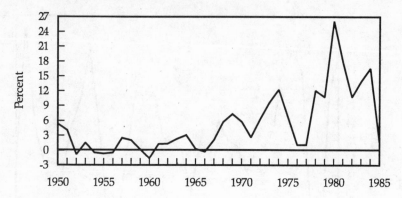

B. Liquidity

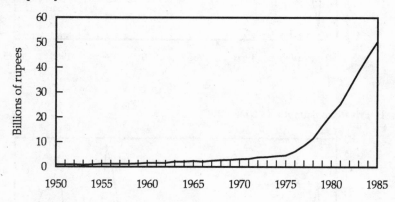

C. Government deficit or surplus

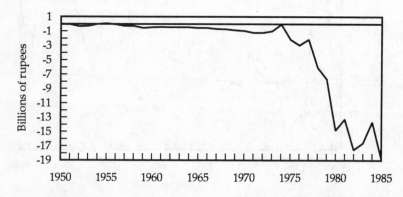

Source: Statistical Appendix, Table A-9.

more fundamental factors affecting growth. Two such factors seem paramount: transformation capacity along with entrepreneurship and decisionmaking in and out of government.

Figure 5-4 provides the general view of money supply, the government deficit, and prices. These three series indicate that changes began to occur around 1970. Sri Lanka had maintained rather remarkable price stability over the 1950s, and the 1960s were only slightly less impressive. The budget deficit was negligible and money supply growth modest by international standards. All of these series began to change markedly by 1970, and by 1975 the deficit and money supply were expanding at a rate much higher than anything Sri Lanka had experienced previously. The consequence was, of course, rapid price rises. Only consumer prices are shown on the chart, but the GDP deflator and wholesale prices would show a similar picture. In the years after 1975 the GDP deflator was increasing at a somewhat faster rate than either of the other series.

The final macroeconomic variable to examine is GDP in constant prices. It is difficult to identify any sort of specific relationship between GDP growth and that of either investment or imports and, at the present level of analysis, no simply stated growth mechanism is readily apparent. The search for this mechanism is one of the major objectives of the following chapters.

Over the entire period 1950–85 GDP in constant prices grew at an average annual rate of growth of about 4.5 percent. Over this same period population increased at an average rate of 2.1 percent, so GDP per capita grew at about 2.4 percent. The rate of growth was, of course, not constant over the period. There do not appear to be very clear-cut growth or nongrowth intervals, but some distinctions are possible. The period from 1950 to 1956 was one of mixed GDP growth owing mainly to the beginning and ending of the boom generated by the war in Korea. The sharp growth in 1951 was due largely to more intensive use of existing rubber capacity in response to its high price. Such intensive use became less profitable (or unprofitable) when prices fell as the war ended.

The years from 1957 to 1960 were years of solid growth of GDP, but were followed by four years of ups and downs, stops and starts. Except for 1965, the years from 1964 to 1970 were impressive in terms of GDP growth for Sri Lanka. The period from 1971 to 1977 was another period of stops and starts. These years are often identified as exceptionally unfortunate and by 1977 the economy was in extremely bad shape, but it is important to appreciate that there were good growth years mixed among the bad even in this period. In 1978 the GDP growth rate leaped up and remained well above average for the following several years. In the years from 1978 to 1985, however, the year-to-year growth rates declined in every year except one. This downward trend in growth rates—in the presence of very large inflows of foreign capital—is another strategic bit of data in any effort to understand the mechanism of growth in Sri Lanka.

The several macroeconomic series show the export-driven, import-adjusting economy fairly clearly. Equally clear is the change in this process beginning in the mid-1970s, a change owing in large part to the sudden availability of substantial amounts of foreign capital. The terms of trade deteriorated over virtually the entire period. The levels of investment, of saving, and of government consumption do not suggest that the availability of investible resources was ever a significant bottleneck to the establishment of new activities. The relationship between GDP growth and investment and between investment and imports is ambiguous, and requires additional study. Part of the ambiguity results simply from the fact that a large proportion of imports (45–50 percent until 1977) were food and drink. Finally, the growth rate of GDP was uneven over the period, but the frequently expressed view that Sri Lanka was (and is) a slow-growing economy is open to question. Especially relevant in appraising the growth rate are the numerous political and social developments over the years. The point now is to emphasize that simply asserting that Sri Lanka was a slow-growth economy from 1950 to 1985 is an incomplete statement at best and calls for considerable elaboration. The real task is to identify the sources of growth, and hence its stops and starts. The late 1960s and the years after 1977 seem especially interesting in this respect.

The charts show that sharp change began in the mid-1970s. The balance of payments changed, money supply growth accelerated, inflation appeared, government deficits and debts jumped, and so on. The basic underlying cause of this great change is this: The Sri Lankan economy had functioned as an export-driven economy for many decades. In the 1970s the essential way the economy functioned began to change. New activities appeared, foreign aid and loans increased, fiscal and monetary policies became more independent of the foreign trade account, and, more generally, the "control" provided by the dualistic, export, colonial economy greatly weakened. At the same time no firm source of control had appeared to replace it. The government was then confronted with unfamiliar issues and problems that it did not yet understand fully and did not have the experience to manage. So the economic indicators began to move in unusual ways. This argument constitutes another major issue in our story.

Before exploring these issues in detail, it is necessary to examine some developments in various sectors of the economy and in the equity of the system.

Sectoral Developments

Agriculture

Agriculture and manufacturing are the sectors of greatest interest. In 1950 almost 40 percent of GDP was classified as agriculture, including fishing and forestry. This ratio declined regularly to 28 percent in 1970. By 1975 it was back up to 30 percent, and hovered between 25 and 30 percent through 1985. From about 1970 on agriculture more or less maintained an unchanging share in the Sri Lankan economy. These ratios are all in current prices, but where constant price data are available they tell essentially the same story. There seems to be no breakdown between estate agriculture and peasant agriculture. Data for growth of output in constant prices are not available for the 1950s. In the 1960s World Bank *World Tables* show real output growing at an average annual rate of 3.0 percent and 3.2 percent in the interval from 1970 to 1982. These averages were well above those for most of the countries in the low-income and lower-middle-income groups. In the 1960s, 13 countries out of 33 had higher average growth rates for agricultural output, and in the 1970s (1970–82), 15 of 55 countries had higher rates. Year-to-year growth rates were, of course, uneven, and in several years output actually fell.

Figure 5-5 shows production indexes for rice, tea, and rubber and the Food and Agriculture Organization (FAO) agriculture production index. A comment or two on each of these series is helpful.

- Except for the years from 1960 to 1970, rubber production was decidedly weak and showed very little growth. At the end of the Korean War boom in 1951, prices fell sharply and remained relatively low until the mid-1950s. Prices in the 1960s were down compared to the late 1950s, and also rose again in the 1970s and early 1980s without eliciting much supply response. It would seem that something other than, or in addition to, world prices was affecting production.
- Tea appears somewhat stronger, but again hardly a leading sector. From 1950 to 1965 production of tea grew quite steadily, if not spectacularly. After 1965, however, it more or less maintained its level until 1970 and then began gradually to fail. Again price series suggest part of the explanation, but not all. One must look for other things as well.
- The paddy series is the most interesting and is of greater direct relevance than tea and rubber to the equity issue. From 1950 to 1970 output growth averaged over 6 percent per year and, with the exception of a few sharp deviations from the trend, the growth was quite steady. In the first half of the 1970s, except for 1974,

Figure 5-5. Agricultural Production in Sri Lanka, 1950-85

A. Rubber

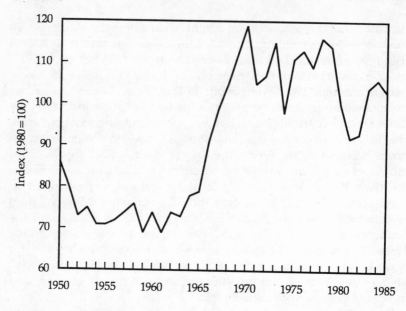

B. Tea

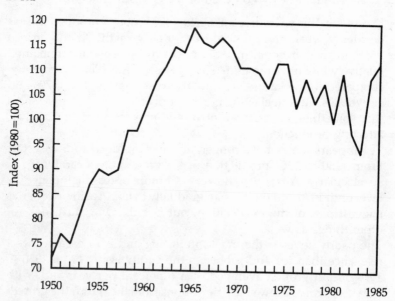

Figure 5-5. (continued)

C. Rice

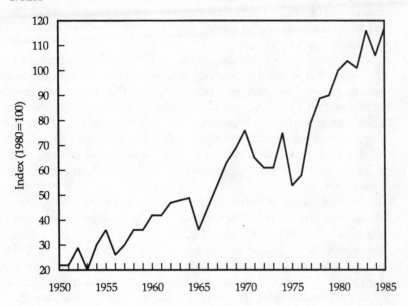

D. All agriculture

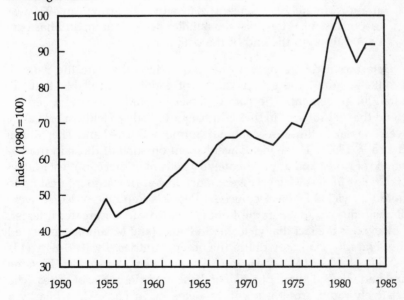

Source: Statistical Appendix, Table A-8.

production was generally falling (in large part because of adverse weather), but from 1976 on growth took hold again, although a leveling off in the 1980s is quite evident. There were fewer fluctuations in world prices for rice than for tea and rubber. In 1974, the year of the rice famine, the Burma price jumped threefold compared with 1973, but in general the prices moved much less abruptly. Again, other factors must be considered. The most important of these other factors are the new rice strains and the more productive sowing, harvesting, and weeding methods that were becoming available in Sri Lanka from other countries. By the early 1980s Sri Lanka was importing only about 12 to 14 percent of total rice consumption compared with one-third a decade earlier and two-thirds two decades earlier. The rubber and tea estates had always been modern sector activities; therefore a period of modernization was unnecessary.

- The overall index of agricultural output smooths out the sharper changes of the individual series and includes a variety of products whose output was relatively small. From 1950 to 1970 growth occurred in a fairly steady way, especially so after 1953. From 1953 to 1970 the average annual rate of growth of the agricultural index was about 3.2 percent, a figure that was higher than that for most of the other countries in the World Bank's low-income category of countries. In the early 1970s this growth stopped, but resumed again in 1974, and with the marked exception of 1976, continued until 1980. In the six years from 1974 to 1980 the index grows at approximately 6.8 percent year, although growth in 1976 was essentially nil. After 1980 the familiar decline set in, and has continued through the end of the data period.

Data on yields are open to more questions than are the data on production, and there is a variety of estimates available that are rarely in agreement. The data in tables 5-1 and 5-2 show a general trend that is probably in the right ballpark. Paddy yields in Sri Lanka were similar to those in Myanmar (formerly Burma) and Thailand in the early 1950s. These yields were about one-half of those in the Republic of Korea and approximately 70 percent of those in West Malaysia. Yields in East Malaysia were much lower. (It is also interesting to note that yields in the Democratic People's Republic of Korea were almost equal to those in the Republic of Korea.) Of greater interest, however, is the fact that yields in Sri Lanka (and Myanmar) increased more rapidly than they did in the other countries. By 1980–84 yields in Sri Lanka, West Malaysia, and Myanmar were more or less the same and had reached about one-half of those in the Republic of Korea. The relatively rapid growth in paddy yields in Sri Lanka is primarily a result of the increasingly widespread use of the new varieties of seeds

Table 5-1. Rice Yields, 1948–84

(hundreds of kilograms per hectare)

Period	Asia	Sri Lanka	Malaysia	Myanmar	Thailand	Republic of Korea
1948–52	14.4	14.2	19.3	14.3	13.1	36.2
1952–56	15.5	15.7	19.6	15.0	13.5	33.4
1961–65	20.5	19.1	25.0	16.4	17.6	41.1
1966–70	21.7	23.2	6.5	16.4	19.2	43.1
1970–74	23.3	23.7	29.3	17.0	19.0	47.7
1974–76	24.9	20.8	30.1	18.5	17.7	53.2
1977–80	27.0	23.5	27.3	16.2	18.9	60.9
1980–84	31.0	28.6	27.3	30.5	19.4	61.6
Rate of growth (percent)	2.1	2.2	1.1	2.3	1.3	1.7

Source: FAO, *Agricultural Yearbook*, various years.

and the greater use of fertilizer. At the same time the great difference between yields in the Republic of Korea and in Sri Lanka suggests that there are additional potentials for still further increases in yields, although climate does play some role in yields. Policy then becomes particularly important in light of the evidence that yield increases can be achieved.

A World Bank report shows higher levels of yields and higher rates of growth than those shown in table 5-1 for the period after 1970. These data show that yields fell sharply in 1971 compared with 1970 and stayed low until they began to rise from 1975. From 1975 through 1983 yields increased steadily at an average annual rate of 5.9 percent—a remarkably high rate by international standards. These data show an average yield of 3,288 kilograms per hectare from 1980 to 1983.

Table 5-2. Tea Yields, 1948–84

(hundreds of kilograms per hectare)

Period	Asia	Sri Lanka	India
1948–52	—	6.3	8.7
1952–56	—	7.0	9.2
1961–65	9.0	9.1	10.6
1969–71	7.5	9.0	11.7
1974–76	6.9	8.5	13.7
1977–80	7.7	8.3	15.2
1980–84	6.9	7.8	14.9

— Not available.

Source: FAO, *Agricultural Yearbook*, various years.

The yields for tea in Sri Lanka are well below those of India, but Sri Lanka yields do compare favorably with those for Asia as a whole. The main point is the absence of any significant increase in yields over the period. (For the years after 1970 the World Bank report shows higher yields than those in table 5-2, but no consistent increase.) Estimates of rubber yields are even more difficult to obtain, but those that are available do not show a consistent increase over the years. The slow and sporadic growth of total production and of yields of rubber and tea suggests that these activities were confronting major technological or demand obstacles. Output in other countries support this argument. Thus the yield of tea in the world as a whole fell from more than 1,000 kilograms per hectare in the early 1970s to fewer than 800 kilograms in the early 1980s. World output of natural rubber increased much more slowly in the 1970s than in the 1960s. Policies, of course, are relevant, but it seems clear enough that technology and demand problems are much more severe in the case of tea and rubber than in the case of paddy.

Manufacturing

Manufacturing accounted for about 10 percent of Sri Lanka's GDP in 1950 in current prices. This percentage reached 15 percent by 1955, and remained approximately 15 to 16 percent until 1970 when it began to climb. It continued to increase until 1977 when it reached 23 percent. From 1977 the ratio—in current prices—fell continuously until 1982 when it seemed to level off at approximately 14 to 15 percent. The general picture is similar in constant prices, but the ratios are almost always lower, and begin their decline earlier.

The manufacturing sector, therefore, was hardly a leading sector that pulled the rest of the economy along. There are no annual estimates for manufacturing in real terms until 1960; evidently the growth rate in the early 1950s was well above that of GDP, but the last half of the 1950s was less impressive. After 1961 the data show a sustained growth of 6.7 percent per year until 1971 when a marked reduction occurred. During the next six years there were three years of absolute decline and three of positive, but modest, growth. In 1978 growth was back up to the level of the 1960s, but immediately slackened, and the stop/go sequence was again in place. The big jump in 1984 (12 percent in real terms) is an exception to the general picture noticed in other series of the leveling off of growth rates in the 1980s. A good part of the increased manufacturing output in the post-1977 years was due to increased utilization of capacity. In 1974 approximately 40 percent of existing manufacturing capacity was utilized, and by 1984 the figure was 75 percent. Even so, the stop and go characteristic was still present.

Manufactured exports prior to 1970 were negligible, and in 1970 amounted to $30 million. They reached $375 million in 1983. In 1970 the major export items were fish and fish products, which accounted for well over $20 million of the total of $30 million. The major growth item, however, was garments. These amounted to about $3 million in 1975 and $197 million in 1983. Garments and petroleum products (largely bunkers and aviation fuel made from imported oil) accounted for $315 million of the 1983 total of $375 million of manufactured exports. In 1984 manufactured exports amounted to about $485 million, some 34 percent of total exports. Of this 34 percent, about 85 percent was accounted for by textile and garments and petroleum products. Ten years previously, in 1974, manufactures were 14 percent of total exports, and textile and garments less than 1 percent. Although manufactured exports began from a very low base, their growth rate is still unusually high compared with other countries in Sri Lanka's income category. The range of manufactured exports was naturally extremely limited.

One other aspect of the manufacturing sector of interest refers to the role of public enterprises. There seems to be no data that show a breakdown between private and public ownership of manufacturing activities over time. It is clear, however, that public enterprises have played an important role in the development of manufacturing activities in Sri Lanka since its independence. In 1979 available data show that value added in the private sector was about twice that in the public sector—Rs2.7 billion compared to Rs1.4 billion. (Billion equals 1,000 million.) Total employment was approximately 84,000 in the public sector and 77,000 in the private sector. The capital-labor ratios were 34,000 in the public sector and 18,000 in the private sector and the capital-output ratios 2.0 and 0.5, respectively. These data suggest that private sector activities used resources more productively than did those in the public sector. Such quickie comparisons must be interpreted with caution, however. Evidently, the type of activities is relevant. We know that capital-labor ratios and capital-output ratios vary widely among activities (and among sizes of activities) in any country. Objectives differ between public and private enterprises. In particular it seems evident that providing employment has long been a major objective of public sector firms. Levels of underutilization also vary between the two categories. It is not clear to what extent either public or private firms benefit from subsidies on various inputs and on infrastructure. It is, however, difficult to believe that the many politically motivated decisions have not had a negative effect on the capacity of the public sector firms to implement their specific assignments. Neither is it possible to determine how efficiently private firms pursue their objectives compared with firms in other countries.

This brief look at agriculture and manufacturing suggests that there

Table 5-3. Composition of GDP, 1950–85

(percent)

Industry	1950	1960	1970	1977	1983	1985
Agriculture	38.7	31.7	28.3	30.7	28.2	27.5
Manufacturing	10.5	15.4	16.7	23.2	14.0	14.6
Construction	2.9	3.9	5.6	3.3	8.6	7.8
Transportation and communications	6.3	9.0	9.5	7.9	11.0	11.1
Trade and finance	18.0	19.3	20.4	19.6	22.8	24.0
Public administration	2.7	4.4	3.9	3.5	3.6	4.3
Other	20.3	16.3	15.6	11.8	11.8	10.7

Note: Agriculture includes forestry and fishing. Ratios are calculated in current prices.
Source: For 1950 and 1960, World Bank, World Tables (1980, 1983, 1987); for other years, Central Bank of Ceylon, Annual Report, various years.

have been no sharp or continuing changes in the broad outlines of the Sri Lankan economy since its independence. Table 5-3 shows this reasonably clearly. It appears from the table that most (not all) of the changes occurred in the 1950s. Manufacturing as a proportion of GDP reached its maximum level in 1977 and declined each year thereafter. (The figure for 1977 is surely too high. In constant prices the percentages for manufacturing is 14.7 percent and that for "other" is 16.0 percent.) Although manufacturing as a proportion of GDP often grows slowly, it rarely declines consistently over a period of four or five years as apparently was the case in Sri Lanka after 1977. In agriculture, both tea and rubber had tough going, and only paddy showed much evidence of dynamism and growth. The yield data on these three activities were especially revealing. And there is the general reduction in growth rates in the 1980s, after the postliberalization spurt of the late 1970s.

Equity

Any sort of general survey of the way equity evolved over the period is not possible, given the great and unyielding ambiguity of the notion. We shall refer to only a few phenomena that either seem to be relevant to or help to illuminate the equity of a society and its change over time. We begin with the distribution of measured income with some reference (brief here) about how transfers affected that distribution. Then, a comment or two follow on employment and wage rates and, finally, some general observations about how the views of Sri Lankans toward equity changed over the decades under review. In later pages, attention will be given to other aspects of equity in the context of specific situations and policies.

Income Distribution

Table 5-4 shows the available data on the distribution of income in Sri Lanka, and its change over time. The nature and extent of the inequality of 1953 has already been discussed. (Note that the estimates here apply to spending units. Estimates for income receivers would show somewhat more inequality.) As measured by the Gini coefficient, inequality was about constant between 1953 and 1963, decreased sharply during the decade from 1963 to 1973, and then increased again to its 1953–63 levels in the late 1970s and early 1980s. The data for 1973 are, for reasons given later, quite misleading. Within the deciles, there were shifts not completely reflected in the Gini coefficients. The lowest decile experienced considerable reduction in its share between 1953 and 1963, and the second decile experienced a similar increase in its share. In addition, the top decile lost modestly to the next three highest. In the decade from 1963 to 1973, the shift was from the top to the bottom. The poorest decile gained proportionately more than any other group, but the lowest five deciles all gained at the expense (largely) of the top. In the increase in inequality that occurred after 1973, the lowest three deciles maintained some of their gains, so their share did not fall back to the 1953 level. Similarly, the top decile did not gain back all that it had lost, so its share in 1981 and 1982 remained somewhat below what it had been in 1953. The middle groups were, in the late 1970s and early 1980s, approximately where they were in 1953. These estimates do not suggest a consistent movement toward increasing equality in the distribution of income. What they do suggest is that over the period from 1963 to 1978 and 1979 there was first

Table 5.4. Decile Shares of Total Monthly Income, 1952–82

(spending units)

Decile	1953	1963	1973	1978–79	1981–82
Lowest	1.90	1.50	2.79	2.12	2.16
Second	3.30	3.95	4.38	3.61	3.55
Third	4.10	4.00	5.60	4.65	4.35
Fourth	5.20	5.21	6.52	5.68	5.24
Fifth	6.40	6.27	7.45	6.59	6.35
Sixth	6.90	7.54	8.75	7.69	7.02
Seventh	8.30	9.00	9.91	8.57	8.69
Eighth	10.10	11.22	11.65	11.22	10.71
Ninth	13.20	15.54	14.92	14.03	14.52
Highest	40.60	36.77	28.03	35.84	37.29
Gini coefficient	0.46	0.45	0.35	0.44	0.45

Source: Central Bank of Ceylon, Statistics Department (1984).

a major shift toward greater equality and then, an even more abrupt shift toward much greater inequality. It may be noted that the World Bank's *World Development Report 1984* gives income distribution by quintile for Sri Lanka for 1969 and 1970, and these estimates are essentially the same as those for 1973 shown in table 5-4. If this evidence is accepted, then the increased equality occurred in the late 1960s and held on until (at least) 1973, before giving way to the forces that generated inequality. Because the estimates for 1973 surely exaggerate the increase in equality, the most appropriate general statement is that over the years since independence income distribution has changed very little.

Table 5-5 is included to provide a later year perspective for Sri Lankan estimates. It is emphasized, of course, that the key consideration is the change over time, and there is not much data to show that for many countries. The data in table 5-5 show that income was more equally distributed in Sri Lanka than in the other countries shown. Only in Malawi did the lowest quintile receive a larger share than was the case in Sri Lanka. Similarly for each of the second, third, and fifth quintiles, there is only one other country for which the shares of the respective quintiles are larger. It possibly is worth noting that the share of the fourth quintile is more nearly equal to 20 percent than is the case for any other quintile in all countries. Indeed the (unweighted) average in this quintile is exactly 20 percent. As noted ear-

Table 5-5. Distribution of Income for Selected Countries in Selected Years, 1969–76

(percent)

Country	Year	Quintile					Top 10 percent
		1	2	3	4	5	
Bangladesh	1973–74	6.9	11.3	16.1	23.5	42.2	27.4
Malawi	1967–68	10.4	11.1	13.1	14.8	50.6	40.1
India	1975–76	7.0	9.2	13.9	20.5	49.4	33.6
Tanzania	1969	5.8	10.2	13.9	19.7	50.4	35.6
Kenya	1967–69	5.6	9.5	12.8	19.6	52.5	37.8
Philippines	1976	5.2	9.0	12.8	19.0	54.0	38.5
Thailand	1975–76	5.6	9.6	13.9	21.1	49.8	34.1
Peru	1972	1.9	5.1	11.0	21.0	61.0	42.9
Turkey	1973	3.5	8.0	12.5	19.5	56.5	40.7
Malaysia	1973	3.5	7.7	12.4	20.3	56.1	39.8
Korea, Republic of	1976	5.7	11.2	15.4	22.4	45.1	27.5
Brazil	1972	3.0	5.0	9.4	17.0	66.6	50.6
Sri Lanka	1969–70	7.5	11.7	15.7	21.7	43.4	28.2

Source: World Bank, *World Development Report 1984*

lier, in 1953 Sri Lanka's income distribution was more unequal than hit-and-miss data suggest was true of other countries.

Employment

There are several aspects of employment that bear on equity in general and on the distribution of measured income in particular.

- Participation in the labor force has changed very little over the years of independence. Available data show a slight decline over the period—from around 36 to 37 percent in the early 1950s to 34 to 35 percent in years after 1960. Participation rates among developing countries vary widely. Jordan, for example, had (in 1980) a rate of 23 percent and Côte d'Ivoire had 50 percent. Many countries also show modest declines in their participation rates over time. The main determinants of labor force participation are the age distribution of the population, the role of women in the labor force, and the demand for labor—that is, the extent of discouraged or fence-sitting workers. The proportion of the population under 14 years of age declined consistently over the period, from well over 40 percent in the 1950s to about 35 percent in the early 1980s. The proportion in the 15 to 64 age group, the working years, increased correspondingly. The participation rate of women rose very slowly after 1960, while male rates remained essentially unchanged. One other point is relevant to the story: the ratio of the number in the labor force to the number in the 15 to 64 age group is relatively low in Sri Lanka and declined regularly after 1960. (Possibly the decline began before 1960, but data are not available before that year.) The only countries for which this ratio (labor force over 15 to 64 age group) is smaller than it is in Sri Lanka appear to be those in which women participate on a very small scale. Sri Lanka's ratio was also well below that for all developing countries and for the countries in its income category. (These statements are based on data shown in various issues of *World Development* and various volumes of the World Bank's *World Tables*.) The low level and decline over time of this ratio bears on income distribution in two different ways: first, it has a downward effect on labor's share, and second, because participation rates vary among ethnic and income groups, income distribution among groups is affected as well.
- In the early 1950s about 60 percent of the labor force was engaged in agriculture and about 8 percent in manufacturing. By 1960 the ratios were 56 and 12, and have shown remarkedly little change since then. Thus there has been no major movement of labor out of agriculture into manufacturing. This is a bit surprising, espe-

cially for the 1960s when manufacturing output grew about twice as fast as agriculture. In the 1970s (as noted above) the stop/go pattern of growth would not be expected to attract labor out of agriculture.

Labor productivity was generally higher in manufacturing than in agriculture and was increasing more rapidly. Rough calculations show that between 1960 and 1980, labor productivity in agriculture grew at an average annual rate of 1 percent and in manufacturing at 2 percent. These data do not provide firm evidence that labor did not move sufficiently rapidly from agriculture into manufacturing, but they do tell us that a large amount of labor remained in an activity where productivity was growing very slowly.

• Some bits and pieces of data from Snodgrass (1966, p.325) indicate that nonagricultural wages rose at a very moderate rate until 1957. Wages in agriculture were fairly constant. The three series—nonagricultural, manufacturing, and agricultural—move together, but agricultural wage rates remained well below the other two series over the entire period. There is no evidence at all of a catching up. Wage controls were in effect, and their implementation and consequence will be part of the explanation of the observed changes in the wage series. Real wages in agriculture were essentially constant through 1971 except for an upward blip in 1968. Yet there was little exodus of labor from agriculture, partly because demand elsewhere was weak and also because many of the Tamils had few options besides agriculture.

• Data on the share of wages in national income over the time period are incomplete and probably not very accurate. They show a fairly constant proportion of national income, about one-half, made up of the wage bill. This rises in the late 1970s to 58 to 60 percent, but falls again. The share of wages affects income distribution only indirectly. If wage income is more equally distributed than is property income, then a rise in the wage share will result in increased equality in the community at large. It is, however, doubtful that this (possible) effect was operative in Sri Lanka to any extent in the years under review.

• Finally, a word on unemployment. A word is all that is possible at this stage as there are no complete time series available for the period. For the 1950s the Snodgrass (1966) series shows unemployment as a more or less constant—11 to 12 percent. The estimates available for later years also imply considerable unemployment. For 1968 a figure of over 10 percent is shown by the data in Richards (1971). The socioeconomic surveys have data as follows: 1973, 24.0 percent; 1978–79, 14.7 percent; 1981–82, 11.7 percent. There was also considerable underemployment as shown mainly by the small number of hours worked per week. The notion of unemployment and underemployment is ambiguous, of course, and the best of surveys convey information that has to be treated cautiously. We are entitled to assume, however, that the economy was never pressing against a labor constraint at any time in the period being considered.

Some More General Aspects of Equity

Inequality of measured income and poverty relief and the provision of employment opportunities are extremely important in the equity story. Other conventional measures are also relevant. Over the period, life expectancy at birth increased from approximately 55 years to more than 70, infant mortality declined from more than 80 per thousand to approximately 35, the literacy rate rose from approximately 60 per cent to almost 90, and calorie supply more than met requirements by the early 1980s. These changes reflect, in a rather direct way, the general approach toward development and development policy that prevailed in Sri Lanka after independence. Other factors were also at play.

The ethnic diversity of the community with the accompanying diversities of traditions, language, religion, and so forth posed difficult problems for defining an acceptable development strategy and development objectives that were consistent with equitable growth. The frequent disturbances, which were sometimes very severe, that occurred during the period call attention to these difficulties. The allocation of investment, especially the land development schemes, reflect an effort to support traditions that were deeply embedded in the Sinhalese society. In some instances, employment and output were sacrificed by investment allocations. In the discussions that follow, we will examine in some detail how the government coped with these great complexities, and, in particular, how investment allocation decisions were affected by considerations of the kind of society and life-styles that were perceived to contribute most to social welfare. The main point to be studied is how the policies followed by the government were affected by the search for the kind of equity that enables a community composed of diverse groups to live together harmoniously.

Summary

This brief review of the period, combined with the equally brief review of background and initial conditions has identified a number of key points. The discussion in the following sections will center around these points.

- The period was characterized by a modest rate of growth of GDP with considerable variations in year-to-year growth rates. The growth mechanism in Sri Lanka is unclear; in particular, it appears that a simple capital accumulation explanation is inadequate.
- The composition of GDP changed in the expected directions, but the changes were surprisingly modest, given the rate of growth of GDP. This is important because there were numerous signals that indicated that the economy needed a strong impetus from new activities—the declining terms of trade, the weakness of tea and rubber, and the continued existence of large-scale unemployment were all very evident signals.
- There is support for the view that the Sri Lankan economy was not pressing against any of the usually identified constraints—saving, import capacity, labor, or land. The ease of taxing estates was one reason for this situation. This point, combined with the previous one, suggests that there were entrepreneurial and transformation problems that impeded change.
- Sri Lanka was an effective democracy, and governments were responsive to the electorate. The history of economic troubles necessitated a strong and direct role by the government in the form of various welfare programs for any government that wished to remain in power. The effectiveness of the democracy also played a significant role in the decisionmaking process of the government, as well as its capacity to implement its decisions and policies. The frequent disturbances made the decisionmaking even more complex.
- The various series show a decided change in the mid- and late 1970s. Previously, the economy adjusted as an export economy. Exports, exogenously determined, drove the system and imports responded; periodic balance of payments–induced stops and starts were almost inevitable. Inflation was essentially nonexistent, there was no foreign debt, and macromanagement was fairly simple. After the mid-1970s, especially after 1977 when foreign capital became abundant, all this changed in a way that made fiscal and monetary policy more complex, and imposed new burdens on the government.
- The distribution of income probably did not change very much over the period if one accepts the argument that the 1973 data are misleading or that that year was something of an exception. The lower-income deciles increased their share a bit at the expense of the highest deciles, but these changes were modest. There were marked improvements in several components of any standard of living index over the period. The most obvious failures were the inability to solve the unemployment problem and to find the

means by which the diverse groups, ethnic and otherwise, could live in harmony.

- No specific, articulated "strategy" of development was established and implemented. The governments found decisionmaking difficult, and any sort of full commitment to a well devised policy essentially impossible.

Over the years the Sri Lankan economy failed to find an indigenous dynamic that would take up the slack resulting from the decline in the tea and rubber estates. This failure can be traced to several sources: an apparent "shortage" of transformation capacity and entrepreneurial talent; governments committed to the role of Transfer State, partly because of heavy pressures from the electorate; the governments were not well endowed with decisionmaking capacity and experience in making and implementing economic policies; and the inherent complexity of shifting an economy from an export-driven, import-adjustment economy dominated by foreign-owned estates to an independent, endogenously controlled economy. Added to this array of difficulties was a population composed of diverse ethnic groups with considerable differences in culture, history, traditions, and ideas about both the good life and what was wanted from development.

We turn now to a more detailed study of these issues in specific time intervals.

6 The 1950s: The Search for a Development Strategy

The years 1950 to 1985 in Sri Lanka were marked by a series of rather sharp changes in policy, and many of these policy changes were associated with changes in government. The two principal political coalitions more or less alternated in power over the years and were quite distinct in their ideas of appropriate development strategy. Many of the changes in economic policy were, therefore, the direct result of a change in the party in power. This was especially true after 1960. At the same time there were numerous policies, some quite basic, to which both parties subscribed. The coalitions are usually identified as the Sri Lanka Freedom Party (SLFP), a Sinhala nationalist left-of-center, more-or-less socialist group, and the United National Party (UNP), a more right-of-center, Western-oriented, multiethnic coalition party that also identified itself as socialist. The two parties took turns running the government.

From 1948 to April 1956. D. S. Senanayake, a leader in the independence movement, organized the first coalition, the UNP, and became Sri Lanka's first prime minister. He served until he was killed in an accident in 1952, after which his son, Dudley, became prime minister. The younger Senanayake, in turn, was forced to resign in October 1953, when his efforts to correct a balance of payments problem and to reduce a government deficit by cutting back on food subsidies resulted in serious social unrest and disturbances. Another leader of the UNP, Sir John Kotelwala, then served until the elections of 1956.

From 1956 to September 1959. The UNP was defeated in the 1956 elections by another coalition put together by S. W. R. D. Bandaranaike, who, until 1951, was a major supporter of Senanayake. The main party in this group was the SLFP, led by Bandaranaike, who then became prime minister.

From 1959 to July 1960. S. W. R. D. Bandaranaike was assassinated in September 1959, and there was considerable political instability (and three elections) between September 1959 and July 1960.

From 1960 to March 1965. The instability was resolved by the second general election of 1960 that put the SLFP back in power and made Mrs.Bandaranaike (S.W.R.D.'s wife) the prime minister.

From 1965 to May 1970. In Sri Lanka's sixth general election in March 1965, the UNP was returned to power with Dudley Senanayake as the prime minister.

From 1970 to July 1977. The alternating of parties continued, and in the 1970 election the UNP was defeated and the SLFP returned to office, again with Mrs. Bandaranaike as prime minister.

From 1977 to 1985. The elections of 1977 resulted in the sixth consecutive transfer of power between the two leading parties. The victory of the UNP was much more decisive than it had been in any of the other elections and gave the UNP a huge majority in Parliament. The UNP was reelected in 1983. A major new constitution was adopted in 1978 to replace the one put into effect in 1972 by the SLFP. The 1978 constitution created a president, elected for a six-year term (later changed to allow the president to seek reelection any time after the first four years in office), to whom the prime minister and cabinet—still drawn from members of Parliament—were subordinate. J. R. Jayewardene, the leader of the UNP, was selected by Parliament to be the first president. The first popular presidential election was held in 1982, and Jayewardene was retained in office.

Throughout these years there were instances of communal conflict, which was sometimes very severe. The conflicts in the late 1950s, immediately after the election in 1977, and in July 1983 were especially traumatic and agonizing. These difficulties show little sign of abating. The elections in Sri Lanka in the 1950s, 1960s, and 1970s were acclaimed for their honesty and integrity and the widespread participation of voters. Those of the 1980s, however, apparently have been cause for question and concern for many observers.

All of this is relevant to a review of economic policy and policymaking in Sri Lanka not only because, as already noted, the two parties had such differing views of development strategy and objectives, but also because the frequent changes in government, combined with the communal disturbances, made policymaking in all areas difficult. Economic policies that need some time to be implemented and to work themselves out are especially vulnerable to an unstable social and political environment. Furthermore, a government has great difficulty in focusing on the development of a long-term economic strategy when other far more urgent difficulties exist.

The most abrupt change in policy occurred with the change in government in 1977. The new UNP government moved quickly to eliminate an array of direct controls and subsidies that had long existed. It also began to seek large-scale foreign aid from Western nations. The changes in government in the 1960s produced fewer abrupt switches in policies, but in each case there were significant modifications in approach and in actual policies followed. Changes during the 1950s were less drastic, and the 1956 election did not represent a major reorientation in policy, although the SLFP did begin to move in the direction of a much greater and more direct role by the government in the economy. It seems fruitful then to divide the discussion roughly by decades, beginning in the 1950s and continuing to the years after 1977.

The Start of the Search

The 1950s were years during which the newly independent country sought a strategy to deal with its widespread poverty and the vulnerability of its export economy and, equally important, to achieve its economic independence. The government did not immediately establish new policies and new approaches that would change—or that were intended to change—the basic structure of the system. Rather, the policymakers searched for ways to make the existing structure more effective—more effective in terms of the role of national economic actors and in terms of the distribution of wealth (especially land) and income.

Independence was accomplished smoothly and painlessly, especially so in comparison with the events on the subcontinent. Prior to actual independence in February 1948, the Sri Lankans had enjoyed considerable freedom in ruling themselves. The British colonial office had concentrated on providing services to the estate sector and had generally ignored the rest of the economy. The most explicit idea that prevailed after formal independence was that the role of the government must be considerably expanded. As already argued, this resulted principally from the universal suffrage in effect since 1931, and the great dislocations created by two world wars and the depression of the 1930s. Universal suffrage meant that the population could exercise considerable pressure on the government to be more directly involved in the economy. On the employment front and on land distribution issues especially, the view was widespread that government action was essential. Then there were the deep-seated matters of language and religion and life-styles, all of which had immediate and long-run consequences for equity and for the economic well-being of the community on which government action was expected. All this the government must do and maintain its role as a transfer agency. Although the government recognized that it must be active and involved, it did not appear to enter the independence years with a clear strategy in mind. Indeed, the evidence suggests that the prime minister and his closest advisers did not appreciate the depth of the feeling among the Sinhalese that the policies of the colonial government seriously threatened those aspects of the nation that they (the Sinhalese) cherished most.

The other side of this view of the role of government was the equally widespread conviction that there were very few entrepreneurs in Sri Lanka. The evidence to support such a view was not explicit, but the point was made frequently by government officials and other people as well. Part of the explanation was the long foreign dominance of entrepreneurial activity, so that Sri Lankan nationals had had little opportunity to learn. The Sri Lankans had, for the most part, pursued unchanging economic activities for decades past, and the idea, not to mention the experience, of taking risks and introducing innovations was not widespread. Most people had long considered government employment preferable to any other activity; it was then easy to assume that the most talented and aggressive people—the people who make the best entrepreneurs—were already employed by the government.

The view was common that the country's political independence was one thing and economic independence another. Therefore, a principal and immediate task of the government was to find ways to replace foreigners with Sri Lankans in all economic activities wherever possible. Finally, there was general commitment to increased government spending on education, health, and food services. Opinions varied widely about strategy, but these basic objectives were held by most people in positions of leadership in both parties.

The first overt act of the independent government was to limit the movement of labor between India and Sri Lanka. The prospect that the Japanese might occupy Sri Lanka during World War II had resulted in the return of large numbers of Indians to India. After the war, Indians returned to Sri Lanka in even larger numbers, but from 1950 on immigration virtually ended, and the net flow of Indians was out of Sri Lanka into India. These were Indians who worked on the estates, and part of the rationale of the population policy was the argument that, were the supply of Indian workers to dry up, the Sinhalese would then find ample employment opportunities on the estates. The policy would also simply reduce the number of non-Sinhalese in the country and thereby help satisfy the Buddhist nationalist groups. The employment effect was not forthcoming, however, as employment on estates was growing very slowly, and natural increases in the estate Indian population amply met the estate demand for labor. The policy did, however, mean that the estates no longer enjoyed the advantages of facing virtually an unlimited labor supply.

The physical infrastructure inherited by the new government was extensive, but somewhat worn down by neglect during the war. It was also largely oriented toward serving the estate sector. The estates themselves constituted a very large stock of capital, of which 40 to 50 percent was owned by British interests. British interests also owned or controlled much of the capital in the service sectors. This capital also was worn down owing to wartime neglect and the uncertainties accompanying the independence movement. Foreign-owned capital, the most productive capital in the country, offered an attractive target for the more devoted nationalists, which meant that the government was under more pressure than it would otherwise have been to take some sort of action. This situation also made it more difficult for the government to move away from the rice and other subsidies as the outlays associated with such expenditures could be financed by taxing the foreign-owned estates. At the same time, government leaders had been reared in a milieu dominated by British conservative colonial policies, and this upbringing had generally been friendly and comfortable.

The First Crisis

Sri Lanka had considerable breathing room at the outset of independence because of the favorable world market for rubber, tea, and coconuts, and an accumulation of foreign exchange reserves, mainly sterling, from receipts earned by wartime services. These reserves were being unfrozen slowly. The export surplus in 1950 was near Rs400 million—almost 10 percent of GDP—and in 1951 it was still a healthy Rs350 million. The increase in GDP in constant prices between 1950 and 1951 was at least 8.4 percent—maybe more. These conditions made it easy for the government to continue its subsidy of rice and to postpone addressing great difficulties that it must have known were on, or just over, the horizon. It was also fun for everyone to permit consumption to increase quickly. The end of the Korean War resulted in a sharp reduction in the price of Sri Lanka's major exports and, hence, in government revenue, as well as in foreign exchange earnings. Large deficits appeared in the trade and current accounts of the balance of payments and in the government's current account in 1952. In 1953 the government reduced food subsidies and other welfare-promoting activities in an effort to eliminate these deficits. This it did even though the price of imported rice was more than 25 percent higher in 1953 than in 1950. This effort illustrated the first of several misunderstandings by the UNP government of prevailing opinion in the country. The resulting unrest and demonstrations forced Dudley Senanayake to resign as prime minister despite a very strong show of support in the elections of the previous October. It seemed clear that the country was committed to food subsidies. The free medical services, housing subsidies, widespread price controls, wage boards, and so forth—all part of the "practical socialism" of the UNP that had been emphasized in speeches and announcements in the years from 1948 to 1951—were also modified in various ways and restrained in their implementation. Less frequently discussed was the idea that the state would reserve to itself the development of basic industries (power, steel, cement, heavy chemicals, and so forth). The term "planning" was used sparingly, and the idea of economic policy as a means of helping the private sector to help itself was increasingly noted. The World Bank's report of 1953 (World Bank 1953) pushed quite hard in the direction of a more market-oriented economic policy and reduced subsidies, and this report was respected by all government officials. The report, however, often showed a lack of understanding and lack of sympathy with Sri Lanka's history, culture, and social objectives.

Aside from the merit of these measures in very narrow economic terms, the policies and pronouncements gave ample opportunities to opposition parties to criticize and to offer alternative strategies. S. W. R. D. Bandaranaike withdrew from the UNP in 1951 to form the Sri Lanka Freedom Party—the SLFP. His withdrawal was not so much a result of domestic economic policy—the major shifts had not become evident in 1951—as it was (in his view) to inadequate attention to the role of the Sinhalese language and traditions, and to unacceptably close links of the UNP with the West. As the UNP began to back away from its "practical socialism," however, the SLFP began to criticize it for that, too. By the mid-1950s, the line between the two parties was clear, and the election of 1956 showed equally clearly the views prevailing among the majority of people in the country as the SLFP won handily.

Growth Strategy in the 1950s

Despite activity in discussions, debates, and political pronouncements, no firm, unambiguous economic strategy emerged. For the most part, the general policies in place at independence were continued, and growth during most of the 1950s, while not impressive, was certainly adequate. After the big increase in 1951, GDP growth averaged about 3 percent a year until the end of the decade. The only real interruption was in 1956 when droughts and floods hit rice production hard, and GDP in constant prices dropped by about 6 percent. Growth quickly resumed in 1957 and averaged 4.4 percent until 1960, when the political instability began to dominate everything. There were severe communal disruptions in 1958, but these did not seem to dampen significantly the economic performance.

The growth mechanism in these years is not clear. Investment in real terms and as a proportion of GDP had a spurt in 1952 but then declined sharply in 1953 and 1954, and rose equally sharply from 1955 to 1957. In the last years of the decade, investment was approximately 15 percent of GDP. Imports moved somewhat similarly, but these imports were dominated by food products, with few capital goods. Even by 1960 consumer goods accounted for more than 60 percent of total imports, and investment goods for less than 20 percent. Machinery and equipment were about 6 percent. These percentages had not changed much over the decade. So the common practice of a developing country's exporting primary commodities and importing capital goods applied only very modestly to Sri Lanka in these years.

Yields of rice and tea increased greatly in the 1950s; paddy yields averaged 3.6 percent growth a year and tea yields 3.0 percent. These growth rates resulted primarily from increased use of fertilizer and improved methods of cultivation, not from physical investment. The paddy story is especially important and is discussed in detail later.

Part of the explanation of the apparently modest role of investment in accounting for the growth of output is found in the composition of investment. By the late 1950s, public investment accounted for almost 60 percent of total investment, compared with 45 percent at the beginning of the decade. Public investment was heavily concentrated on school buildings, sanitation and water supply schemes, hospitals, and housing. Such investments have little immediate effect on output and, even over a longer period of time, effects on output growth are indirect at best. Investment in land development, another activity with a long gestation period, also took place, but much of this investment extended the area of the relatively low productivity of peasant agriculture (Corea 1965, p. 57). Public sector investment outlays also included subsidies to private rubber and tea producers for replanting with higher-yielding clones, and these outlays also could yield only modest increases in output until much later. Finally, of course, there were conventional infrastructure investments—transport, power, communications, and so forth—that, in themselves, have little immediate and direct effect on output. All these arguments are consistent with public investment accounting for a very small part of the observed growth in output.

Less is known about the composition of private investment. Manufacturing had experienced a spurt during World War II, as it did in many countries, but after the war, when imports again became available, most of it died out. No effort was made to nurture or protect the new war-created activities. The government announced intentions to invest in "basic industries," but backed away during the 1953 crisis. The government then began to encourage private investment and private industrial activity, and some of the publicly owned industries were to be sold to the private sector.

The government in the early 1950s, however, did not greatly encourage private investment in manufacturing activities. Although it seemed to acknowledge that a strong domestic manufacturing sector was essential to diversification and economic independence and to resolving the employment problem, its support of new nonagricultural activities was fairly limited. It offered some tax incentives for new investment and introduced some tariffs that were intended to protect infant industry. Tariffs on capital goods and raw materials were reduced. The government also participated, or announced that it would participate, with private capital in some new ventures, and also guaranteed bank credit. The policy toward private foreign investment remained somewhat ambiguous until a clear statement was issued in 1955, just before the UNP government lost the election. This package of policies was not sufficiently strong to induce significant private investment in manufacturing, but neither did it distort the economy the way the economies in many other countries were distorted. Sri Lanka did not plunge heavily into the kind of import substitution strategy that other countries in the area found so attractive. That it did not do this is of some interest, and is examined in more detail later.

The new government elected in 1956 was much less sympathetic with the move toward increasing reliance on the private sector. The election itself is relevant to our story only insofar as it explains the reason for the defeat of the UNP. Wriggins (1960, p. 328) has the following illuminating paragraph:

> The defeat of the UNP was as astonishing to the victors as it was to the vanquished for all indications seemed to point toward a strong return of the ruling party, although with a slightly reduced majority. The Prime Minister had recently returned from a world tour where he had been received by many of the world's leading statesmen and his ideas on foreign affairs had been widely quoted abroad. Independence and equal status in the world of nations was dramatized as recently as December 1955 when Ceylon entered the United Nations. Unique among South Asian countries, Ceylon's decade of independence was without civil war or protracted public disorders. Health services had improved spectacularly. The school system had expanded over the decade, and the school-going population had nearly doubled. Ceylon's practice of universal free education was more extensive than any other country in South Asia. Over a dozen quayside berths had been provided to improve the Port of Colombo and the cumbersome and costly system of lighterage could be eliminated. The Gal Oya project, modeled on the TVA [Tennessee Valley Authority] in the United States, could show a river tamed, turbines producing more electricity than could yet be completely tapped, and thousands of families settled on new and well watered land. The island's staple food, rice, was being produced in much larger quantities than eight to ten years previously; tea and coconut production had increased as much as 30 percent

and 15 percent respectively. Improved capital assets and increased productivity, internal peace and political stability had all been achieved during the years of UNP rule.

This paragraph is doubtless a considerable exaggeration, but it conveys an accurate picture of development in Sri Lanka at the time of the election. The main omission in the statement is any reference to the employment problem. Given this experience, why was the ruling party so soundly defeated? Almost all analysts answer in terms of language, religion, culture, and traditions. The SLFP offered more convincing evidence that it would preserve and, indeed, further the traditions of the Sinhalese culture and language. The low income of the Sinhalese, especially the Kandyans, compared with most other groups in the country gave the emphasis on language a narrow economic content. There seems little doubt, however, that there was more at work than this narrow economic interest. The Sinhalese were apparently willing to sacrifice some GDP to maintain the traditions to which they had been attached for so many years. This was an important lesson that the election outcome made unambiguous.

The new government was dubious about emphasizing private investment, foreign or domestic, and some ministers even spoke of the nationalization of foreign-owned tea and rubber estates. The new government also was much more sympathetic with formal planning than the UNP had been. The campaign platform of the SLFP announced that it would give "top priority to the preparation of a real plan for development as well as social services, and recast our taxation system according to the needs of that plan, relieving the poor and the middle classes from the burden that now falls on them . . . and by adjusting the other taxes in a manner that will ensure the greatest possible stimulus to economic development" (Oliver 1957, p. 59). The platform also said that the government would accept responsibility for housing, that all "key industries" would be run by the state, and that small, cottage industries would be in the hands of the private sector. Land development would be accelerated and social services would be expanded.

This list implies that a major change in direction in Sri Lankan general policy was anticipated, but communal difficulties, divisions among ministers, droughts, and floods made it impossible for a planning effort to be effectively implemented. A document of considerable competence was produced, but had few practical implications. In the years from 1956 to 1960, the SLFP was clearly seeking to modify the general strategy that had been followed from independence to 1956, and to make the role of the government more direct as well as more extensive. Beyond a few relatively mild measures, however, the new government did not move aggressively in this direction. Economic policymaking suffered both because of attention given to more urgent problems and because the decisionmaking process within the government was yet to be firmly established. An added role was filled by the still strong estate sector that did not like policies that interfered with foreign trade. The fact that both tea and rice were doing unusually well, combined with a sharp increase in imports, probably was the main reason that there were no greater difficulties in the late 1950s. Neither government was able to establish a firm stance on the role of the private sector relative to that of the government. Therefore, no clear policy emerged that was designed to encourage private sector activity, especially in new activities.

Consequently, the manufacturing story in the 1950s is ambivalent. Manufacturing output grew more rapidly than did GDP, but some significant part of this increase was in the processing of export products. Employment also increased. Data from Snodgrass (1966) indicate that employment in manufacturing almost doubled during the 1950s. Such an estimate is probably too high. The 1950 base was, of course, quite small, but even so the growth rates of employment and output were high enough to matter. It is interesting to note that Sri Lanka received much advice on these matters. The World Bank report has already been mentioned. In the late 1950s a number of distinguished economists from Europe and the United States gave lectures in Sri Lanka, and most of them encouraged industrialization. Under the Colombo Plan, Sri Lanka had a number of resident experts to advise on development strategy and to assist in designing specific policies. The evidence about the contributions of such advisers is, one must add, unclear.

It is helpful to consider one development strategy in particular—that centered around an unambiguous commitment to an open economy with a strong emphasis on exporting combined with great reliance on market forces to produce growth. Sri Lanka in the 1950s was a very small economy, and there appeared little reason for anyone to believe that sustained growth based primarily on the domestic market was at all possible. Why then did it not move strongly in the open economy direction? There is, of course, no neat answer to this question, but some points are relevant. The international sector had dealt harshly with Sri Lanka during the forty years before independence. No one believed that during the decades after 1950 world trade would grow at rates unmatched in history. Indeed, almost all projections showed world trade returning to something like that of the 1930s. Similarly, most economists were extremely conscious of market failure, at both macroeconomic and microeconomic levels, principally because of recent history. Direct government action in the form of a major "development plan" was pushed by the World Bank and other lending and aid agencies. The instruments by which to encourage (subsidize) exports were not well understood, nor was free trade acceptable, because of perceived inadequacies in markets and entrepreneurship. The great reliance on imported rice to feed the population put pressure on both parties to make rice sufficiency a paramount objective.

For all these reasons, an open, export-oriented economy was simply not feasible, nor was it thought to be feasible. Indeed, it is doubtful that the leadership of either major coalition seriously considered it.

A similar question is this: If by 1960 it was evident that world trade was booming, why did not the governments then switch to the open economy strategy? The main answer lies in the great difficulties both parties experienced when in power with decisionmaking and policy design and implementation, combined with an increasingly apparent determination to reduce the role of foreign enterprises in Sri Lanka. There were also strong views about other aspects of nationalism and a general (that is, not only in Sri Lanka) lack of understanding about how to create an open, export-oriented economy that would be invulnerable to outside events and that would not violate established traditions and social arrangements, which were important sources of social welfare.

All these considerations are understandable, especially in light of the conventional wisdom of the 1950s about how development could take place.

The Paddy Story

The most dynamic sector of the 1950s was not a new, import-replacing activity, but the most traditional of activities in Sri Lanka—paddy farming. Paddy output was the same in 1951 as it was in 1950, but after 1951 it increased handsomely. Output in 1960 and 1961 was almost twice that of 1950 and 1951, yields were up by almost 50 percent, and area cultivated by approximately 40 percent. This strong showing occurred despite two bad years, 1956 and 1957, when output and yields were below the 1955 level. While rubber and coconuts were struggling, paddy and tea were doing well. Tea was largely a foreign-owned plantation crop, and it is paddy production that is of greatest interest in understanding the real Sri Lanka rural development.

There were several factors at work to explain paddy's good showing. The first prime minister was committed to the idea that a thriving rural sector was the single most important component of a development strategy, and, although his death came before any major policy initiatives were in place, he did affect the way in which the government prepared for its expanded role. The paddy society was almost entirely Sinhalese, an important source of support of both parties. The government was also familiar with the paddy society and culture, and the widespread poverty there was generally recognized. Irrigation and land development had occupied attention since the 1930s, and there were people available who were experienced and trained in these activities. The community as a whole understood paddy farming, and as fertilizer, new seeds, and new methods of cultivation appeared farmers could absorb them with relatively modest disruption to routines and practices. It was also known that paddy yields in Sri Lanka were much lower than in other countries, so it seemed evident that there were established ways to raise yields relatively quickly. Finally, self-sufficiency in rice was a major goal of both political parties. The paddy sector was then an obvious place to begin any sort of development program.

There were two parts to the paddy policy—land settlement and irrigation and a guaranteed price scheme. About one-quarter of federal development funds went to the construction of irrigation facilities and to helping people settle on newly irrigated lands during the 1950s. Demand for new land increased markedly as it became evident to everyone that malaria was almost eradicated and as population pressure on already occupied land increased. In many instances the land development took the form of restoring or enlarging existing "tanks," some of which had been built centuries earlier. The tasks of improving the tanks, clearing the jungle, and building roads, houses, and public buildings were all undertaken by the relevant government authority located in Colombo. Settlers were also provided with credit, subsidized inputs, and technical advice. The World Bank (World Bank 1953, p. 386) estimates that such efforts cost between Rs12,000 and Rs15,000 per settler, including irrigation costs of Rs3,000 to Rs5,000. The variance is high, of course, but in any event, it meant that the government was subsidizing the settlers in sizable amounts. This approach meant that the land settlers in Sri Lanka were being handed a largely ready-made scheme.

The first large-scale irrigation and land settlement project was the Gal Oya River Valley. This project, aimed at capturing the runoff in a 770-square-mile area, represented a very large effort. Foreign firms built the complex of dams, but other aspects of the project were implemented by the Sri Lankan government. Costs per settler for this project were apparently much higher than for the smaller units, and yields were disappointingly low because the soil proved less suitable than had been expected. There were numerous other unexpected difficulties (World Bank 1953, pp. 395–96; Harriss 1984, p. 318) that increased costs and reduced benefits. The evidence suggests that the design and execution of this size project was beyond the capacity of the organizational and technical skills available. A committee, chaired by B. H. Farmer, studied the Gal Oya project in considerable detail and concluded that the present value of costs greatly exceeded the present value of benefits. (These results are reported in Harriss 1984,

p. 318.) The Gal Oya project had lessons for the Mahaweli Ganga project of more recent years.

The other aspect of the paddy policy was the guaranteed price scheme. Snodgrass (1966) firmly credits this scheme with the increased yields, but other observers (for example, Wriggins 1960) are less confident of its role. In this scheme the government authorizes a producers' cooperative to buy paddy from the farmer at a government set price—Rs12 per bushel over the 1950s. The cooperative then sells it to the government at the guaranteed price plus a commission and a fee for transportation. The government ships it to a mill, and the rice is distributed to consumers under the rationing program. Snodgrass's data show that in 1950 1 percent of paddy output was sold in this way and by 1960 it was over one-half. The increase is attributable partly to changes in the guaranteed price relative to the market price and partly to increased administrative efficiency. There were numerous difficulties and violations, which always accompany such schemes.

The basic idea of the scheme was, however, powerful. It created a major incentive for the rice farmers to search and learn ways to increase output. Learning takes time and effort, and the Sinhalese peasant had much to learn about row planting, use of fertilizer, control of water, weeding, and so forth. Extension work was helpful, but most of the learning had to be done by the farmer on his own, on a trial and error basis. The rationale of the guaranteed price was in part simply to raise incomes of very poor people, but its most significant effect was to induce the search and learning that raises productivity. The argument is especially applicable for farmers who owned their own land, as did over one-half of paddy farmers during this decade. Where land tenure was less clear or where share-cropping arrangements discouraged efforts to search for ways to increase yields and output, the price incentive was less effective. Efforts to modify rental arrangements where they did not encourage such effort were part of the paddy package, but changes in these kinds of arrangements always take time. It seems fair to conclude that this part of the paddy policy did raise the income and the productive capacity of the rice farmer, who belonged to a very poor group in Sri Lanka in the 1950s. It is also fair to say that it was costly. Another very tentative hypothesis may be advanced: the large-scale land development and irrigation programs were less effective—in terms of return on outlay and in terms of effect on yields—than was the price support program. The main justification for such a hypothesis is that the price supports acted directly and immediately on experienced farmers and set in motion a search and learning process that often paid rapid returns. In a longer term, this hypothesis might be less defensible.

One could argue that the guaranteed price scheme was the equivalent of an investment that eventually produced marked increases in yields and output. As such it was an effective investment, although any calculation of rate of return is impossible. As long as the scheme produced increased yields, the "investment" paid at least some return. The move toward self-sufficiency in rice was also part of the return. Presumably the original intention was not permanent guaranteed price and logistical support of the paddy farmers, but rather an attempt to bring them to the point where they could proceed on their own. As just noted, the large-scale irrigation projects did not appear to be as productive an investment and, for the most part, were probably premature.

The Six-Year Programme of Investment

Sri Lanka published two documents, one in 1946 and one in 1951, that were similar to plans, although they were largely simply lists of intended development expenditures. Another document was published in mid-1957, but this was principally a discussion of various issues rather than an attempt at planning as such. The most serious document was prepared and published in 1955 by the UNP, and although the SLFP paid it little heed after it came to power in 1956, the *Six-Year Programme of Investment, 1954/55–1959/60* (Ceylon 1955) is an impressive report and a comment or two is helpful to our understanding. The *Programme* refers only to government investment. It allocates 16 percent of the expenditures to social services (health, education, and housing mainly) and 76 percent to "economic" projects, almost all of which were public utilities and agriculture and irrigation. Only 4 percent was earmarked for industry. Obviously the UNP was not emphasizing industrialization. Indeed, it observed (p. 28) that "the policy of the government in this field [industry] is to encourage activity in the private sector." There was even a hint of privatization as governmental enterprises were to be "converted to public corporations with the participation of private capital," and foreign investment was also encouraged. The other 8 percent of expenditures was to be used for administration and defense.

There is a good discussion of the role of capital formation in development, and of the capital goods sector, but also a recognition of the crucial role of productivity growth, in addition to a short analysis of the existence of the underutilization of capacity. There is essentially nothing about income distribution and little on general policies—that is, tariffs, taxes, and so forth. In this respect, the *Programme* was not unlike other planing documents of the era. The main point here is that this document—though owing a great deal to the World Bank study (World Bank 1953)—represented a set of ideas and insights of relevance and understanding. It seems reasonably clear, however, that these ideas and insights did not affect policymaking in any significant way in the 1950s. It is doubtful whether it would have even had the UNP remained in power.

Social Welfare Policies

The fall of Dudley Senanayake in 1953 and the election results in 1956 made abundantly clear that the majority of the Sri Lankan population believed firmly that the government should continue to play a direct role in social welfare. The origin of this belief was studied in the discussion of background and initial conditions in this report. Social welfare activities and the search for equity on the part of the government in this period fall into two broad categories: the first included expenditures on education, health, food subsidies, and land development; the second category refers to policies and other activities that were intended to "Ceylonize" the economy to an increasing extent. This latter objective included the search for a national language other than English, the effort to maintain and extend the great Buddhist culture and traditions, and to increase the extent of Sri Lankan ownership of the means of production relative to that of foreigners.

Subsidy and transfer payments (other than interest on the public debt) doubled between 1950 and 1952, but were reduced sharply in 1953 and 1954. As a percentage of total government expenditures they increased from about 17 percent in 1950 to 25 percent at the end of the decade (Central Bank of Ceylon, *Review of the Economy*, various issues). Most of this increase occurred after 1955. These figures do not include outlays on education and health facilities and their operating costs. Current account expenditures on these items in addition to agriculture, transportation, and other industry amounted to between 40 and 50 percent of the total government spending over the decade. Government fixed investment apparently was essentially a residual reflecting both the unclear policy with respect to industrialization and the priority of claims that the government accepted.

Government revenue was largely derived from import and export duties; corporate and social security taxes contributed far less. The government's current account was positive until the period from 1958 to 1960 when it became moderately negative. When the capital account was added in, the budget was negative in almost all years of the decade, especially so in those years after 1957.

The most volatile issues, however, were not those that required large outlays of money, but rather were those associated with language and with finding the most convincing way to reconcile the culture and life-styles of Sri Lanka's several ethnic groups. A comment or two on four specific topics is important for our story.

Language

Language is an even more complex issue than religion in the equity question. The presence of a number of religions may have few disadvantages for the practitioner of one particular religion, but the presence of two or more languages complicates many aspects of economic and social activity. Further, language reflects and affects many aspects of the society. The role that English had played, the advantages that it had given to those who had mastered it, was recognized and often resented. The Sinhalese language was most widely known and used, which argued for its adoption as the national language. Similarly, Sinhalese was the language of the great majority of those who followed the Buddhist faith and culture, and had been linked closely with that faith and culture through history. Finally, it seemed essential that Sri Lanka have its own language—if only as evidence of its independent existence. Sinhalese was also the language of most of the people in the lowest income groups, and many believed that making it the national language would contribute to the reduction of inequality and poverty.

At the same time it was also appreciated that many Sri Lankans spoke Tamil and were part of a Tamil culture within which they felt comfortable and satisfied. Simply to ignore this group would be called equitable by few observers. Yet there was no obvious solution that could be provided that everyone would accept as equitable.

One may argue that a full commitment to English inevitably would have been far more advantageous in narrow economic terms than any alternative solution. Sri Lanka, a small island nation, necessarily engaged in a great deal of foreign trade, would surely find it economically profitable to conduct all of its activities in a world language. A third language would also relieve the tension among groups that would be created by selecting either Tamil or Sinhalese or both as the national language. Yet no one could seriously push this solution (English), given Sri Lanka's history and culture and its ideas of what constitutes independence. The great majority of the population wanted Sinhalese to be the national language, and any government that ignored that fact would surely be ejected from office. The emphasis on Sinhalese, however, did not relieve the tensions nor did it remove a major source of difficulty for the government policymaker. The situation also meant that those people with full command of English possessed advantages over those who did not. A source of income inequality was thus maintained.

Education

Education is similarly messy. Both parties were strongly committed to universal free (to the student) education. The origin of the interest in education in Sri Lanka is to be found in the story told earlier in the background section. The idea at independence was essentially to reduce the inequalities of income, job opportunities, and advancement that the inequalities of education appeared to have created. There is no evidence that anyone in government argued that increased formal education was an important source of increased real output growth in Sri Lanka in the 1950s.

This origin had a marked effect on the kind and quality of education that was offered and on the attitude of the majority of the students who participated. The colonial administration wanted clerks who were efficient and content, who spoke English, and who would help maintain stability. Thus, the colonial school system was designed to produce an administrative elite (Dore 1972, p. 500). It was also limited to a very few. When the idea of universal primary education was introduced, it was difficult to move away from the idea that the purpose of education was to qualify the student for a government job. The increase in such administrative jobs, however, could not possibly keep pace with the supply of applicants. So standards in terms of years of education were raised, and the demand for higher education increased. There were some changes in fields of study, away from law and administration and into the sciences. It is doubtful, however, whether these changes were significant. Education remained a means of obtaining a job with status and income. Dore quotes a Ceylonese Commission of Inquiry of 1963 to the effect that the engineers who emerge from training are "lacking in practical skills and often averse to working with their hands" (Dore 1972, p. 501).

Added to this heritage was the fact of a general shortage of available educational resources. The limited supply of teachers, teaching materials, and buildings made it impossible to provide for all those students who were eligible to attend if universal education were to be achieved. "Free education" cannot in any event cover all the expenses associated with attending school. The additional expenses had to be met by the families themselves, which meant that many children of poorer families could not attend school on a regular basis, or indeed at all. By 1960 approximately 60 percent of the school-age population was actually enrolled in schools compared with around 40 percent at independence.

These observations make it doubtful that the expenditures on education and the education itself contributed either to the growth of output or to equity, or even to increased equality in the distribution of measured GDP in these years. Few observers would question that the emphasis on education exacerbated the employment problem, which in turn exacerbated the social tensions that prevailed in the country. Unemployment among the youth may have been a relatively short-lived problem in many cases, but, given the general atmosphere in the country in this period, this unemployment still contributed to the existing tension. (Psacharopoulos and Woodhall 1985 have a good general discussion of education and unemployment.) For any country seeking to effect a sharp change in its educational program that is beyond its capacity to implement quickly, the result will be either a concentration of effort or a general effort that falls far short of the intent. In the former case, inequality is increased; in the latter case, little is accomplished. This also is true of other similar activities, especially health and medical care.

At the same time, it is crucial to the present study to emphasize that the allocation of resources to education and the effort to achieve universal school attendance were necessary in a democratic society that enjoyed universal suffrage and had had the history and the experience of Sri Lanka. Hla Myint (1971, p. 233) notes that "These [language and education] are some of the social values which the Southeast Asian countries may legitimately wish to pursue even at some cost to the most efficient functioning of their educational system for economic development." It may also be noted that relatively few economists in the 1950s (or 1960s) would have argued against this educational policy and its objectives, or even its method of implementation. Chapter 9 in Myint (1971) is a good discussion of how countries with pluralistic societies often seek to use education, language, and similar characteristics as instruments of social integration. His discussion also illuminates how complex the issues are in achieving such integration with such instruments. There is also a useful examination of the difficulties of designing an appropriate education strategy in that book (chapter 8). It is one of the earliest works (it was first published in 1965) that expressed some doubts about the extent to which formal education can contribute to development (see also Myint 1972).

It must also be emphasized that much was accomplished. Many new school buildings were constructed and opened and many new teachers were hired. The literacy rate increased and the measured student-teacher ratio declined. All this occurred as the intractable difficulties noted above surfaced. The point, we think, is that to seek to change, or to begin to change, anything so long in place and so deeprooted as education (or language) creates problems that are likely to be more severe and widespread than anticipated and, therefore, considerable time is required before advantages of the change can be realized.

Subsidies

The food subsidies in Sri Lanka have attracted much attention, and have frequently been severely criticized. Rice was the major food subsidy item in the budget. Data reported in Karunatilake (1975, p. 208) show the net subsidy on rice at about Rs111 million in 1950–51 and over Rs246 million in 1960–61. This was approximately 15 percent of the government's current expenditures. It was considerably lower in the years from 1952 to 1956 with the political consequences already noticed. The subsidy was in the form of a free ration to everyone or a ration provided at a heavily subsidized price. Most of the rice provided under the schemes was imported, and the cost, therefore, varied with the world price. The imported price of rice (at the official exchange rate) during the 1950s was below the guaranteed price of Rs12 per bushel. After 1953 the world price was rarely much more than one-half the domestic price. As already reported the guaranteed price was a relevant factor in accounting for the relatively high rate of growth of output and yield of paddy over these years. Domestic output doubled and imports were about 10 percent higher at the end of the decade than at the beginning.

The rice subsidies raised the nutritional standards of a large number of the low-income groups, and thereby contributed significantly to alleviating poverty. Because there was no means test required, rice was provided to many people who could have easily paid the market price. Consequently, it was obviously unnecessarily costly, although the administrative costs of a means test may have been high. The government, however, had ample numbers on its payroll to have implemented a means test without hiring more employees. Karunati-lake (1975) notes that many individuals who acquired rice on the ration then sold it on the open market to increase their money income.

The World Bank 1953 report (World Bank 1953, p. 185) states that "Food subsidies impose an unending drain on the country's financial resources." It further argues that "if there were no subsidies, food prices and wages would be higher, whereas profit margins and consequently the yield of export duties would be smaller" (p. 185). During the 1950s, with a low world price for rice, the imported price was well below the domestic price. In the absence of a much tighter labor market, it is uncertain whether wage rates would have been higher without the rice subsidy. The major issue seems to be that tree crops—tea and rubber especially—were taxed heavily (in part because they were foreign owned) and grew more slowly than they might with aggressive replanting. Although the rice subsidy used foreign exchange, it is difficult to believe that it thereby depressed domestic investment as well as a higher growth rate of aggregate output—especially manufacturing—and employment. The rice subsidy was shown earlier to be a political necessity, at least in this decade. The government's great difficulty in finding and implementing a coherent development strategy was the basic source of problems, not simply lack of resources in the conventional sense.

Land Development

Land development projects are the last major social welfare program to be discussed. The broad outline of the land development program was given a few pages back. The objective here is to comment briefly on the social welfare and equity implications of this program. The growth aspect of land development was the simple fact that agriculture was familiar to everyone, land was more or less abundant, demand conditions were deemed hopeful, and the rural life was certainly the choice of many Sri Lankans. The equity side of the issue was also compelling to most observers, but more complex and more entwined with the new nationalism and with politics.

It was easy for Sri Lankans to believe that the so-called "waste land" ordinances of the nineteenth century by which the colonial government took title to large areas of land and then sold the land to the highest bidders—British planters—were both illegal and immoral. Such lands had been utilized as pasture and as a source of fuel, and often for slash-and-burn agriculture. The lands also, of course, provided areas into which expansion was possible as rural population increased. As Oliver (1957, p. 14) notes, these lands were "reserves akin to the commons of pre-Tudor England," and as such performed an important function in the community, even if they were ostensibly idle. This attitude, apparently widespread and frequently referred to in Parliament, not only made nationalization a live issue, but also made the immediate development of any available lands by the Sri Lankans attractive. Some observers (for example, Snodgrass 1966) believe that plantation development did not really constitute a land constraint for small-scale operations, but there is no doubt that most Sri Lankans perceived it as such. Samaraweera (1981) has a great deal of evidence to show that many people viewed land ownership as the source of most of Sri Lanka's problems. Thus, land development and policy mattered greatly.

The main rationale with respect to equity of land development, however, was that there were many landless people in rural Sri Lanka and many people with extremely small holdings. As population increased, the situation would get worse unless new lands were made available. Such development would also help protect and restore peasant agriculture, which many Sinhalese believed to have been severely damaged by the expansion of the plantation economy. Because most of the new land development was in the Dry Zone, where the ancient Sinhalese civilization (the Kandyan kingdoms) had been located, the land development had considerable historic and nationalistic appeal from independence.

The two main climatic areas of Sri Lanka are usually identified as the Dry Zone and the Wet Zone. The latter is in the Southwest quarter of the country, spreading out from Colombo, and rainfed agriculture is common. The Dry Zone is most of the rest of the country—approximately 60 percent of the total. In this area rainfall is variable (although in some areas considerable) and cannot be relied on to be adequate to support agriculture. In addition, the soil does not hold water well and evaporation is rapid so that some form of irrigation is essential. It was also a great place for malaria. It was in this area that the ancient Sinhalese kingdom, beginning around the third century B.C., had built its impressive array of irrigation tanks and developed its "hydraulic" society. This civilization had declined over the twelfth and the thirteenth centuries for reasons that are not fully documented, but the spread of malaria doubtless was a major factor. As the population pressure developed in the Wet Zone, the idea of rebuilding and renewing the great irrigation arrangements of the past was an obviously appealing development strategy. Some work began during the 1930s and World War II, but a more sustained effort began in the late 1940s when it became evident that malaria was under control and population pressure became increasingly evident. Colonization of the Dry Zone then became an objective of both political parties.

The first approach was that of renovating the old irrigation "tanks" that had been used in the distant past; the Gal Oya River project was the only large-scale "new" irrigation project. According to the *Six-Year Development Programme of Investment* (1955), approximately 200,000 acres of Dry Zone lands were opened for cultivation between 1945 and 1955, and around 100,000 people moved into the newly opened areas. During the 1950s the basic idea had simply been to bring new lands under cultivation, and modest attention was given to increasing yields. After 1960 or so, a shift appeared in government thinking that began to emphasize yield.

The basic idea of the colonizing plans was to provide poorer people with a small plot of land on which they would raise rice. The Land Development Ordinance of 1935 introduced the main principles that have since guided settlement policy. Land is leased to settlers with restrictions on its use, transfer, and subdivision. The government in these early years cleared the land, built the house, the irrigation ditches, and roads. The settler was obliged to improve and fence the land, to build interior irrigation facilities, and to maintain production at an acceptable standard. If this was done and a modest charge paid, then the settler gained full title after several years. In 1957 the government began to do less of the initial work, and the settler undertook substantially more. This change was intended to reduce the cost to the government and to increase the rate at which land was occupied.

The main qualification for selection has been, from the outset, landlessness, and this often resulted in giving land to people with rather modest land management experience. It has also meant, according to some observers, that a rather heterogeneous group of families suddenly came together, which made cooperation difficult and sometimes led to conflict. Settlers often ran quickly into debt and had to borrow from local moneylenders at extremely high interest rates. Survey results reported in Harriss (1984) indicate a strong resistance to the creation of small, new villages because it would induce conflict and jealousy and violate important ideas of "social distance" from other groups. Finally, there were complaints that the government's policy and the style and manner of the government agents were often unpleasantly paternalistic, which tended to dampen the interest of the new settlers in finding and learning their own way.

On the more technical side of production, water management was perhaps the major difficulty. Water management is a complex task in all activities where irrigation is crucial and where the most effective use of water is not well understood. Management is especially difficult if there is no, or only a small charge for it, because "too much" water can help keep down weeds and make other aspects of cultivation easier as well. Proper methods of fertilizing and planting are also demanding, but apparently less so than water management.

The discussions and parliamentary debates of land development and the policies that eventually emerged suggest that the primary objectives were welfare and historical and cultural concerns. The latter refers to the general belief that the small-scale farmer in an agricultural community was one of the truly fundamental features of Sri Lankan social organization. The objective of self-sufficiency in rice was sought, but was given less weight than the other objectives. Initially, less attention in terms of policy formation was, therefore, given to production and productivity growth than to other considerations. This meant that a situation was created in which the land development programs—at least in the 1950s—were largely a transfer payment rather than an investment. This is an important distinction, and is relevant to the difficulties that Sri Lanka experienced later, especially in the 1960s. One must not push too hard on this argument, however, because paddy output and yields did increase during the 1950s in Sri Lanka. Most of these increases, however, probably had little to do with the land development of the period.

The land development story implies that for the full fruits of the program to be realized a great deal of learning was necessary. One may put the argument this way: the land development program in the 1950s (and later) created a situation where search and learning would pay very high returns. The task then was to ensure that the search and learning in fact took place among the farmers themselves and among government officials. One issue in particular on which learning was especially important had to do with what the government can and cannot do. The government tried to do too much in the 1950s and thereby tended to discourage individual effort. Yet the government could not do all that it sought to do, not only because of lack of resources, but also because of lack of organization, skills, and understanding. The idea must be, therefore, to learn what the government can accomplish that the individual farmer cannot, and how then to induce the farmer, or potential farmer, to learn to do that which only he can.

The land development programs—like the education effort—ran into many problems because the economy was unable to respond to unexpected and unplanned needs. This sort of difficulty, common in many developing countries, arises from creating a large new something—such as dam, factory, university, and land development—that will necessarily generate a strong demand for a great variety of intermediate goods and services that the economy is not equipped to supply. This situation may induce additional investment and learning that resolves the problems in acceptable time periods, or it may produce bottlenecks or unmanageable amounts of imports. Which it does depends primarily on whether the innovation is so alien, so far from existing practices, that adjusting and responding are impossible, (Bruton 1989).

The last points may be illustrated by a reference to the large-scale river control and irrigation projects. These projects began with the Gal Oya scheme in the 1950s and reached a mighty climax with the huge Mahaweli project initiated in 1970. These projects, especially the latter, were enormously demanding of skills such as organization, flexibility, and adaptiveness, as well as skills of agronomy to develop seeds and fertilizers, and water management capacity. Other things such as foreign exchange, extension service, and credit to farmers were necessary as well. So demanding were the big irrigation projects that the economy simply could not absorb them, could not respond to them, and, hence, could not learn how to exploit fully their potential. Compare this situation with tank irrigation of ancient Sri Lanka, which was an indigenous part of that society and culture, so the tanks proved to be more suitable and more productive than the more elaborate modern irrigation projects. Indeed one observer (Wijesinghe 1981) has argued that almost as much new land could be developed by an aggressive effort to repair and maintain some 7,500 tanks as will be developed by the Mahaweli scheme. Costs, of course, would be much lower and the demands placed on farmers would be much more manageable. Other observers (Farmer 1957, Bandara 1984) have argued that there were major unexploited opportunities in the use of well irrigation, especially in the highland areas of the Dry Zone. Here, too, the irrigation and water arrangements would have been cheaper and, more important, more conducive to learning and productivity growth than were the super projects.

One major lesson can be said to have been implicit in the experience of the 1950s—a lesson that probably was not appreciated by either political party or by outside observers. Welfare programs that were simply transfer payments, which were financed by the tax receipts from tea, rubber, and (to some extent) coconut plantations with little attention given to the means of raising the productivity of the low-income groups, could not continue indefinitely. The emphasis had to be placed on finding ways to increase the productivity of the low-income groups, which would solve the welfare problem. If ways could be found to induce and enable the farmer to increase his productivity, the welfare problem would be solved. This basic point was undoubtedly recognized in some circles, but it probably was not thoroughly absorbed by the appropriate government officials and even less so by much of the population.

7 The 1960s: Ideas of Equity in a Changing Economic Environment

The SLFP party governed Sri Lanka from July 1960 to March 1965, when the UNP returned to power, and governed until the next election in May 1970. Over the decade GDP increased at an average annual rate of almost 5 percent, 3.8 percent during the first five years and 5.9 during the second. Population growth averaged 2.4 percent per year, so GDP per capita growth was a respectable 2.5 percent per year. Table 5-3 in chapter 5 shows that the equality of the distribution of measured GDP increased markedly from 1963 to 1973. Not only did the Gini coefficient fall from 0.45 to 0.35, but, more important, the share of each of the first five deciles increased, and their combined share rose from 21 percent to 27 percent. It was also argued that the 1973 estimates are misleading and do not reflect any fundamental change in the performance of the economy. The lowest decile's share of income rose from 1.50 percent to 2.79 percent.

There were, however, some problems, which were especially evident in the foreign sector. The current account, which had turned negative in the late 1950s, remained so throughout the 1960s except for 1965. The trade balance was also negative in the early years of the decade, and became strongly negative in the last half. Reserves were low throughout the period, and during the past five years were equal to, or less than, two-months' imports, compared with about six months in the early 1960s. The unemployment problem remained severe, and, by the end of the decade, the growth rates of money supply and the price level were showing signs that they could begin to be a problem. The terms of trade moved more or less consistently against Sri Lanka over the decade. This fact indicates a lack of success in generating new exports to replace or to add to tea, rubber, and coconuts—all of which were experiencing weak or declining prices while import prices were rising. This failure to develop transformation capacity is extremely significant to our story. It is perhaps the single most important issue in the story of the 1960s (and 1970s). The other major issue is the apparent difference in the performance of the economy between the two halves of the decade.

Both of these issues—the transformation problem and the differences between the first and second half of the decade—are reflected in the fact that the strongest sectors were paddy and other food products, and the weakest were the tree crops.

Industry

With regard to industry, it is convenient to consider the first and second halves of the decade separately.

1960–65

The industrialization effort began to be evident in the late 1950s, but it was not until after 1960 that industrialization policies became an important part of development strategy. The restrictions on imports, which had been modest, were increased in 1961 largely in response to a sharp balance of payments problem. Exports in current prices were down Rs100 million in 1961 compared with 1960, and although they regained a bit in 1962, they fell back to the 1961 level in 1963. Imports in current prices fell more rapidly, from Rs1,966 million in 1960 to Rs1,700 million in 1963. In 1964 they were back up again to the 1960 level, but declined again sharply in 1965. In terms of volume, imports in 1965 were 64 percent of the 1960 level. Because over 60 percent of imports were consumer goods (40 percent were food) in these years, the reduced level of imports necessarily impinged on consumption. (In 1962 the government tried briefly to reduce subsidies, but gave up quickly when it became evident that the community would resist strongly). Export volume increased, so the main immediate source of the difficulties was a fall in the world price of the major exports, especially that of rubber and tea; the price of coconuts was more or less steady. The export price of rubber fell constantly from Rs3.55 per kilogram in 1960 to Rs2.13 in 1967. This was a 60 percent decline in seven years. The price of tea fell less sharply, from Rs5.88 per kilogram in 1960 to Rs4.90 seven years later. This then was a made-to-order situation for an aggressive import substitution effort.

Manufacturing as a proportion of GDP changed little over the decade. It was about 14 percent in 1960 and 17 percent in 1970. Manufacturing output in constant prices averaged 6.2 percent growth over the decade, 5.8 percent for the first half and 7.4 percent for the second. The available data on employment show little or no change in the proportion of the labor force engaged in manufacturing, and little change in the distribution of the population between urban and rural areas. These data also indicate that employment in manufacturing grew only about one-sixth as fast as manufacturing output. For the economy as a whole, employment growth was about 40 percent of output growth.

The government was, however, explicitly committed to industrialization through an import substitution policy. *The Ten-Year Plan* (Sri Lanka 1959b) states that industrialization was the solution to the employment and balance of payments problems of the country. On page 32 in this document one reads: "The stage is already set for initiating a process of industrialization on the basis of import substitution." On other pages attention is given to the possibility of exporting industrial products processed from domestic agricultural output and from imported raw materials. *The Ten-Year Plan* emphasized, however, that it was much easier to initiate a full-scale industrialization program on the basis of import substitution than trying to enter export markets immediately. The Ministry of Planning and Economic Affairs stated that the development strategy for the last half of the 1960s was to replace imports of consumer goods with their domestic production. *The Ten-Year Plan* was never a firm guide to policy, but it did reflect the thinking of the policymakers at this time.

It is important to appreciate that in emphasizing import substitution to the extent that it did, Sri Lanka was following common practice in many other developing countries. Similarly in the late 1950s and early 1960s development economists generally did not question such an emphasis. For example, several World Bank reports and *Papers by Visiting Economists* (Sri Lanka 1959a) emphasize the importance of industrialization to Sri Lanka, and indicate that the way to accomplish this was through import substitution. Foreigners were generally careful to hedge their advice, but it is fair to say that their main conclusion was that Sri Lanka should push import substitution in industry. This policy position was supported by the country's factor endowment, especially its abundant, literate labor force. Its geographic position on well-traveled sea routes suggested to some a possible advantage in seeking to enter world industrial markets.

Given all this one might have expected an all-out import substitution policy package to be quickly implemented. A significant move was made in this direction, but there was no internally consistent, well-designed policy package established and pursued. The government did move away from its fairly liberal import policy of the 1950s and imposed higher tariffs and a variety of quantitative controls to make it clear to potential investors that the domestic market was firmly protected. There had been tax incentives in the 1950s, but these were not deemed sufficient to induce domestic entrepreneurs to swing into action. The view that entrepreneurship was a bottleneck in Sri Lanka, especially so with respect to industrial activity, meant presumably that the incentives to invest in new industries had to be strong and evident, and the community had to be convinced that the protection was long term.

There was then a commitment to import substitution in general, but its design and implementation was largely in response to the immediate task of correcting a balance of payments position that could not be sustained, and no carefully crafted strategy emerged. The result was that the protective structure that evolved did not seem to have been designed in a very coherent way. As in most other countries, heaviest protection was given to so-called luxury goods. Some of the new activities apparently used a substantial number of imported intermediate goods, which did not contribute much to the solution of the balance of payments problem. In general, however, the new industrial activities that appeared—as a substantial number did in the period from 1960 to 1963—were simple consumer goods common to many countries in the first phases of an industrialization effort. These were mainly private sector activities, while the government began to invest increasingly in the more basic industries, especially textiles and construction activities. The main objective, however, seemed to be to protect the balance of payments rather than to initiate an industrialization process.

Between 1964 and 1966 no new approvals were issued for private investment, apparently because of the balance of payments situation. Another common feature of the early stages of an import substitution strategy—underutilized capacity—became evident in 1964 and continued through 1965. The underutilization resulted largely from the lack of intermediate goods caused by the inability to import. The SLFP, in power from 1960 to 1965, did not have confidence in foreign private investment, and no specific effort was made to attract it. In 1964 a moratorium on the remittance of profits of foreign enterprises was introduced—as a balance of payments measure.

Evidently this was not a good beginning, but it is a crucial part of this story to recognize explicitly that, at that time, the correct policy was hardly readily apparent. Although the generalities of the foreign observers were not incorrect, they were so vague that they led to little in the way of specific policies, or to a specific policy package, other than the one that was followed. Recall that the situation in the early 1960s included: widespread unemployment, especially among the young and literate with definite ideas about appropriate jobs; a traditional export sector that faced falling (assumed to be long-run) prices for its products and that accounted for 90 percent of foreign exchange receipts; a heavy reliance on imported food and consumer goods in general; a very modest amount of foreign exchange reserves; a labor force with little experience in nonagricultural activities; and a democratically elected, inexperienced, and insecure government facing a society that had become accustomed to a number of heavily subsidized consumer goods and services, especially rice. In addition, ethnic (including language, traditions, and values) divisions prevailed in the country. The problems were thus severe and the constraints on the government numerous and firmly entrenched.

One may expect in this situation that "transformation capacity" in the economy would be extremely limited. At the same time, it was abundantly clear that new, nonagricultural activities were essential to a resolution of the employment and balance of payments problems and to any sustained increase in social well-being. The general policy of the 1950s, supported by both parties, was to tax the estates, and then use the revenue to subsidize consumers and paddy farmers in various ways. As the estate sector declined, this was no longer a viable policy, and hence the transformation question became paramount.

Transformation capacity refers to the efficiency with which an economy can move resources from one sector to another. Sri Lanka, with the long years of dependence on tree crops and rice, had produced an economy that was strongly oriented around these activities. The factors used in these sectors were quite specific to them, as were the infrastructure and financial institutions. Factor markets were not very well integrated, and markets in general were not complete. Thus developing new activities was a demanding task, and establishing the proper incentives to push resources into the new activities placed heavy demands on the policymaker. There is little doubt that this transforming process should have begun earlier, but for both political and economic reasons it did not. In addition, a policy package to effect such a transformation process without penalizing exports was not very well established, so there was much difficulty not only in designing, but also in implementing, a new strategy.

1965–70

One of the earliest changes in policies instituted by the new UNP government after it took office in March 1965 occurred in foreign investment policy. Foreign investment was to be welcomed as a means of increasing the rate of investment, helping to resolve the balance of payment difficulties without penalizing capital imports, and also overcoming any entrepreneurial shortages and improving the technology and technical knowledge in the country (Sri Lanka 1966). The policy statement announced that foreign enterprise would not be discriminated against compared with domestic firms, that profits and interest could be sent out of the country, that nationalization was not anticipated, but if necessary full compensation would be made to the investors. Certain activities—the manufacture of cement, steel, or fertilizer and the refining of petroleum, for example—were not open to the foreign investor, but would remain as public activities. Activities that produced items for export were especially welcome as were those that used domestically produced intermediate goods rather than imported ones.

To initiate a flow of foreign investment into new activities, however, is no small matter, and Sri Lanka's recent history (including the nationalizing of some estates) constituted a considerable barrier that had to be offset, and mere policies can rarely accomplish this quickly. Foreign investment, therefore, played little role in the expansion of industry in the last half of the 1960s. The policy reversal did, however, illustrate the difference between the two parties with respect to views and positions on the role of the foreigners in Sri Lanka.

The new government also gave greater attention to industrial exports than did the previous one, but import substitution remained the primary strategy. A policy statement issued in 1967, when approval of new private investment was resumed (after the suspension in 1964), stated that priority would be given to projects "where expanding domestic demand for essential commodities and possibilities of import substitution justify the creation of new capacity" (*Economic Bulletin for Asia and the Far East* 1972, pp. 30–31).

In 1966 a more direct effort began to induce exports. Specific minor exports were given import vouchers equal to 20 percent of their value. At least 25 percent of the intermediate inputs into such products had to be produced in Sri Lanka. The vouchers were transferable, and could be used only for the importation of a select list of items approved by the government. This instrument, which seemed to have had very little impact, was replaced in 1968 by a major new exchange rate policy. (There was a 25 percent devaluation in 1967 relative to the dollar so that the rupee could retain its relationship to the British sterling.) The new policy was a partial devaluation of the Sri Lanka rupee and the creation of a dual exchange rate system. Two categories of imports and exports were established. Essential imports (mainly food items) and traditional exports were to continue to use the official exchange rate (Rs5.9 per U.S. dollar). About 60 percent of imports and 90 percent of exports were in these categories. The other category of imports required a foreign exchange entitlement certificate (FEEC) to be surrendered when purchasing foreign exchange. The FEEC could be purchased for Rs44 for a Rs100 certificate initially, and then in 1969 the price was raised to Rs55 for the Rs100 certificate. Exports of nontraditional products received a claim on certificates equal in value to these same prices. Most (but not all) of the imports in this latter group also remained subject to government licensing.

There seem to have been two basic arguments for this approach rather than an outright devaluation. The assumption that devaluation would not produce increased short-run foreign exchange earnings from tea, rubber, and coconuts was doubtless correct and an across-the-board devaluation in addition to an export tax was probably not considered or, if considered, was deemed administratively and otherwise infeasible. The other argument referred to the possible inflationary impact of a devaluation. A devaluation would raise the rupee price of imported items, and substantial amounts of food items were imported and their prices were, of course, politically sensitive. To the extent that the government imported many of these items, the threat of inflation or even the price increases of individual goods could have been circumvented, although the administrative demands may have created some difficulties. The government clearly did not want the rupee price of these imported items to rise, a decision presumably based on political and welfare considerations. This decision may also have alleviated any pressure on the government to seek ways to reduce its own demand for imports. In this case the government clearly was thinking in terms of a quantity of imports—the quantity fixed by political and welfare considerations—and then sought to import this quantity in the least costly (in rupees) way. It is unlikely, of course, that a higher rupee price for foreign exchange would, in fact, have reduced government demand by very much. In this latter case, exchange rates played no role in determining the level of imports, so presumably the rupee could have been appreciated for these commodities, which would have further eased the financing problem.

The FEEC policy then rested on the assumption that an across-the-board devaluation would reduce total foreign exchange receipts because major exports—tea, rubber, and coconuts—faced an inelastic demand. Substantial numbers of imports were also inelastic with respect to price because the government determined their quantity on the basis of political and welfare considerations. Therefore, an attempt was made to protect these products from the devaluation, while subjecting the other parts of the economy to the higher price for foreign exchange. This situation is, of course, found in many developing countries, and a foreign exchange policy similar to that described here has frequently been followed. It is a completely valid approach within the terms of the arguments used. There was, however, no reason to believe that the prevailing exchange rate was the correct one. Indeed, as just noted, an appreciated rate would have been appropriate for some items.

These arguments, however, are essentially demand side arguments. A major consequence of devaluation should be on the allocation of new investment, especially new private investment. Private investment (and total investment) increased markedly in 1967 relative to 1966 and especially in 1969 compared with 1968. The share of private investment in this rising total remained in the neighborhood of 50 to 55 percent. In 1970 it was 57 percent compared with 60 percent in 1961 (*Economic Bulletin for Asia and the Far East* 1972, p. 35). A devaluation makes investment in export activities more profitable than it was at the old exchange rate and may make overall investment more profitable in general. This investment allocation effect is much more important than is the distribution of the output of existing capacity between the domestic and export markets, if the investment rate is strong in activities that seek to earn as much profit as possible. Even if foreign demand for the product is inelastic with respect to price, devaluation may result in increased income in domestic currency for the producer. The FEEC was designed, however, both to satisfy government concern about the balance of payments and to keep certain food prices low.

This exchange rate policy episode clearly illustrates three related points that are helpful in understanding policy and policymaking in Sri Lanka. The first refers to the great difficulty for government in solving urgent problems without exacerbating longer-run problems. A balance of payments problem is evident to all and requires immediate attention, and the government's attention is directed to it at the expense of other, more fundamental problems. Not only are these more fundamental problems pushed aside, but, as just noted, their resolution is often impeded by the way in which the urgent problem is solved. Second, the episode illustrates the cost of a stop-and-go situation. The great role of prices and markets is not primarily intended to achieve maximum output from given resources and technology by ensuring stability in a range of marginal equalities. Rather, it is to ensure that the appearance of bottlenecks does not force the economy to stop (or slow perceptibly) for their correction. The evidence seems clear that productivity growth occurs most effectively when the economy is experiencing relatively uninterrupted growth. A further tentative hypothesis may be stated: the single most important instrument available to the Sri Lankan government at this time was the exchange rate. To have concentrated primarily on managing a single, large devaluation might possibly have quickly turned the investment allocations toward new directions. It is doubtful that it was seriously proposed by anyone. This policy instrument is reviewed in detail later.

In the third place the episode raises the question of why the UNP government did not go further in the direction of decontrolling the economy and relying much more on the market at this time. This is to say, why was not the policy package of 1977 installed in 1967? The answer would appear to be that neither the government leaders nor the society at large was prepared to effect such a market change with the traditional approach to economic governance. More evidence had to be accumulated; more had to be learned.

Agriculture

Agricultural output averaged approximately 3 percent growth a year during the 1960s—a bit lower in the first half; a bit higher in the second half. In the early 1960s about 39 percent of GDP originated in agriculture, including forestry and fishery. Over the decade the ratio in current prices declined more or less steadily, but by 1970 was still around 33 percent. In the middle of the decade, it was about 37 percent. Data for employment in agriculture are less plentiful and less reliable. Those estimated by the Department of Census and Statistics show that about 53 percent of the labor force was directly engaged in agriculture in 1963 and 50 percent in 1971. Much of the employment in manufacturing and services was indirectly linked to agriculture. Employment in the sector increased by almost 8 percent over these years. In what Thorbecke and Svejnar (1987) identify as the "organized sector," agricultural employment increased by 28 percent, and was 78 percent of total employment in agriculture in 1963 and 69 percent at the end of the decade. Employment in unorganized agriculture declined modestly over the decade. Tea, rubber, and coconuts accounted for 93 percent of exports in 1960 and 90 percent in 1970. Tea alone accounted for about 60 percent of total exports. In general then, agriculture held its own with other sectors during this decade despite the commitment to industrial import substitution.

The story, however, was not the same over the entire agriculture sector. Paddy (and other food crops) led the way, as they had in the 1950s, but the tree crops, except rubber, ran into problems. This discussion will concentrate on the role of policy in accounting for these results. Differences in policy between the two parties were less defined with respect to agriculture, and the period will be treated as a unit with few exceptions.

Figure 5-5 in chapter 5 shows the broad outline of production of tea, rubber, and paddy over the years of the 1960s. That picture is reasonably clear. Paddy output increased briskly over the decade, except for the period from 1965 to 1966. Rubber production grew almost as well, and tea hardly at all. Coconut production increased sharply for four years and then declined until 1970 when output again shot up. Rates of growth per year of output and yields using the average of the two end years are shown in table 7-1.

Table 7-1. Growth Rates of Tea, Rubber, and Paddy, 1960–70
(percent)

Crop	Output, 1960–70	Yield 1960–65	1965–70	1960–70
Tea	0.7	2.6	−1.2	0.5
Rubber	4.6	6.4	6.3	6.7
Paddy	5.2	0.7	4.6	3.5

Source: Calculated from data compiled by the Department of Census and Statistics.

The area under cultivation increased slightly for tea (and coconuts) and declined by over 15 percent for rubber. Paddy acreage rose by over one-quarter. Output per land unit for tea declined from 1964 to 1970 and rose only moderately during 1960–65. Rubber and paddy yields showed impressive gains; rubber over the entire decade, and paddy over second half in particular. The volume of paddy that was marketed rose even more rapidly than did total output, especially from 1964 on (Thorbecke and Svejnar 1987, p. 36).

The growth in acreage and yield of paddy clearly reflects government policy. The land development schemes begun in the 1950s had opened up substantial new lands for cultivation, and the rising yields were made possible by the increased use of the high-yielding varieties of seeds. In the 1960s the initial versions of high-yielding seeds were available, which created a great potential for increasing yields. Along with the high-yielding seeds, fertilizer was provided at a subsidized price, and the guaranteed price scheme continued throughout the decade. As already discussed, water use and management were severe problems that reduced the effectiveness of the new seeds. In addition, fertilizer was mainly imported, and when balance of payments difficulties forced reduction in imports, paddy output suffered. Distribution problems also impeded effective use of all the imported fertilizer. By the end of the 1960s, power was also something of a problem. Tractors had been increasingly imported during the period, and reduced imports of spare parts caused a substantial portion of the tractor fleet to become immobilized. Meanwhile, the buffalo herd was declining, presumably on the assumption that the tractorization of paddy would continue (Hewavitharana 1980). The difficulties of shifting—of transformation—are particularly evident in this specific case.

The increase in the rate of growth of yields in the second half of the decade relative to the first seems to result from better organization and institutions. Credit availability was improved as were extension services and marketing through the guaranteed price scheme. Village-level planning was more effective as well. The basic policy package, however, was no different in the second half from what it was in the first half of the period.

For all these reasons, paddy was increasingly vulnerable to the country's capacity to import at the same time that output was growing. The capacity to import intermediate goods was largely dependent on two things: the exports of tea, rubber, and coconuts and the reduced imports of rice. Self-sufficiency in rice remained a major national objective (of both parties), but the achievement of this objective required, at least temporarily, considerable capacity to import. In U.S. dollar terms, rice accounted for 12 percent of imports in 1960 and 15 percent of a smaller total in 1970. Imports of rice were 90 percent of domestic production in 1960 and fluctuated markedly over the decade.

They were 109 percent in 1966, 29 percent in 1969, and back up to 50 percent in 1970. Figures vary rather widely among various sources, but general trends are similar. Given the limited transformation capacity in Sri Lanka, imports of intermediate goods were likely to be necessary for some time to maintain this growth. The paddy sector and other field crops also had to absorb considerable amounts of labor if the employment problem was not to worsen. A further aspect of the transformation problem in Sri Lanka (and the hold that the paddy culture had on the community) is illustrated by the relative slowness with which nonpaddy field crops expanded despite apparently strong economic incentives. Some implications of this situation will be discussed after a comment or two on the plantation crops.

The output and yield patterns of tea and rubber were quite different. Rubber grew at an impressive rate and tea essentially not at all. Government policies were more or less the same with respect to both products. Export taxes on tea amounted to over 40 percent of the Colombo price in each year. In 1969 and 1970 the tax was 56 and 50 percent, respectively. The tax on rubber was generally between 25 and 30 percent, less in 1967 and 1968, and 36 percent in 1970. Revenue from tea taxes was, of course, several times larger than that from rubber. Prices of tea remained quite stable over the period, while those of rubber fell consistently through 1967 when they rose for two years before dropping again in 1970. The government provided both tea and rubber plantations with a replanting subsidy, but these subsidies were relatively modest compared with the taxes that the plantations paid. Approximately 4 percent of the total tea area was planted with high-yielding varieties in 1960 and about 10 percent in 1970. For rubber the percentages were 31 and 70, respectively (Thorbecke and Svejnar 1987, pp. 110 and 123).

To what extent is it appropriate to say that tea and rubber were penalized by government policy and, therefore, were less dynamic than paddy? It is clear (as noted above) that paddy production and consumption were heavily subsidized and tea and rubber heavily taxed.Thorbecke and Svejnar (1987) show that the net tax receipts from tree crops (gross taxes minus subsidies for fertilizer and replanting) just about covered the cost of the food (mainly rice) subsidies (consumer and producer) plus the domestic costs of the irrigation projects. At least two-thirds, and usually more, of the net taxes came from the tea sector. It seems then that the tree crops, especially tea, were taxed to subsidize the paddy sector and all consumers. (This was the practice generally followed in the 1950s as well.) If the taxes were the main source of the poor showing of tea, and if the paddy subsidies (for production and irrigation) did little to create a paddy sector that could pay its own way, then evidently major problems would appear at some point. If, however, the paddy sector was being equipped to go it alone and tea's problems were owing to factors other than taxes, the story would be quite different.

One cannot answer this question with any degree of confidence, and it is doubtful whether the government's decisions rested mainly on these specific considerations. It is, however, important to emphasize that the land development and irrigation projects, almost entirely concerned with the paddy sector, were major investments. The objective of self-sufficiency in rice was established and accepted, the paddy farmers were among the lowest income groups and were strong politically, and comparison with paddy yields in other countries suggested that there were possibilities for increased production in Sri Lanka. Finally, to repeat, the paddy culture was dominant and indigenous and the appeal of its further development was strong in both parties and in large sections of the population. These considerations suggest that the policy was genuinely successful.

On the other side, the long-run prospects for tea and rubber appeared dim and, one might argue, the heavy taxes and modest replanting subsidies were simply helping to phase out these once mighty sectors. They were also primarily foreign-owned holdings that were in no sense indigenous to the culture. Diversification and Ceylonization—also major objectives of both parties—required a reduced role for the two main tree crops. The difference between rubber and tea is instructive. Rubber was less heavily taxed and its output and yield growth rates were much higher than those for tea. The difference in performance, however, was so great that it is difficult to explain it solely, or even primarily, in terms of differential rates of taxation. Had the more realistic incentive exchange rate (FEEC) applied, the sectors would have received more rupees and possibly pushed harder to find ways to export. There is little doubt that profits from tea production were well below those deemed necessary to induce aggressive replanting and marketing efforts (Hewavitharana 1980). Profit figures are always suspect, of course. Tea acreage under high-yielding varieties was only about 10 percent in 1970 compared with 70 percent for rubber. Fertilizer (largely imported) and its distribution were problems throughout the decade, and were especially important for the tea sector. Fertilizer use in Sri Lanka was well below the average in other countries for both tea and rubber. Foreign exchange difficulties also meant that machinery, spare parts, and other equipment were often in short supply. Sri Lanka's share of world tea exports declined from about 36 percent in the first half of the decade to 30 percent in 1970. The share of rubber in world exports remained more or less constant, at the much lower figure of 5 to 6 percent.

What one sees then is a reasonably successful paddy and rubber decade, but a very poor one for tea (and coconut). The success of paddy can be attributed to the solid government commitment to this sector, and that of rubber to the achievement of rapid replanting schedules. The basic source of the failure of tea was simply that replanting was very slow. Other factors, noted above, compounded the problem, but they affected rubber as well. Why did the rubber sector replant and the tea sector not? Profits were (as noted) probably lower for tea, but market prospects were somewhat brighter than they were for rubber over most of the period. One could argue that had the replanting subsidy been greater than it was, the rate of tea replanting would have been greater. This is surely correct, but does not, in itself, constitute a compelling argument for higher replanting subsidies. In 1970 about 70 percent of the tea area was owned by companies registered in Sri Lanka, but over 40 percent of output was produced by companies registered in the United Kingdom. The latter companies tended to produce the higher-priced teas. For rubber, less than 15 percent of the registered area was owned by U.K. companies. This may have mattered (as nationalization was in the air), and there was uncertainty about compensation schemes and other aspects of a nationalization effort. It is impossible to gain much insight into the importance of this consideration in the differing performances of tea and rubber. The difference in the general policy approach between the two parties was modest and does not seem to be an important explanation. Tea output and yields grew adequately in the period from 1960 to 1965. Evidently the complex of factors surveyed above had a far greater dampening effect on tea (and coconuts) than on rubber. A reversal would require changes in numerous aspects of the economy that affected replanting decisions in tea and coconuts.

Food Subsidies in the 1960s

There were many direct and indirect subsidies in Sri Lanka in the 1960s. Of course, this statement applies to any country at any time, but the subsidy picture for Sri Lanka is especially relevant to the main theme of this story. It is probably correct to say that subsidies in a number of other countries were more pervasive than those in Sri Lanka and the distortions created more extensive, although we have no very satisfactory way of comparing degrees of distortions. The point in mentioning all this is to emphasize the fact that, although Sri Lanka's subsidies have attracted a great deal of attention, subsidies of many kinds were common to developing countries, especially in the 1950s and 1960s. Here attention is concentrated on the food subsidy. Previous sections have reviewed the origin of these subsidies, and the commitment of both the major coalitions to them.

In 1960 and 1961 gross food subsidies were 17 percent of the central government's current expenditure, and during the rest of the decade they were slightly more than 20 percent (Peebles 1982, pp. 247–48).

These subsidies amounted to almost the entire cost of financing the rice programs, and a sizable portion of the program involved rice imports. To the extent that the exchange rate understated the cost of earning foreign exchange, these figures also understate the cost to the economy of the rice program. Profits were made by the government on the sale of sugar (and, to a very minor extent, on the sale of flour). These sugar profits, which in some years were substantial, were used to offset the debit on the food subsidy account of the treasury. Thus, net subsidies (gross minus profits from sugar sales) were around 15 percent of current expenditures in most years, though markedly higher and lower in 1964 and 1965. Even with net figures, the subsidies constituted a major item in the budget. The gross subsidy figure was the largest single item of current expenditure in each of the years of the decade.

These subsidies were direct outlays by the central government, and hence affected the government budget and its financing. Because of this, their size and their existence were evident to everyone, while other subsidies, more indirect and not involving an explicit financial outlay, have attracted less attention. Food aid from abroad did not become a significant factor in the story until the 1970s.

Rice rationing began in Sri Lanka in 1942 to help alleviate the difficulties created by the war. The Food Commissioner's Department obtains rice through imports and purchases of domestic supplies, and then issues the rationed rice to authorized distributors, including retail cooperatives and a smaller number of private distributors. The Price Controller's Department in the Ministry of Trade is responsible for policing the distributors to ensure that the legislated price is observed. Other products (especially flour and sugar) that have long been rationed are managed through the same arrangement. As noted, profits were made on sugar throughout the 1960s.

Table 7-2 shows that from 1954 until 1966 the rice ration was four pounds per week per person over one-year old. There was no free rice, but the price paid varied widely. More important, the ratio of the subsidized price to the imported price varied widely. For a brief interval in 1953 the ratio was over 90 percent, but, as noted, this brought down a prime minister. In some years the ratio was as low as one-quarter, but at all times there was a subsidy for which the government had to find a means of payment. By the mid-1960s, three-quarters or more of the rice consumed in Sri Lanka passed through the rationing system, and rice purchases in the open market declined more or less continuously. Essentially then the Sri Lankan population depended almost exclusively on rationed rice in the years until 1966.

As of December 1966, the ration was reduced from four pounds per person per week to two pounds, which were distributed at no cost to the consumer. The result was a sharp fall in the proportion of rice that

Table 7-2. The Rice Ration Program, 1952–78

Date of change	Pounds per person per week			Price per pound (cents)
	Free	Paid	Total	
September 1952	0	2.0	2.0	12.5
July 1953	0	2.5	2.5	35.0
October 1953	0	2.5	2.5	27.5
November 1954	0	4.0	4.0	27.5
May 1955	0	4.0	4.0	25.0
October 1955	0	4.0	4.0	12.5
May 1956	0	4.0	4.0	20.0
June 1958	0	4.0	4.0	17.5
June 1959	0	4.0	4.0	12.5, 22.5[a]
April 1960	0	4.0	4.0	12.5
December 1966	2.0	0	2.0	0
September 1970	2.0	2.0	4.0	37.5
February 1973	2.0	2.0	4.0	50.0
October 1973[b]	1.0	2.0	3.0	100.0
April 1974	1.0	1.0[c]	2.0	115.0
August 1974	1.0	1.0	2.0	110.0
December 1974	1.0	1.0	2.0	110.0
March 1975	1.0	1.0	2.0	110.0
November 1975	1.0	1.0	2.0	100.0
1977	1.0	3.0	4.0	100.0
1978[d]	1.0[d]	3.0[d]	4.0[d]	100.0[d]

a. The price for the first two pounds was 12.5 cents and for the next two pounds 22.5 cents.

b. As of this date, income-taxpayers were no longer eligible for free ration.

c. In the urban areas of rice-deficit districts, two pounds of paid ration rice were issued.

d. In 1978 a uniform ration of four pounds a person a week was provided to households earning less than Rs300 per month. One pound was provided free and three at Rs1 per pound.

Source: Gavan and Chandrasekera (1979), p. 28.

the rationing authorities obtained and a corresponding increase in the quantity of rice sold through the open market. Similarly, rice imports declined sharply, but wheat imports rose. Total rice consumption fell by about 125,000 tons in 1967 compared with 1966, and annual per capita consumption dropped by about thirty pounds. By 1970, however, per capita consumption was ten pounds above the 1966 level, but still below the average of the early 1960s. The years 1967 to 1970 were years of good rice harvests and (as we have seen) good GDP growth. There is no doubt that the good harvests were crucial in preventing the halving of the rice ration from having serious consequences for the lower-income groups. Although there appear to be no data directly relevant to the point, the reduced rice consumption probably was concentrated on the lower-income population.

The 1966 modification in ration arrangements (which continued until September 1970) was induced by the increasing difficulty of financing. There is no evidence that it was changed as a matter of policy to remodel the entire rationing program. The cost to the government of the program continued to rise until 1970, mainly because the reduced ration was distributed free. The quantity imported in 1969 was about half the level of 1963 to 1965, but world prices had risen, so the import costs did not decline very much. Evidently, had the ration not been reduced from four to two pounds, the imported costs would have been higher than they actually were. The 1966 change amounted, therefore, to a relatively modest change in management rather than a change in basic policy.

A major portion of the resources available to the government were allocated to the rice rationing program. Any sort of firm evaluation of this use of these resources is difficult, but some observations may be justified.

- Although data are not very clear on the issue, it is surely safe to assume that the program enabled the lower-income groups to achieve a higher level of food consumption than they otherwise would have. From data obtained in the 1969 to 1970 Socioeconomic Survey of Sri Lanka, Gavan and Chandrasekera (1979) determine that the value of the rice ration to the lowest-income decile amounted to 16 percent of the average income of that group. The percentage falls slowly as incomes rise, so that even in the sixth-decile income group the rice ration added an estimated 10 percent to average income. These authors also estimate (p. 42) that the rations provided about 5 percent of the calorie requirement for the lowest-income decile. At higher incomes, the rice ration resulted in a reduction of market purchases of rice, so that a net increase in calorie levels for the community as a whole was small. Thus the main consequence of the program was to help alleviate the effects of poverty on nutrition, not to increase the level of calorie consumption. The 1969–70 year had a good harvest, and, as the country became more dependent on domestic production, a marked interaction between the harvest and the contribution of the ration program developed. The better the local crop, the less important was the role of the program (Gavan and Chandrasekera 1979, p. 45).

Because the rice ration was available to everyone, irrespective of income, the cost of delivering the rice to the lowest deciles was extremely high. Gavan and Chandrasekera (1979) work out some interesting estimates of the exact cost of reducing the calorie deficit in 1969 to 1970. These estimates are, as the authors emphasize, open to question, but they support the commonsense view that the cost of supplying the very poor was very high. One of the genuine puzzles in the Sri Lanka story is why, especially after 1966, the government persisted in making the rice ration available to everyone. Some administrative problems were solved, but it is unreasonable to assume that problems of limiting the rations to targeted groups were genuinely insurmountable. The explanation that the two political parties were seeking support is perhaps the most convincing one. Indeed the 1969–70 survey data show that ration use among middle-income groups was greater than among the lowest-income groups for both paid and free rations. This was presumably a consequence of administrative difficulties in distributing the ration cards. The evidence also suggests that even the lowest-income groups purchased some rice in the market even though they had not exhausted their rations. Gavan and Chandrasekera (1979) explain this result largely in terms of the difference in quality between rationed and free-market rice. The latter was considered markedly superior. Even so, the case remains that the rice (and wheat) ration program made an important contribution to alleviating some of the effects of poverty, but was accomplished at an unnecessarily high cost.

The costs were covered, as noted above, by taxing tea and rubber. The ambiguity of the effect of the taxation on tea and rubber has also been noted. A less expensive ration program would have permitted reduced taxes on the plantation crops, especially on tea, and one might easily argue that this would have resulted in a higher rate of replanting. This result is uncertain, however, and from 1966, saving rates were rising; except for a downturn in 1968, the investment rate (in the economy as a whole) and total investment rose from 1965 on. These data suggest, at least, that investible resources were not a significant bottleneck, at least during the last part of the decade. The price level remained under control throughout the decade. The balance of payments was weak, and reserves fell continuously over the decade, except for 1967 when they recouped a bit compared with 1966. Imports in constant prices also declined steadily. Even so, tea replanting did not require large-scale foreign exchange outlays. The taxes did have a significant effect on after-tax profits, and tea profits were more often low and negative than were those of rubber. Such effects may have been important, but doubtless there were other equally important factors, such as the possibility of nationalization and exchange rate policy. It does seem more or less safe to argue that the government's rice-rationing program was not financed at the expense of the availability of investible resources for tea or other activities.

- Did the rice ration program have any effect on labor productivity that would justify its classification as mainly an investment? For most income groups the answer to this question is surely no, and for the lowest-income groups, maybe. Even if rations did raise the productivity of the lower-income groups—through improved nutrition—it was an expensive way to achieve it. There is the further question of whether the ration program dampened the enthusiasm unemployed people had for searching for and accepting jobs that were identified. This seems to be very doubtful. The heaviest unemployment was among first-job seekers who had had some education. Such people were concentrated in urban areas and were members of higher-income families. Any such effect as this was surely modest.

- One concludes that the exact form of the rice ration program was determined largely by the jockeying for support by the political coalitions. Neither party, in the 1960s, felt secure enough—or possibly appreciated the issues clearly enough—to act decisively on this issue. It may also be noted that, although numerous World Bank missions and other advisers informed the government of the unnecessary costliness of the ration program, the leaders of neither party understood or "heard" such advisers. Often the language used included language and concepts that government authorities did not appreciate. Indeed, the frequent reference by outsiders to the rice program as a "burden" was misleading in the context of Sri Lanka's racial and political situation of this period. The program was not considered a burden nor indeed was it, given the attitude toward the provision of products and services of all kinds by the government and the main source of financing. Until much heavier economic pressure on either party developed, the parties would compete for votes by supplying rice at zero costs or at a greatly subsidized price. There is no evidence that either coalition thought about educating the population about the cost of the ration system even to the extent of limiting the program to low-income groups.

Equity in the 1960s

The several aspects of equity were addressed in various ways during this decade. Consider first the distribution of income. Table 5-4 in chapter 5 shows that the distribution of measured income improved (that is, became more equal) significantly between 1963 and 1973, although the 1973 estimates must be discounted. (The data on income distribution for these two dates are much more complete than they are for the beginning and end years of the decade itself. The discussion, therefore, will be based from 1963 to 1973. The less complete data for the years from 1960 to 1970 shown in table 5-5 indicate that much of the change reflected in the 1973 data had, in fact, occurred by 1970). The share of the lower deciles increased and those of the top two deciles decreased. The share of the lowest decile increased by more than 80 percent and the top decile declined by about one-quarter. Such large changes are unusual in a ten-year period; although the data are suspect, some equalizing forces were doubtless at work. These changes are especially noteworthy considering that virtually no improvement had occurred during the preceding decade. Before trying to identify the forces that produced these changes, some more details on distribution are useful.

The increased equality seemed to pervade the economy, so no single development is adequate to explain the change. The ratio of the median income to the arithmetic mean provides a rough guide to distribution. The nearer the two are to each other, the greater the equality as extremely high or low levels affect the mean, but not the median. So if the two measures are near each other in value, there are no, or only minor, extreme values. Median and mean values are available on a sectoral basis for 1963 and 1973. This ratio increased by 16 to 40 percent for the largest sectors. It declined or increased only slightly for some small sectors—mining, transport, and electricity. Construction is the largest sector to experience a decline. The ratio in this sector had risen from 0.51 in 1953 to 0.78 in 1963, and then declined to 0.64 in 1973. No immediate explanation is available for this sector's different results. Construction is also a very small sector, constituting about 5 percent of GDP in 1970. The main point, however, is that inequality seemed to fall pretty much across the economy in this period.

The socioeconomic survey data also classify income recipients into broad occupational groups—farmers (owner-operators), semiskilled and unskilled, clerical, and so forth—for the two years. If one leaves aside the category "professional," then the "managerial" category had the highest income in both years. The ratio of every other category, save one, to managerial income was higher in 1973 than in 1963. The exception was the "technical" category, where the ratio declined from 0.44 to 0.39. These ratios refer to total income—that is, income from main occupation plus income from all sources. Income from main occupation for the technical category actually declined by more than 16 percent, while all others increased by substantial percentages. In the absence of a specific explanation of this decline, it is a bit suspect. One of the reasons for the catching up was that income from sources other than the main source was larger in 1973 than 1963 for the lower-income recipients than for the managerial category. The professional category, however, enjoyed a threefold increase over the

Table 7-3. Income for Income Receiver by Ethnic Group, 1963 and 1973

	1963		1973		Ratio of median to mean income	
Ethnic group	Mean income (rupees)[a]	Percentage of all island	Mean income (rupees)[a]	Percentage of all island	1963	1973
Sinhalese						
Kandyan	218	81	422	93	0.63	0.89
Low-country	292	109	520	114	0.68	0.82
Tamils						
Ceylonese	327	122	470	103	0.60	0.82
Indian	148	55	225	49	0.80	0.80
Moors and Malays	414	155	670	147	0.60	0.70
Other	819	306	982	215	0.57	0.64
All island	267	100	455	100	0.62	0.79

a. Income for two months.

Source: Central Bank of Ceylon, *Report on Consumer Finances and Socio-Economic Survey* (1973).

decade, and all other categories declined relative to it. Professionals became unusually well paid by 1973, but, of course, were relatively few in number.

Finally, something can be said about income changes among and within ethnic groups. Table 7-3 shows the basic data. The Moors and Malays and "other" category are both relatively small groups, and the income of the latter is strongly affected by that of a few Western residents. The income of Indian Tamils is by far the lowest and in 1963 was more equally distributed than that of any other group, to the extent that equality can be indicated by the ratio of median to mean income. The Indian Tamils are almost all estate workers, and constitute the only large group of people who are not allowed to vote. Estate workers are all paid very similar wages, so the relatively high degree of equality is to be expected. For the same reason, any increase in equality would not be expected.(Calculations of the Gini coefficient for estate workers for the two years show an increase from 0.27 to 0.37. This change, however, is owing to a different sampling procedure in 1973 that resulted in managers and households with a smaller number of workers having a greater probability of being included than was the case in 1963.) The Kandyan Sinhalase, with the next lowest average income in 1963, experienced the largest percentage increase in income over the decade as well as a sharp increase in the median-mean ratio. The low-country Sinhalese achieved the second largest percentage increase in average income and a significant increase in the measure of equality. Both Tamil groups experienced markedly lower percentage increases in income, but the Sri Lankan Tamils achieved the largest increase in the median-mean ratio. Note, however, that in 1973 Kandyan Sinhalese still, on the average, had a lower income than did the Sri Lankan Tamils, but the low-country Sinhalese passed the latter group by a sizable margin over the period. The Sinhalese groups were the only ones to increase their income relative to that of the nation as a whole. Finally, it is evident from comparing columns two and four that incomes were more equally distributed among the ethnic groups in 1973 than in 1963.

One last piece of evidence may be cited. Income originating in the various sectors changed only slightly over the decade. Approximately 41 to 42 percent of income originated in the primary sectors including agriculture, fishing, and mining in both years (and also in 1953). The share of the entire secondary sector actually declined a bit, but that of manufacturing increased by a similar bit, as did the services sector. One may then conclude that the change in the distribution of income was not produced by significant changes in the structure of the economy.

Given this general picture of changes in distribution over the period, one must now ask about the forces that produced them. The changes have, as noted, been large and reflected in a variety of ways. The most revealing data are those in table 7-3. The period was characterized, one might say dominated, by the improvement in the relative position of both groups of Sinhalese. The various programs designed to raise rice yields and open new lands produced this increase. The various capital outlays on irrigation and other infrastructure in rural areas, in addition to the guaranteed minimum price and various subsidies for intermediate goods, all combined to raise income of rice farmers. Estimates of the Gini coefficients for the rural areas show a decline of about 16 percent, compared to a decline of just over 18 percent in urban areas. The decline in inequality in the urban areas seems most likely due to a narrowing of wage differentials. Wage income is the dominant form of income in urban areas, and government controls on wages were largely responsible for this narrowing.

Two other developments were important. Emphasis has already been placed on the extent to which the estate sector was taxed to pay for much of the investment in the paddy sector as well as support of food subsidies. Therefore, tea and rubber profits declined; for tea, the decline was sharp and severe, so people whose income depended mainly on profits from these plantations were penalized. They were few in number, of course, and included many foreigners and other higher-income groups. The other point to note is that the import-substitution push was fairly mild. Perhaps it is better to say that the results from the import-substitution policies were modest. No great source of rents was, therefore, created, and rents are naturally often a major source of inequality.

One must also note that Indian Tamils, largely estate workers, remained at a very low income level. Their average (nominal) income increased over the decade by a solid 50 percent, but they averaged not much more than 50 percent of the income of the next lowest income group. Sri Lankan Tamils lost ground relatively, but they had enjoyed a higher than average income in 1963. The average income of low-country Sinhalese had been slightly higher than the national average in 1963, and it was higher still in 1973. These statements are all based on the data in the table.

The conclusion, then, is that the changes in the distribution of income can be accounted for in a reasonably satisfactory fashion by specific policies. It can also be said that these policies were specifically aimed at equalizing income distribution and that this effort had the support of the majority of the population. It seems clear that the quest for political support was a major reason for these policies. The neglect of the Indian Tamils also reflects the extent to which policy was dictated by the government's interpretation of what the majority of the population wanted.

The various changes in distribution are so large, however, that it is doubtful that they represent a fundamental change in the way the economy worked, although arguments supporting the change seem valid. The main difficulty is with the year 1973—a bad year in a number of respects. In the next chapter, 1973 is examined more closely to identify the special circumstances of that year. The story just told, however, seems applicable in broad terms. It does not, however, describe fundamental changes in the way that income was distributed in Sri Lanka.

Not only did the Sinhalese want more income, they also wished to preserve the paddy culture. In this sense, the development strategy of seeking to preserve the paddy culture, while making it more productive, was a strategy that sought to preserve the life-style and the ancient harmonies, which were such an important source of welfare to the Sinhalese. In this sense, equity was genuinely served by the development. In neglecting the Indian Tamils, however, it is not unfair to say that the approach was not equitable. Their lack of political clout accounts for, but does not justify, that neglect. The data on educational attainment also show that estate workers, who were well below every other group in 1963, were even further behind in 1973.

One may also raise the question of intertemporal inequality. The argument was made above that the tea and rubber estates were taxed, and the taxes were used to subsidize the paddy sector and food supplies. It should be recalled that it is not clear whether the tax policy was the basic source of the difficulties of the tea sector. It is, however, clear that the expansion of the paddy sector was inadequate to offset the decline of tea as a leading sector to provide the basic source of dynamism to the economy. The failure in the 1960s to create new sources of output and employment meant that the future had to be penalized. The 1960s was the time to begin that process. Intertemporal equality (or inequality) is even more impalpable than other kinds, but it does seem legitimate to argue, in the present instance, that the policies of the 1960s unduly neglected the future in an effort to concentrate on the present. This neglect does not seem to be a result of inadequate saving capacity or foreign exchange bottlenecks or any other specific bottleneck. Rather, it is attributable to a decisionmaking process and a political and cultural heritage that prevented either political group from taking a long view and acting decisively on it. Similarly, both parties tended to respond to what they saw as the majority's wishes, and did little either to guide those wishes or to address the policy and equity questions. In this respect the two parties were similar to most political parties in the world, but quite dissimilar to the governments in the very rapidly growing economies of the Republic of Korea, Taiwan, and Singapore and, to a somewhat lesser extent, Malaysia. It was not until difficulties became unmanageable in the mid-1970s that more aggressive policy action was taken. The decisionmaking was made more complex because of the difficulty of the transformation problem. To induce a beginning of the transformation would have required well-defined and well-executed policies, and these could not be forthcoming in the 1960s.

8

1970 to 1977: Difficulties and Changing Attitudes

In the election of May 1970, the UNP was defeated and the SLFP returned to office, again with Mrs. Bandaranaike as prime minister. The SLFP margin of victory was decisive although, as in 1956, developments in the economy during the three or four years before the election were unusually favorable. The 1970s were troubled years indeed for Sri Lanka owing, in part, to some bad luck (for example, weather) and to the continuing difficulty of formulating and implementing a decisive economic policy package that would begin to create new sources of strength in the economy. In this section, we first review the general developments of the period that are most directly relevant to the story and then examine policies that seemed to be especially important in accounting for these developments. An effort is also made to explore ways in which the events of these years created circumstances that enabled the big revolution in policy to occur in 1977.

The General Picture

The average annual growth rate of GDP in constant prices over the years from 1970 to 1977 was about 3 percent. Year-to-year rates fluctuated markedly. There was essentially no growth in 1971 relative to 1970, and in 1975 and 1976 growth was somewhat less than 3 percent, while in 1977, the rate reached a strong 4.2 percent. In 1978, it was over 8 percent.

The investment rate, which had reached a postindependence peak of over 19 percent in 1969, declined through 1973, and then hovered around the 15 percent level until 1978, when it rose at an exceptionally rapid rate. Saving and consumption followed the time path that corresponds to this investment pattern (figure 5-3 in chapter 5). From 1973 to 1976, the consumption rate was well above that which had prevailed for the preceding seventeen or so years, and similarly, the saving rate fell below its traditional levels. Although incomes in Sri Lanka were, of course, low in these years, per capita income did not fall (except in 1971), and there appears to be no urgent health or other reason for consumption to increase the way the data show that it did. This evidence suggests that there was an unrealized saving potential. The balance of payments remained precarious during the entire period, and reserves were always a modest proportion of imports. Consumer good imports, however, were over 50 percent of total imports until 1974, when petroleum imports in value terms skyrocketed. Even after 1974, had consumption not risen so sharply, the balance of payments would have been under much less pressure. Therefore, a major question is why investment did not remain at its high 1969–70 levels. Numerous factors are relevant, but we will consider only the major ones.

The Difficulties in Agriculture

Rice

Paddy production was a major factor in accounting for the poor years. From a rather high level in 1970, production declined in each of the following three years, and after a sharp upturn in 1974, fell severely in 1975 and remained low during 1976. It was only in 1977 that paddy production surpassed the 1970 level. A series of droughts in the years from 1971 to 1973 years and again from 1975 to 1976 was largely responsible for these results. Acreage did not fluctuate much, so yields declined over most of the period. Fertilizer per acre sown was well up in 1971 to 1974 compared with the late 1960s, so weather problems seem to account for almost all of the reduced yields. From 1975 to 1976, fertilizer was reduced as balance of payments difficulties forced a curtailment of imported fertilizer, but there were also distributional problems. The institutional support (credit, extension services, and so forth) that began in the late 1960s also began to decline mainly owing to inexperienced leadership in the new government. Water management continued to pose major difficulties.

Difficulties were compounded by two other events. The price of imported rice rose remarkably quickly. The "world" price of rice more than doubled in 1973 compared with 1972, and rose another 60 percent in 1974 before beginning to fall. In 1977 it was still more than double the 1971 price. Because of the problems on the domestic production side, rice imports were large during each year. In 1975, the peak year in terms of value, outlays on rice imports were five times their value in 1972 and amounted to 20 percent of total imports. They had been approximately 10 percent.

The other event was the change in the rationing programs. The newly elected SLFP government increased the weekly rice ration to four pounds a person in September 1970. The promise to do so had been emphasized by the SLFP in its campaign in the 1970 election. Two pounds were distributed at no cost to the consumer and an additional two pounds were made available at a heavily subsidized price. Although subsidized, the price was almost three times higher than it had been during the mid-1960s before the free ration went into effect. From 1971 to 1973, a large part of the paid quota was not utilized, and even some of the free rice was not claimed. Presumably, the latter result was owing to administrative and logistic difficulties.

Such a scheme was obviously very expensive. Per capita consumption of rice had declined from 1965 through 1969, but rose strongly in 1970 and 1971. The costs to the government also rose—absolutely and as a proportion of total government expenditures—and many of the cost outlays were in foreign exchange. Modifications were necessary. In early 1973, the ration price was raised as the price of imports continued upward, and in the autumn of that year, the free ration was reduced to one pound per person per week. At the same time, income-taxpayers, a relatively small group, were made ineligible for the free ration. In April 1974, the paid ration was also reduced to one pound (except in rice-deficit urban centers) and the price raised again. Even so, net food subsidies in 1975 were twice the amount that they were in 1971 and 1972.

Gavan and Chandrasekera (1979, p. 33) point out that consumption of wheat and rice combined seemed more closely related to domestic production of rice than to changes in the ration. The data show that the market price of rice was quite stable from 1967 through 1973, despite the bad harvests and lower availabilities of 1972 and 1973. This could reflect a drawing down of stocks accumulated in the good harvest years of the late 1960s or it could simply mean that the available price quotations were too low (Gavan and Chandrasekera 1979, p. 33). The market price almost tripled in 1974, a fairly good harvest year, as the ration amounts declined. If stocks had been drawn down in the preceding two years, there may well have been a rebuilding in 1974—that is, part of the measured rice consumption was really an increase in stocks.

It may again be noted that the changes in the ration program were forced on the government by circumstances more or less beyond its control. There does not appear to have been an appraisal of a range of policy options, followed by a choice based upon fundamental economic considerations. Decisionmaking remained difficult.

Tea and Rubber

The weak showing of tea continued in the 1970s, and rubber, which had done moderately well in the 1960s, suddenly began to experience major difficulties. The output of rubber that was achieved in 1970 has not been equaled since; in 1977 it was about 10 percent below the 1970 level. The output of tea was up a bit in 1971 compared with 1970, but declined again and remained below the 1970 level for the rest of the period (Central Bank of Ceylon, *Review of the Economy*, various issues). Marketed coconut sales increased through 1972, at which time they reached a maximum not yet reached again. Yields per planted area for all three products were lower in 1977 and 1978 than in 1969 and 1970, even though the proportion of the total area (of tea and rubber) using high-yielding varieties of seeds increased over these years by a sizable amount. The falling yields seem best accounted for by reduced availability of fertilizer, although the evidence is not completely clear. Note also that yields per acre harvested performed better, especially for rubber. The share of the world market for tea supplied by Sri Lanka fell by approximately 15 percent, while rubber and coconuts just about held their own. Despite this rather unfortunate showing on the output side, export earnings held up reasonably well for all three items, as export prices rose somewhat to compensate for changed volume.

The government did establish (in late 1973) an investment fund of over Rs600 million for the tea sector to be spent over a five-year period. It also raised rubber replanting subsidies and lowered the export duties on rubber and coconuts at this time. Such policies, of course, made good sense but were not strong enough to offset to any degree other forces at work in other directions.

The fertilizer bottleneck for tea and rubber was not simply a consequence of an overall shortage resulting from limitations on imports. It was only in 1971, 1972, and 1976 that imports were reduced sharply. Prices were pushed up, also. The quality of the fertilizer that was available may have declined somewhat compared with earlier years, and the distribution system, largely public, was such that occasionally fertilizer did not arrive at the farm or estate until it was too late to be fully effective. Much more important, however, was the government's decision to favor paddy farmers at the expense of tea and rubber in making fertilizer available. This was a reflection of the continuing policy of all governments to beef up the paddy sector at the expense of the tree crop sector. Credit and extension services also favored paddy at the expense of tea and rubber.

The other important policy that had a direct effect on the tree crop sector, especially that of tea, was land reform. There were important land reform laws passed in 1970, 1972, and 1975, but changes had occurred in land holdings from the time of independence. At independence in 1948, there were approximately 3.2 million acres of land under cultivation in Sri Lanka. About two million of these were devoted to the tree crops—tea, rubber, and coconuts—and approximately 900,000 acres to paddy. The rest was given over to a variety of minor crops, some of which (cinnamon, citronella, cardamon, and so forth) were exported. By the early 1970s, acreage under cultivation had increased to 4.5 million, of which paddy accounted for 1.4 million—a slight percentage increase compared with 1948. Plantation crops occupied 2.2 million acres—a far lower percentage from that of 1948. Land devoted to vegetables more than doubled over these years. From independence to the early 1970s, there was continued transfer of plantation land from foreign to Sri Lankan ownership. In 1948, almost 70 percent of tea land was held by companies registered in the United Kingdom and by non–Sri Lankans; by 1972, the figure was 30 percent. For rubber, the percentages were 38 and 13, and for coconut, 11 and 4. (All the data in this paragraph are from Peiris 1978). Tax policies, difficulties with transferring profits abroad, and a general atmosphere of impending nationalization dampened the enthusiasm of British investors to retain (or increase) these holdings. Joan Robinson (in Sri Lanka 1959) asserts that "the strongest argument in favor of nationalization at the present time is simply the fact that it is expected."

As this Ceylonization occurred, the importance of the large-scale units declined. Tea estates of more than 100 acres, which had dominated this activity at independence, were significantly less important by 1972. Similarly, rubber and coconut estates had become smaller, although coconut estates were never as dominant as tea and rubber estates. Peiris (1978) suggests that this breakup of estates was largely a matter of private land speculation. The size of paddy holdings, however, apparently rose a bit from 1948 to 1972.

Along with the reductions of foreign ownership, there was also a significant increase in the government ownership of the plantations. The State Plantation Corporation was established in 1957, which enabled the government to engage in commercial agricultural activities as well as to continue its research and extension services. Some cooperative farming also began in 1971 as an instrument for decentralized agricultural planning and rural development.

All of these developments indicate, therefore, that the new laws of the 1970s were not infringing on a long-static landownership situation. Things had been happening over the years at a fairly steady rate. The changes were all in a fairly consistent direction as well. The land reform laws of the early 1970s had, however, a more far-reaching impact and imposed changes more abruptly than had previously been the case. The laws in the latter two years resulted in a transfer from private to public ownership of more than 60 percent of the area under tea cultivation. The Land Reform Law of 1972 reduced the maximum size of private paddy holdings to 25 acres and mixed holdings (paddy and other crops) to 50 acres, only half of which could be paddy land. This law was implemented in 1973 and 1974, and about 560,000 acres were acquired by the Land Reform Commission for distribution to people who owned no land. Approximately one-third of this land was jungle or generally uncultivated, 60 percent was planted in tree crops, and only 3 percent was paddy land. The State Plantation Corporation, District Land Reform Authorities, and various cooperatives were given a large proportion of these lands, so an extremely small percentage was, in fact, made available to landless individuals.

The 1975 law called for the nationalization and allocation of the lands of the large companies, both rupee and sterling companies. This phase included another 415,000 acres—almost entirely plantations—nearly all of which were in the wet zone of the country. As was true earlier, no paddy lands were affected. Initially, the Agency Houses, the long-term managers of the estates, were kept on to run them. The government guaranteed the prevailing salaries as well as other benefits of superintendents and managers for nearly a year, and the Agency Houses continued to do all the marketing. Compensation was provided to farm owners, although the terms of the compensation were often disputed. There was apparently little opposition by the estate owners to the nationalization, and there is some evidence that British owners and the British government welcomed them (Fernando 1980a).

The world is not exactly filled with successful land reforms. At the same time, inequality in landholdings is frequently a major source of inequity, not only of income, but of various kinds of influence. Land tenure arrangements may also be a factor in accounting for differential rates of increases in yields. In the absence of alternatives to paddy farming or employment, landlessness was an evident problem at this time. The distribution of paddy lands, however, was reasonably equal. At least there were no very large holdings of such lands that could be broken up. Land tenure arrangements on paddy lands varied widely, principally because so many such arrangements involved family members, so formal tenant-landlord laws were virtually impossible to enforce. The Paddy Lands Act of 1958 had sought to establish a fixed rent that the landlord could not vary willy-nilly. Such an arrangement would encourage the tenant to seek ways to increase output because he (the tenant) could keep everything over the fixed rent figure. When harvests were poor, however, the tenant might well suffer greatly, and insurance schemes were (and are) extremely difficult to design and administer. The act also declared that tenancy rights were permanent and transferable. In any event, the conditions of the act were not enforced, primarily because of the extent to which tenant-landlord relationships were entrenched in the social structure of the rural community. It may well be that these relationships were an impediment to increased yields and that the tenancy laws, if implemented, would have resulted in greater productivity, but such laws seemed unenforceable within the community at that time. The experience also demonstrates how difficult it is to effect land redistribution or a change in tenancy laws when labor is so readily available.

The estates were, of course, large-scale operations, and were an obvious target for nationalization by the government in the 1970s. Nationalization of the estates had been discussed for years, and one must conclude that the uncertainty created by such talk was a factor in replanting decisions and other matters that contributed to the difficulties of the tree-crop sectors. The new policies could not be implemented expeditiously, and management practices undoubtedly deteriorated as the authority and responsibilities of private owners weakened (Fernando 1980a and 1980b; Sanderatne 1974). There is abundant evidence that political considerations often led to the selection of managers and other estate personnel who were ill-equipped for the tasks. Fernando (1980b) calls attention to the great difficulty of restructuring a long-standing, deeply rooted socioeconomic system such as the tea and rubber estates involved. To have accomplished this restructuring quickly and effectively would have required a great deal of what we have argued Sri Lanka lacked—strong, effective, decisionmaking ability, a long view that permitted careful step-by-step action, and continuity of purpose and commitment. Yet, political pressure was strongly in favor of nationalization. The newly elected government had discussed land reform in its election campaign, and the employment and balance of payments position in the early 1970s made its implementation even more attractive. The Kandyan Sinhalese had long been strongly opposed to the estates because they believed that the lands the estates occupied were rightfully theirs. The insurrection of 1971, essentially an urban, youth-led event, made it still more attractive and urgent. So, the government felt obliged to pursue an activity that it was ill-equipped to manage. Given the social status and living conditions on the estates (and the availability of the rice ration), any employment opportunities that land reform might have created would be very unattractive to the urban, educated young people who led the insurrection.

The difficulties of the tea and rubber sectors were part of the explanation for the continuing low income of the estate workers. Data are not very clear, but underemployment very likely increased and the demand for additional workers was expanding very slowly, if at all. Because nationalization of the estates was not initiated because of the relative deprivation of their workers, little attention was given to their plight after nationalization. In addition, the absence of political power of the estate Indians was not significantly modified by the nationalizations. The government did mandate an increase in the wages of estate workers by over 50 percent in the mid-1970s. This had some effect, but was partially offset by the weak demand for labor and by rising prices, especially for flour, which is a more important item than rice for many Indian Tamils. Increasing wages during a period of slack demand for labor is not an effective way to raise labor income.

In addition to the general unemployment problem, there were other labor problems. As villagers (in contrast to estate residents) became an increasingly important source of labor supply, language difficulties arose, training had to be more explicit, and transportation to and from the estate was a problem. Short-term adjustment problems on the labor side were, therefore, significant and exacerbated the complexities of realizing any benefits of the land reform acts.

It is not possible to determine the impact of the land distribution programs on the output of tea, rubber, and coconuts. Annual output did not change significantly in the late 1970s compared with earlier years. Yields of tea and rubber fell from the early 1970s to the early 1980s, but as previously mentioned, other factors, especially fertilizer, were responsible for reduced yields. Yet, most observers seem to conclude that the several land distribution programs had an adverse effect on yields and on the long-run prospects of tea and rubber, especially. The effort to establish effective cooperatives apparently failed. Peiris (1978) states that some of the cooperative farming ventures begun in the reform years were already abandoned in the late 1970s, and in other years cooperative principles really were not applied. Numerous individuals and organizations, both in and out of Sri Lanka, urged against dismantling the estates, principally because of scale economies and the importance of experienced management and marketing personnel.

The SLFP government undoubtedly knew all this and presumably concluded that these costs were worth the social and political gains resulting from an effort to alleviate landlessness, to break down the long-standing and socially disruptive distinction between the estate sector and small-scale peasant sector, and to achieve gains in employment from a more intensive cultivation of the land. These arguments were not at all nonsense; indeed, they made a great deal of sense in the context of the political economy and the traditions of the Sinhalese society. The great difficulty was simply that the program imposed on the government tasks that it could not implement in a sufficiently efficient manner to achieve these objectives.

The Difficulties in Industry

Manufacturing also had its share of difficulties. Output in 1977 was slightly more than 7 percent higher (in 1970 prices) than it was in 1970. This yields an annual growth rate of 1 percent. Year-by-year growth rates varied widely. Those for 1973, 1974, and 1977 were negative, and that for 1972 was less than 2 percent compared with 3.7 percent for 1971. For the other years, the growth rates were almost 5 percent. Manufacturing hovered around 15 percent of GDP over all these years. Manufactured exports grew rapidly from a very small base, from about $5.0 million in 1970 to around $30 million in 1977. (The several sources of data vary widely, but it seems safe to say that manufactured exports were small, yet growing rapidly. These data are all those of the Central Bank.) It should be noted that petroleum imports and reexports increased considerably after 1973, but it does not appear appropriate to include these items under manufacturing. The major manufactured exports were fish and fish products and garments. In 1977 these two categories accounted for over 70 percent of total manufactured exports. Exports were also concentrated in a small number of firms. Employment in this sector expanded slowly, and the data suggest that the share of total employment provided by manufacturing remained more or less constant, and perhaps even declined. At the same time, the data available indicate that open unemployment was at least 15 percent and probably considerably higher, especially in the early 1970s. Manufacturing was still not providing a leading sector to compensate for the weak performance of the tree crops in either the domestic economy or as a source of foreign exchange. The transformation problem was unambiguously evident.

The government that came to power in 1970 did not undertake a major change in the industrial policy that it inherited from the preceding government. There were, however, some changes in style and approach, and the environment of the 1970s made it increasingly evident that further changes were needed.

The policy statement of the UNP in 1966 had emphasized the importance of new industries that would stimulate agricultural development, use primarily indigenous raw materials, and have export potential (Sri Lanka 1969). The SLFP government did not dispute these objectives, but it did place additional emphasis on developing "basic" industry by the public sector, locating new industries in depressed regions, and attacking unemployment directly. Attention was also given to appropriate technology—a technology that took advantage of Sri Lanka's factor supplies (Sri Lanka 1971a and 1971b). These objectives were spelled out more completely in *The Five Year Plan 1972–76* (Ceylon 1971). From the mid-1960s to the mid-1970s, the share of value added in manufacturing produced in the private sector declined from 90 percent to about 50 percent. These data surely overstate the decline, as very small-scale manufacturing is less well captured by surveys than are larger-scale units. The data do, however, indicate that the government role in manufacturing was increasing rapidly. The 1972 to 1976 plan assigned about 15 percent of total planned investment to industry and 55 percent of this to public sector industry. The plan, however, never became an actual guide to investment decisions.

The objectives were convincing, and the government undoubtedly had the best intentions, but implementation was no small matter. The failure of the tree crops, the rising price of imports, and the consequent pressure on the balance of payments, combined with the bad paddy harvests, all demonstrated the need for a strong, labor-intensive, local manufacturing sector using local raw material. Although this need was apparent, achieving such a sector was virtually impossible. Thus to relax import controls or to lower the rates of protection would have created an intolerable balance of payments crunch in the short run.

Estimates of the effective rate of protection as of 1970 by Pyatt and Roe (1977) present a picture common to most countries that have pursued an import substitution development strategy. Rates varied widely from sector to sector. Tea, rubber, coconuts, paddy, and a number of other products had negative protection, principally because of export taxes. Some other rates were very high; for example, dairy products, 400 percent; distilling, 750 percent; tobacco, 193 percent, and so forth. Oils, fuels, and transport equipment showed negative value added at world prices. All such estimates are open to many questions, of course, and Pyatt and Roe are careful to call attention to difficulties in their calculations. In particular, they do not include the effect of quantitative restrictions in their calculations. It can, however, be concluded with considerable confidence that protection was substantial and had a distorting effect, and that there was a considerable bias against exporting, especially those products of nontraditional activities. Two points are relevant, however. The first is simply that this pattern of rates is very similar to those in many other developing countries. The second is that the key issue is not the existence of protection; rather, it is what happens behind that protection (Bruton 1989). If productivity growth in the protected industries is strong, then protection can be considered a form of investment. The costs imposed by the protection result in an economy that not only has rising productivity over many industries, but is also more flexible and responsive. This leads us back to the problem of transformation and the way the economy responds to incentives.

If the Pyatt and Roe data provide a reasonably accurate picture of protection in Sri Lanka at the beginning of the 1970s, any significant modification in that picture would certainly have resulted in a quick increase in imports. And, as already emphasized, Sri Lanka was in extreme need of foreign exchange in the early 1970s. To offset the bias against exporting, which was created by the protection, with a cash payment would have been administratively difficult and would have exacerbated the budget deficit and the threat of inflation. A subsidy to exports in the form of tax relief on profits earned from exports would have had modest effects at best and would also have worsened the deficit and inflation problems. It is hardly surprising, therefore, that the government tightened controls, and policy turned even more inward. It is doubtful if, at this time, any alternative policy was possible. At the same time, it was also evident that the economy was in deep trouble and that the trouble was worsening daily. In such a situation, foreign aid could have been extraordinarily helpful; however, aid was available only in modest amounts, mainly because of political matters that are reviewed in the next section.

During these years, there were several specific aspects of the industrialization process that are especially relevant to our story.

Underutilization

One of the most frequently observed consequences of distortions and misallocations is the appearance of underutilized capacity. The evidence is clear that during the 1970s, underutilization was common. It probably increased in the early part of the decade and declined from 1974 until the end of the decade. Central Bank data show that, as of 1974, the utilization rate in manufacturing was 40 percent. It ranged from 9 percent in the chemicals (petroleum, coal, rubber, and plastics) category to 78 percent in nonmetallic mineral products other than coal and petroleum. It was 65 percent in the largest sector—food, beverages, and tobacco. The overall percentage rate of utilization rose to 54 percent in 1975, 64 percent in 1976, and dropped back to 60 percent in 1977. During the last three years of the decade it continued to rise, but only very slightly. Variation among sectors seemed to fall somewhat over these years. Utilization rates were a bit higher in the state-owned corporations, and also varied widely from corporation to corporation. Estimates of utilization rates are, of course, open to doubts, and the data used here may well represent an overestimate of utilization.

There are many reasons for underutilizing capacity. The most obvious reason is the lack of imported intermediate goods. Available data on imported raw materials suggest that activities that relied more heavily on imported raw materials often experienced lower rates of utilization. The relationship is far from complete, however, and obviously other considerations were at work. Undoubtedly, there were demand problems. If a firm cannot export because its costs are too high (or because the domestic currency is overvalued), then it can readily run into a demand constraint, especially if it is operating in a small country. Although one cannot document that this argument is applicable to Sri Lanka, the general evidence supports the view. Unavailability of parts or the inability to repair a machine that is down can create a bottleneck. Both of these problems could presumably be eliminated by a larger supply of foreign exchange. Even with ample foreign exchange, maintenance and repair can cause a continuing bottleneck simply because downtime is frequent and inevitable. We also know that rising wage rates can result in underutilization in a profit-seeking firm, if ex post factor substitution is limited (Winston 1974). Most observers consider foreign exchange difficulties to be the main source of the underutilization. This conclusion is reasonable, though doubtful, because after 1977, when high levels of aid removed the foreign exchange bottleneck, underutilization continued to a surprising extent. In addition, public sector companies were favored in the allocation of foreign exchange in the early 1970s, and they, too, operated well below rated capacity.

Idle capacity means, of course, sacrificing output that is technically possible. It also means that employment will probably increase more slowly than anticipated from a given rate of investment. The most important consequence of this kind of situation, however, is that it is characterized by a stop/go pattern that is very damaging to the learning that produces productivity growth. For example, when a firm cannot export and must depend entirely on the domestic market, and capacity utilization fluctuates for any of the aforementioned reasons, available evidence suggests that productivity growth will be adversely affected. This was certainly true in Sri Lanka at this time.

Manufactured Exports

Another aspect that is relevant to the impact of an early industrialization effort is the increase of manufactured exports. It has already been mentioned that exports of manufactured goods were concentrated on fish and fish products and garments and involved only a few firms. Some thirty to thirty-five firms account for about 80 percent of all manufactured exports over these years. Private firms did almost all of this exporting. (Public sector firm exports of petroleum products is a large item that, for reasons noted above, is not included here.)

Tax advantages were offered for exporting, and the previously discussed FEEC applied to the products of this sector. The fact that manufactured exports were so modest and so concentrated suggests that the manufacturing sector was not oriented to them. The FEEC and tax inducements had some effect, but could not overcome the general problems of creating new, export-oriented activities in a society unaccustomed and ill-prepared for the task. The policy of the government to build modern basic industries (steel, and so forth), which it had essentially no prospect of exporting, made the objective even more difficult to achieve. Both the export and the underutilization situations call attention to the effect of structure, created by previous investments, on the impact of new policies. A structure that is inflexible and unyielding cannot readily react and adapt to a new policy environment. This is especially true where the existing structure has been created by "artificial" means—means that imposed on the economy a set of activities incompatible with the resource endowment and learning capacity of the society. These factors are part of the content of transformation capacity, and lead to two additional issues associated with Sri Lanka's industrialization strategy: entrepreneurship and protection.

Entrepreneurship

Mainstream economics has difficulty finding a place for the entrepreneur. Casson (1982, p. 9) notes that the entrepreneur "has been surrendered by economists to sociologists, psychologists, and political scientists. Indeed, almost all the social sciences have a theory of the entrepreneur, except economics." The reasons given for this state of affairs are that economists tend to define the problem away by assuming perfect knowledge and an unambiguous objective function (Baumol 1968; Leibenstein 1968). With all this, there is no need for an entrepreneur, as the only task is that of calculating the production levels and setting the price that maximizes the objectives function. The economist has been mainly interested in the characteristics of the outcome of this process—the equilibrium in both its partial and general form. Austrian economists, whose approach places great emphasis on the entrepreneur, give primary attention to the competitive "process" in contrast to the outcome, in which process analysis the entrepreneur has a crucial role. Their approach, however, is so thoroughly subjective that, after claiming that the entrepreneur is crucial, they have little illumination to offer (Kirzner 1973, 1979). At the same time, however, one must agree that the notion is necessarily quite subjective.

In the Sri Lankan industrialization story, the entrepreneurial function may be defined simply as the source of decisionmaking that leads to the establishment of a new enterprise or to a significant change in the routine of an already existing firm. The capacity to perceive—to identify profit opportunities that arise from doing something new or something old in a different way—is at the heart of the matter. Ignorance is rampant and the perceiving must take place in an environment where most markets (factor, product, and money) are incomplete and imperfect, where data are absent (or out of date), where government policy is often unclear and tentative, and where considerable ethnic unrest is endemic. Entrepreneurship is important in our efforts to understand Sri Lanka partly because of frequent comments, referred to in earlier sections, that it was an important impediment to the country's development and partly because of the difficulties, just discussed, of overcoming the transformation problem in Sri Lanka.

There are no data that are helpful, so all observations are necessarily somewhat speculative. It would, however, be even more misleading not to speculate.

The main issue is simply the lack of Sri Lankan experience in entrepreneurial activity except in very small-scale activities, mostly in rural areas. The long history of tea and rubber estates owned and managed, to a large extent, by foreigners, on the one hand, and small-scale paddy farms, on the other, did not create a cadre of Sri Lankans well equipped to identify investment and other profit opportunities in the industrial sector. The general need for diversification was acknowledged, but identifying specific activities that could function in Sri Lanka called for a kind of experience and knowledge that working in a paddy, coconut farm, or tea estate did not provide. There was similar inexperience concerning organizational skills and management capacity. The incomplete and imperfect markets rendered all these tasks more complex than they were in countries whose people were more experienced and whose markets were better established. Introducing industrialization in such a situation is no small undertaking. A cautious and gradual approach, combined with some protection, would be required.

The other important aspect of entrepreneurship concerns the social and psychological conditions of the society and its individuals. Many observers have suggested (or asserted) that the traditional Buddhist society does not produce many individuals whose personality, style, and interests are adapted to effective entrepreneurship. (It may be emphasized that this is not to say that economic factors in Sri Lanka are or are not responsive to market signals. On this point, it seems clear that there is a response, though perhaps slower and more guarded than in, say, Korea or Singapore.) There is surely something in this position, but it is difficult to clarify it or to distinguish it from lack of experience. The previous discussion, especially the background section, offers evidence and argument to support a view that the Sinhalese tended to resist, or perhaps were not interested in, entering new activities and assuming the risks involved in such endeavors. Therefore, any effort or search was limited, although traditional opportunities were becoming exhausted and increasingly recognized as such. The government policies with respect to food rations may have facilitated, at least to some extent, this nonsearching. One may accept the idea that a strong commitment to a given culture and tradition means that individuals must make a major decision to do something different. It also should be noted, however, that government policy can facilitate, and ease the risks associated with, such undertakings. That the government chose not to do so, but instead actively supported "basic" publicly owned industries as well as tea and rubber estate nationalizations, appears to have been dictated by political arguments, and to have exacerbated whatever entrepreneurial barrier might have existed.

Three other points may be briefly noted. The first is the common hypothesis that outsiders—those who do not have easy access to the established ways of the community—are more likely to be entrepreneurs than are people who are an essential part of the society. There is little evidence on this point for Sri Lanka. The Moors and non-Buddhist Sinhalese, in general, had higher incomes, but this tells us little about their entrepreneurial activities relative to those of other groups. The same is true of the Sri Lankan Tamils. This latter group was also commonly involved in activities other than paddy farming or estate labor. Experience and job training were more common among this group; thus, new undertakings were perhaps more agreeable to them than to Sinhalese Buddhists.

The second point refers to the government as an entrepreneur. Governments of both political parties had made statements from the time of independence implying that entrepreneurship was a bottleneck in the private sector and, therefore, the government must assume this role. The major difficulties with this argument are well known: the government can acquire large amounts of liquid funds more easily, but there is no reason to expect government officials to be better able to identify investment opportunities than private individuals. The same problems apply to both. Given that the government has the capacity to mobilize large amounts of capital, it is indeed more likely to try to undertake activities that impose more severe and more complex entrepreneurial and organizational tasks on available talents than would be the case in the private sector. It must also be acknowledged that the government can absorb risks more safely than most private individuals and firms, probably has more information and data, and may be able to draw on a wider pool of skills than could most private firms in a country just beginning to industrialize. One must conclude that government companies have a role to play, but it is a role not much different from that of the private sector.

The third point refers to education. Formal education is not a great source of entrepreneurship or a great means of acquiring entrepreneurial skills or the entrepreneurial personality. Indeed, a better argument can be made that formal education tends more to dampen, or even defeat, the entrepreneurial spirit than it does to develop or release it. Formal education may well instill uniform attitudes among students and deemphasize individualism and diversity of views. The common tendency in much of formal education is to study questions that have a ready and generally accepted answer, and not include issues for which answers are not known (Casson 1982, p. 356f). The mind of the student is rarely led into uncertain and unexplored territory, where insight and tension prevail and innovation is considered. This argument seems especially applicable to educational institutions and programs that are concerned essentially with providing certification for a job, especially a government job. The entrepreneurs and entrepreneurial activity, however, are presumably concerned with questions that have no established solution, no real category into which all the arguments fall, and where considerable risk is an inevitable part of the exercise. Thus, Mark Casson (1982, p. 357) concludes that these arguments illuminate "why it is that academic training—and the use of academic qualifications—has a very limited role in developing and screening entrepreneurs."

Landless peasants and educated unemployed young people do not constitute the pool from which entrepreneurs emerge, and it was these groups that were in ample supply in Sri Lanka in the 1970s.

Protection

A brief further comment on the protection of industrial activity is helpful. The case for protection in Sri Lanka in the period from 1960 on seems convincing. Protection was necessary to provide learning time, to help potential entrepreneurs fulfill that potential, and to isolate the society sufficiently to give it a chance to find its own desired consumption patterns rather than simply imitate those of richer countries. Protecting the balance of payments also made a great deal of sense in this period. There are, however, many kinds of protection and certain kinds can so distort and penalize the economy that it is led into blind alleys and dead ends. In such a case, little learning takes place and rent-seeking becomes a popular pastime.

The main point to be added to the earlier discussion refers to exchange rate policy. In the context of the Sri Lankan story, one can argue that the most feasible and efficient form of protection would have been a strongly "undervalued" domestic currency. Such an exchange rate makes imports costly, which makes finding domestic substitutes lucrative. Incentives are thus created to search for import replacements of both intermediate and final goods. It would also help create evident profit opportunities in export opportunities. Some minor tariffs, essentially the same across the board, are acceptable, but the burden of protection would rest on the undervalutation of the exchange rate. Undervaluation would mean, almost by definition, that foreign exchange would be accumulated. Availability of foreign exchange is not a constraint in this context; rather, its limitation is an instrument of inducing search, in aiding the entrepreneurial activity, and in effecting transformation. This argument is similar to that which Hirschman (1958) developed. Hirschman was concerned mainly with the investment criteria question, a hot topic in 1958.

The undervaluation and the induced search would also help the Sri

Lankan potential industrialist identify activities that he could create and manage. The temptation to undertake activities that were largely imitations of those in other countries could not, in general, be yielded to. The new activities would "fit" better the Sri Lanka factor and cultural environment, and learning would be a much more probable outcome. Import substitution would occur, but in a way that helped produce a flexible, responsive, learning economy and created little distortion.

Although numerous economists urged devaluation on Sri Lanka in the 1970s, there does not appear to be any instance of a recommendation to maintain an undervalued Sri Lankan rupee as a protectionist instrument. The idea was widely accepted that foreign exchange was a crucial means of capital formation, and, along with saving, constituted the two-gap model. In all this, the "correct" exchange rate was one that valued exports at their real cost. The present argument is quite different, and rests heavily on the importance of the protection provided by undervaluation for learning (Bruton 1989).

Over the years from 1960 to 1977 the exchange rate "deflated" by the wholesale price index changed little. Only in 1967 and 1968 did the rate value domestic currency substantially lower than in other years. In 1974, the data show a distinct appreciation of the Sri Lankan rupee, and it was not until the late 1970s that significant devaluations occurred relative to other years. Even this devaluation hardly produced the kind of undervaluation needed to provide adequate protection, and it was soon offset by continuing inflation and large-scale capital imports.

There is no doubt that Sri Lanka "needed" foreign exchange in the early 1970s, and that the heavy balance of payments pressure made maneuvering difficult and any policy experimentation appear dangerous. Undoing the quantitative restrictions would have led to a spurt in imports even with a wholesale devaluation. It was argued earlier that this set of circumstances made understandable the government's tightening of import restrictions and increasing the reliance on quantitative controls, but contributed little to a long-term solution.

Aid and Other Administrative Complications

It has been argued that transformation capacity, decisionmaking ability, and implementation competency were crucial factors in the Sri Lankan story from independence onward. Efforts have been made to explain the reason for this as well as the consequences of such difficulties on growth and equity. In this section, an attempt is made to examine another aspect of both of these issues, which is reflected in the use of foreign aid and in the evolution of the Mahaweli Ganga Irrigation Project. This latter project, an enormous one with a long history, became an important part of development strategy in the early 1970s. Its story illuminates, in an especially helpful way, a number of issues affecting Sri Lanka's story. The story of the project also brings foreign aid into the picture for the first time in an important way. The present discussion goes a bit beyond 1977 on this particular topic only, but consideration of later years helps to identify a number of issues not evident if 1977 is used as the cutoff date.

Foreign aid was of some significance to Sri Lanka from the mid-1950s. Its availability appears partially linked to political considerations. In the first half of the 1960s, aid commitments averaged around $15 million a year, and in the last half, with the more Western-oriented government of the UNP coalition in office, commitments from the aid group alone were $50 million for two years and then reached $60 million; in 1969 commitments were almost $130 million and fell sharply after that until 1973, when they again increased. In 1975 commitments from the West (the aid group) were about $250 million. (These data are from Levy 1985.) That aid commitments from the West resumed strongly in 1974 and 1975 disputes the simple version of the argument that aid was largely determined by which party was in power. However, the West's aid commitments increased by unusually large amounts from 1978 on. There were additional commitments from centrally planned economies, and, after the big jump in oil prices, from a number of oil-rich Arab sources and from Iran. Disbursements were generally smaller, often much smaller.

Two considerations are pertinent to our story. The first concerns the uses for the aid and the second deals with the role of the aid donors on economic policy in Sri Lanka.

The uses for aid are always difficult to pinpoint. Aid funds may replace domestic resources, which then can be used for projects that, without aid, would not have been funded. Then, the "use" of aid is essentially determined by the use given the released domestic resources. There are qualifications to this argument, but the general point is valid. The data show that nonproject aid accounted for over 75 percent of total aid commitments from 1965 to 1975, about one-half in the period from 1975 to 1977, and one-third from 1978 to 1983 (Levy 1985). Project aid was dominated by the Mahaweli Ganga undertaking in most years.

The shift to project aid suggests that the aid group was increasingly concerned with the uses for their aid. The most frequent argument was that the aid was being used to finance consumption instead of investment. Figure 5-3 shows that the investment rate increased sharply in the late 1960s and then fell equally sharply from 1970 through 1977. It was argued above that a considerable part of this decline was a result of bad rice harvests and to the weak state of the tree crop sector. The latter difficulty was not, in general, a matter of availability of investible resources—that is, had aid not been used for consumption, it would not have been used for investment in tree crops. It was also argued that, except for the years of the bad rice harvests, there was no great pressure on aggregate resources. Investment was in trouble, as already argued, not because of too little potential saving, but because of policy matters. This, then, leads to the second consideration—the role of the aid donors in policymaking in Sri Lanka.

The members of the aid group, chaired by the World Bank, were generally critical of Sri Lankan economic policy. Although this criticism may have increased after SLFP regained control of the government in 1970, it had also applied to policies followed in the 1960s. The World Bank apparently tried to have little to do with the SLFP government. The basic theme of the criticisms had always been that too many resources were being allocated to social services and food subsidies, and, consequently, too few to investment; and somewhat later, that the inward orientation of the development strategy was preventing the expansion of exports. In 1971 the World Bank apparently decided to end all further commitments to Sri Lanka until there were major policy changes, especially with respect to subsidizing consumption. Levy (1985) states that the Bank's senior representative to the aid group complained in 1973 that the Sri Lankan government promised major reforms, but that after donors made their commitments, no reforms were implemented. It was later in 1973, however, that (as discussed above) major changes were made, especially with respect to food subsidies. It is unclear whether these changes were made in response to aid donor pressures or to a growing recognition that it was virtually impossible to continue large-scale subsidies in the face of poor rice harvests and declining revenues from tea and rubber exports. It probably was unclear even to the government itself at that time. Aid commitments in 1974 exceeded most pre-1970 levels and were doubled in 1975. In the mid-1970s, Sri Lanka began to receive aid from some of the OPEC countries. Amounts involved were not large, except for the $50 million in 1975, but the appearance of a potential new source of aid further weakened the aid group's capacity to influence policy in Sri Lanka. It was about this time that the aid group began to shift from program aid to project aid, presumably to seek greater influence on how aid (if not total investible resources) was used.

The aid group (except for Sweden), especially the World Bank, was interested in giving advice and, of course, was confident that the advice offered was "right." Two points seem relevant. The first is that much of the advice given was of a very general, textbook sort. This is virtually necessary, but it did mean that details of policy changes remained to be worked out. General policy prescriptions and strategy are always easier to define than are the details that will implement those guidelines. The capacity of Sri Lanka to accomplish these latter tasks was, of course, limited. The very fact that members of Parliament and other government officials felt free to comment and intervene made such tasks even more difficult. It is not helpful for outsiders to tell a government that it should improve the management of its "something-or-other" and reduce the role of political considerations in appointments. Such advice is doubtless "correct," but also doubtless otiose.

The second point refers to objective functions and the constraints on their achievement, those of aid donors and those of Sri Lankans. They surely were different. In particular, aid donors were not affected in their views, their thinking, and their feeling by Sri Lanka's history, its culture, its ethnic complexity, its eagerness to be truly independent. To some extent, the group viewed the Sri Lankan policymaking scene as a tabula rasa on which any new policy could simply and effectively be established, and was disappointed when it was not. Actual objectives of the government were complex and ill-defined, and there were constraints (real and imagined) at every turn in identifying and understanding specific policy changes.

In the numerous World Bank reports on Sri Lanka there is a great deal of sensible advice, but little discussion of how aid might be used to underwrite a policy change or to help ease the costs of such change. Language used often seemed to imply that aid was considered to be a reward for the government's changing its policies in the way the donors liked, rather than a means of effecting the changed policies. The shift from program to project aid was an implicit recognition by the aid group that its capacity to use aid as a lever to force Sri Lanka to change its policies was extremely limited. This, of course, is not unusual. Aid donors have seldom had much luck using aid as a lever to induce a country to change policy, at least not until the country had already decided to make the change.

The Mahaweli Ganga Irrigation Project illustrates a number of aspects of the role of aid and of decisionmaking in the Sri Lankan government. Some of the problems that accompany large-scale irrigation works have already been noted, and these applied with even more intensity to the Mahaweli project. The main point here has to do with aid and policymaking.

Both political parties pushed the Mahaweli project. The Mahaweli Ganga, the country's largest river, has its headwaters in the Wet Zone highlands and flows across the Dry Zone. The first large-scale commitment was in 1969 when $60 million was made available by the aid group. The basic idea of the project was in the air as far back as the late nineteenth century, and the World Bank looked into possibilities in 1961. To use the water of Sri Lanka's largest river to provide irrigation for large tracts of land in the Dry Zone was an obviously attractive idea. When completed, the project would just about double the irrigated land area of the country, and would eliminate the need for any rice imports. The ruins in the Dry Zone provided continuing reminders of the great Sinhalese civilization of the past and the irrigation works that made that civilization possible. Much of the area that would be affected was populated largely by Sinhalese, a constituency whose support both parties sought. The Wet Zone was already densely populated and new available land in the Dry Zone was considered a solution to many difficulties in Sri Lanka.

The project also excited everyone's imagination and deflected attention from the great range of deep-seated problems that resisted quick, specific cures and that were socially and politically upsetting. Foreign aid could do little to help with these latter problems. Sri Lanka, like many developing countries (and much of development economics), placed great emphasis on the assumption that having large capital projects would resolve other problems that were difficult to confront directly. In addition, a substantial part of the project, especially the very beginning, would have to be accomplished by foreign engineers and other experts. Little burden, therefore, would be placed on the government itself because the work could all be farmed out, and this too was a major attraction.

The project could not be implemented without a great deal of outside help. A big project has considerable appeal to donors because it reduces the apparent complexity of identifying the use for the aid funds and facilitates monitoring that use. It was also evident to donors that there were not very many well-designed projects available in Sri Lanka. At the same time the aid group had some misgivings. The most complete plan for the development of the Mahaweli had been drawn up during the last half of the 1960s by a group supported by the United Nations Development Program and the Food and Agriculture Organization. These plans turned out to be misleading and incomplete in their own right, and, in any event, needed modification because of changes in relative prices and other data of fundamental importance to understanding the impact of the project. The aid group, especially the World Bank, therefore, preferred to move slowly, to attempt to determine the effects of the projects, and to explore a variety of alternatives. Bureaucratic pressures and procedures among the members of the aid group, however, produced incentives to move ahead. Similarly both political parties, the UNP in the late 1960s and the late 1970s and the SLFP in the early 1970s, were also eager to proceed with the project as rapidly as possible for the reasons reviewed above. For these reasons, in addition to the eagerness of the West to maintain an important presence in Sri Lanka, the project moved ahead more rapidly perhaps than effective management and support would dictate. The major difficulties occurred after the UNP resumed power in 1977. The point here is to call attention to the great complexities created by such an enormous project. These complexities arise partly from the inevitable imperfections in the analysis of the project itself. But, as Levy notes in his excellent study, the major difficulties were a "consequence of the particular sets of goals, constraints and bureaucratic pressures within which both the Sri Lankan government and aid donors made their decisions" (Levy 1985).

It should be emphasized that the Mahaweli project has had a number of favorable consequences, and doubtless will have more. The point is rather that the aid group found itself not only unable to affect policy decisions on Mahaweli (as well as on other matters), but indeed found itself supporting a project about which it had major doubts. The evidence also supports the view that other investment projects would have contributed more (in some sense) to social welfare than even a completed Mahaweli—and certainly more than an incomplete Mahaweli. Given the context as it had evolved over the years, these alternative projects, along with modified policies, were essentially impossible. As noted, even the World Bank, said to be objective and nonpolitical, became so caught up in the situation that it, too, acquiesced. It can be argued that such a large-scale, imaginative project was important in its effect on morale and hope within the government and among the population. It may have been true that less imposing projects would not have attracted aid. This is a useful point, but it must be acknowledged that the project created tasks that could be managed less well than tasks associated with smaller, more indigenous projects.

The Insurrection of 1971

A brief review of the insurrection that occurred in the spring of 1971 helps our understanding of Sri Lanka's complex society and of the difficulty of economic policymaking in that society. The purpose of this discussion is not to review the details of the insurrection as such, but to point out a few aspects of the situation that illuminate matters concerning our main theme. Most observers agree that the movement that led the insurrection, the People's Liberation Front (PLF), drew almost all of its support from the sixteen-to-twenty-five-year-old Sinhalese and Buddhist students in the secondary schools and universities. Very few students came from other ethnic and religious groups. Many women were apparently directly involved. Most of the participants were reasonably well educated and either were unemployed or were working in jobs that they deemed inappropriate. Apparently there were few workers and peasants in the PLF, despite its avowed Marxist background. The leaders were educated Sinhalese and had little to do with the other political parties, most of which had long ago agreed to play according to mutually accepted rules of the political game. A. J. Wilson states that the PLF members were "schooled more in the ruthlessness of Marxian intolerance than in the scientific and humanitarian aspects of its socialism" (Wilson 1972, p. 371). It is difficult to believe that this kind of attitude could have emerged without considerable intervention from outside Sri Lanka.

The PLF emerged in the mid-1960s and supported the SLFP in the 1970 election. It became disillusioned with Mrs. Bandarnaike's government program almost immediately after the election, and demanded far more severe measures—more nationalizations, more direct controls, more subsidies, and so forth—than the government was willing or able to take. The direct cause of the insurrection was the lack of jobs suitable for educated young people, lack of upward mobility, the presence of rich foreigners, and the apparent inability of the government to act decisively to alleviate these problems. The PLF was especially strong in its condemnation of the plantation sector and the alleged lack of economic independence. In a sense the insurrection pitted a new and more violent left against an old, more established, and less violent left. The great problem, of course, was that neither the left—nor anyone else—offered a very convincing policy package that would resolve Sri Lanka's economic difficulties.

The insurrection was severe and frightening, and it was defused with considerable authority. That it failed seems clear. It did not attract support from any other group in the society, and the evidence suggests that all other groups rejected it. Some commentators (for example, Wilson 1972; de Silva 1977) argue that Sri Lanka's democratic tradition—the fact that governments were elected in honest, open voting and were unrepressive—made it especially difficult to arouse the general population to a wholesale revolt. It may also be noted that numerous countries—including India, the United States, and Britain—provided immediate help to the government.

Two points are pertinent. The insurrection had its roots in the late 1960s. Toward the end of those years, the economy was showing some signs of significant improvement, although by 1970 the balance of payments was in trouble and little had been done to alleviate the employment problem. The UNP government was soundly defeated, and the SLFP was elected by a great majority. The insurrection occurred in less than a year after the SLFP took office. Evidently there was tension and distrust in the society that resulted in such an odd array of events. The second point refers to the effect of the insurrection on the policy of the SLFP. Although the insurrection failed to achieve its own goals, it is surely true that it resulted in an acceleration of a number of policies, especially the land reform laws and the establishment of basic industries under government ownership and control. These policies were difficult to design and execute in any circumstance and especially so when accomplished hastily and under considerable pressure. The government seems to have become more authoritarian, or, more accurately perhaps, a number of emergency measures adopted at the time of the insurrection were continued long after they were no longer needed. The government that took over with confidence and optimism was, thus, almost immediately pushed into an insecure position and forced to decide upon extremely complex issues with undue haste.

Equity in the 1970s

Equity in these complex and troubled years was an even more difficult notion than it had been in earlier years. Undoubtedly the new government believed that the policies that it sought to implement were contributing to a more equitable society than were the policies of the previous government. The nationalization of the estates, the land reforms, the food (and other) subsidies, the effort to establish "basic" industries, and so forth, were based on the belief that their application would increase equity. The principal objective was to create a truly national, independent Sri Lanka grounded in Buddhism and a humanistic sort of socialism. Such an objective had great appeal. The land reforms especially were intended to break a great source of wealth and thereby a great source of power. Equity was the major objective, equity and the preservation and expansion of a revered life-style, not simply an increased output. It is possible to question, however, the extent to which the non-Sinhalese were helped by the policies and indeed the extent to which they were intended to be helped. Some observers have suggested that these policies may well have exacerbated rather than resolved the ethnic problems and rivalries. From this standpoint, it is doubtful whether a major source of equity—racial harmony—was actually served.

Distribution of Income

The 1973 estimates are, as noted several times, of doubtful validity, but it is helpful to look quickly at what they show. From 1973 to 1978–79 the Central Bank's survey results show a sharp increase in inequality. Data for 1978 and 1979 are used, as are those for 1973, though neither year is exactly what we would like. In 1978 and 1979 the new government had been in office a year or so, but it is doubtful whether the new policies could have had affected distribution so quickly. Gross domestic product did increase sharply in 1978, and that would have had some effect, but it seems reasonable to assume that the general picture of distribution shown by the data is a consequence of the polices and strategies of the 1970–77 government. The Gini coefficient (for spending units) rose from 0.35 to 0.44, and the share of the highest-income decile increased from 28 percent to almost 36 percent while the share of all other deciles was declining. The lowest decile's share fell by 25 percent, the eighth and ninth by about 5 percent. The mean income in current prices of all deciles at least doubled, but the percentage increase was lower, the lower the decile. It would seem then that the highest-income groups profited at the expense of the very lowest. The level of GDP in constant prices was about 30 percent higher in 1978 than it was in 1970, and per capita GDP was about 15 percent higher.

These data show that inequality increased in both the rural and urban sectors, but declined rather impressively in the estate sector. Mean income of all estate income receivers in all quintiles was much lower—approximately 50 percent—in 1973 than other rural income receivers, and by 1978 and 1979, the lowest quintile of estate income receivers had a higher average income than did other rural workers; in other quintiles, except the highest, the relative difference between estate and rural income had narrowed considerably. Evidently estate workers had gained in this period, in part, possibly in large part, because of the government's wage policies and the change in ownership. Wage increases helped to alleviate some of the costs of the change in rice rations. These results for the estate sector affect the income/education relationship as well. Almost one-half of the income receivers with no formal education are in the estate sector, and the relatively large increase in the income of estate workers meant that, for the nation as a whole, the incomes of those with little or no education increased more, in percentage terms, than they did for those with much more education. The median income of people with a "passed degree" achieved the smallest percentage increase between 1973 and 1978–79. In general the data show that the variance of income among educational levels was much less in the latter year than in the former. This evidence is consistent, at least, with the view that as education was becoming so widespread it was also becoming less a determinant of income than had been true earlier.

The relative increase in the income of estate workers is difficult to reconcile with the jump in inequality. In 1973 Indian Tamils had a mean income about one-half that of the next lowest category—the Kandyan Sinhalese. This evidence—in addition to the direct comparison among the estate, rural, and urban groups in 1973 and 1978–79 referred to above—would suggest that income should have become more equally distributed between the two years. The fact that such a large part of the increased inequality was reflected in the big jump in the share of the top decile suggests a hypothesis or two. Perhaps the major source of increased income was associated with the big land development (including Mahaweli) projects and the investments in the new public-sector basic industries. Large-scale, concentrated investment projects can easily result in a situation where very few people profit handsomely relative to others, at least until the projects are fully operative. Worker remittances had begun to be significant by 1978 and 1979, and those who went to work in the Middle East received very high wages relative to wages in Sri Lanka.

One final point may be relevant. The unemployment rate in 1978 and 1979 was much lower than in 1973. The largest reductions in unemployment were, of course, in the fourteen-to-twenty-five age group. These newly employed people would, for the most part, be among the lowest-paid employees, and hence contribute to the increased inequality. (Presumably in the earlier period the unemployed would have had zero income and so contributed even more to inequality. This may have happened, but it seems that young people who were unemployed were less likely to be included in the sample than were young people who were employed).

These kinds of arguments make sense, but there is little direct support that can be offered in their favor. Now a more specific comment on the quality of the 1973 data. The changes in decile shares and in Gini coefficients from 1963 to 1973 to 1978–79 are unusually large compared with the experience of most countries. Income distribution usually changes much more slowly than these figures indicate was the case for Sri Lanka. The argument, therefore, has been made that 1973 was an odd year, and the estimates were less reliable than those for other years. It has already been mentioned that the years from 1971 to 1973 were poor for paddy and the tree crops, measured unemployment was 24 percent, the balance of payments was in trouble, the effects of the insurrection were still evident, and new manufacturing activities were in trouble. Given all these difficulties, 1973 was an unusual year, compared with 1963 and 1978–79. The decile distributions of 1978–79 and 1963 for income receivers are remarkably similar, as are the Gini coefficients. For spending units there is less similarity between the two years, but it is still much more marked than that between 1978–79 and 1973. Perhaps, then, the distribution of 1973 was a fleeting event, dependent on rather short-term phenomena that were associated with the depressed state of the economy, and perhaps the basic determinants of the distribution of income really did not change much between these two years. The comparison of decile shares between 1978–79 and 1953 also shows relatively modest changes. This comparison shows that the lowest decile had gained substantially, as had the third, fifth, and eighth, largely at the expense of the top decile. From 1953 to 1963 to 1978–79 the share of the top decile falls, and the share of other deciles fluctuates modestly. One then concludes that the major change that occurred during these years was the decline in the share of the very rich, and that this was proceeding at a steady, but modest, pace. This conclusion is consistent with previous arguments that transformation was occurring slowly and rather painfully in Sri Lanka.

It is difficult to say much about what happened to low-end poverty in these years. The mean income in current prices in each of the lowest three deciles of spending units more than doubled between 1973 and 1977. A deflated series of income per income receiver (Unicef 1958, p. 22) shows the same figure for the lowest decile for 1973 and 1978–79, and increases of 20 to 25 percent for the next four deciles. The fact that the data show that there was no increase in the real income of the lowest decile doubtless means that the income of many people in this group declined. At the same time it does seem fair to say that there was no large-scale increase in low incomes and poverty in these years.

Social Services and Food Subsidies

Expenditures on these items as a percentage of the government's current expenditure and of GDP declined slightly over the years from 1970 to 1977. Central Bank data show that in 1971 and 1972 they were over 11 percent of GDP, having risen from 10 percent in 1969 and 1970. They fell to just over 9 percent in 1973 and remained there until 1977. Health and education outlays (on current account) seem to have declined more than food subsidies, but any difference is quite modest. These minor changes do not represent a change in policy or strategy by the government. The SLFP remained committed to such an approach to the end of its term in office.

Social Indicators

The period under review is too short to expect significant changes in the usual array of social indicators, but a couple of points may be noted. Available data show that the school enrollment ratio for the five-to-fourteen age group declined steadily from essentially 100 in 1970 to 80 in 1976. This may reflect the economic difficulties of the period, but it may also reflect some growing disillusionment with education by families and students. One must note with respect to this latter argument, however, that the ratio was back up to 98 percent by 1982. Even so, the fact that elementary education was sacrificed somewhat during the tough times implies something about the priority given to it by the society.

Life expectancy, infant mortality, crude birth rate, various health indicators, female labor force participation rates, and so forth, all moved slowly in the generally approved direction. Despite the trou-

bles of the period, improvements in these important variables continued at a steady pace. Given that these variables were already at unusually favorable levels for a country with Sri Lanka's per capita income
in 1970, it can be concluded that virtually all income groups were
included.

Other Aspects of Equity

Undoubtedly, the general philosophy of the SLFP fit well with most of
the Sinhalese, as indeed it had in the years from 1955 to 1965. The
search for genuine economic independence combined with a rather
relaxed approach to economic development was congenial to the traditions and values of this community. The ready availability of the estate
sector to tax in an effort to support this approach was also satisfying
and consistent with prevailing ideas and views. As the estate economy
declined, as population grew, as literacy and awareness increased
among the Sinhalese population, and economic problems became increasingly severe, this kind of an approach became less and less effective. For the SLFP to modify its strategy was essentially impossible
given its makeup and the other problems—the insurrection, weather,
decline in aid, and so forth—that occurred during these years. As
these difficulties increased, the government became increasingly authoritarian, very much contrary to traditional political practices in Sri
Lanka.

In the 1970s it became evident to virtually everyone that the traditional approach was no longer possible. In this broad sense, then,
there emerged a significant tradeoff between economic growth and
equity. Here equity refers to the maintenance of a social organization
and social environment that is deemed by the community to be appropriate and honored. Something had to give, and it had to be these
ideas of what constituted a good life-style. The new government in
1977 was vastly freer to act than any government had been in the
past—freer both in terms of pressure from its constituents and,
equally important, in terms of its own capacity to acknowledge that
change was necessary and that the ideas that dominated the past had
to be relinquished.

Two Final Points

First, this idea of equity that had prevailed so long had done little to
contribute to ethnic harmony. Pluralism was never established, and,
given the history of the society and the emergence of the strong and
devout attitudes among all groups described earlier, this failure was
not surprising. It was, however, a blank spot in a notion of equity that

was otherwise exceedingly appealing. The agonizing ethnic conflicts of the 1980s emphasized this blank spot.

Second, in these years emigration of labor became a factor to be considered. Emigration in the early 1970s was mainly concentrated in high-skill groups—doctors, engineers, architects, and so forth. Most of these people went to the United Kingdom, the United States, Canada, or Australia. In the mid-1970s skilled and unskilled workers were emigrating to the Middle East. Data compiled by the World Bank show that by 1979 more than 20,000 Sri Lankan workers had emigrated to the Middle East. Slightly more than one-half of these were classified as unskilled, and the others as skilled and "middle-level" white collar people.

The full impact of this (and later) migration is difficult to discover. There were good and bad sides. Accumulating evidence for other countries suggests that the bad may well outweigh the good (Bruton 1980). The main point to emphasize here is that this emigration had both a push and pull side. The nature of the pull is obvious. The push suggests that as changes began to occur in Sri Lanka, sizable numbers of people began to look elsewhere, and the appeal of the traditional life-styles began to weaken. These were traumatic years and traumatic experiences for Sri Lankans. It does not help to say that had different policies been followed in the preceding twenty-five years, the trauma would have been averted. Such policies were unavailable, and, had they been known, they could not have been implemented.

9 1977 to 1985: A New Strategy

The UNP was swept into power by an unprecedented majority in the election of July 1977. The SLFP, which had ruled the country in the preceding seven years (1970–77), had its parliamentary strength reduced from 91 seats in a Parliament of 151 seats to a mere 8 seats in an enlarged parliament with 168 seats. The UNP won 140 seats.

For the first time Sri Lanka's Marxist parties failed to secure a single seat. Only two other parties won any seats in Parliament. These were the Tamil United Liberation Front (TULF), which was an ethnic party representing the Tamils in the northern and eastern parts of the country, and the Ceylon Workers' Congress (CWC), representing the estate workers of Indian origin. The TULF won eighteen seats and secured 6.8 percent of the total vote. The CWC, which was allied with the UNP, contested two seats and won a single seat.

The Political Setting

There were several aspects of the electoral results that markedly contrasted with previous elections. For the first time in Sri Lanka's electoral politics, a single political party secured over three-fourths of the parliamentary seats. Also for the first time, a single party secured over one-half of the votes cast. The rejection of the SLFP regime was made clear by the fact that the former prime minister retained her seat by a much reduced majority; only one other SLFP cabinet minister secured a seat, and the two Marxist parties—the Communist Party and the Lanka Sama Samaja Party—which formed part of the SLFP-led coalition government from May 1970 until March 1974, did not secure a single seat. This was the first time that these two parties had not secured a single seat in Parliament.

In interpreting this convincing victory of the UNP, it is easy to fall prey to the simplistic view that it was entirely owing to a rejection of the economic policies pursued by the SLFP and its coalition regime. It is clear, of course, that the economic results achieved by the SLFP regime were so meager and the gap so wide between the expectations and the reality that the people rejected the government in no uncertain terms. Other considerations, however, were important, and a comment or two will help to clarify numerous post-1977 developments.

From 1956, when the UNP was first defeated at the polls, it was not by the strength of the SLFP alone, but by a coalition of parties. The SLFP faced the 1977 election without such a coalition. The parties that formed the coalition government between 1970 and 1977 were, by 1977, in bitter opposition to the SLFP; consequently, the SLFP was particularly weakened at the polls. Although the UNP obtained more than 50 percent of the total vote for the first time in Sri Lanka's political history, the SLFP was able to obtain only about one-third of the votes—the same that it had achieved in previous elections. The seven-year period of being out of office had enabled the UNP to reorganize itself under its new leader, J. R. Jayewardene. The party projected a new image of being youthful and energetic, and was especially successful in establishing itself in the rural areas.

Some observers have argued that, as Sri Lankans were in the practice of changing governments every five years, the extra two years between the 1970 and 1977 elections made the electorate even more eager than usual to change. It is also important to recognize that a number of problems of the 1970s resulted from matters over which government policy had no influence—particularly the 1973 oil price increase and the bad weather. The failure of the land reform programs to fulfill expectations created additional problems for the SLFP at the election, but the idea of land reform and the nationalization did not. All of these factors, combined with the unfortunate experience of the economy during the years from 1970 to 1977, placed the SLFP in a virtually impossible position for the election.

Thus, no single explanation of the outcome of the election is adequate. A mixture of political factors, failed economic polices, a harsh international situation, and bad weather all contributed to defeat of the SLFP. The UNP was able to exploit these conditions and results, the deficiencies in economic management, and the apparent corruption. The UNP took over the government not only with a large majority, but also in a good position to advance a radically different policy package from any that had been tried previously.

The New Economic Policies

The package of policies introduced by the UNP in November 1977 was intended to transform the Sri Lankan economy from an inward-looking, closed economy, which was managed through direct administrative controls, to one that was outward looking and market oriented.

The main consequences expected of this new approach were a higher growth rate of GDP and a major expansion of employment opportunities. The principle features of the new policy may be listed.

- Trade and payments were liberalized. Import controls were largely abolished and tariffs rationalized. Export licensing was to be similarly phased out, and the export duty structure reformed. Export promotion and diversification were emphasized.
- The rupee was devalued from about Rs8.8 to Rs16 per U.S.dollar. The exchange rate was tied to a basket of currencies and allowed to float as the basket floated, and the balance of payments was to be protected mainly by movements in the exchange rate.
- The devaluation and import liberalization would have immediate revenue and expenditure effects on the government budget; therefore, the government budget had to be adjusted.
- The private sector was encouraged to participate in all aspects of the economy, and public sector monopolies were to be ended. Price controls were eliminated over much of the economy and there was a greatly increased reliance on market signals to determine resource allocation. Tax concessions and other investment benefits were made available to private sector agents. Private foreign investment was also encouraged and a free trade zone was established.
- There was to be large-scale public investment in transportation, telecommunications, and energy facilities.
- Agricultural pricing policies were changed to create and maintain strong producer incentives to increase output. The guaranteed price of paddy paid to producers was raised from Rs33 to Rs40 per bushel, and the guaranteed procurement price of other subsidiary agricultural products was also raised.
- Fiscal policy was to be redesigned to channel more resources into investment and simultaneously reduce the current account deficit, which in turn required some reduction in subsidies and transfer payments. There was no change in the publicly supported education and health programs, and the subsidized food ration, already available only to those who did not pay income tax, was further restricted to households with an income of Rs300 a month or less. It seems clear that the long-established food subsidies could not have been completely abolished without creating great unrest. In the best of circumstances it would take some time for the expected increase in investment and employment to eliminate need for some sort of help to the lowest income group.
- To encourage saving, the interest rates on saving deposits were increased from 7 to 8 percent to 12 to 18 percent on 6-to-18-month deposits. The financial market was liberalized, and interest rates became important as a market-clearing instrument.

The new policy package of 1977 was evidently different from any that Sri Lanka had experienced in its independent history. The new package had most of the ingredients for which aid donors had long been pressing. The fact that the government undertook such a radical reform in such a short period doubtless reflects the expectation that aid donors, especially the World Bank and the International Monetary Fund, would offer substantial support. These expectations were realized as large amounts of foreign capital became available almost immediately.

Results of the Policy Reform

The charts in chapter 5 show that several series took off in the mid-to-late 1970s. It would appear that the post-1977 performance of the economy was fundamentally different from what it had been prior to that date. An important question arises, therefore, about whether the performance was really different.

Growth and Employment

Table 9-1 summarizes the main indicators. The growth rate of GDP in these years averaged about 5.7 percent per year compared with about 3.0 percent in the 1970 to 1977 period. The investment rate increased sharply, from around 14 to 16 percent in the years before 1978, to 20 percent in 1978, and to a peak of 33.7 percent in 1980. The average for the period was over 27 percent, well above any rate experienced in Sri Lanka's history. The ratio of national saving to GDP was actually lower in most years of the period than it had been in 1976 and 1977. The exceptionally high investment rate and the much lower saving

Table 9-1. Macroeconomic Indicators for Sri Lanka, 1978–85

Year	GDP[a] (millions of rupees)	GDP growth (percent)	Investment-GDP ratio	Saving-GDP ratio	Export volume index	Import volume index
1978	59,246	8.7	20.0	14.8	101	71
1979	62,876	6.1	25.8	13.3	102	87
1980	66,728	6.1	33.7	12.1	100	100
1981	70,386	5.5	27.7	11.2	103	103
1982	73,975	5.1	30.7	12.7	113	107
1983	77,645	4.9	28.8	13.3	110	128
1984	80,800	4.1	25.8	17.5	128	132
1985	84,805	4.9	25.8	14.2	134	123

a. At 1980 prices.
Source: Central Bank of Sri Lanka, *Annual Report* (various years).

rate meant, of course, that foreign assistance in one form or another was a major feature of the post-1977 years. The Central Bank estimates that during the years from 1971 to 1977 foreign financing amounted to about 20 percent of investment and from 1978 to 1985 the figure was about 40 percent. Export volume increased slowly, but there were big jumps in 1984 and 1985. Imports rose quickly over the first years of liberalization, then leveled off a bit, before rising sharply again from 1983. The share of public investment in total investment rose from less than one-half in the 1970 to 1977 years to almost 60 percent in the years after 1977. The investment boom, therefore, was very much a public sector, foreign aid phenomenon.

Two additional characteristics of the general picture stand out. After the big spurt in growth in 1978, the annual growth rates began to decline from one year to the next until 1985. The estimate for 1985 shows the growth rate for that year about equal to that for 1984. These growth rates declined despite the continued high rate of investment and a splurge in the volume of imports after 1982.

The other characteristic to note about this growth period is that it produced virtually no changes in the composition of GDP. Agriculture and manufacturing were about the same proportion in 1985 as they were in 1970 (see table 2-9, chapter 2). Trade, finance, and construction increased a bit, but essentially one concludes that there was no change in the composition of GDP in this period of unusually rapid growth and marked change in policy. In particular, it should be noted that no new activities emerged as leading sectors. The increased role of construction reflected government investment in infrastructure, housing, and urban renewal. Questions about transformation capacity and entrepreneurship continue to be relevant. The absence of change in composition, however, meant that all sectors participated in the rapid growth. That agriculture held its own with other sectors is extremely relevant in our story.

The new policy was explicitly aimed at increasing the rate of growth of measured GDP and reducing the rate of unemployment. Unemployment, a major problem throughout Sri Lanka's history, had reached alarming proportions in the 1970s. New jobs were as urgently needed, as was increased output. Large-scale public investment programs were expected to generate a big increase in the demand for labor. The unemployment rate as measured by the consumer finance and socioeconomic surveys of the Central Bank was 24.0 percent in 1973, 14.7 percent from 1978 to 1979, and 11.7 percent from 1981 to 1982. It should be noted here, however, that the fall was costly in terms of investment per job created. The decline was also greatly facilitated by the fact that perhaps 200,000 people migrated to the Middle East to work for extended periods and approximately 337,000 persons of Indian origin in the estate sector left for resettlement in India under the India–Sri Lanka Agreement. The employment effect of the new strategy must then be considered carefully.

Some Further Details

The accelerated growth rates and reduced unemployment solved some problems and created others. A short review of some of these will help to identify a few more of the forces at work in the economy.

INFLATION. Price increases as shown by official indices in the 1970s were above those of the 1960s, and it is probable that these indices understate the actual price rises. Even so, it seems correct to say that inflation was not a serious problem before the late 1970s. As the charts in chapter 2 show, money supply and the government deficit rose sharply and this produced the pressure on prices. The expansion of credit to both public and private sectors and the financing of an increasing government deficit led to money supply increases of as much as 30 percent a year. Although the government was committed to reduced current account expenditures, success was hard to come by. Transfer payments to government corporations continued to grow until 1983, and household transfers grew rapidly throughout the period. Tax collections proved to be quite inelastic with respect to GDP growth, and there was increasing resort to indirect taxes, which always have some distorting effects. About 70 percent of the government resources were obtained from indirect taxes and only about 20 percent from direct taxes. Devaluation in addition to large-scale foreign aid create inflationary pressures and add to the complexities of monetary management. The circumstances of 1977 and 1978 illustrate the point made earlier that during these years the old order was breaking down and the new was not yet in place. Economic management was inadequate to guide this transition without major problems, such as inflation, as rapidly as resource availability would allow. The general evidence suggests an inadequate effort to widen the tax net and strengthen the tax administration to facilitate collecting taxes from the people who benefited directly from the new development strategy. This inadequacy had consequences not only for the government budget, but also for income distribution.

BALANCE OF PAYMENTS. If there is no access to foreign loans or foreign assistance, foreign exchange expenditures must be matched by foreign exchange earnings. In the past, Sri Lanka had usually maintained this equality by squeezing imports when it was forced to do so because of reduced foreign exchange earnings. The greatly increased availability of foreign assistance and loans beginning during the late 1970s made it possible to have a large deficit in both the trade balance and the current account.

Imports increased sharply in volume and value with liberalization of controls and increased aid in the late 1970s. They more than doubled in value in 1978 compared with 1977. Volume grew slowly after 1980, but import prices rose steadily, so that by 1985 they were approximately eight times higher than in 1977, and more than twice their 1980 value. Food, including rice, continued to be imported, but declined sharply as a percentage of total imports. Intermediate and investment goods became an important component of total imports. In 1985, for example, foodstuff was just over 10 percent of imports, while investment and intermediate goods (omitting petroleum) constituted about one-half of all imports. This shift in composition reflects the availability of foreign assistance and the more severe growth orientation of the new policy.

Exports, of course, were much less affected. It was not until 1984 and 1985 that volume increased by very much. Tea, rubber, and coconuts continued to dominate the export structure, accounting for about one-half the total in 1985. A major disappointment with the new policy was its failure to generate nontraditional exports in substantial amounts. Garments continued to be far and away the largest new export item, and most of these were produced in the investment promotion zone by a very small number of firms. The term of trade improved during 1983 and 1984, but fell sharply again in 1985. This export picture reinforces the conclusion reached earlier that the new policy had not made great strides on the transformation and entrepreneurial objectives.

The foreign debt, as shown in figure 5-1, began to rise during the late 1960s, accelerated in the mid-1970s, and then took off in the 1980s. The Central Bank data show that the foreign debt in rupees more than doubled in the 1980s (and increased by two-thirds in SDRS). The debt service as a percentage of exports of merchandise and services rose from about 15 percent in 1980 to over 22 percent in 1985.

The final development to note in the balance of payments is the large increase in "private transfers"—largely remittances from Sri Lankans who went to the Middle East to work. These amounted to R56 million (SDR6 million) in 1976, Rs2,200 million (SDR105 million) in 1980, and between SDR240 and SDR270 million from 1982 to 1985. Earnings from tourism declined sharply in the 1980s because of the ethnic disturbances. Such remittances eased the immediate balance of payments pressure and the unemployment difficulties of the 1980s, but in no way did they solve any of Sri Lanka's fundamental problems.

These balance of payments developments reflect a new kind of vulnerability in the great dependence on foreign assistance and worker remittances and the small success in implementing new activities.

EXCHANGE RATE. Despite the persistent deficits in the balance of payments, import restrictions were not reimposed. The main instrument of adjustment was the exchange rate with some help from a rationalization of the tariff structure. The rupee fell regularly over the period in nominal terms. The sharp devaluation in 1977 lowered the value of the rupee from 10.2 per SDR to 18.9, and by 1985 there were Rs30 per SDR. As it was more or less tied to the U.S. dollar, it fell less rapidly against the dollar.

The data show, however, that the exchange rate, corrected for differentials between Sri Lanka's inflation and that of its trading partners, appreciated sharply in 1980 and remained above the 1977 level throughout the rest of the period. The appreciation in 1985 was especially marked. It seems clear, therefore, that the efforts to achieve an effective devaluation were largely unsuccessful.

The foreign assistance in addition to worker remittances further complicated the exchange rate picture. They not only made possible the large import surplus on the trade account, but also supported the exchange rate at a level that misrepresented the productivity of the Sri Lankan economy, except possibly for the tree crops. The appropriate exchange rate policy was less clear than it had been earlier. The dominance of tea and rubber (plus controls) had made it possible to have an exchange rate that overstated the productivity of the rest of the economy. The dominance of tea and rubber continued, but now they were supported by foreign assistance and remittances, so that the rupee, although falling in nominal value, remained high and often rising when corrected for inflation. The exchange rate, therefore, probably offered only modest incentives for nontraditional activities to emerge, to grow, and to export. The exchange rate policy and the effort to rationalize tariffs illustrate the great difficulty of designing concrete blueprints to effect a general policy position, and Sri Lanka, not unlike all governments, had trouble in this area.

AGRICULTURE. The rice sector continued to be the most dynamic of the agricultural activities. Production was more than 50 percent higher in 1985 than in 1977, so growth averaged slightly less than 6.0 percent a year, despite two years when production actually fell. Yields also rose steadily, and, despite a sharp fall in 1984, were more than one-third higher in 1985 than in 1977. The guaranteed price was increased regularly over the years, and by 1985 was more than double the 1977 price. The "world" price was still higher than the guaranteed price in most years, and the purchases under the guaranteed price scheme declined rather steadily. Consumer prices rose faster than this, but even so, the rising guaranteed price was an important inducement to increase output. More widespread irrigation, the greatly increased use of high-yielding varieties of seeds, and the even larger increase in the use of fertilizer all help explain the growth of paddy production. The rice program had long been supported by both parties, and these years were in some sense the culmination of a program begun much earlier.

The program was expensive, and some aspects of it, especially the large-scale irrigation projects, could probably not be justified on a narrow cost-benefit analysis. On more general criteria the program was surely a success. The objectives of self-sufficiency in rice and of raising the income and employment opportunities in the rural, nonestate areas were served by the program. Rice imports were 543,000 tons in 1977 and fell steadily to 27,000 in 1985. This was an important objective of the post-1977 government, as it had been for all previous governments.

Tea and rubber continued to have their troubles. The replanting of tea with new, higher-yielding clones remained slow, and even by the mid-1980s less than 20 percent of the total tea area had been replanted. Yields grew virtually not at all, despite strong prices, especially after 1982. The good tea prices did result in a substantial increase in the minimum wages of estate workers in 1984 although output growth was essentially nil. Although replanting was much more extensive for rubber than for tea, yields did not increase significantly.

It is difficult to determine the main source of the continued weakness of tea and rubber production. Estimates of the costs of production published in the *Review of the Economy* for 1985 by the Central Bank show that substantial profits were available at prevailing prices. Undoubtedly, long-range projections for rubber were weak, but those for tea were probably less so. Most of the estates had become publicly owned by the early 1980s, and it can be argued that the government simply made a decision to push rice production hard and allow the estates to follow, at least for a period of time. This neglect took the form of inexperienced management, fertilizer shortages, and some labor difficulties. This approach could have been justified had projections been poor for both tea and rubber, and had an aggressive effort been made to create new leading sectors. The latter did not happen, so the major foreign exchange earners declined before any alternative leading sectors appeared.

Coconuts, the other tree crop, enjoyed some success. Output in 1985 was about 60 percent above the 1977 level, although the 1985 figure was exceptionally high. Coconuts are also primarily a product of small farms, and some advantages may have accrued to their production for this reason.

MANUFACTURING. The manufacturing component of GDP averaged over 5.0 percent growth a year from 1978 to 1985. Although this growth was much larger than the 1 percent average of the 1970s, it was still disappointing. There were several factors accounting for the failure of this sector to flourish. Public investment was heavily concentrated in infrastructure with the expectation that the improvements in transportation, power, communication, and so forth would make private (domestic and foreign) investment sufficiently profitable that substantial new manufacturing activities would appear. This did not happen. Public sector ventures, a large weight (about 60 percent) in the determination of overall manufacturing growth, remained sluggish and privatization efforts had not taken hold by 1985. The quick increase in imports created competition to which many domestic firms had difficulty responding. Central Bank data show that current transfer payments to public corporations averaged about 10 percent of total current expenditure in the years from 1978 to 1985. The long period of protection and government support had made it costly to adjust to the new environment. As already noted, petroleum products and garments accounted for a major share of output and of manufactured exports. Because much of the garment output was produced in the investment promotion zone, few linkages with the rest of the economy were created.

To get the tariff "rationalized" was a major objective of the government when it took office in late 1977. This effort proved to be difficult. A Presidential Tariff Commission studied the tariff structure in 1984 and found numerous anomalies and inconsistencies. A new tariff structure, which sought to eliminate redundant protection as well as increase the protection afforded certain activities that seemed to have a higher value added, was introduced in 1984. The government also found itself subjected to pressure by individuals for more protection, which hampered the achievement of a full and neat rationalization.

In terms of numbers of branches and transactions, the banking system grew rapidly. The growth, however, was concentrated on relatively low-risk, fast-yielding areas, such as import financing and other short-term lending. This cautious approach of the banking system posed additional handicaps to the manufacturing sector in diversifying and expanding.

SERVICES. Activities usually defined as services (transport, storage, communication, wholesale and retail trade, banking, and insurance) increased their share of GDP by a sizable amount—from 27 percent in 1977 to about 35 percent in 1985. The investment in this sector has been dominated by state enterprises—much of it associated with foreign trade and the other increased movement of goods.

Table 9-2. Employment by Sector, 1977–82

(thousands of persons)

Sector	1977	1980	1982
Estate	510	530	192
Tea	431	442	388
Rubber	68	73	88
Coconut	10	14	16
Government	423	476	486
Semigovernment	617	769	792

Source: Central Bank of Ceylon, Statistics Department (1984).

EMPLOYMENT. An additional word on employment is helpful. Table 9-2 shows some data on employment for estates and the government. The falling employment on tea plantations is evident, as is the growing demand on rubber and coconut estates. The decline in tea, however, was so large that total estate employment fell from 1980 to 1982 by almost 8 percent. Government employment increased by approximately 22 percent between 1977 and 1982—most of which had occurred by 1980. There are no data for the other sectors of the economy. Table 9-3 shows the breakdown of unemployment among ethnic groups. The one point that stands out is the difference in unemployment rates between the two major ethnic groups. Both Tamil groups had markedly lower unemployment rates in all years than did the two Sinhalese groups. Indian Tamils, largely employed on estates, had the lowest unemployment rate. They also had the lowest wages and the most unsatisfactory living conditions.

Table 9-3. Labor Force and Unemployment by Community, 1973–82

Community	Labor force as a percentage of population			Unemployment as a percentage of labor force		
	1973	1978–79	1981–82	1973	1978–79	1981–82
Kandyan Sinhalese	30.6	39.8	33.8	23.0	13.9	11.3
Low-country Sinhalese	35.3	37.4	34.6	30.0	18.5	14.6
Sri Lankan Tamils	29.8	31.4	30.3	17.7	10.9	6.7
Indian Tamils	51.1	51.9	51.2	12.3	5.6	4.9
Moors	25.5	27.0	24.6	21.3	13.8	10.4
Malays	25.8	32.3	33.3	43.5	10.8	22.6
Total	33.9	38.0	34.3	24.0	14.7	11.7

Source: Central Bank of Ceylon, Statistics Department (1984).

The unemployment rate had been greatly reduced by 1982, but naturally was still high. Unemployment among the fourteen-to-twenty-five-year-olds was only slightly smaller in 1981 and 1982 than in 1978 and 1979. The educated unemployed problem also continued with its implications for social and political stability.

Of the educational categories, the two with the lowest unemployment rates were "no schooling, illiterate" and "no schooling, literate." Approximately 40 percent of undergraduate degree holders were unemployed in 1981 and 1982 compared with 50 percent in 1978 and 1979. All these estimates are based on sample survey data obtained from the socioeconomic surveys.

As noted earlier, some 200,000 workers had migrated to the Middle East on a long-term assignment, and about 337,000 persons of Indian origin had returned to India. The labor force in Sri Lanka in the mid-1980s was approximately 5 million, so about 10 percent of the labor force had left Sri Lanka. There is little doubt that, had the large-scale migrations not occurred, unemployment rates would have been markedly higher after 1980. Indeed, a stronger statement is possible: The improvement after 1978 and 1979 was simply a consequence of the migrations. The economy itself did not generate a significant number of new jobs.

There are no data for the period after 1982, but general evidence suggests that unemployment has risen since that year. The growth rates have declined—especially those for tourism and construction. The growth of agricultural output has reflected mainly increases in productivity. Finally, the outward migrations have essentially stopped because of both the large-scale cutbacks in spending in the Middle East oil-producing countries and the inability of India to accommodate returning workers. All of these developments support the view that unemployment in 1985 was substantially greater than in 1982.

Conclusion

What can one say in conclusion about these developments? A rather hopeful conclusion would be along the following lines. The large-scale infrastructure investments by the government, including irrigation projects such as the Mahaweli project, have a long gestation period; even after completion, there is a further lag before a long-shackled private sector can respond with directly productive employment-creating investment. The continued communal disturbances in addition to the slowdown in the world economy in the early 1980s dampened potential foreign as well as domestic investment. The ethnic disturbances have also distracted the attention of the government from long-term economic matters to resolving the communal strife. The disturbances have added to the government's budget problems as additional outlays for defense became necessary. The achievement of near self-sufficiency in rice, the increase in power-generation capacity, the expansion of housing, and the development of trade and financial activities as well as the good GDP growth rate, have all been noteworthy achievements. Once the ethnic problems are solved and the world economy is fully recovered, the economy will begin to respond more effectively than it has so far. So policy was essentially right.

This argument is important and relevant, but must be qualified in several respects. It is difficult, of course, to appraise the impact of the civil disturbances. Their effect on tourism and foreign investment clearly has been extremely negative. That the private sector has responded so slowly demands additional questions. The transformation and entrepreneurial problems manifested themselves in various ways during these years—especially in the manufacturing sector, which could not establish itself effectively. The government could not halt the subsidies to the public corporations, nor could it seem to make privatization work—further evidence of the transformation problem. Exchange rate and tariff policies seemed intractable, and the big investment boom, heavily financed from abroad, created inflationary pressures that were difficult to manage. In addition, the foreign debt shot up, traditional exports lagged, and few new exports appeared, so the economy became even more vulnerable than it had been, and depended heavily upon foreign assistance and worker remittances. The exceptionally high growth rates in the years from 1978 to 1980 were the easy phase of the liberalization policy. The big splurge of imports solved a number of shortages, and allowed output to expand quickly for a few years. The decline in the growth rate reflects the fact that the basic limitations of the economy had not really been solved. The government, with a huge majority in Parliament, still could not act decisively and effectively, which was further evidence that the decisionmaking problems of the government had not been solved.

This argument is also important and relevant. Before trying to reach a conclusion on these two arguments, equity during this period must be studied.

Equity and the New Policy

The main focus of the new policies introduced in late 1977 and 1978 was the acceleration of growth and the expansion of employment. Distribution as such was given less explicit attention and the intention was to modify and reduce food and other subsidies. Strong growth, combined with a rapidly growing demand for labor, was to make such subsidies completely unnecessary—or at least greatly reduce their role in the pursuit of an equitable society. Growth and employment were discussed in the previous two sections; now, a study of the impact of such policies on equity is necessary. As usual, we begin with income distribution and poverty, and then move on to the more complex issues of equity.

Income Distribution

Table 9-4 shows the distribution of income by decile of spending units for four years—1963, 1973, 1978–1979, and 1981–1982. There are no estimates available for years after 1981 and 1982, so it is not possible to say anything in quantitive terms about distribution after 1982. Given the long lag between policy change and its effect on income distribution, this is a serious gap in our story. In the earlier discussion, the point was made that 1973 was an unusual year in many of the respects that would be expected to affect the distribution of income. For these reasons, it was argued that 1973 data should not be taken as reflecting a fundamental change in relation to 1963 in the way the economy distributed its income. Even given this interpretation of the 1973 data, there were some changes between 1973 and earlier and later years (assuming the data have some accuracy) that are part of the story.

The data for the three years other than 1973 are remarkably similar. If the two later years are compared with 1973, then there is little doubt that distribution became less equal after 1973. In particular, the top decile had gained at the expense of every other decile by 1978 and 1979, but especially did it gain at the expense of the two lowest deciles.

The top decile continued to gain after 1978 and 1979, and most of

Table 9-4. Decile Shares of Income, 1963–82

(percent)

Decile	1963	1973	1978–79	1981–82
Lowest	1.50	2.79	2.12	2.18
Second	3.95	4.38	3.61	3.55
Third	4.00	5.60	4.65	4.35
Fourth	5.21	6.52	5.68	5.24
Fifth	6.27	7.45	6.59	6.35
Sixth	7.54	8.75	7.69	7.02
Seventh	9.00	9.91	8.57	8.69
Eighth	11.22	11.65	11.22	10.71
Ninth	15.54	14.92	14.03	14.52
Highest	36.77	28.03	35.84	37.29
Gini coefficient	0.45	0.35	0.44	0.45

Source: Central Bank of Ceylon, Statistics Department (1984).

the gain was at the expense of the lowest five deciles. Only the lowest deciles did not lose between 1978–79 and 1981–82. This continued gain, in addition to the rapidity with which distribution returned to the pre-1973 state, not only lends support to the notion that 1973 was an exceptional year, but also supports the view that the new policy did, at least in these first years, contribute to increased inequality. This inequality was especially characterized by an increasing share for the highest income deciles. There are several reasons that this result is to be expected.

- Although data for wage rates are incomplete, the available evidence suggests that real wages rose very little. Indeed, from 1980 through 1984 they probably declined over most sectors. Tables 9-5 and 9-6 summarize data that have been compiled by the Department of Labor and the Central Bank.

  Table 9-5 shows wage-rate indexes for the three major sectors of the organized sector—central government, government schoolteachers, and those trades in the private sector and corporations that are governed by wage boards. The real wages have been obtained by deflating the nominal wage series by the Colombo consumer price index. This index surely understates the price rises over these years, so the real wage index in the table overstates real wages. Even so, real wages fell sharply after 1979, and, for teachers and Wage Boards Trade Employees, did not regain 1978 levels until 1985. Wages of central government employees began to rise in 1982. When nominal wages are deflated by a more

Table 9-5. Indexes of Lowest Wages in the Organized Sector, 1978–85

(December 1978 = 100)

Year	Wage boards trade employees		Central government employees		Government schoolteachers	
	Nominal wage rate index	Real wage index	Nominal wage rate index	Real wage index	Nominal wage rate index	Real wage index
1978	100.0	105.2	100.0	105.2	100.0	105.2
1979	119.6	112.9	117.2	111.2	112.3	106.6
1980	147.3	111.1	129.1	97.2	120.1	90.5
1981	152.2	97.1	146.1	93.2	133.1	84.9
1982	152.2	97.1	187.8	108.0	166.4	95.7
1983	188.8	95.5	215.7	109.0	188.1	95.1
1984	224.3	96.9	246.6	106.6	211.4	91.4
1985	244.1	104.1	284.3	121.2	247.3	105.4

Source: Central Bank of Ceylon, *Annual Report* (various issues).

Table 9-6. Annual Average Daily Wages in the Unorganized Sector, All Island, 1979–85

(rupees)

Sector	Gender of worker	1979	1980	1981	1982	1983	1984	1985
Paddy	Male	13.55	14.27	15.04	15.04	15.69	14.77	14.81
	Female	9.48	9.89	10.73	10.82	11.54	10.90	10.57
Coconut	Male	13.46	13.85	14.62	15.75	16.19	14.05	14.72
	Female	7.60	7.98	8.70	8.95	9.22	8.53	8.86
Rubber	Male	12.19	13.60	13.74	12.85	13.65	12.67	12.72
	Female	9.10	9.80	9.85	9.44	9.56	8.78	9.49
Tea	Male	10.88	11.42	11.10	10.64	10.20	10.14	10.73
	Female	7.64	8.09	8.21	7.50	7.19	7.89	8.40
Construction								
Carpenter	Male	22.16	23.60	25.36	26.38	25.68	23.95	25.47
Mason	Male	21.81	22.89	24.00	20.60	24.99	23.33	24.77

Note: Wage rates represent payment in cash without meals.
Source: Central Bank of Sri Lanka, *Annual Report* (various issues).

accurate price index, the declines are sharper and recovery in 1985 does not bring real wages back to 1978 levels except for central government employees.

Table 9-6 provides some evidence on real wages in the unorganized sector: smallholder tea, rubber, coconut, paddy, and two construction activities. They are based on survey data from about 100 representative centers in the country. These series show some modest increases in wages over these years, especially until 1981 or 1982, after which some weakness and even decline sets in. Again, here the deflator employed most probably understates the price rises, and so the figures in the table overstate the increase in real wages in these years. It is not, however, exactly clear what price index would be especially suitable to deflate these series. It seems safe to conclude, in any event, that real wages in these sectors did not rise at all or rose very little as the new policy became effective.

Nominal wage rates rose more or less everywhere, but the continued increases in prices held down, or eliminated completely, increases in real wages. Given the devaluations, the big jump in foreign assistance, and the main content of the investment programs, substantial inflation was essentially inevitable. It also seems likely that additional wage increases would have produced additional pressure on prices.

The more or less constant real wages may have contributed to the employment objective. The employment from the large-scale public investments, however, was probably not greatly affected one way or another by wages. The employment effect on small-scale nonagricultural private firms would be expected to be important. That these activities did not take off with the new policy is one important explanation of the employment problem.

- If real wage rates remained more or less constant over these years, and employment grew slowly and GDP rapidly, then the share of wages in GDP must have declined. Other sources of income—rents, interest, dividends, profits—must have increased as a proportion of GDP. The initial impact on distribution of the massive public investment program, with the heavy concentration on infrastructure development and construction, would be expected to benefit property owners and contractors. The removal of internal and external trade barriers, the abolition of price controls, the revision of interest rates, and the new tax incentives would all have a more immediate effect on nonwage income than on either wages or the demand for labor. The decline in the growth rates after the first few years tended to slow down the spread effects of those activities that were directly and immediately affected by government policy and government investment. So, wages were weak and unemployment continued, and nonwage income rose to make inequality increase. The fact that the Gini coefficient of income receivers in relation to that of spending units in 1981 and 1982 was higher than in all previous survey years, except 1973, is consistent with this view. So, also, is the fact that inequality within the urban areas, as measured by the Gini coefficient, increased in 1981 and 1982 compared with 1978 and 1979, while it remained unchanged (and lower) in the rural areas and on the estates.

- Data that permit a very complete story about poverty in these years are not available, but a few observations on the subject are possible and may aid our understanding.

Several studies directly aimed at estimating the incidence of poverty all produce similar figures: approximately 20 to 25 percent of the population lived in poverty. The figure does not change very much over the decade from 1973 to 1981–82. The changes that do occur show that the percentage of the population living in poverty was larger in the early 1980s than in the early and mid-1970s, but differences are all so small that it is probably best to ignore them. These studies use either an income level as the cutoff point or are based on a calories per person norm.

All studies show that the incidence of poverty was much greater in rural areas than in urban centers, and was least prevalent on the estates. Although wages were very low on the estates, there was greater job security for the workers than for rural labor in general. Also, women and children on estates have more employment opportunities than do the rural poor. The poor fall into two general groups—landless labor in rural areas and workers in small-scale industry on the one hand, and small farmers cultivating food crops with family labor and small-scale traders, carpenters, weavers, and household servants on the other. Even among paddy producers, approximately one-half had such a low level of output that they had to buy rice in the market. As the market price rose, their real income—and consumption—declined.

In 1978 and 1979 approximately 89 percent of poor households were headed by a person with a full-time job, and two years later the figure was 93 percent. These results are compatible with the evidence that unemployment was heavily concentrated among the very young. They also underline the importance of creating an environment in which productivity is rising throughout all sectors of the economy.

A final bit of evidence that also supports the view that poverty has not declined since 1977 is price data. Low-income households in Sri Lanka spend from 70 to 75 percent of their income on food, and food prices have risen more rapidly than the other components of the general price indexes. To deflate incomes of all income levels with the same index will, therefore, produce a result that overstates the real income of the lower-income groups. Thus, the available data on levels of income in various income deciles most probably overstates that of the lowest groups. Because these measured income changes were modest at best, it is reasonable to conclude that the real income of many low-income people actually fell over these years.

There are no data on distribution and poverty for the years after 1981 and 1982. The evidence from GDP composition and growth rates, inflation rates, the composition of investment, term of trade, nontraditional exports, and imports do not suggest that there should have been any significant change in distribution or in poverty alleviation in these years. The civil disturbances after 1982, of course, added to the complexity of achieving changes anywhere in the system, but especially so with respect to distribution and poverty relief. It can be assumed that the picture for these variables described for 1981 and 1982 more or less continued through 1985.

As was true with respect to the growth discussion, it can be argued that the strategy and its implementation were basically "right," but there is a long and painful lag before the effect on distribution and poverty relief is realized. It is possible to claim that the general policy and (especially) its specific details are themselves the source of the failures, but before considering these issues directly, two other topics associated with equity should be reviewed.

Food Subsidies, Education, Health, and Housing

The first three items had been the major components of Sri Lanka's welfare program since its independence. The new policy cut back sharply on food subsidies, but did not change education and health very much. It added improved housing as one of its major social priorities. A brief comment on each of them follows.

- The most significant change in social welfare policy was the replacement of the rice ration program with the food stamp program that became effective in September 1980. (In February 1978, the rice ration had been limited to those families with an annual income below Rs3,600 per year.) The objective of the food stamp program was to reduce the food subsidy outlays and try to maintain them at a relatively stable level. Recipients were given food stamps that they could spend on selected food items, the prices of which were to reflect their full costs. The value of the food stamps was fixed in nominal terms, so it was possible to set the rupee allocation with some certainty. Such allocations were about Rs1,500 million from 1980 onward. The food subsidy program in 1978 and 1979 had cost over Rs2,100 million in each year. Under previous schemes there was a built-in tendency for costs to rise with increases in the cost of rice imports and with population. Evidently, as food prices rose, the real value of the stamps fell. If the program was about "right" when it was established in 1979, then within a couple of years it was surely inadequate. This new program, therefore, contributed to the inequality and poverty problems that were discussed in the preceding section.

  The food stamp program represented a major change in Sri Lanka welfare policy, which the government was able to accomplish in 1979 because of its great majority in Parliament and because the community in general acknowledged that drastic action was necessary. The real costs for the lower income deciles were, however, severe. It may also be noted that transfer payments to cover deficits in the operation of public enterprises rose rapidly over the period, increasing by a factor of more than twelve between 1977 and 1983. The government could not act completely freely even then.

- The new government did not change the three-decade-old policy of providing universal free education through secondary school. The numbers of students increased rapidly, rising an average of almost 3 percent a year from 1978 on, and pressure on budgetary allocations increased correspondingly. The rapid rise in numbers reflected not only population increase, but also the weak labor market for young people. Unemployment makes education cheaper for the student. Adequate numbers of qualified, well-motivated teachers proved impossible to find, as did the provision to many schools of supporting facilities. There is some evidence to suggest that an increasing proportion of students was leaving school before completing the six-year cycle. The most common reason given was that low family income made it impossible for children to remain in school. Certainly the relationship between leaving school and income level was negative in the early 1980s. To meet this issue the government has, in recent years, expanded the lunch and the textbook program.

The emphasis on investment by the government after 1977, and the effort to maintain firmer control of recurrent expenditures, led to increased capital outlays on education even as operating budgets were penalized. This awkward pattern partly reflected the increasing reliance on foreign assistance. Foreign aid is generally more readily available for buildings, equipment, and vehicles than for teachers' salaries and maintenance costs. There seems little doubt, therefore, that the quality of primary and secondary educations declined in these years compared with that earlier years.

Similar arguments apply to university education. The allocation of capital expenditures clearly favored higher education at the expense of primary and secondary schooling. The number of higher education institutions continued to grow, but quality surely suffered.

The declining quality of public educational institutions led to the appearance of schools and colleges that charged tuition. This development, as might be expected, created controversy among students and the general public as it violated a long-standing policy of equality and free access for all students. The relaxation of exchange controls facilitated education abroad for members of the higher-income families, and this, too, disturbed the equality of opportunity principle. Finally, the more liberal environment enabled the professionally qualified—including teachers and university professors—to migrate in search of higher pay.

The difficulties with education thus continued. The social environment did not allow a specific policy of retrenching on the availability of educational opportunities, so school enrollments continued to rise, quality deteriorated, and the educated unemployed problem was exacerbated. Private tuition and education abroad contributed to inequality of opportunity. The government again had great difficulty taking actions that would relieve these problems, but that would not simultaneously contribute to an even more unmanagable kind of social unrest. In such a situation, perhaps the best approach is not to act explicitly on education, but rather to create ample job opportunities. If jobs are readily available for all levels of educational achievement, attending school becomes expensive—but expensive in a palatable way. So once again the employment problem emerged, and its link with the development strategy followed. We are also reminded of the difficulties of policy change in the Sri Lankan situation, even for a government with a large and unqualified majority.

• Similar observations apply to the government's health policy. Essentially, there was no deviation from the long-standing commitment to state-supported free health services. In the 1960s and early 1970s, health expenditures on current account were about 2 percent of GDP, but this amount began to decline well before the election of 1977. The new government, therefore, did not begin the reductions, but it did continue them. As was the case with education, there was a sharp shift in favor of capital expenditures. In the early 1970s, capital expenditures were 11 to 15 percent of current outlays and after 1978 they were much higher—approximately 80 percent in 1980 and 60 percent in 1983. The figure fluctuated from year to year, but was always much larger than in earlier years. This emphasis on investment in health facilities is partly explained by the availability of foreign aid for capital projects, but not for recurrent expenditures. Foreign aid accounted for about 5 to 7 percent of the health budget prior to 1977, rose to over one-half in 1979, and averaged approximately 20 percent from 1980 to 1985.

Budgetary allocations on current accounts rose in nominal terms, of course, but it seems clear that the availability of health services deteriorated over the period. Many of the better-trained doctors migrated and the training of new people could not keep pace with population growth or with the newly available capital equipment. Private practice by doctors was permitted, and doctors were enticed from government hospitals to these higher paying private clinics. A number of private health care centers evolved very quickly and existed alongside the government centers. Some of the former became very well equipped and very high priced. Some observers found evidence that even within the government, hospital fees were being charged and tips expected by hospital personnel. The rupee price of medical supplies, especially drugs that were imported, rose as the rupee depreciated, and government dispensaries often could not supply them.

It is important to emphasize that health-related demographic indicators showed improvements during these years. Infant mortality and the crude death rate, both already low in the early 1970s for a country with Sri Lanka's per capita income, declined still further. These national averages, however, tend to hide the inevitable increased disparities among regions and income groups.

• A major change in social policy in the post-1977 period was the new emphasis on housing development. Housing and urban development became major projects in the public investment programs. Initially the government built houses directly, but soon shifted to an aided self-help arrangement. Before 1977, housing was a negligible item in the government budget and averaged 9 to 10 percent between 1978 and 1985. A large part of this increase was concentrated on low-priced housing in rural villages and fishing communities. Along with aiding in housing, the government supplied improved water and sanitation facilities. By 1985 more than 80 percent of the urban population had access to safe piped water, as did 50 percent of the rural population. These major improvements had direct effects on health levels, and must have reached low-income groups.

It is possible to conclude from all this that the food stamp program of the new government added to the penalties of being very poor in Sri Lanka. Similarly, education and health services available from the government probably deteriorated over the period, while those available in the private market improved. Housing, including water and sanitation facilities, however, probably improved for the lower-income categories. The more open economy, especially the free import policy, made it easier for the higher-income groups to flaunt their riches with imported consumption goods, foreign travel, and foreign education and health services. The significant size of the migration of skilled medical people and some other categories of professional people exacerbated the inequalities by making them evident to everyone in the societies.

Other Aspects of Equity

The continued attention given to the development of paddy production—price support, irrigation, and land development—reflected not only the commitment to rice self-sufficiency, but also to the idea that maintaining the Sinhalese rice culture was itself an important social objective. It would provide a source of stability and some employment in the rural areas, and it was the kind of activity with which the government was familiar. The large-scale irrigation works were also attractive to aid donors. It is not surprising, therefore, that the government continued to emphasize this area of development.

The wages of estate workers were raised in 1984, and this, along with giving them a representative in Parliament, was an important change in policy. Their income and living conditions, however, remained the worst in Sri Lanka. The government elected in 1977 was unable, as were previous governments, to resolve this major source of inequity. The inequity was even sharper at this time because so many estates were owned and operated by the government.

The great ethnic issues that divided the Sri Lankan Tamils and Sinhalese also continued and showed few signs of resolution. The issues that underlie this conflict include virtually all aspects of social relationships, and it is probably true that by the 1980s economic policy as such was not a basic tool. Meanwhile, it is important to notice, as in previous sections, that the strong commitment to the Sinhalese culture made it difficult to design an economic policy that was equally appropriate for both major ethnic groups. The new policies established in late 1977 and in 1978, which were intended to liberalize and to open the economy, did not achieve this to the extent that all ethnic groups were equally affected. Indeed, it can be argued, although the evidence is quite inadequate, that one of the reasons that the new policy approach had so little effect on the private, nonagricultural sectors was that the policies were less applicable to Tamils than they could have been. A weaker statement can be made with more confidence: The development strategy followed by the new government was determined in part, possibly in large part, by the nature of the ethnic issues in the country. This fact, to an unknown degree, affected the extent to which new activities emerged and old problems, such as the educated unemployed, could not be attacked.

The most explicit way in which the new policy deviated from that of the preceding thirty-seven years was with respect to evidence of inequality. Evidence of measured income distributions have shown that there was relatively little change over the entire period from 1950 to 1985, except for the misleading 1973 estimates. After 1978 and 1979, as the liberalization of the economy began to take hold, consumption inequalities became more open and more widely observed. These inequalities probably were especially important in terms of their effect on health, education, and other matters that affect current welfare and access to future opportunities. The increase in the migration of the better-trained professional people also highlights the inequalities of income and opportunity.

The developments with respect to equity can be summarized as follows: Inequality in the distribution of income increased—certainly compared with 1973 and very probably compared with other years for which there are data. Public evidence of inequality increased much more and exacerbated the tensions within the society. There may have been an increase in poverty; surely there was no decrease. Policies with respect to food subsidies, health, and education probably made the consequences of poverty harsher than they had been in earlier years. Housing policy, however, may have helped to alleviate some of the consequences of poverty. No headway was made on the deep-seated problems arising from the ethnic diversity of the nation. It is probably correct to argue that the increased openness of the economy, at least in the form that it took, exacerbated the intractableness of these complexities.

Before an attempt is made to examine the policy issues in a more general way, the Malaysian story must be told.

III Malaysia

10 Background to the Economy of Malaysia

At its independence in 1957 what is now referred to as Peninsular Malaysia was, by Southeast Asian standards, a rich and thriving nation. It was also a nation with a range of difficult and long-standing social problems. The deep-seated nature of these problems and their long history meant that almost everyone in the new nation was committed in one way or another to a specific point of view or to a specific approach to possible solutions. Similarly, the economy had great strengths, but was also vulnerable in various ways. All this meant that there were specific entrenched interests that liked the status quo, and other entrenched interests that did not. The newly independent state and its government, therefore, did not begin life with a clean policy slate on which to write whatever a careful, objective, informed analysis of the situation dictated. The government as such and the individuals who composed it were constrained in many ways, and could, in no sense, begin ab initio to remake the economy and society as they might wish. Indeed in the economy bequeathed to the Malaysians, the history and prevailing circumstances were such that it is doubtful whether "the government" had a specific, detailed vision of its own about the direction and content of the policies it would follow. The next several pages present a broadly outlined sketch of certain aspects of this history that affect the post-independence story to be told.[1]

As in Sri Lanka, Malaysia's colonial period included times during which the Portuguese and the Dutch were dominant. Their influence was short-lived and slight, and it was not until the end of the eighteenth century, when the British came, that a genuine colonial status began slowly to evolve. Britain came first to Penang Island and then to Malacca and, with Singapore, these constituted the Straits settle-

---

1. Material for this survey is taken from a number of general studies. Especially helpful were Chee (1983), Fisk and Osman-Rani (1982), Golay (1969), Lim (1973), Ness (1967), Andaya and Andaya (1985), and Snodgrass (1980).

ments, a part of the East India Company, and the entire area became a significant trading region. The long series of civil wars in the late eighteenth and early nineteenth centuries—in part over the succession of the rulers in the several states and in part over control of tin mines—interfered sufficiently with trade that Britain became interested in a more direct and significant governing role. The Straits settlements came under the jurisdiction of the British Colonial Office in 1867, and in 1874 a treaty with the Sultan of Perak gave the British the right to establish in that state a resident who was given power over everything except matters related to Malay religion and culture. This treaty was then repeated with other states. In 1895 the Federated Malay States was established to facilitate British control. This federation included four states, but a separate arrangement with Johore was essentially the same. In 1909 Thailand relinquished her claims to the four northern and western states, which in turn accepted British residents with powers similar to those in the other states. British control of the peninsula was then complete. These arrangements were often referred to as indirect rule, but for the most part the British influence was clear and unambiguous, if not direct.

Europeans thought of the region largely in terms of trade until well into the nineteenth century. Singapore, founded by Thomas Stamford Raffles in 1819, quickly became the center of trade in the area. Trading between India and China and between India and the Malay States had naturally occurred over the centuries. The trade involved many nationalities, but the Chinese long had dominated most trade and trading routes. Malay wood products—aromatic woods, resins, rattans, and so forth—were major items in this very early trade, as were sea shells (for example, cowrie shells, mentioned in old texts on money), shellfish, and coral. There was also apparently some gold that attracted widespread attention. The region was once identified as "Golden Khersonese," and several historians link the use of yellow as a royal color with the presence of gold in early Malay courts. Gold was exciting, the rainforest wood products were interesting and pleasant, and the sea products were fascinating, but it was tin that really mattered.

Tin mining is an old industry in Malaysia. Apparently, there is evidence that it was mined as early as the fifth century and was shipped to India to be used in making bronze religious icons (Andaya and Andaya 1985, p. 12). Because tin was so plentiful, it could be mined simply and profitably by very primitive techniques—merely washing the tin-bearing soil. Tin smelting was equally simple. These techniques apparently had changed little over the centuries. It was in the middle of the nineteenth century, when new rich deposits were discovered in Perak and Selangor and world demand increased sharply, that major changes in technology occurred. The Chinese had mined some tin for many years, but now they moved in force. They developed a new and much more productive technology, and also brought in a large Chinese work force to perform the unpleasant tasks that had to be done. The Chinese proved to be extraordinarily efficient, and quickly dominated the activity; thus began the first great influx of Chinese into the area. For example, there were virtually no Chinese in the Larut Valley of Perak in 1850 and by 1870 there were about 40,000 (Young and others 1980, p. 12). By 1911 there were 196,000 tin miners in the Federated Malay States, more than 95 percent of whom were Chinese. At this time Malaysia was producing half of the world's output of tin (Snodgrass 1980, p. 17). It was the continued warfare among Chinese secret organizations that caused the problems that led to the British being invited by the Sultan of Perak to help maintain order.

There had been numerous Chinese in Malaysia from the earliest periods for which there are records, but the rapid increase in the middle of the nineteenth century was quite another matter. The Chinese who came were generally seeking to get away from their extreme poverty in China. Also, the unsettled conditions in South China—most of the immigrants came from the southeast provinces—encouraged them to seek other areas. They left extreme poverty, usually traveled under equally harsh conditions, and then found an environment which, for them, was extremely unhealthful. A great many died at a relatively early age. This experience may well have meant that survivors were people of unusual strength and determination; indeed, the stuff out of which entrepreneurs are made.

The Chinese dominated the tin industry until the bucket dredge was introduced in 1912. These dredges were much more efficient at taking tin from low-content ore than were the existing methods, but they were costly and required skilled labor. They also could be profitable only with large, long-term leases that assumed continued access to ore-bearing areas. The cost of the new technology meant that only the larger international mining companies could finance and manage its use. The British then began to replace the Chinese as the major operators in the tin industry. Chinese-owned mines produced about 75 percent of Malaya's tin in 1912 and less than one-third (of a much larger output) in the mid-1930s. This development on the technology and finance front had the important consequence (for our story) of pushing Chinese out of tin mining and into other activities, such as agriculture and a variety of services. It also pushed them toward urban centers, a move further induced by their virtual exclusion from the development of uncleared land and the protection of cultivated land for Malays.

Tin was first; then there was rubber. There had been commercial agriculture since the mid-to-late eighteenth century. Pepper, gambier (used in dyeing and in the tanning of leather), tapioca, and spices were grown, as were sugar and coffee. Pepper, grambier, and tapioca were raised on plantations, largely by Chinese planters. These efforts all more or less petered out by the end of the nineteenth century as world prices fell, and the soil was exhausted by the agricultural methods that the Chinese employed. Rubber had been tried, but was not working well until a plant from Brazil that was sent first to Kew Gardens in Britain to germinate, and then to Singapore to multiply, turned out to be remarkably successful. It was first planted commercially on plantations in Malaysia in the 1890s, initially by coffee planters discouraged by the low prices of coffee. It was an instant success. This supply-side breakthrough was accompanied by a demand boom as the electrical, bicycle, and then automobile industries—all great rubber users—expanded rapidly. About the only other source of supply was Brazil's Amazon Basin where rubber trees mainly grew wild. By 1908 rubber was planted in every state in Peninsular Malaysia on more than 100,000 hectares of land (Andaya and Andaya 1985, p. 214). Plantation rubber was concentrated on the west coast where the infrastructure—chiefly roads, railroads, and ports—were already in place in response to the needs of the tin industry.

The rubber industry was British from the beginning, but as it became established and evidently successful, Chinese and Indians began to participate. At the outset the latter groups were generally involved in plantation rubber, but later on they included rubber in their smallholdings as well. Rubber was a useful adjunct for the Malay smallholder. Its gestation period was seven or eight years, a long time, but rubber trees could be interplanted with other crops that matured much more quickly. Once it reached a stage to be tapped its productive life was twenty-five to thirty years, and it provided the peasant with an extra source of income at little extra cost.

The land suitable for growing rubber was made available to British investors, but the labor supply was another matter. In the early years, Malays were not employed on the rubber plantations and were slow in developing smallholder rubber. The explanation for this crucial issue is difficult to nail down, because there were numerous contributing factors. The British policies discriminated against the peasants in favor of planters. For example, in the alienation of land with road frontage, instructions were issued to all district officers to refer all applications by Asians to the British resident. This policy seemed to be established at the instigation of the planters, and was later extended specifically to discourage application for land plots of fewer than twenty-five acres, where such land possessed a road frontage. Roads and drainage works also favored plantation interests.

The Malay Reservation Enactment of 1913 imposed limitations on the commercial transactions of peasant Malay land—that is, land within a Malay reservation was not to be sold, leased, or disposed of in any way to a non-Malay. There were cultivation restrictions as well on the use of reservation land.

There was also official hostility to the cultivation of rubber by the peasants. This hostility, which had increased markedly by 1916, included the closure of land office books to peasant rubber land applications, withdrawal of lands alienated to peasants on temporary occupation licenses and found to be planted with rubber, and the prohibition on rubber cultivation in certain areas. The Depression of the 1930s in particular convinced the colonial rulers that peasants should not depend on cash crops, which, therefore, were to be discouraged. Paddy cultivation by the peasant was to be further encouraged, while the Chinese were politically discouraged from it.

It seems fair to add to this set of policies by the British the argument that the Malays greatly preferred a less regimented, less disciplined life than was possible on the plantations. They were reluctant to move onto plantations, and, to a lesser extent, to give up their rice culture. In the early period—before World War I—it is probably correct to say that wage payments to plantation workers were below what most of the Malays could earn in their rice kompongs and fishing villages, and this also made the plantations less attractive.

Evidently then, several factors were at work that resulted in Malays not being fully absorbed into rubber activities. The planters then turned to the Tamils of South India where a large supply of people was eager and willing to migrate to Malaysia and work at relatively low cost to the British planters. So Indians moved into Malaysia in substantial numbers, which added more complexity to the already complex plural society.

Indians had, of course, been present in Malaysia before the big rubber boom. They had come to work for the British as traders, clerks, and public servants. They were especially active in the Malaysian railroads and Public Works Department. Indians in these activities, however, arrived over a longer period of time, and were fewer in number than those who were brought to work on the rubber plantations. By the 1920s both tin and rubber were firmly established and doing extremely well. Demand for both products was expanding, and supply conditions continued to be equally favorable. Malaysia had become, as Snodgrass (1980) emphasizes, a prime example of a colonial export economy. It looked good in the 1920s, and it was devastated by the Depression of the 1930s. This devastation affected the objectives and thinking of the government in significant ways at independence in 1957. In addition to being a relatively prosperous and well-run export economy, it was a plural society, which was composed of three main ethnic groups in addition to a variety of other groups. In 1911 data collected by Snodgrass (p. 24) show that 48 percent of the 2.3 million people in Peninsular Malaysia were Malays and another 6.5 percent were "other Malaysians." Approximately 30 percent were Chinese and 10 percent were Indians. Ten years later the proportion of Indians had risen to 15 percent and that of Malays had declined moderately. It is important to note that in both of these years Chinese and Indian men greatly outnumbered their female counterparts. Obviously this situation, a product of the rapid immigration of these groups, could not continue for any length of time. Similarly, in 1921 about 20 percent of the Chinese and about 12 percent of the Indians in Peninsular Malaysia had been born there. Here, too, one observes a source of potential instability.

The Malays remained in agriculture and were the principal growers of rice. Demand for rice rose strongly with the tin and rubber boom; thus, paddy growing was often a fairly lucrative occupation. The Malays surely found the paddy culture much more compatible with the other aspects of their life-styles than were tin mining and rubber plantation work. Their commitment was strengthened as it became evident that rubber made a profitable smallholding venture that occupied idle, jungle lands or, in some instances, replaced paddy land. Labor in smallholder rubber was largely family, or other, labor that was also employed in growing paddy. The British thought of the Malays as rice farmers and fishermen, and indeed created some obstacles to keep them out of rubber. There was little research effort aimed at rice, and the government provided only modest infrastructure or credit to support the paddy farmer. The Malays did not generally take advantage of the growing demand for vegetables and poultry, which were principally raised by the Chinese. Table 10-1 summarizes data on the distribution of ethnic groups by occupation that Donald Snodgrass (1980) has gathered from various censuses. The data are, of course, incomplete and not fully comparable among the years; they are different in some instances from data from other sources, but the overall picture that the table presents seems accurate.

Several observers have emphasized that the Japanese occupation of British Malaya during World War II was an important factor in the creation of nationalism and in the beginning of difficulties among the ethnic groups. The Malays were recruited into the police and armed forces during this period, and an anticolonialist attitude was aggressively advanced by the Japanese. The Japanese were also strongly anti-Chinese, and their treatment of the Chinese in Malaya was frequently harsh. This harshness seemed to contribute to the emergence of hostile feelings between the Malays and Chinese. The Indians in Malaysia were also encouraged by the Japanese to fight for Indian independence from Britain. Three other events are an essential part of the preindependence story—the efforts of the British to establish the Malayan Union, the actual establishment of the Federation of Ma-

Table 10-1. Distribution of Occupations among Ethnic Groups
(thousands)

Group and occupation	1911	1921	1931	1947	1957
Malay					
Padi planters	108	452	366	417	—
Agricultural laborers	29	95	—	—	—
Agricultural owners and managers	18	30	—	—	424
Rubber cultivators	—	—	123	147	247
Laborers	3	8	17	19	33
Fishermen	3	35	35	41	41
Proprietors and managers	—	11	—	—	14
Other	51	146	214	235	245
Total	212	777	755	861	1,004
Chinese					
Miners	149	71	79	30	—
Agricultural laborers	40	144	—	—	—
Fruit and vegetable growers	17	26	51	91	—
Rubber cultivators	—	—	175	153	177
Proprietors and managers	—	37	37	36	35
Laborers	12	43	56	18	51
Other	142	259	339	389	496
Total	360	580	737	717	759
Indian					
Agricultural laborers	80	213	—	—	—
Laborers (unspecified)	11	16	51	26	32
Proprietors and managers	—	8	9	7	8
Rubber cultivators	—	—	189	141	129
Other	52	103	132	126	138
Total	143	340	381	300	307

— Not available.
Source: Compiled from data in Snodgrass (1980), pp. 32–33, 38, 41.

laya in 1948, and the insurrection led by Chinese communists that also began in 1948.

The short-lived Malayan Union, which the British established as of April 1, 1947, did much to convince the Malays that they could exercise considerable political pressure. The Union lasted less than one year because of strong opposition from the Malay community. It sought to replace the old treaties between Britain and the several sultans, and to lump all the states together into one union. In this union the Malays would have no special privileges and all of the races would occupy an equal position in terms of the law. Finally, the sovereignty and prerogatives of the sultans would be substantially reduced and British jurisdiction would be paramount generally. The Malays strongly opposed the Union, and clearly voiced their opposition to a British Parliamentary Commission sent to Malaysia to review political conditions (Ness 1967, p. 51). Neither did the Chinese nor the Indian communities demonstrate much enthusiasm for the Union, although they had much to gain from it. Silcock and Aziz (1953) suggest that the Chinese were not especially interested because there were better opportunities in business than in politics, and because success in politics resulted in publicity and extortion from the Chinese communists, who were gaining strength at this time.

The important result of this brief Union was to convince the Malays that their interests could be protected and supported by organized efforts. It led to the creation of the United Malay National Organization (UMNO), the political party that has dominated Malaysian politics since the late 1940s. Several observers emphasize that it was principally the opposition to the Union and the effectiveness of this opposition that galvanized the Malays politically and launched Malay nationalism. The Union was replaced in February 1948 by the new Federation of Malaya Agreement that, among other things, restored the position of the sultans and tightened citizenship requirements.

The Federation of Malaya was established to bring order to the virtual chaos that followed the end of World War II and the rejection of the Malayan Union. The sultans kept their positions, but a strong central government emerged in Kuala Lumpur. There was a federal legislative council and an executive council over which the British high commissioner (not governor) presided. There were chief ministers in each state, but the British resident had considerable power. Everyone was eligible for citizenship who had been born in the country or who had lived there for fifteen of the past twenty-five years and who declared their intention to live permanently in the Federation, *and* who spoke Malay or English.

The Malayan Communist Party rejected the continuation of the colonial government, and went underground. Many of its members took to the jungle and sought to conduct guerrilla warfare against the government. This movement had considerable strength for a number of years, but by 1952 or so it was under control, although the insurrection did not officially end until 1960. In the present context there was one far-reaching consequence of the "Emergency," as it was called. In an effort to cut off support to the insurrectionists, the government moved hundreds of thousands of Chinese from their small rural villages into new villages located near urban centers. The Chinese, who had lived mainly in rural areas, suddenly became urbanites (Young and others 1980, p. 15). This relocation was not reversed after the Emergency ended. It seems inevitable that the fact that the Emergency involved mainly British and Malays on one side and Chinese on the other added to the difficulties of achieving and maintaining racial harmony, as well as reaching a consensus on the meaning of equity.

Education is the final aspect of the preindependence years that is extremely relevant to understanding the equity issue at independence. This is a complex issue and brief discussion can only call attention to a few of the major ideas and developments that seem most directly relevant to our story.

Two assumptions seemed to underlie British ideas about education in Malaysia. The first was that the Indians and Chinese were temporary residents, and the second was that Malays were paddy farmers and should remain such for the indefinite future. There was, therefore, little effort to create a national educational system; rather, the idea seemed to be to allow each ethnic group to take care of itself. Indian students attended schools provided by the estates for the most part, with some schools established and run by missionaries and occasionally by local communities. The government took some interest in the Tamil schools by the late 1940s, but was not interested in much more than agriculture and handicrafts (Andaya and Andaya 1985).

The Chinese were also left to their own devices for many years, and early schools were conducted in a variety of Chinese dialects. After the revolution in China in 1911, the Chinese of China began to try to influence Malaysian Chinese. After 1911 a common Chinese language was spoken, and great emphasis was placed on teaching Chinese culture and tradition. It seems to have been this latter emphasis that led the Malaysian government to begin to pay close attention to the education of the Chinese. The decline in Chinese participation in tin mining and their consequent move into agriculture and urban pursuits demonstrated that numerous Chinese viewed Malaysia as their home. The Chinese firmly resisted efforts to control or direct their schools, even if money were also made available. In particular they wished to continue to emphasize China's history and culture and to resist emphasis on Malaysian studies, although the Chinese viewed Malaysia as their home. The Chinese, more so than either the Indians or the Malays, offered their children a great variety of training and apprenticeships in Chinese-run businesses.

The Malay schools were intended to help Malays become better paddy farmers and fishermen. The long tradition of education, centered around reading and memorizing the Koran in Arabic, did little to help students in any practical way. Although Malays often realized that their best prospect for advancement was in government work, Malay-language schools were ill-suited to provide the necessary training.

The only education that mattered much in terms of economic advancement was English-language education. Although there were such schools, they were generally located in urban areas where it was inconvenient and expensive for Malays to attend. Yet Malay parents acknowledged that the ability to speak English was virtually essential for employment outside of paddy and fishing. For postelementary education, English was the only possibility. Although the Malays, as noticed above, were committed to their kampongs and their Islamic traditions (just as the Chinese were committed to their traditions), it seems fairly clear that most Malays would have taken advantage of educational opportunities with economic benefits had such opportunities been available to them. There were some efforts to create a Malay-language school that included vocational training along with the traditional Koranic studies, but such schools were unusual, and attention was generally concentrated on religious training.

It was only in English-language schools that the three main ethnic groups attended the same class. It was in such schools that some commonality among the groups was created, although, as noted, Malay attendance was small. Malays accounted for approximately 15 percent of total enrollment in 1936, while about 50 percent of the students were Chinese and 30 percent Indian. Data in Snodgrass (1980, p. 243) show that at independence in 1957, less than 10 percent of Malay men between the ages of twenty-five and forty-four had postprimary education, while more than 20 percent of Chinese and Indians had such education.

A brief comment on the social and religious characteristics of the three principal ethnic groups will complete this background section. One characteristic common to all three was the commitment to the family system. Strong family links exist and are observed, and the extended family was extremely important in each group. Obligations of respect and obedience to elders, especially to parents, is demanded of all children.

Within the Malay community, the Islamic religion was of paramount importance in all activities. A highly extended family, including three generations plus cousins and distant relatives, was not uncommon at this time. Religious education on the fundamentals of Islam formed an important part of education, at school and at home, for the Malays. The strong commitment to Islam was a principal factor that made interethnic marriages rare. It was necessary for the Chinese or Indians to become Muslim to marry a Malay, and few among the former groups felt it possible to do this. The relative infrequency of interethnic marriages has contributed to each group's maintaining its social arrangement very much intact.

Malay society is essentially a cooperative society, based on "gotong royong," a term meaning mutual help. This cooperation exists both in social and economic spheres. The offer of help or service is expected to be reciprocated later. Closely related to this is the concept of "umrah," Islamic religious community, whereby fellow members are expected to help each other at any time, anywhere. Various social customs also help bind the Malay community together and feelings of solidarity arise among the Malays as a result of observing these social customs. Another important concept in the Malay value system is that of "malu," or self-respect; every Malay is to maintain self-respect at all times.

The basis of the Chinese social structure is also the family system. As with the Malays, the extended family system is very important. For the Chinese, however, the family group tends to be larger, with strong emphasis on respect and consideration for ancestors and elders, implying obedience and a sense of responsibility for family members. Kinship plays an important role in family relationships. Belief systems among the Malaysian Chinese vary considerably, but the majority subscribe to Confucianism, Buddhism, or Taoism, with a small Christian minority. Whatever the doctrinal adherence, however, respect and responsibility to ancestors is a common attitude.

Malaysians of Indian origin can be divided into various subcommunities where ancestry can be traced to a single village or region in India. The majority of Indians in Malaysia are Tamils, Malaylis, or Telugus. The customs and practices of Dravidian India predominate, which emphasize Sivaism and the worship of the female deity in its various forms. Indian immigrants to Malaya were employed primarily on estates, which resulted in a special pattern of settlement whereby most estates employ groups of Indians who come from the same village or region in India or who have a similar linguistic background. Through an elaborate network of kinships, ties are still maintained with the village of origin in India. A constant two-way movement of Malaysian Indians between India and Malaysia still exists and has helped to enhance the Indian identity among the Malaysian Indians. There also exists a considerable number of Malaysian Indians who are Muslims and are commonly known as Indian Muslims. This has given them a special place in their relationship with the Malays.

These brief observations suggest, at least, the difficulties faced at independence when Malaysia attempted to create a more unified society. It seemed clear then that a plural society was necessary, that Malaysia could not be a melting pot, and that this plurality would long prevail.

11 The Initial Conditions: Malaysia at Independence

Malaysia achieved full independence from Great Britain in 1957. Available data make it more convenient to try to establish the statistical picture as of 1960. The GDP per capita estimates of Summers and Heston (1984) begin with 1955 for Malaysia, and for that year their figure is 784 in international prices. In 1960 it was 888. This is a bit higher than that of Sri Lanka, higher than the figure for Taiwan, and about equal to the figure for Iran. During the five years from 1955 to 1960, GDP growth in 1970 prices averaged just over 3.0 percent a year. (Sri Lanka's figure for this period was 3.8 percent.) In 1960, therefore, the Malaysian economy was growing, but at a very moderate rate. Its overall level of per capita output, however, made it a relatively prosperous nation by South and East Asian standards.

The Foreign Trade Sector

The data in table 11-1 show the great dependence of Malaysia on its foreign trade sector. Exports were more than one-half of GDP, and rubber and tin exports accounted for 70 percent of foreign exchange earnings and over one-quarter of GDP. These ratios had not changed over the preceeding five years in any significant way. The price of rubber had risen in 1959 and remained favorable in 1960. The price in 1960 was higher than at any time in the 1950s, except for 1951, and approximately equaled the 1955 price. It fell sharply the following year. Tin prices were also slightly higher in 1959 and 1960 than they had been in recent years. They were on a rather clear upward trend at this time. Imports were a smaller proportion of GDP, and the balance of trade was in particularly good shape. This had also been a characteristic of the Malaysian economy for the decade prior to 1960. About one-half of Malaysia's imports were consumer goods, and about one-quarter were foodstuffs. The data show that about 18 percent of exports were classified as manufacturing goods. In 1959 some 45 percent of the rice consumed was imported, and Lim's data (1973, p.121) show

Table 11-1. Macroeconomic Indicators of the Malaysian Economy, 1960

Indicator	Measure
GDP (millions of ringgits)	7,025[a]
GDP per capita (ringgits)	860
Exchange rate (ringgits per U.S. dollar)	3.06
Trade and debt (millions of ringgits)	
Merchandise exports	3,633
Rubber	2,001
Tin	508
Logs	169
Palm oil	61
Petroleum	147
Merchandise imports	2,786
Balance of trade	847
Foreign exchange reserves	1,089[b]
Foreign currency debt	360
Current account balance, 1961	−16
Average annual price change, 1955–60 (percent)	0.3
Money supply growth, 1955–58 (percent)[c]	0
Government budget deficit	132
Percentage of government expenditure	14.4
Demographic features, 1957	
Population (millions)	6.2
Population growth, 1947–57 (percent)	2.5
Labor force participation (percent)	34.1
Age distribution (percent)	
Under 14	43.8
14–64	53.3
Over 64	2.9
Ethnic composition (percent)	
Malay	49.5
Chinese	37.2
Indian	11.7
Other	1.6
Land area (square miles)	50,713

a. 6,566 million ringgits in 1970 prices.

b. $356 million, the equivalent of five months' worth of imports.

c. A change in measurement procedure makes post-1959 data not comparable with 1955–58 date.

Source: World Bank, *World Tables* (1980) IMF, *International Financial Statistics Yearbook* (various years); Lim (1973); and Young and others (1980).

that 81 percent of the total supply of food was imported in 1959, but this seems unbelievably high. About one-quarter of total imports were capital goods or materials used mainly for capital goods. Given the level of investment for 1960, most of the physical capital accumulated was in the form of imported capital goods, and virtually all machinery and transport equipment was imported. Rubber replanting was a large component of investment in the economy, especially in the earlier years. In 1963 it accounted for as much as 40 percent of total investment, but was much less than that by the end of the 1960s. Gross fixed capital formation in the agricultural sector consisted largely of land improvement, plantation and orchard development, and breeding stocks. Malaysia was unambiguously an export economy in 1960. Its exports were primary goods and its imports were foodstuffs and manufactured goods, some of which were capital goods.

Although the price of rubber in 1959 and 1960 was reasonably favorable compared with the preceding several years, the future of rubber was generally considered to be quite dim. The growth rate of the volume of rubber exports had averaged slightly more than 2 percent a year during the 1950s. Between 1955 and 1960 the industrial consumption of synthetic rubber in the world had increased from 36 percent of total rubber consumption to 52 percent. In the United Kingdom it increased from 8 percent to 39 percent, in the Federal Republic of Germany from 15 to 42 percent, in Japan from 4 to 27 percent, and in the United States from 58 to 69 percent. It was, therefore, easy for the policymaker to convince himself that Malaysia's future did not lie with the continued heavy dependence on rubber.

The demand for tin was considered reasonably strong, but there were major concerns about the supply. Known reserves were becoming smaller and smaller and there was a marked decline in the quality of the ore being mined. World War II and the long Emergency period had interrupted the necessary prospecting that had, in the past, gone on almost continuously. There was also the great difficulty of land use decisionmaking. Much of the land that potentially contained tin deposits was also especially suitable for agriculture. In the easiest of situations such a decision is exceedingly complex. The complexity was greatly increased by the program to set aside lands as Malay Reservations. These areas were often thought to be rich in tin deposits, but Malays were extremely reluctant to commit themselves to an activity that required considerable investment and in which they had little experience (Lim 1973, p. 28). Further, as already emphasized, the Malays had generally found mining a less congenial activity than agriculture. These complications, therefore, made it difficult to exploit whatever tin was available, and also made it appealing for the government to look elsewhere for a source of dynamism to move the economy. Oil palm, logs and timber, and petroleum were still of relatively minor importance.

It is relevant to emphasize that the economy—the infrastructure, the trading and banking companies, the quality of much of the labor—had evolved around and with rubber and tin, and the export-import economy. In addition, the tin and rubber estates were all located on the west side of the peninsula, so that the infrastructure could provide few services to the east coast areas where the majority of the paddy farmers and fisherman lived and worked. Similarly, despite the explicit recognition by government policymakers that rubber and tin were questionable leading sectors, it was also true that they wanted to believe that rubber and tin could stage a comeback. This seems true because policymakers in all countries find it comfortable to maintain the staus quo—fully aware of the difficulties and costs associated with making significant changes that would affect economic performance. Another consideration was that such changes would necessarily have numerous implications for racial harmony in the new nation. It was also evident that the Malaysian situation was sufficiently favorable that there was no urgency to act.

Other Macroeconomic Variables

Other data in table 11-1 support the view that the Malaysian economy around 1960 was in good shape. Inflation was essentially nonexistent. The consumer price index had actually declined over most of the 1950s, and there was no built-in inflation process at work. The government budget was virtually balanced, and the rate of growth of the money supply was remarkably low. There was no reason to expect any inflation pressure in the future, unless it came from outside the country. The current account balance reflected the strength of the trade balance. The foreign currency debt was 10 percent of annual exports and foreign exchange reserves were adequate, if not ample. Besides all this, foreign credit was good. The new government seemed to have plenty of room to adjust and test.

The Composition of GDP

Output

Department of Statistics data show that more than 40 percent of GDP originated in agriculture in 1960. Other estimates place the figure somewhat lower, around 35 percent or so. A percentage of 35 to 40 for agriculture in 1960 would be about twice the average for the twenty-two countries that the World Bank includes in Malaysia's income category, upper-middle-income. Korea's percentage is about equal to that of Malaysia, but in all the other countries a much smaller proportion of GDP is produced in agriculture. Malaysia's ratio reflects both the great role of rubber in the Malaysian economy and the fact that a very large proportion of the Malay community with incomes well below average were engaged in rice farming and fishing (included in agriculture) as well as in smallholder rubber. Thus the unusually high proportion of GDP produced in agriculture in 1960 represents not so much an anomaly as a reflection of the dual nature of the Malaysian agricultural sector. The estate rubber sector was, of course, a modern-sector activity. In 1960 something less than one-half of the mature acreage devoted to rubber was on estates, and about 60 percent of total rubber output was produced on estates (Young and others 1980, p. 222).

The 8 to 9 percent of GDP originating in manufacturing in Malaysia is, therefore, very small compared with the other countries in the upper-middle-income group. The average for the countries as a group was 25 percent, almost three times the figure for Malaysia. The reason, of course, is the obverse of that given for the relatively large size of the agricultural sector. The other major sector was trade and finance. The size of this sector reflects the importance of exporting and importing in Malaysia as well as the long history of the area (including Singapore) as a major trading region.

It will be argued later that the existence of a relatively high-income agricultural sector alongside an exceptionally small manufacturing sector added to the difficulties of restructuring the economy to accommodate the long-term weakness of rubber. The point is that concentrating the more productive resources in agriculture did little to encourage the flexibility and adaptability needed to effect a change in the economic structure without reducing real income.

Employment

At the time of independence in 1957, almost 60 percent of the labor force was classified as employed in agriculture (and fishing). This share, so much larger than the share of output originating in agriculture, is a consequence of the low productivity of the rubber smallholders and the rice farmers. Value added per person in rubber in the smallholdings was about one-third of that on the estates and yields were less than one-half of that of the estates. Value added per acre and per worker on rice farms was also well below the estate average. The rubber smallholders and the rice farmers constituted much the largest group in agriculture; consequently, the ratio of employment in agriculture to total employment greatly exceeds the ratio of output in agriculture to total GDP.

The employment and output ratios for manufacturing suggest that the productivity in this activity was not very much higher than the average for the economy. The ratio of the two ratios for Malaysia is lower than it is for most of the countries in its income group or a lower income group. Korea, for example, in 1960 had 9 percent of its labor force in industry, while industry produced 20 percent of GDP. In Chile the ratios were 20 and 35, in Egypt 12 and 24, in Thailand 4 and 19, and so on. This diversity reflects mainly the differences in agricultural productivity among the countries. In the case of Malaysia, it reflects the high productivity of labor in the rubber estates, and, in 1960, the rather limited state of the manufacturing sector in the country. This picture emphasizes the point that the great difference in productivity was not between manufacturing and agriculture, but between modern estate rubber agriculture and smallholder rubber (and coconuts), rice farms, and fishing.

Open unemployment in 1960 was on the order of 6 percent (Young and others 1980, p. 51), but there was a great deal of underemployment in all sectors of the economy. The estimates are of the rough and ready sort. There is no evidence that the economy was pressing against any sort of labor constraint, but neither was there evidence that unemployment had reached dangerous proportions.

Investment

The investment rate averaged 12 percent over the last half of the 1950s, increasing from 9 percent in 1955 to the 14 percent shown in table 11-2. This is a low figure. For 1960, among the countries in the World Bank's upper-middle-income category, only Korea, then still in very bad shape, and Singapore had a lower rate. The average for the whole group of countries was 22 percent. The saving rate, however, was quite high, which was to be expected, given the large export surplus and the balanced budget. In both 1955 and 1960, gross national saving was well over 20 percent of GNP. It is not completely clear what to make of this low investment, high saving rate. It suggests that the demand for investment was relatively modest considering the available investible resources. The economy was not pressing against any sort of real constraint as such terms are usually understood. Malaysia had grown at a modest rate over the 1950s, and yet there were untapped investment resources available. Presumably resources existed in sufficient amounts to allow for a faster rate of growth, but this potential was unrealized. A possible explanation exists in terms of the characteristics of the economy just summarized. In the modern sector, the adverse expectations with respect to rubber, the supply problems of tin, and the modest size and growth of the manufacturing sector did not encourage investment. The rubber and coconut smallholders, the paddy farmers, and fishermen had little access to investible funds

Table 11-2. Other Indicators of the Malaysian Economy, 1960

Indicator	Amount (thousands of ringgits)	Percent
Composition of GNP		
Private consumption	n.a.	64.7
Government consumption	n.a.	11.3
Gross domestic investment	n.a.	14.7
Exports	n.a.	55.7
Imports	n.a.	−42.4
Net factor payments abroad	n.a.	−4.0
GDP by industrial origin		
Agriculture	n.a.	40.0
Mining	n.a.	6.0
Manufacturing	n.a.	8.6
Construction	n.a.	3.0
Transport and communication	n.a.	4.3
Trade and finance	n.a.	23.2
Other	n.a.	14.9
Employment, 1957		
Agriculture	1,245	58.5
Mining	58	2.8
Manufacturing	136	6.4
Construction	68	3.2
Commerce	195	9.2
Transport and communication	75	3.5
Services	320	15.0
Other	30	1.4
Total	2,127	100.0

n.a. Not applicable.

Source: Employment data, Lim (1973), p. 112; composition data, World Bank, *World Tables* (1980).

even had they wished to invest; therefore, exporting kept the economy moving. An additional hypothesis is offered later.

The Equity Issue

Distribution of Measured Income

The equity issue is no less complex for Malaysia than it is for Sri Lanka. It is convenient to begin with an examination of the distribution of measured national income. Table 11-3 shows Malaysia's income distribution at independence for the nation as a whole and for the urban areas. Two other countries and one province are included for compari-

Table 11-3. Distribution of Income in Selected Economies in Selected Years, 1957–60

(percent unless otherwise noted)

Decile	Malaysia, 1957–58		Zambia, 1959	Iran, 1959	Taiwan, 1959–60
	All	Urban			
Lowest	2.2	2.7	2.6	0.9	2.3
Second	3.5	4.3	2.8	2.6	3.3
Third	4.6	5.3	3.5	3.7	4.2
Fourth	5.4	6.3	4.1	4.6	5.1
Fifth	6.5	7.5	4.9	5.7	6.1
Sixth	7.7	8.7	6.2	6.8	7.5
Seventh	9.2	10.4	7.7	8.3	9.1
Eighth	11.1	12.6	10.0	10.3	11.5
Ninth	15.0	15.9	14.2	13.6	15.5
Highest	34.8	26.3	44.0	43.5	35.4
Top 5 percent	17.2	16.1	33.7	34.4	24.5
Gini coefficient	0.44	0.35	0.52	0.54	0.45
Per capita GDP[a]	888	—	657	1,015	733

— Not available.

a. Estimated, in 1960 international prices.

Source: For Zambia, Iran, and Taiwan, Jain (1975); for Malaysia, *Household Survey, 1957–58.* All data are based on household income. Summers and Heston (1984).

son purposes, and table 4-2 in chapter 4 provides additional comparisons. Several observations are relevant. As is true of most income distributions, the lower end of the distribution is more unequal than the upper-middle—that is, the sixth, seventh, and eighth deciles get approximately their 10 percent share, while the ninth and especially the tenth decile get much more than a 10 percent share. The large share of the top deciles, therefore, is at the expense of those in the lower half of the income distribution. Note, however, the huge difference between Malaysia and Taiwan in this respect, on the one hand, and Zambia and Iran, on the other. Much of the income of these latter countries originated in rents from natural resources. In Thailand in the early 1960s the top decile received a larger share (42.6 percent) than was the case in Malaysia, and Thailand, of course, is not a natural-resource-dominated economy. Malaysia's Gini coefficient suggests that overall inequality was, at independence, not greatly different from that of most developing countries. It was much higher than that of India, for example, somewhat higher than those for Bangladesh and Burma, and lower than for most Latin American countries, Thailand, and most mineral-rich countries.

Table 11-3 shows also that urban incomes are distributed more equally than are incomes for the nation as a whole. The greater equality arises from a reduction in the share of the highest income group that is spread over the first eight deciles. The greater equality in the urban areas is contrary to the usual evidence, and is disputed by other evidence cited below.

Data are available for 1957 and 1958 that permit a decomposition of the inequality into a variety of categories: between and within ethnic groups, among races within a given region, and between regions for a given ethnic community. Yukio Ikemoto (1985) has recently prepared a number of estimates showing how these various considerations contribute to inequality in Malaysia. For 1957 and 1958 Ikemoto's calculations show that considerations other than race were much more important than race in accounting for the measured inequality. For the whole of west Malaysia, about one-quarter of the measured inequality was owing to racial inequality and about 15 percent was a result of rural-urban inequalities. Within the rural areas about one-quarter of the measured index is accounted for by racial inequalities, while in the urban areas racial inequality was negligible, accounting for about 3 percent of the total inequality. These results tell us two things. The first is that there is considerable inequality within ethnic groups. Second, these results mean that race as such is not an important source of inequality. Indeed, what such a statement would mean is unclear. When it is demonstrated that rural-urban differences account for a certain proportion of total inequality, it must also be noted that two-thirds of the population in the rural areas are Malays. So the inequality between rural and urban was in large part also inequality between Malays and other ethnic groups. Similar observations hold for decompositions based on education or experience or other comparable considerations.

These observations are clearly demonstrated in table 11-4, which gives estimates for the income distribution within each major ethnic group. (The data in the total column in table 11-3 differ slightly from those in table 11-4 because of some adjustments of the former series by Snodgrass. The differences are negligible.) The three distributions are quite similar on a decile-by-decile basis as well as on the basis of a comparison of Gini coefficients. The Malays have a slightly lower Gini than do the Chinese and Indians as well as a smaller percentage of income accruing to the highest decile. If the data are broken down between rural and urban for each ethnic group (table 11-5), the inequality within the urban Chinese and Indian groups is greater than that of the urban Malays, and is also greater than that in the rural areas. Average urban incomes are also higher than rural incomes. Thus average income of urban Malays was twice that of rural Malays. Indian rural and urban incomes were almost equal, and urban Chinese received on the average about 20 percent more than their rural counterparts. Overall average income of the Chinese was more than twice

Table 11-4. Income Distribution among Ethnic Communities, 1957–58

(percent unless otherwise noted)

Decile	Total	Malay	Chinese	Indian
Lowest	2.1	2.7	2.6	3.0
Second	3.6	4.4	4.2	4.6
Third	4.6	5.7	5.2	5.6
Fourth	5.6	6.7	6.0	6.5
Fifth	6.7	7.6	7.0	7.4
Sixth	7.8	8.6	8.1	8.5
Seventh	9.5	9.9	9.6	9.5
Eighth	11.5	11.9	11.5	11.2
Ninth	15.4	14.9	15.3	14.2
Highest	33.2	27.6	30.5	29.5
Gini coefficient	0.41	0.34	0.37	0.35
Mean monthly income (Malaysian dollars)	215	139	300	188

Source: Snodgrass (1980), p. 71.

Table 11-5. Income Distribution among Urban and Rural Ethnic Groups, 1957–58

(percent unless otherwise noted)

Decile	Malays		Chinese		Indian	
	Rural	Urban	Rural	Urban	Rural	Urban
Lowest	2.0	1.9	1.8	1.6	2.4	1.8
Second	4.6	4.4	4.1	3.7	5.5	4.0
Third	5.7	5.4	5.2	4.7	6.5	5.0
Fourth	6.7	6.3	6.3	5.7	7.4	5.8
Fifth	7.8	7.2	7.5	6.8	8.4	6.7
Sixth	9.0	8.7	8.8	8.0	9.4	7.7
Seventh	10.5	10.4	10.4	9.5	10.6	9.5
Eighth	12.5	12.2	12.7	11.6	12.1	12.4
Ninth	15.2	15.0	15.9	15.2	14.3	17.0
Highest	26.0	28.5	27.4	33.2	23.4	30.0
Gini coefficient	0.34	0.36	0.36	0.41	0.29	0.39
Average monthly income (Malaysian dollars)	122	249	266	320	213	225

Source: Ikemoto (1985).

that of the Malays, and Indian average income was a solid 35 percent higher than that of Malays. In general, however, it is correct to say that inequality within ethnic groups is about the same.

If one examines income distribution data for other developing countries, one sees a pattern similar to that for Malaysia. Rural-urban differences are substantial, educated-noneducated are equally so, as are differences owing to the relative importance of one language compared with another, and so on. The picture for Malaysia is essentially the same. The difference, of course, is that members of the Malay community were more heavily represented in those categories that were at a disadvantage. Malays were especially dominant in smallholder rubber and coconut, in rice, and in fishing. All of these activities were low-productivity activities no matter which ethnic group was involved. It is for this reason that the historical, political, and cultural issues briefly summarized in the background section are so crucial to an understanding of the inequality as of independence. In large measure the question is not so much—or at least not only—why there was inequality in 1957, but why it was that the Malays were so heavily concentrated among the poorer income groups. One may also phrase the question in terms of the failure of the productivity in small-scale agriculture (including fishing) to increase. It will be argued later that Malaysia was not unlike a natural-resource–rich country in that it had a strong export sector (rubber and tin) that carried the system in general (at least in the view of the colonial power); further, no incentive was present for any increased flexibility or new source of dynamism to emerge. In particular, given the apparent slack in the economy (excess of saving over investment and underemployment especially, and no inflation or balance of payments pressure), an exchange rate that protected the balance of payments offered little inducement for import substitution or for finding new exports in addition to tin and rubber. This point helps to explain the inequality itself, rather than the reason that the Malays were in low-productivity activities. The great rubber estates and the tin mines were largely foreign-owned at independence; hence, profits accrued to foreigners. Much of the inequality, therefore, was a consequence of differences in wages, rather than because of the concentration of profits in the hands of a few, although specific evidence on this point is not presently available.

Data on poverty, as distinct from inequality, always have a considerable component of arbitrariness about them. Snodgrass (1980, p. 80) has calculated the percentages of households with an income of less than $120 a month from data in the Household Budget Survey for 1957–58. His findings are consistent with the inequality story just told, as shown by the following data.

Other estimates show slightly different totals, but the relationship among the several groups is essentially the same as that of Snodgrass. Thus more than one-half of the Malays were below this $120 a month line, compared to one-fifth of the Indians and one-eighth of the Chinese. It is probably correct to assume that the real income of the Malays, especially those in rural areas, is more likely to be understated than is the income of the other ethnic communities. Even so, the general picture shown in the Snodgrass data is doubtless a fair representation of the 1957–58 reality.

Group	Percentage of households earning less than $120 a month
Malays	55.7
Chinese	13.1
Indian	19.8
Rural households	44.2
Urban households	16.8
All households	34.9

Employment and Wages

Data in table 11-2 gave the industrial breakdown of employment. The present task is to try to determine how employment and wages contributed to equity. The general distribution of the labor force by ethnic group is shown in table 11-6. In agriculture Malays were heavily concentrated in small-scale production units, in fishing, and in rubber tapping. Smallholder agriculture had, in general, a lower productivity than manufacturing and services, and the Malays were concentrated in the lower productivity sectors of agriculture. In the service sector, teaching was a common occupation of Malays, and teaching is hardly a dynamic, well-paid activity in any society. Malays constituted a great

Table 11-6. Ethnic Distribution of the Labor Force, 1957

(percent)

Ethnic community	Agriculture[a]	Manufacturing[b]	Services
Malays	73	9	18
Chinese	40	28	32
Other	47	18	35
Total	57	18	26

a. Includes fishing.
b. Includes mining, construction, utilities, and transport.
Source: Young and others (1980), p. 118.

majority of the civil service, which in 1957 had very few Chinese or Indians. Both of the latter two communities were more heavily involved in commercial and financial activities than were the Malays. Table 11-6 largely confirms the ethnic employment picture already described—the Malays were concentrated in activities with low productivity that had little prospect for increased productivity in the years ahead.

The wage bill was something less than one-half of national income. It has been noted that a substantial share of profits went to foreigners. In the case of the smallholder the distinction between wage and property income is often quite ambiguous. All of this means that the measured value of the share of wages in national income is of dubious relevance for the economy as a whole.

Other Aspects of Equity

The distribution of measured income, to repeat an old refrain, is not the only component of equity. The background survey made it clear that the Malays strongly favored maintaining their kampongs and smallholdings and a life-style that they found compatible with their commitment to Islam. The unity of the Islamic tradition means that the idea of a secular state is generally unacceptable or undesirable; equally unpalatable are other distinctions between Islam on the one hand and economic, social, or cultural matters on the other. In addition, there were educational and other policies, which were followed during the colonial period, that effectively denied Malays access to the more modern and more foreign—more export oriented—sections of the economy. Meanwhile, it was the Malays who had become dominant in the government and worked with the British in achieving independence. These Malays constituted a strong minority of individuals who seemed to argue that, given Malaysia's plural society, a secular state was necessary. Many of the Malay leaders had been educated in Britain. To these political leaders the task was to recognize the plural nature of the Malaysian society, to design a political system, and work out an economic strategy that accommodated this plurality. Also, a substantial number of Malays interpreted Islam not only to permit, but indeed to encourage, economic advancement (Chee 1983). At the opening of a Conference of Moslem Theologians in April 1969, the Yang di-Pertuan Agong (king) identified three attitudes in the practice of Islam that Malays needed to cultivate—the spirit of investigation, the spirit of unity, and the spirit of pioneering (Chee 1983, p. 263). These ideas were pushing Malays to be more active, more searching, and less content, without losing their commitment to Islam. Such a statement acknowledged and emphasized the fact that Malays were uninvolved in the new developments that were taking place in the world, and that they must begin to change.

At independence, therefore, this difference existed within the Malay community in addition to economic and cultural differences between the Malays and the other ethnic groups. There was also history—a history of an economy that, from one point of view, had worked well. Consequently, there were firmly entrenched institutions, routines, and ideas that limited what was easily changed and, in particular, limited what the new government considered changeable. Thus, development involved a continuing process of adjustment, of adaptation, and of learning in this diverse environment. In this context, there were several issues that appeared high on any agenda a policymaker might have—the apparent long-run weakness of rubber and tin and their instability, even in the absence of long-term weakness; the importance of finding new activities in an economic system centered principally on tin and rubber; and the increasing recognition of the difficulties of managing a plural society in general and the complexities of the income distribution and equity issues in particular. In this environment, what strategy made sense?

12 Growth and Equity in Malaysia: A General Survey

In this chapter we seek to establish a general picture of the development that took place over the years from 1960 to 1985. As in the case of Sri Lanka, the objective is to provide the broad outlines of how those variables of greatest relevance to our story evolved over this period. The following chapters will then add more detail and seek to explain this evolution in terms of the policies followed and the political economy that affected the choice of policies.

Macroeconomic Variables

Exports and GDP

Exports were 53 percent of GDP in 1955 and 1960, 53 and 57 percent in 1979 and 1980, and a bit less than 50 percent in 1985. In between these years they were below 50 percent in each year from 1962 through 1975. The lowest figure was 36 percent in 1972; 1967 was the only other year that the percentage fell below 40. The sharp increase in the ratio of exports to GDP in 1976 was a result of a general rise in the price and quantity of all major exports, except palm oil. Exports in current prices jumped 45 percent in 1976 compared with 1975, and this increase raised GDP by 11 percent. During the years from 1962 to 1975, export volume continued to increase at a fairly steady rate, but the unit price index was generally weak. Even so, a 40 percent ratio of exports to GDP is high by international standards, and only the mineral-producing countries (and Hong Kong and Singapore) have ratios higher than that for Malaysia. Of equal importance to later argument is the continued export surplus in the trade balance over the period. Such a surplus prevents a bottleneck, which allows the economy to operate uninterruptedly.

There were, however, important changes in the composition of exports. Rubber in the early 1960s constituted over 50 percent of total exports, and by the mid-1980s it was falling below 10 percent. The big gainers were palm oil, logs and timber, and petroleum. These three items constituted about 45 percent of total exports in the early 1980s; and in 1985 petroleum exports accounted for almost one-quarter of foreign exchange receipts, and rubber constituted 7 percent. Similarly the five major exports (rubber, palm oil, tin, logs and timber, and petroleum) accounted for about 75 percent of total exports in the early 1960s and from 1980 to 1981, but by 1985 they were accounting for less than 60 percent. Diversification was occurring then, as exports increased, in the 1960s and 1970s, and seems to have accelerated in the early 1980s. The rapid development of petroleum and its large price increases were, of course, major factors in the continued strength of exports.

Part of this diversification was reflected in the increase in the exports of manufactured commodities. In 1961 they were less than 5 percent of total exports, in 1970 they were 7 percent, and by the mid-1980s were approaching one-third. Thus manufactured exports were growing much more than were total exports. In the 1970s manufactured exports grew much more rapidly than in the 1960s. Indeed in the 1970s the growth rate was over 30 percent a year even before a big jump in 1977. The main point, however, is that total exports grew well, and that manufactured exports, a negligible figure in 1960, had become a significant item by 1980. In the early 1980s, however, new difficulties appeared.

Growth and Investment

Figure 12-1 shows that GDP has grown at a remarkably steady rate over the quarter-century since 1961. Annual rates of growth in constant prices fell below 5 percent in only five years—1964, 1967, 1969, 1975, and 1985. Only in 1975 was the growth rate essentially zero. During the twenty-four years the average annual rate of growth was over 7.0 percent—one of the highest in the world for such a long period. Within that period the variance was generally small. Over the years from 1967 to 1974, the growth rate averaged 7.7 percent, and from 1975 to 1981 the average was 8.3 percent a year, but in general the growth rate was high and remarkably stable by international standards over the whole period. The relatively high and steady rate of growth of GDP meant that Malaysia was able to avoid the stop-go routine that is such an impediment to achieving sustained growth and, more important, to increased productivity. An important question is, of course, why no growth-stopping bottlenecks appeared. The answer seems to be in terms of the general absence of a balance of payments bottleneck and, until recently, the absence of inflation.

Figure 12-1. GDP and Its Components for Malaysia, 1960-85

A. Volume of imports

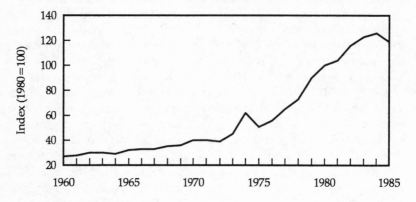

B. Volume of exports

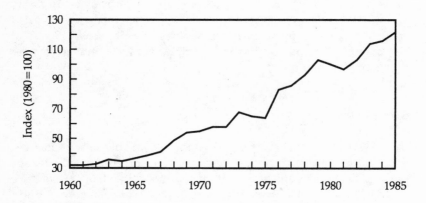

C. GDP (in 1980 prices)

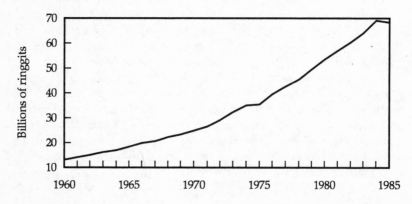

Figure 12-1. (continued)

D. Investment (in 1980 prices)

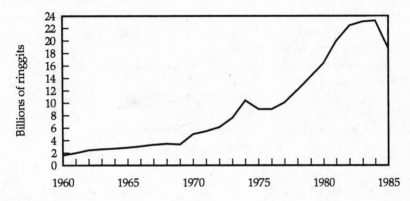

E. Terms of trade

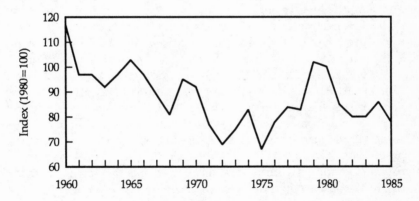

Source: A, B, and E, Statistical Appendix, Table A-21; C and D, Statistical Appendix, Table A-18.

More on this issue later. The point here is to emphasize the steadiness of the growth, and the advantage that steadiness has for productivity growth as well as for the design and implementation of policies and plans. Steady growth at 4 or 5 percent is more advantageous than high rates today and stops tomorrow. If a country can design and implement a set of policies without having to stop and direct its attention to a short-run bottleneck, the economy is more likely to have time and opportunity to respond to the long-run policies. Thus steadiness—the absence of stop-and-go—is a major advantage, even if the steady growth rate is a modest one.

The other question is about the source of growth in Malaysia. What was it that moved the system? Investment, as shown in figure 12-1, experienced a modest fall in 1969 and an abrupt jump in 1974, but for the rest of the period was surprisingly (for investment) stable. The graphs in figure 12-2 shows that the ratio of investment to GDP—again ignoring 1969 and 1974—rose fairly regularly at an average rate of about 2.7 a year from 1960 to 1976, and then took off mightily (9.0 percent growth a year) for the next six years. In the years from 1960 to 1979 saving rates were usually slightly higher than the rate of investment, but from 1980 investment exceeded national saving by a considerable margin, and foreign saving became important as a means of financing the investment.

Using conventional formula one arrives at a rough estimate of the rate of growth of the capital stock over this period of at least 5 percent. This figure, rough though it is, is evidence that the capital-labor ratio was rising at a sizable rate, as employment grew at possibly 2.5 percent a year. Capital-labor ratios for an entire economy are of dubious meaning, but these estimates do indicate that more and more physical capital was becoming available per laborer. More relevant perhaps is the simple fact that throughout the period capital formation was proceeding at relatively high rates with only minor, short-lived interruptions. Additional support of this evidence is the apparent steady rise in the ICOR until it was well in excess of four by the 1980s. The investment graph in figure 12-1 does show some tailing-off in the 1980s, although in the early years of that decade the rate of investment was unusually high.

The other general point to note about investment is its changing composition over the period. Sectoral investment data are not available, but it is clear that investment in nonperennial crops (rubber; oil palm mainly) fell over the period, and investment in nonagricultural activities increased. Investment in infrastructure, especially transport and communication, became increasingly important. Also, public investment rose, most notably after 1970, compared with private investment.

Foreign Trade and Growth

Exports and imports in constant prices also increased at an unusually
steady pace. The rate of growth of export volume was a bit less steady
than is expected from a small country whose exports are largely primary goods. The fluctuations suggest that there were some adjustments on the supply side as prices in world markets changed. Over
the entire period export volume averaged 7.2 percent growth a year
and imports 6.6 percent. Export growth, therefore, just about matched
GDP growth, while imports lagged slightly, but only slightly. Two
intervals seem somewhat distinct. During the first, from 1960 to 1969,
exports averaged 5.7 growth a year and imports 3.3 percent. This
suggests that in these years the economy was becoming—or starting
to become—less foreign-trade oriented. The next section seeks to explain how and why this occurred. In the second period, from 1975 to
1984, the rate of growth of exports jumped to 9.7 percent and that of
imports to 10.5 percent. There was a bit of a decrease in 1984. The
years in between, from 1969 to 1975, were somewhat unsettled—a
couple of years of very low or negative growth and then three years
of very rapid growth, followed by a sharp decline. These were the
beginning years of the New Economic Policy, a matter that will occupy
considerable attention in later pages. Both exports and imports moved
along in a remarkably similar fashion to investment, but with somewhat less severe fluctuations, at least in the 1969-to-1975 period.

Saving

Saving rates fluctuated, as figure 12-2 shows. There is something of an
upward trend from 1964 to 1969 and again from 1972 to 1979, but there
are sharp reversals so it is inappropriate to speak of a trend. Of more
relevance to the story is the fact that from 1955 to 1961 national saving
exceeded gross investment by a substantial margin. During the decade
from 1950 to 1960, savings were almost twice investment and from
1960 to 1970 exceeded investment by about 13 percent. It was not until
the early 1980s that Malaysia began to depend on foreign savings to
any extent. The government budget was more or less balanced until
1970 when deficits began to increase. As a proportion of GDP the deficits remained modest by international standards until the late 1970s
and early 1980s. Finally, the corollary to what has happened on the
saving front is, of course, consumption. Private consumption as a
proportion of GDP declined steadily from the early 1960s with a blip
here and there. Something more than an upward blip occurred from
1980 to 1982, but the downward trend was then resumed. Government consumption as a proportion of GDP remained around 15 percent
over the entire period.

Figure 12-2. Macroeconomic Indicators for Malaysia, 1960-85

A. Investment - GDP

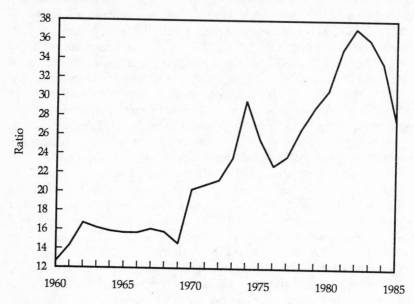

B. Government consumption - GDP

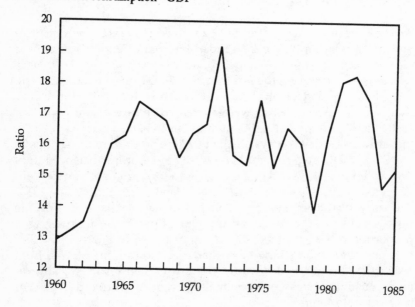

Figure 12-2. (continued)

C. Savings - GDP

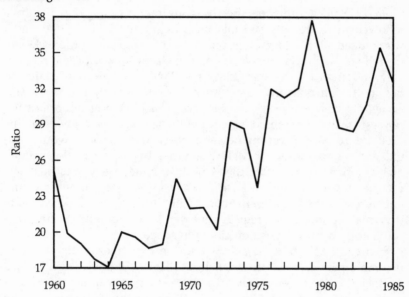

D. Private consumption - GDP

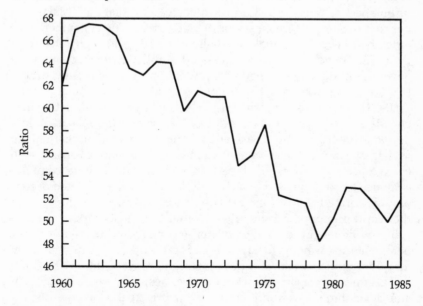

Source: Statistical Appendix, Table A-19.

All of this seems to indicate an unusually cautious fiscal policy specifically and development policy in general. It would appear that resources were available for an even higher rate of investment and, presumably, a higher rate of growth. These resources were not exploited. From another perspective, one might argue that Malaysia followed an extremely sensible macroeconomic policy. Investment was indeed high and grew rapidly, as did GDP. No bottlenecks appeared, and the economy—at the aggregate level—performed remarkably smoothly. The economy stayed well within its resource availabilities, both domestic and foreign. This result is related to the ethnic issues discussed in previous chapters. The following important hypothesis will be explored subsequently—growth was lower in the 1960s because the government was concerned that growth would benefit non-Malays more than Malays and thereby exacerbate the inequalities between races. After the New Economic Policy was in place, growth was accelerated because it was believed that that policy would ensure that the Malays participated fully in the growth. Needless to say, this hypothesis will require considerable examination before anything approaching a position can be reached.

Figures 12-1 through 12-4 show that some changes in this clear and favorable picture began to occur in the late 1970s. The most explicit evidence is the acceleration in the increase in the consumer price index and in the size of the budget deficit. Similarly the current account of the balance of payments began to suffer sharp reversals at this time, and foreign debt began to increase at an accelerating rate. More recent data confirm that Malaysia's smooth ride is running into considerable turbulence, as data for 1985 show a decrease in real GDP. Malaysia's dependence on its foreign sector remains great. The consumer price index had begun to rise at unusually (for Malaysia) high rates from 1973. The money supply also increased at this time even though the government deficit remained well under control. The money supply in the 1970s grew at over 18 percent a year, about twice the rate in the 1960s. There were other signals as well. The improvement in the merchandise trade balance in 1983 and 1984 was principally a result of slow import growth reflecting a weakened domestic demand rather than the growth of exports. Malaysia then seemed to experience a considerable change in its macroeconomic performance in 1980; more accurately, evidence began to appear of a change in the way that the macroeconomy performed. Part of the explanation of this involves the state of the world economy, but there were other factors at work as well.

It may be useful to anticipate later argument and make one point here about the way the Malaysian economy worked—as measured by macroeconomic variables—in the 1960s and most of the 1970s. Colonial regimes were generally cautious regimes, partly because growth and development were not among their principal concerns. Institutions and attitudes evolved then that produced policies that kept the economy operating well within its resource constraints and firmly controlled deficits and money supply. These attitudes and corresponding policies continued into the early history of independent Malaysia. As they changed and as the policymaker became more concerned with development, problems appeared that could not be managed either in the traditional way or by new instruments available to the policymaker.

This review combined with the four figures suggests a sharp change in the late 1970s in the way the economy performed similar to that observed for Sri Lanka. Variables that had been moving steadily in the 1960s and early 1970s, suddenly seemed to be subjected to new forces that caused them to move in unexpected ways. The general explanations of this turn of events is similar to that offered for Sri Lanka. The economy was moving away from its traditional mode of functioning, and this shifting process, as just noted, introduced problems that could not be managed in traditional ways. So the macroeconomic indicators began to move in unexpected ways. This is an issue that will be considered again in the following pages, and especially in the last section.

Some Changes in the Composition of Output

In 1960 agriculture accounted for 36 percent of GDP (in current prices) and trade and finance for 26 percent. Manufacturing and mining each amounted to 5 percent. Over the next quarter-century agriculture's share declined in the traditional manner, and the share of trade and finance also declined, somewhat nontraditionally. The rather high share of trade and finance in 1960 reflects the continuing role of Malaysia, especially the Chinese community of Malaysia, as traders. The decline in the role of agriculture was, however, less than in other countries with Malaysia's level and rate of growth of per capita income. In the early 1980s, therefore, Malaysia continued to be much more of an agricultural economy than any other country in its income category. For example, agriculture in Malaysia accounted for 24 percent of GDP in 1982; in Korea it accounted for 16 percent, in Mexico 7 percent, and in Chile 6 percent. All these countries had approximately the same per capita income at this time.

There are two general factors that seem to explain, or help to explain, the strong role that agriculture continued to play in a relatively rich and growing economy. The first is the effective development of new, higher-yielding strains of rubber as well as the development of new uses for natural rubber. Both of these helped to keep natural rubber reasonably competitive with synthetic rubber in world markets. Even so, of course, demand for natural rubber was lagging be-

Figure 12-3. International Transactions for Malaysia, 1960-85

A. Current account balance

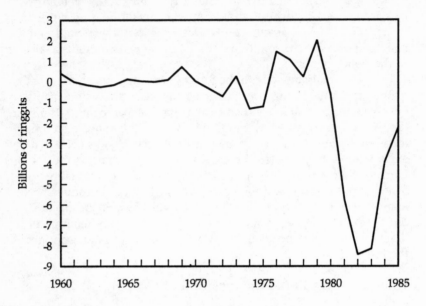

B. Balance of trade

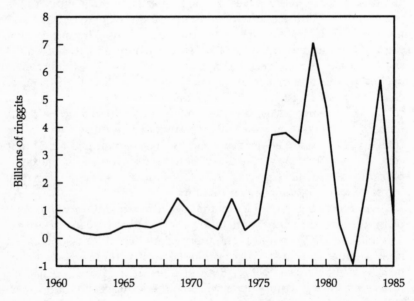

Figure 12-3. (continued)

C. Foreign exchange reserves

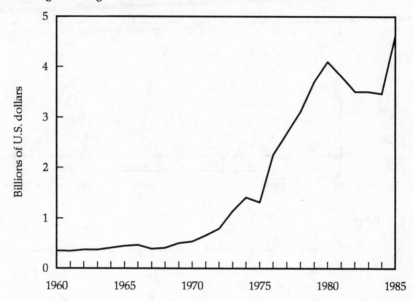

D. External debt

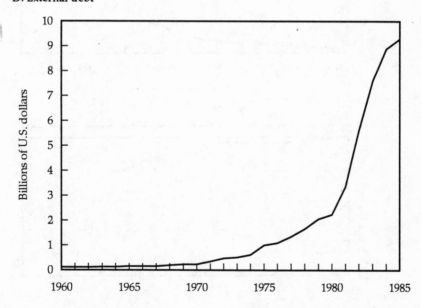

Source: A and B, Statistical Appendix, Table A-21; C and D, Statistical Appendix, Table A-22.

Figure 12-4. Money and Prices in Malaysia, 1960-85

A. Change in the consumer price index

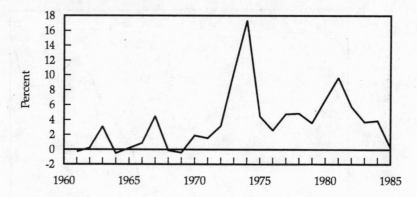

B. Liquidity

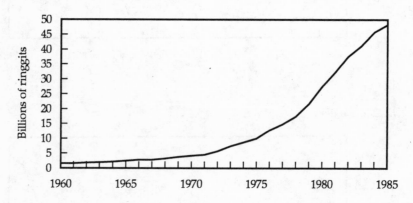

C. Government deficit or surplus

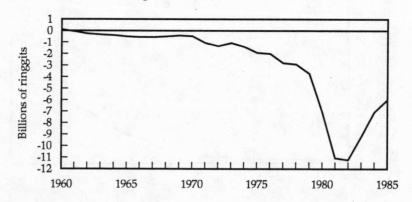

Source: Statistical Appendix, Table A-26.

hind that for synthetic rubber. In the mid-1950s the consumption of natural rubber was 55 percent of the world's rubber consumption, and in 1980 it was approximately 30 percent. Production of rubber grew at an average annual rate of 5.7 percent in the 1960s, but less than one-half that rate in the 1970s, and began to decline absolutely in the 1980s. The volume of rubber exports followed a fairly similar pattern. Although rubber was a lagging sector, it is important to emphasize that the improvements in yields and the increase in the variety of uses were impressive and helped to prevent an abrupt collapse of Malaysia's rubber sector.

The other factor that helps in understanding the reason that Malaysia's agriculture sector has remained strong was the successful shift from rubber to palm oil. Palm oil production increased more than fortyfold over the period, and by the end of the 1970s had replaced tin in fourth place (after petroleum, timber, and rubber) among Malaysia's foreign exchange earners. Thus estates were able to move rather readily out of the lagging rubber sector into the thriving oil palm sector. Tin was failing, of course, throughout most of the period.

These arguments about the strength of agriculture apply largely to the estate sector. Rice and fishing did not experience such growth. In particular rice yields increased very slightly over the period. They were about 2,500 kilograms per hectare in the early 1960s and 2,600 in the early 1980s. They reached 2,900 to 3,000 kilograms in the first half of the 1970s, but then dropped back to the lower levels as the decade wore on (FAO, annual b).

There is another question of relevance. Why did not the Malaysian government provide heavy protection at independence and thereby push up the rate of growth of manufacturing output. Details on this are to be covered later, but it is pertinent to note several things here. The estate sector, which was (and had long been) a strong political force, would have opposed any policy that penalized exports or made importing difficult. Any policy that tended to increase wages would also have been opposed by the estates. The success of the rubber innovations combined with the shift from rubber to palm oil enabled the estate sector to continue to be strong and to exercise its political influence. Along with these developments came timber and petroleum as major sources of foreign exchange receipts. The rapid growth of exports of these two items more or less relieved any balance of payments pressure to turn inward.

Three points have been made to explain agriculture's continued strong position—the success in prolonging rubber's competitive position and the successful shift to palm oil; the strong political role of the estates that would have been hurt by protection; and the appearance of logs and sawed timber and petroleum as important foreign exchange earners relieved balance of payments pressure to invoke protection. A fourth factor is doubtless of great importance, although it is difficult to pin down specifically. It was widely believed that a much greater emphasis on industrial development in the 1960s would bene-fit principally the non-Malays, especially the Chinese. The govern-ment, therefore, was reluctant to provide protection that would most likely have penalized Malays, because of increased prices of the manu-factured products that Malays bought, and helped only the non-Malays.

The continued strength of agriculture meant that the manufacturing sector grew a bit more slowly, in relation to GDP, than was the case in other rapidly growing countries. The ratio of manufacturing output to GDP tripled between 1960 and 1980, and the growth rate was fairly steady over the period. Other sectors grew along with GDP in more or less the expected manner. Trade and finance lagged somewhat, but it was already an unusually large sector at the time of independence.

Equity

The story just summarized defines an unusually favorable develop-ment process. The very fact of this good showing, however, contrib-uted to the increasing complexity of defining and achieving equity in the multiracial society. In other words, if GDP had not grown so smoothly and rapidly, the inequalities in its distribution would not have appeared to be so stark, and the price paid to maintain traditional life-styles would not have appeared so high. In this section the broad outlines of the income distribution changes and the employment pic-ture are summarized, and an effort is then made to discuss equity in a somewhat wider context.

Income Distribution

There are three recent books that provide complete and careful studies of income distribution (Anand 1983; Snodgrass 1980; and Tan 1982). All of these books discuss the quality of the available data and de-velop a number of arguments and hypotheses explaining the reason that income distribution changed the way it did. The objective in the present context is much more limited. An effort is made to present a general picture of how the distribution of income changed over the 1960-to-1985 period, and then to examine some of the factors that appear especially strategic in terms of more general considerations of equity.

Table 11-4, in chapter 11, shows the distribution of income among ethnic communities and for the nation as a whole in 1957 and 1958.

Table 12-1. Income Share of Households for Selected Years, 1957–84

(percent unless otherwise noted)

Decile	1957–58	1970	1976	1979	1984
Lowest	2.2	1.2	1.2	1.3	1.4
Second	3.5	2.8	2.1	2.4	2.8
Third	4.6	3.2	3.2	3.6	3.8
Fourth	5.4	4.5	4.6	4.6	4.8
Fifth	6.5	5.5	5.1	5.5	6.0
Sixth	7.7	6.8	6.7	7.0	7.2
Seventh	9.2	9.1	8.4	8.6	9.3
Eighth	11.1	10.7	11.4	11.2	11.5
Ninth	15.0	15.1	15.7	16.5	16.6
Highest	34.8	41.1	41.9	39.3	36.6
Gini coefficient	0.42	0.50	0.53	0.51	0.48
Mean monthly income (ringgits)	220	275	513	693	1,095
Median monthly income (ringgits)	156	170	313	436	723

Source: Government of Malaysia, *Household Survey* (1957–58), *Post-Enumeration Survey* (1970), *Agricultural Census* (1977), *Household Income Survey* (1980, 1984).

Table 12-1 shows comparable estimates for four other years. There are, as always, many questions about the quality of the data. It is probable that inequality is understated for Malays and overstated for Indians. The estimates for the Chinese, and for the nation as a whole, seem less likely to be biased in either direction. Given all the difficulties with the data, one might conclude that they cannot be used at all to tell us how distribution changed over the period. Anand (1983, chapter 2), after a detailed argument, does in fact reach this conclusion. Snodgrass (1980, pp. 76–77), however, is convinced, and offers equally good reasons for his view, that the data do serve to inform us that inequality has changed in just about the manner indicated in the tables. Snodgrass and Anand's comments refer to the first three sets of data. There is little evidence one way or the other to lend outside support to the other two years. The general position taken here is that the data do indicate with reasonable accuracy the direction of change and more or less the extent of change. The main reason for this point of view is that the story that can be told to account for these changes is convincing, given other data and information about the period. Qualitative information fit well with these data. It is possible, then, to proceed on the assumption that the data reveal something that has really happened in Malaysia between 1957–58 and 1980.

DISTRIBUTION IN THE NATION. The main data are shown in tables 12-1 and 12-2. Table 12-1 refers to the nation as a whole, and table 12-2 refers to the three main ethnic communities. The general picture is clear. Between 1957–58 and 1970 inequality increased. The simplest illustration of this is that the share of the highest 10 percent rose while that of the lowest ten percent declined. This is true for the nation as a whole as shown in table 12-1 and for each ethnic community as shown in table 12-2. For the nation as a whole the share of each of the poorest eight deciles declined over the period. The eighth and ninth deciles gained fractionally. Therefore, it was largely the top deciles that gained over the period, and gained mainly at the expense of the lower deciles. The top 5 percent received 22 percent of the income in the first period and 28 percent in 1970. The Gini coefficient rose correspondingly from 0.42 to 0.50—a 22 percent rise over the thirteen years, which is a rapid rate of change. The mean monthly income rose moderately over the period—most rapidly apparently between 1967–68 and 1970. The median, as a proportion of the mean, declined, which is to be expected as inequality increases. In 1957 and 1958 the mean income of the top decile was eight times the mean income of the lowest 40 percent. In 1970 it was 14 times as high.

From 1970 to 1976 the Gini coefficient for the nation as a whole rose a bit further, but there were minor gains by some of the lower deciles. The top two deciles also gained a bit. In addition, Snodgrass (1980, p. 77) points out that large portions of private income are never included as household income because they are retained by the firms. His data show that such income rose much more rapidly than did personal income. If this income were included in household income, virtually all of it would accrue to the top deciles, thereby increasing the measured inequality. It is, therefore, difficult to conclude from these results that inequality of measured income distribution decreased over the first years of the New Economic Policy.

After 1976 there appears a consistent movement toward greater equality. The share of the top decile falls by about 15 percent between 1976 and 1984, and the first four deciles each gain a modest share. Other measures are also consistent with the conclusion that the economy began to produce a more equal distribution after 1976.

It is important to remind oneself that the distribution of measured pretax income is not a very satisfactory measure of the distribution of welfare and equality. In particular, some adjustment for tax incidence and the availability of public goods and services must be made, as both of these have differential effects on the various income groups. The data in table 12-1 (and table 12-2 as well) do, however, reveal something about how growth itself—before taxes and before transfers, public goods, and so forth—affected distribution. More accurately, it indicates the distribution aspects of growth. This is impor-

Table 12-2. Change in Household Income Distribution by Ethnic Community, for Selected Years, 1957–59

(percent unless otherwise noted)

Decile	Malays				Chinese				Indians			
	1957	1967	1970	1979	1957	1967	1970	1979	1957	1967	1970	1979
Lowest	2.7	1.8	0.8	1.0	2.6	2.2	1.5	1.0	3.0	2.6	1.5	1.1
Second	4.4	4.2	2.9	2.6	4.2	3.9	3.1	2.6	4.6	3.7	3.4	2.8
Third	5.7	5.0	4.0	3.6	5.2	4.9	3.1	3.6	5.6	4.6	4.3	3.9
Fourth	6.7	6.0	5.0	4.7	6.0	6.0	6.2	4.7	6.5	5.4	5.1	5.0
Fifth	7.6	6.8	6.2	6.0	7.0	6.9	6.2	5.9	7.4	6.6	6.0	6.2
Sixth	8.6	7.8	7.6	7.5	8.1	8.1	7.3	7.5	8.5	8.1	6.9	7.8
Seventh	9.9	8.8	9.2	9.5	9.6	9.5	8.9	9.5	9.5	9.6	8.4	9.7
Eighth	11.9	11.4	11.8	12.5	11.5	11.8	11.1	12.4	11.2	11.3	10.2	12.6
Ninth	14.9	15.5	16.3	17.7	15.3	15.0	15.5	17.7	14.2	15.4	14.6	17.6
Highest	27.6	32.7	36.2	34.9	30.5	31.7	37.1	35.1	29.5	32.7	39.6	33.2
Gini coefficient	0.34	0.40	0.47	0.47	0.37	0.39	0.45	0.47	0.35	0.40	0.46	0.45
Mean monthly income (Malaysian dollars)	139	163	177	—	300	349	399	—	237	260	310	—
Median monthly income (Malaysian dollars)	112	120	122	—	223	261	269	—	188	191	195	—

— Not available.

Source: For 1957–58, 1967–68, and 1970 estimates, Snodgrass (1980); for 1979 estimates, Ikemoto (1985).

217

tant, of course, as it is difficult indeed to offset to any significant degree the distribution generated by the functioning of the market, especially where the economy is as open and market oriented as it is in Malaysia. It should also be noted that the data in table 12-1 are household data. Probably per capita data would show a lower Gini ratio and possibly more evidence of improvement over time than household data.

DISTRIBUTION WITHIN ETHNIC GROUPS. The data in table 12-2 tell a story for each ethnic group very similar to that which table 12-1 tells for the nation as a whole. These data, especially those for 1979, are probably less reliable than those used in the previous table. For each community the Gini coefficient rises until 1970 and then seems to remain more or less constant for the following decade. Similarly, it was the top two deciles that gained, and they gained largely at the expense of the lower four or five. So whatever mechanism produced the rising inequality for the nation as a whole seemed also to be present within each ethnic community. It may be noted that at the time of independence the data indicate less inequality within the Malay community than within either of the other two major groups. The Malay Gini coefficient was a bit lower in 1957 and 1958 than that in the Chinese and Indian communities, and the share of income accruing to the top three deciles was 54.4 percent among Malays, 57.3 among the Chinese, and 54.9 percent among Indians. The share going to the lowest three deciles was greatest for the Indian community and least for the Chinese. Diferences are obviously very small. By 1970 the Gini coefficients were essentially the same in the three communities, and the share of the top three deciles was about 64 percent in each. By 1979 the share of the top decile had fallen somewhat in each community, but the share of the top three deciles had risen marginally for the Malays and Chinese and declined marginally for the Indians. Essentially, it can be said that the share of the highest decile fell over the 1970s, while the share of the top three deciles remained fairly constant. The share of the lowest three deciles declined from 1970 to 1979, slightly for the Malays and Chinese, and rather significantly for the Indians.

Table 12-2 contains information about average income in the three communities. In all periods the average—mean or median—of the Malay community is the lowest of the three and the Chinese the highest. The relative position of the Chinese increased a bit between 1957–58 and 1970, especially in relation to the Malays. Estimates from Malaysia (1979, p. 44) show that the ratio of the mean of household incomes of the Chinese to that of the Malays was markedly higher in 1976 than in 1970. Median income ratios changed less, but the small change that did occur was in favor of the Chinese. The fact that these

"disparity ratios" increased much less when calculated from the median than when calculated from the mean suggests that the income of
the rich Chinese increased more rapidly than did the income of the
rich Malays.

The Fifth Malaysia Plan (1986, p. 99) provides data on household
income by ethnic group in 1979 and 1984. These data show that between these two years the average income (in 1970 prices) of Bumiputera grew at an annual average of 5.3 percent, more rapidly than did
that of the Chinese at 3.7 percent or the Indians at 1.7 percent.
Clearly, the relative position of the Indians was deteriorating. For all
three groups, the median income grew more rapidly than did the
mean over the 1979 to 1984 period. This, too, is consistent with increasing equality in these years.

What should one conclude from these data? There are very few
estimates of changing income distribution over an extended period
in other countries with which to compare the Malaysian experience.
Generally, it is believed that distribution changes rather slowly, but
the effect on distribution in a growing economy obviously depends
on how and why the growth occurs. In a rapidly growing economy it
is easy to see that inequality can increase quickly. It would appear
that, on the basis of very rough comparisons with other countries,
there were fairly rapid changes in income distribution in Malaysia
over these years. It also seems to be true that inequality in the nation
as a whole and within each ethnic community increased until about
1976, after which the data show equality increasing. By the 1980s there
was probably still greater inequality than at independence. The rapid
growth in the 1960s clearly benefited the highest income groups at the
expense of the lowest, and through most of the 1970s the sixth through
ninth deciles gained at the expense of the highest. One might argue
that, in the late 1970s, the income began to "trickle down," and that
the New Economic Policy had begun to have an effect. Data for 1979
and 1984 support this view. The other important aspect of the distribution story is that there was inequality within each community, not just
among the communities.

POVERTY. To discuss changes in the incidence of poverty requires a
definition of poverty, and any definition is sure to be arbitrary. Estimates for the 1970-to-1984 period in the Fifth Malaysia Plan are perhaps the most satisfactory. They are reproduced in table 12-3. The
specific definition of poverty is not given, and the plan document
identifies numerous difficulties with the data. The estimates do, however, seem to be a reasonably accurate indicator of changes in poverty
over these years, but some of the changes appear extremely large.
These data show a sharp decline in the incidence of poverty across
the whole economy during the fifteen years after 1970. The only excep-

Table 12-3. Incidence of Poverty by Area and Activity, for Selected Years, 1970–84

(percent)

Area and activity	1970	1976	1984
Rural	58.7	47.8	24.7
Rubber smallholders	64.7	58.2	43.4
Paddy farmers	88.1	80.3	57.7
Estate workers	40.0	—	19.7
Fishermen	73.2	62.7	27.7
Coconut smallholders	52.8	64.7	46.9
Other agriculture	89.0	52.1	34.2
Other	35.2	27.3	10.0
Urban	21.3	17.9	8.2
Manufacturing	23.5	17.1	8.5
Construction	30.2	17.7	6.1
Transport and utilities	30.9	17.1	3.6
Trade and services	18.1	13.9	4.6
Agriculture	—	40.2	23.8
Mining	33.3	10.1	3.4
Other	—	22.4	17.1
Total	49.3	39.6	18.4

— Not available.

Note: Data are ratios of poor households to the total number of households. For 1970 data are per capita poverty lines and for the other two years gross poverty line incomes. Estimates are based on data from *Post-Enumeration Survey* (1970), *Agricultural Census,* (1977), and *Household Income Survey* (1984). Data for estate workers for 1970 were based on indirect sources and are not completely comparable to data for 1984. These estimates are different from the estimates published in previous plan documents. They show less poverty and a more rapid fall in poverty than do previous plans. The Fifth Plan explains that these differences are the result of its use of better data and a clearer conceptual basis.

Source: Government of Malaysia (1986), p. 86.

tion is the sizable increase among coconut smallholders between 1970 and 1976. Between 1976 and 1984 incidence of poverty declines sharply here as well. The location of poverty remains the same over the period; it is very common in the rural areas, and within the rural area it is concentrated among paddy farmers and fishermen and rubber and coconut smallholders. The reduction in the estimates of poverty among fishermen is truly remarkable. In all of these four categories of poverty concentration, Malays are overwhelmingly in the majority.

Snodgrass (1980, p. 80) has a table that shows the proportion of the households with an income below $120 a month for 1957 to 1958, 1967 to 1968, and 1970. About one-half of Malays, 13 percent of the Chinese, and over 20 percent of the Indians have an income below this level at each of these time periods. The incidence was much greater (around 42 percent) in rural areas, approximately 16 percent in the urban areas, and a bit over one-third for the economy as a whole. The main point is that over this thirteen-year period the incidence of poverty, so measured, changed virtually not at all. Thus if the data in table 12-3 are accurate indicators, an important result appears—little or no poverty reduction occurred from 1957–58 to 1970, but after 1970 its incidence fell rapidly across virtually the entire economy. There was no change in the activities where poverty was most common and only minor changes in the states where poverty was greatest. These were the activities and the states in which the Malay community constituted a large majority. Such large reductions in poverty could not have taken place without considerable help from government policies, and much later discussion is devoted to how policies, especially the New Economic Policy, helped to alleviate poverty. It may be noted that these changes in the incidence of poverty, especially between 1976 and 1984, are large by international comparisons. That poverty declined after 1975 or so has been established, but that it declined to the degree indicated by the table is doubtful.

In addition to these data on income, the data on school attendance, health facilities, water and electricity supply, and other overhead items show increases of such magnitude over the twenty-five years that all income groups were affected, at least to some extent.

Employment and Wages

To repeat another old refrain, open unemployment is not a very helpful notion in developing countries. The various estimates for Malaysia show little evidence of increasing open unemployment over the period. Estimates seem always to be around 7 to 9 percent until 1980. The Third Malaysia Plan (Malaysia 1976, p. 141) estimates unemployment at 7.4 and 7.0 percent for 1970 and 1975, and the Fifth Plan shows 5.7 percent in 1980 and 7.6 in 1985. The unemployment rate among Malays declined from 8.1 to 6.9 percent between 1970 and 1975, while the rate of the Chinese and Indians rose slightly. Unemployment among the Indian community was markedly higher than the rate among the Malays and Chinese.

At the same time there appears to be evidence that there were considerable numbers of people who did not have a job but who wanted to work if the right job became available. The labor force grew at an average rate of 2.8 to 3.0 percent over the period from 1960 to 1985, and estimates of employment levels in various years (Young and others 1980, p. 118) suggest an employment growth rate of about 2.5 percent a year. The open unemployment was concentrated on people hunting for their first job, which always makes it more difficult to fit the supply of new jobs with the composition of the demand for those jobs. In October 1971 almost 23 percent of the fifteen-to-nineteen age group in the labor force were unemployed, and by 1974 the rate had fallen to something over 16 percent. All rates are markedly higher in rural than in urban areas. On the basis of very general and impressionistic information, it appears that this compositional complexity increased in the early and mid-1980s. It is obvious, of course, that solving an unemployment problem owing to compositional or "structural" matters is a more difficult task than solving one resulting from an aggregate demand problem or to the lack of capital. The kind of job an individual wants—especially an individual just entering the labor force—is a function of many things. Education is perhaps most frequently noted, but other factors are also important. In the case of Malaysia, issues related to the objective of occupational restructuring were, as is discussed later, of great importance.

Unemployment may also be indicated by numbers in those jobs that are viewed as "jobs of last resort." Tan (1982, pp. 115–20) estimates that in 1970 there were approximately 50,000 hawkers in Malaysia, and argues that the number has doubtlessly increased since then. Few choose to be a hawker voluntarily, and virtually all people in this category are there because there is no better alternative available to them.

Underemployment was widespread over the entire period, although there are no data giving unambiguous documentation. It can be concluded, then, that a fairly loose labor market has prevailed in Malaysia since independence. The major complication is an important one—the complexity of generating a demand for jobs that the unemployed wished to fill.

The distribution of labor among the producing sectors changed over the period, but surprisingly slowly, given the rate of growth of GDP. Table 12-4 shows that the proportion of the labor force in agriculture was 57 percent in 1957, and by 1985 had fallen to 36 percent. (The World Bank's *World Tables* show 63 percent in 1960 and 50 percent in 1980.) Even if the lower percentages are used, the figure for the 1980s

Table 12-4. Distribution of Labor Force by Category, for Selected Years, 1957–85

(percent)

Category	1957	1970	1975	1980	1985
Agriculture	57	50	46	40	39
Industry	17	20	22	28	29
Services	26	30	32	32	35

Source: Young and others (1980), p. 118, and Government of Malaysia (1986), p. 138.

Table 12-5. Distribution of Occupation by Ethnic Community, for Selected Years, 1957–80

(percent)

	1957		1967		1980	
Activity	Malay	Non-Malay	Malay	Non-Malay	Malay	Non-Malay
Agriculture	61	39	62	38	68	32
Rubber estates	19	81	24	76	—	—
Rubber smallholdings	62	38	65	35	—	—
Other	79	21	73	27	—	—
Industry	22	78	25	75	39	61
Mining	18	82	20	80	30	70
Manufacturing	19	82	26	74	40	60
Construction	32	68	26	74	32	68
Commerce	17	83	26	74	30	70
Public administration	73	27	69	31		
Service	29	71	35	65	62	38

— Not available.
Source: Snodgrass (1980) and Ikemoto (1985).

is still high compared with the other countries in Malaysia's income group that have comparable rates of growth. This result is owing in large part to the strong showing of agriculture to which reference has already been made. Manufacturing's share of employment remains at about 15 percent from 1970 or so through 1985, and the Fifth Plan projection for 1990 is still 15 percent. Another aspect of this occupational structure refers to urbanization rates. Malaysia's urbanization rate in the 1960s and 1970s was one of the lowest in the world. As of 1984 about one-third of Malaysia's population lived in urban areas. To find a comparable figure in another developing country one must look for countries with very much lower per capita incomes. It is possible to conclude, then, that there was less rushing to the cities in Malaysia than was the case in most other developing countries. People in rural areas are often classified as agricultural workers even when they do very little work at all or spend a good part of their time in nonagricultural activities.

Table 12-5 gives some information on the allocation by ethnic community of the labor force over the period. The 1980 data are especially open to question. The picture there is compatible with previous discussion. The labor force in agriculture was heavily Malay throughout the period, and within agriculture the Malays were concentrated in the least productive sectors—rubber and oil palm smallholdings and paddy production and fishing. The data for 1980 show that 40 percent of the people working in manufacturing were Malays compared with 19 percent at independence. The 40 percent is surely too large, but there was certainly a significant increase. The same observation applies to services. On the basis of table 12-5, one gathers that there was considerable restructuring of the labor force over the period in the sense that the Malays were much more appropriately represented in nonagricultural activities than they had been twenty years earlier.

Data for labor's share of national income are not adequate to provide much of a picture of developments over the period. During the 1960s wage share seemed to hover around 47 to 49 percent with little evidence of a trend. No estimates appear to be available for the past fifteen years. Wage rates were certainly higher in Malaysia than in any other country in South and Southeast Asia, save Singapore. At the same time, it seems clear that the Malaysian government kept a close watch on wages. In the 1960s there was an employment tax, and the government could have taken action to increase the demand for labor. The International Labour Organisation has a number of cases showing that the Malaysian government seemed to be impeding the emergence of strong labor unions. Policies to dampen the power of labor unions were often justified on grounds of national harmony. There appears no evidence of a strike by any group in Malaysia.

Wealth Ownership

A final aspect of the distribution question refers to the role of foreign ownership and to wealth holdings in general. There appear to be no estimates of wealth holdings over any interval. Data are available for 1970 that tell something about the distribution of the ownership of share capital in limited companies and are shown in table 12-6. Two things stand out in the table. The first is the dominance of ownership

Table 12-6. Ownership of Share Capital by Sector, 1970
(percent)

Type of owner	Rubber	Tin	Manufacturing	Financial institution	Trade	All
Malay	10	4	2	3	1	2
Chinese	13	9	22	24	30	23
Indian	1	0	1	0	1	1
Government	0	2	1	3	0	1
Other residents	7	19	14	17	4	13
Total resident	22	33	40	48	36	39
Foreign	78	67	60	52	64	61

Note: Totals may not add because of rounding.
Source: Snodgrass (1980), p. 99.

by foreigners, nonresidents, or foreign-controlled companies. For all industries combined, over 61 percent of share capital was owned by foreigners, and in some individual activities the proportion in foreign hands was even higher. Since wealth, by definition, is a source of income, these data mean that a great deal of income generated in Malaysia was accruing to foreigners.

The second thing to note about the data in table 12-6 is that the holdings of members of the Chinese community were very large compared with holdings by Malays and Indians. The Chinese share in manufacturing, trade, and finance was substantial (though much smaller than that of foreigners), and provided a strong base from which to accumulate even more wealth. Share capital was a relatively small proportion of total capital in the country, but it was the capital that probably yielded the highest returns.

It was the situation represented by these data that led to the New Economic Policy objective of a restructuring of wealth ownership in Malaysia. The initial target was both ambitious and controversial. It called for the Bumiputera (the Malays and other indigenous people) to own at least 30 percent of share capital of limited companies by 1990, other Malaysians to own 40 percent, and foreign interests 30 percent—less than one-half of their 1970 share. The table shows what an ambitious target this was.

Some interesting complications may be noted. Malays were much more likely to own their own homes than were members of either of the other two communities. Sewing machines and radios were also very common among all communities. These two items have long been popular among all Malaysians, while the importance that Malays attach to home ownership reflects their commitment to a rural life-style of which this is one aspect. Note that this does not mean Malay homes are generally larger or more comfortable than those of other communities. Of more modern forms of consumer durables and assets—bank account, life insurance, camera, car, and so forth—the Chinese had (in 1967–68) many more than did the Malays. Television sets, however, were also more widely available among Malays than a simple look at relative incomes might suggest. Thus, these differences are partly explained by variations in income levels, but another factor is a difference in life-styles. (Data in this paragraph are from Snodgrass 1980, p. 101.)

Similar data for other years do not appear to be available. The picture before 1970 would have been very much the same as that just described. For the period after 1970, changes were beginning to occur. The most important of these changes is the decline in both the role of foreigners and foreigner-controlled enterprises. The fall in the foreigner's share of the Malaysian economy was largely, but not entirely, matched by a rise in that of the Malays. This change has probably been relatively slow, although firm data are not yet available.

The wealth data add still another dimension to the distribution and equity issue. The large role of foreign holdings makes understanding the consequences of distribution more complex and calls attention to an array of quite productive assets that appear to offer a possibility of redistribution (to Malays) without creating severe tensions within the country. Meanwhile these assets were controlled and managed by well-trained, experienced people who would not be available if foreign interests were significantly reduced. Similarly there were few Malaysians and no Malays who could purchase such assets outright. It was generally believed to be quite inappropriate to allow foreigners such a large role in wealth ownership when Malays had such small holdings of their own.

Some Larger Issues of Equity

There was an unequal distribution of measured income in 1957 and 1958 and the inequality increased through the 1960s, with some evidence of a trend toward greater equality in the late 1970s and early 1980s. Although most measures of inequality in the 1980s showed it to be greater than at independence, this inequality was present in the nation as a whole and within each of the three main ethnic communities. There were also significant differences in the average income of the three groups. The Chinese average income was much higher, the Malay was much lower. The low income of the Malays resulted principally from their concentration in low-productivity sectors—smallholdings of rubber, oil palm, and coconuts; paddy farming; and fishing. Poverty was largely a rural phenomenon. Malay employment was correspondingly concentrated in rural areas and traditional activities. Finally, foreigners held a substantial share of the most productive wealth, the Chinese held some, and the Malays and Indians very little indeed.

When one recognizes that there are much broader aspects of the equity issue than the distribution of measured income, complexities naturally arise in any country. The main one in the Malaysian context is that of life-styles. One may argue that most of the members of the Malay community had an opportunity to opt out of their existing occupation and life-style and thereby gain higher incomes, but at the same time commit themselves to pursue a markedly different life-style. If the Malays actually had that opportunity, but chose to stay with their traditional life-styles and low incomes, the presumption must be that they consciously preferred this arrangement. Evidence to this effect can be found in the refusal or reluctance of the Malays to accept employment opportunities on the estates and in tin mines, the slow movement from kampongs to urban centers, the apparent frequent rejection of employment opportunities in modern sector activities, and the interest in and commitment to a variety of traditions that were inconsistent with the modernization process. In a fairly open economy, and indeed open society such as Malaysia was and is, one may well conclude that the great majority of the members of the Malay community did not wish to give up their life-style and their culture simply for the higher measured income that could be obtained in an environment that they found exceedingly distasteful.

The inequality within the Malay community was often recognized as part of this valued tradition. This point refers not only to the high incomes of the members of Malay royalty, but to that of a wealthy landowner or some such individual who performed many social functions, such as financing important religious feasts, providing emergency transportation and communication arrangements, or sharing the great rewards of a journey to Mecca, which made his riches not only socially acceptable, but also socially desirable. Thus the disutility attached to the inequality was limited, and poverty was recognized as part of the circumstance of the traditional Islamic community. In most Malay villages, especially rice villages, a claim on an adequate amount of rice was generally accepted as a basic right, and a tenant, for example, had a recognized claim on some of the landlord's rice in case of difficulties. Poverty and the threat of poverty were, therefore, tempered by these and other traditional institutions that evolved to cope with the poverty.

Similarly the introduction of technical and biological innovations that would increase rice yields or increase the catch of fish impose costs that often seemed high indeed for some Malays. Traditional rice varieties have taller and stronger plants with heavier grains than do the new higher-yielding strains, and are more tolerant of too much and too little water. They allow much more flexibility in the timing of transplanting, thereby giving the farmer greater opportunity to use locally available labor and to time his farming activities to mesh with his other activities. The taller plants help defeat weeds, while the shorter, fertilizer-responsive strains seem to encourage weeds. The more extended period for planting, transplanting, and harvesting also means that the draft animals can be used more sparingly and with greater attention to the animals' need for rest. Thus the traditional rice varieties were much more compatible with the established routines and the availability of complementary resources than were the new varieties. Surely it is appropriate for the rice farmer to move slowly and cautiously into new technologies, even though they might increase his yields. It is helpful to compare this situation in the rice village with that on the rubber and oil palm estates. On the estates, management was often foreign and, foreign or not, was much less concerned with fitting the work routines into the rest of the daily life than was the case in the rice villages. Change in the technology used by the estates was, therefore, more rapid and more accepted by those who were committed to the estate life, and appeared quite unappealing to those committed to a rice culture.

One can tell a similar story about fishing villages. The introduction of boats powered by diesel engines meant that the fishermen had to buy diesel fuel that came from outside the village and usually had to establish new marketing arrangements. These links with economic activity and economic agents in other parts of the country added to the uncertainty of an activity already faced with many uncertainties. The diesel-powered boats also imposed new routines, required different nets and other equipment, and so forth. The shift to power was a major event with far-reaching consequences in many directions, and hence was often resisted.

Conner Bailey's book (1983) has a number of studies of village life in Malaysia that illustrate these and other issues in illuminating detail. Such studies are fundamental to any effort to understand equity in a society that is changing with increasing rapidity. Increased income or an increased share of available income may well not be adequate compensation for relinquishing those things that are so much a part of one's life. So inequality in measured income may not mean inequity in any important sense. (See also Nagata 1979, 1980, and 1984.)

There are two important qualifications. The first is that poverty frequently impedes or prevents people from having what would, and what they acknowledge would, greatly enrich their lives. With additional money it might indeed be possible to gain more from the traditions than is otherwise possible. So poverty as such is hardly an advantage, and obviously it is not the preservation of poverty and inequality that is the objective. Rather, the objective is to reduce poverty in a manner that neither violates nor penalizes traditional values and social arrangements. This task is far more complex than simply raising yields on a modern estate. Naturally, equity does not mean poverty; rather, it means finding a way to relieve poverty that recognizes both the context within which it exists and the fact that this context is, itself, a source of welfare. When poverty or inequality is relieved in ways that are inconsistent with the traditional environment, there may be no increase in welfare, and equity may suffer.

All of this does not mean that change is always and permanently resisted. It does mean that rapid, sweeping change, which destroys the acceptable old before a preferred new can be found, is costly in terms of sacrificed welfare. It is useful to note that it took the West over a century to absorb the industrial revolution and to reorganize the society and working arrangements to take full advantage of the rewards that it could produce. Even so, many changes were painful and costly. The contemporary developing country is faced with the task of trying to absorb new ideas and technologies that are even more different from most prevailing practices than was the case in the West in the eighteenth and nineteenth centuries—and to absorb them in a far shorter time. Resistances, difficulties, and misunderstandings are to be expected and should be taken into account by policymakers. One then sees a tension, an ambiguity, that inheres in a process of rapid change, especially when that change is imposed largely from the outside. It is an ambiguity and tension arising from the appeal of the established and known contrasted with possibilities of the better and more satisfying.

The second qualification is a point similar to that made with respect to the Sinhalese and Tamils in Sri Lanka. A community could have little concern for its own inequality and its poverty, yet find it difficult to accept the fact that other groups are becoming increasingly well off. This is especially true when the several groups are ethnically distinct and members have little social contact with each other. It is made still more difficult if the rich groups are creating an environment that is alien to the one that the poorer group seeks to establish or maintain. Charles Kindleberger (1984, chapter 2) argues that the optimal cultural area is smaller than the optimal currency or production area. In the Kindleberger analysis, this leads to an eventual homogenization of cultural characteristics—and hence lower welfare—after a period of some form of conflict. In postindependence Malaysia, there were similar cultural areas, and the fact that one—that of the Chinese—seemed to be characterized by higher measured income exacerbated the cultural conflict. Perhaps more important was and is the fact that the differences in measured income among the ethnic groups is an easily identifiable difference that, if eliminated, one is tempted to believe, can relieve the cultural conflict. It cannot, and seeking to do that in the wrong way can, of course, worsen the cultural conflict. The problem is to identify the right way.

Summary

Malaysia's development over most of the twenty-five years after 1960 has had many characteristics of success. The growth rate was high by international standards, unemployment was not excessive, the balance of payments was strong, inflation was low, and poverty reduction proceeded at a favorable rate. There was inequality, but it was not at a disturbing level. Yet there were grave and deep-seated difficulties. These difficulties were associated with two closely related phenomena. There were such pronounced differences of income and position between the Chinese and Malays that the difficulties between the two major ethnic groups became increasingly severe and intractable. The deadly racial disturbances of 1969 were the clearest evidence of these difficulties, but the distrust and suspicion were reflected in many other ways. The second phonomenon arose from the necessity in the Malay community of changing its life-styles in an effort to redress the imbalances of income and position between itself and the Chinese community. These changes produced tensions within the Malay community and ambiguous objects for its advancement.

Malaysia had a market economy from the beginning. The government's role was important, but generally indirect. It was not until after 1970—after the New Economic Policy—that the government entered directly into economic activity, and implemented and managed investment and production activities. Even then the language of socialism was eschewed, and the government remained explicitly committed to widespread use of the market. Policies were conventional—tariffs, tax holidays, subsidies of various kinds, infrastructure investment, and so forth. Although these policies produced fairly smooth growth, they did not prevent the great riots of 1969. In addition, the policies did not produce a transformation capacity that was sufficient to generate efficient new activities to relieve the dependency on rubber, tin, oil, palm oil, and timber. It was this failure that led to the difficulties of the 1980s. To accomplish this diversification was one major economic task. The other complex policy issue was concerned with achieving an economic balance—redressing the imbalances—between the Malay and the non-Malay communities. The detailed study of the effort to accomplish these tasks is the major objective of the following pages.

13

1957 to 1970:
Development Strategy
in a Multiethnic Nation

The review of the years from 1957 to 1985 indicated several instances of significant and fairly abrupt changes in the several variables studied. Most of the more evident ones occurred in the period after 1975 and change seemed to accelerate after that date. The 1960s, however, appear less volatile and the series show smoother and more even growth sequences. The most overt event that affected virtually all aspects of policy and policymaking in independent Malaysia was the racial disturbance in Kuala Lumpur in 1969. The attitude and general philosophy of the government changed sharply, profoundly, and permanently as a consequence of this event. Given the relative smoothness of development in the 1960s and the immediate changes induced by the racial disturbance, it seems reasonable to consider the period from 1957 to 1970 as a unit, and to examine the policies, their rationale, and their consequences for this period. Then the 1970s and the New Economic Policy will be considered in detail. The post-1980 years will be studied as the last chapter of the Malaysia story. Of course, any division of time into segments to be treated has some artificiality about it, and one must be alert to avoid identifying as an abrupt change that which has been in the process of change for a considerable period of time. Because one cannot discuss everything simultaneously, one must risk making false distinctions or miss noting an important change when it actually exists. This is inevitable and hardly need be mentioned except to remind the reader that the possibility of these difficulties always exists and is acknowledged.

There are, then, three detailed chapters ahead:

1957–69: the data cover mainly 1960–70
1970–80: the years of the New Economic Policy
1980–85: the years of new issues and new problems.

The same coalition was in power during the entire period and faced no real threat of losing an election. At the same time, the coalition was composed of hetrogeneous interests, and there was the considerable task of balancing these interests to maintain harmony and cohesion within the coalition.

The growth rate of GDP in the 1960s averaged about 6.5 percent with only minor fluctuations from year to year. There were no balance of payments problems, and the price level was virtually constant over the entire decade. There were few obvious price distortions in the economy. The investment rate averaged about 18 percent a year and the saving rate was even higher. Private consumption averaged about 4.3 percent in growth—at least 1.5 percentage points above the growth in population. Government consumption grew at over 7 percent, but there was a surplus on the government's current account in each year. The share of the manufacturing sector in GDP increased from 10 to 16 percent, and agriculture's share fell from 45 to 37 percent. The decade then appears almost as a textbook example of growth with stability.

At the end of this decade of textbook growth, there was a dreadful race riot in Kuala Lumpur, in which at least several hundred people died and millions of dollars (as the monetary unit was in the 1960s) of property was destroyed. The riot was not, of course, entirely a result of economic factors, but such factors did play an important role.

Between 1957 and 1970 inequality of measured GDP increased to a significant degree. That increase was shown unambiguously in table 12-1. The increase in inequality was pervasive—between and within racial groups and among regions. Unemployment also resisted resolution. Employment growth in manufacturing was especially disappointing. Along with this increased inequality and a difficult employment situation, there was the beginning of the breakdown of the old order, and any new order had yet to establish itself. In particular the Bargain of 1957, the modus vivendi for racial harmony, was eroding. The arrangement permitted the Chinese (and Indians) full freedom in their economic pursuits and established the understanding that the government would be essentially a Malay government. Although the economy, according to conventional indicators, performed exceedingly well, equity was ill-served and deep-seated difficulties emerged that led to the riots and to a big change in policy after 1970.

In this chapter we study some of the more specific strategies and policies that were followed in the 1960s, as well as the way in which these policies affected the textbook growth and contributed to the breakdown of order in 1969. There are three major categories of policy to be examined. The first, and in some sense the most important, is the rural development policy; the second is educational policy; and the third is industrialization policy. There are naturally many other policies, but these appear to be the most strategic in accounting both for what actually happened and for the objectives of the Malaysian government. Similarly, there are countless details about these policy categories that could be studied. The purpose here is not to study detail but, as implied in the discussion of the policymaking question, to examine broad characteristics of policy, their origins and rationale, and their consequences.

Rural Development

The primary concern of the British in Malaysia was maintaining order. There were several aspects of order and its achievement. Of special importance was the notion that order was served by a balanced budget, a strong balance of payments, low taxes, and zero inflation. Achieving these objectives would not only make maintaining order easier and more secure, but it would also be the best means of attracting the principal source of development—foreign capital. This capital would be invested mainly in primary production on the estates, so output and exports, as well as government revenues, would increase. The increased government revenues would, in turn, allow for additional social services that would also contribute to maintaining the order objective and serve the estate economy in a variety of ways. Although growth was not a specific objective of the British, their general approach did, in fact, result in the rapid growth of the rubber and tin sectors. It was this general strategy that enabled independent Malaysia to begin its life as a strong, relatively rich (in overall terms) nation.

The national government of independent Malaysia recognized these economic arguments, but at the same time the new government also appreciated that an expanding economy was a necessary part of its "objective function." In particular, the new government was aware that for it to maintain its position in the country, a significant rural development effort was necessary. The new constitution explicitly recognized a special position of Malays in the plural society. The implementation of this recognition involved several means (such as scholarships, employment quotas, business permits), but by far the most significant was rural development. Rural development was appealing for various reasons. The great majority of rural residents were Malays, and a set of policies that aimed at increasing output in rural areas would raise the income of the Malays and have little or no adverse effects on the established economic interests of the Chinese. (In general, rural did not include rubber and the oil palm estates, and the rural population refers to those who live in villages or communities with fewer than 1,000 inhabitants.) Finally, an increase in the output of rice would contribute to the self-sufficiency in rice production—a major objective of the new Malaysian government. As a consequence, almost one-half of development expenditures in the first two plans (1956–60 and 1961–65) were allocated to rural development.

The most important thing to note about this strategy is that it is built on the notion that the Malays would remain paddy farmers, fishermen, and smallholder rubber farmers. There was to be no large-scale shift from rural to urban areas and activities. This strategy partly reflected the old British idea that Malays should be primarily in these rural activities, but also doubtlessly reflected a genuine preference among Malays for the kampong life. The idea was to raise the income in these rural activities, not to shift the Malays to other, more profitable activities, and not to try to create new activities in the rural areas. To accomplish these objectives, the government had to take a much more active role than was the case under the British. The British colonial officers, in general, attributed the low income of rural Malays to their character and their value system. The new government, while generally agreeing that the old values and old life-styles of rural Malays must change, emphasized that the real source of the prevailing inequalities was the policies followed by the colonial government. The important change, therefore, was to be in the activities and attitude of the government.

There were several components of the government policy, two of which are especially important in the present context—land development and the paddy program. Both programs were intended to increase output and to raise the income of the poorest group, the rural Malays.

Land Development

Malaysia has always had ample land relative to its population, and land reform in the sense of taking land from landowners who owned large amounts to give to those with no land has never been a major issue. Land development meant opening up lands not currently under cultivation. Opening up included clearing the land of trees and undergrowth, building roads and (often) irrigation facilities, and providing household water and housing. Although there have been several methods of approaching land development, the most important by far has been the work of the Federal Land Development Authority (FELDA). This authority was initially created in 1956 as something of a planning and financing agency to help the individual states with land development. This limited role was soon expanded as it became evident that, because of different population densities among the states, different state laws, and implementing capacity, a strictly state-run land development program was inappropriate. By 1960 FELDA was actually conducting land development under its own control and management.

The land development undertaken by FELDA has by and large accomplished the basic objective of opening up new land, mainly for rubber and oil palm production. The initial idea was for settlers to clear their own land, but this notion did not prevail very long. Land clearing was given over to contractors. By 1960, contractors were also responsible for planting the first rubber trees and caring for them initially, as well as for constructing the houses for the settlers. To have left all of these tasks to the new settlers would have involved an unacceptably long period of construction and work before any output could have been realized. Settlers did work for the contractor for wages, and as Snodgrass (1980, p. 179) notes, the early stages of such a project were very similar to an estate investment project. After the project was put into running order by the contractor, the settler took over and operated the plot that was provided to him. He was obliged to repay some of the costs of the land development after the trees began to bear, but the repayment was well below the cost of the development, so the settler received a substantial subsidy.

Several points about land development in general and FELDA in particular are relevant to growth and equity in the late 1950s and early 1960s in Malaysia.

- There have been several estimates of benefit-cost ratios and internal rates of return on land development in Malaysia, (Lim 1973, p. 194). These estimates are extremely sensitive to the rate of interest employed and to the price of rubber and oil palm chosen, and they undoubtedly do not include all costs and all benefits. Even so, the calculations indicate that yields were acceptable—that is, benefit-cost ratios exceed unity and internal rates of return are at least 10 percent.
- The fact that professional contractors (including Chinese and expatriates) did so much of the work is relevant. As noted above, the original idea was for Malays to clear the land themselves, but this plan was quickly abandoned. Then the intent was that the new settlers would plant the first trees, but this, too, was quickly abandoned. As finally arranged, the new settlers were more or less handed acreage that was all set to function as a going concern. There is little doubt that the procedure followed resulted in an increased output more quickly than would have been the case under the original plans. Several observers, however, have argued that the FELDA approach was an especially unfortunate form of paternalism, and instilled the idea among rural Malays that the government would provide the wherewithal for a higher income. A more revealing way to frame the issue is in terms of learning. The rural Malay community, as emphasized above, had a life-style in which all parts were mutually compatible. This life-style

included a relatively low per capita measured GDP and considerable inequality in its distribution. To shift anyone abruptly from this environment to a quite different one may raise their income, but it may also impede a learning and adapting process that is necessary for the people to realize the full advantage of this new environment. In some respects the FELDA approach is similar to a turnkey project by a foreign firm. The foreign firm builds the factory and hands it over to the nationals, who then are supposed to make it go, despite the fact that they could not build it initially and had no genuine experience in operating a similar plant. Such an approach effectively avoids the lengthy learning, trial and error process that is so crucial to building a strong, flexible economy.

• Learning enters the story in another way. The yields per hectare and productivity per worker on the estates have always been higher than on the smallholdings. In large part this was a result, since the 1950s at least, of the fact that the estates were able to replant with the higher-yielding clones on a much larger scale than were the smallholders. The very fact of being a smallholder made replanting difficult, because it meant withdrawing some of the small amount of acreage from current production, which the smallholder was generally reluctant to do. This specific problem can be resolved without much difficulty given sufficient funds and the appropriate institutional arrangements. Some changes in institutional arrangements were made toward this end, but even the new government acted slowly in removing some government-imposed obstacles for replanting by the smallholders. The First Malaysia Plan estimates that by 1965 approximately 80 percent of the rubber estates had been replanted with the high-yielding clones, while fewer than one-half of smallholder plots had been replanted. The percentage of the very small plots that had been replanted was still lower, so that the poorest rubber growers were, for the most part, still using lower-yielding varieties. For example, of holdings with fewer than ten acres in 1968, about 30 percent had high-yielding clones (Tan 1982, p. 76). There were, however, problems of greater complexity than money and institutions. These problems resided in more fundamental characteristics of the rural society. Essentially they arose from the sharp demarcation between the modern estate sector and the smallholder sector. The latter was unable to accumulate experience—to learn and to move slowly, step by step, over a long period of time—to increase productive activity. So when the new clones became available and the tasks of replanting were upon them, the smallholders were ill-prepared to make the very big jump from existing practices to the newly available high-yielding techniques. Yet the existing social and political environment necessitated such an effort. Given the head start of the estates and absence of contact between them and the smallholders, it was unrealistic to expect that it would be possible for the latter groups to catch up simply by subsidizing replanting and new planting. The FELDA approach may have exacerbated this difficulty by, in effect, seeking to create an estate environment for a group that was unprepared for it and that resisted it for several reasons.

- Despite these strictures, one must conclude that an overt role by the government was essential. Given the way things looked to the Malaysian policymakers in the late 1950s, a major land development program was unambiguously the correct policy choice. The decision of FELDA to have professional contractors do so much of the initial work also seems understandable, in light of the slow pace that would result if things had been left largely to individual smallholders. This last point may be questioned if one believed that the political situation was less edgy than apparently the central government believed it to be.

There is the further question of whether the government's approach to land development was that most likely to help the very poor in the rural areas. A brief comment on this issue is in order, but the more general discussion is postponed until after the discussion of the rice price support program and technical assistance. The FELDA approach, as well as the other land development projects, consisted mainly in creating an infrastructure. This is not surprising. Constructing roads, irrigation ditches, and water plants, clearing the jungle and building "low-cost" housing are activities that the government can perform in a fairly straightforward way. In the later 1950s and early 1960s, "development economics" placed great emphasis on infrastructure. The Hirschman arguments against a concentration of government on infrastructure had yet to make an impact. So, to the extent that the professional opinion of economists was relevant in the government's decisionmaking, it would have undoubtedly supported the emphasis on infrastructure. Finally, it also seems to be a fact that the rural elite—mainly those who occupied significant political positions or those who owned more land than the average—supported an infrastructure approach. Some observers (such as Gibbons 1985) argue strongly that political elites or loyal supporters of political elites had preferred access to newly opened lands. For FELDA lands, successful applicants were always vetted by the Menteri Besar (chief administrative office) of the relevant state before a final decision was made. The evidence for this does not, however, seem clear. Technically a point system was in effect—based on various considerations that sought to measure poverty and need—that determined who obtained FELDA plots. More likely is the frequently made claim that politically loyal contractors were the ones who were rewarded with the land-clearing contracts. It is impossible to say how important such factors were, but clearly the particular approach to land development that was followed was partly determined by these kinds of considerations. Virtually all new settlers were Malays.

There were, however, two important consequences of this emphasis. The first is the well-known point that rural infrastructure investment always benefits those with much land relative to those with little land. (The same is true, of course, for subsidized inputs—fertilizer, lime, and so forth.) It is quite unlikely, therefore, that the land development programs as such would contribute significantly to reducing inequality, given the land distribution, although possibly they could help to relieve poverty. The other consequence of the infrastructure investment is less clear-cut and is linked to the previous discussion of searching and learning. Infrastructure and subsidized inputs do little to induce search and trying new techniques. The general basis of the argument in favor of infrastructure investment is that the provision of such capital will itself make the relevant groups more productive. Evidence on productivity growth denies this. Rather, there must be learning, and learning requires inducements to search actively and explicitly—not simply to accept passively that which is provided from the outside.

It is also useful to note in this connection that the taxes for replanting and research were higher for smallholders than for estates. As argued by Tan (1982, p. 96), collecting a replanting cess and then providing a replanting grant is a kind of forced saving, if the replanting grant that is received equals the total payment of the cess. If, however, the rubber grower does not replant at all or replants only part of his land, then the cess becomes a tax. Because, for reasons already summarized, the smallholder is much less likely to replant than is the estate, and the really small smallholder is less likely to replant than the medium-size smallholder, the replanting cess was, in effect, a regressive tax. The same argument holds for the research cess levied on rubber production in these first years of independence. The Rubber Research Institute (RRI), has been supported by a cess on rubber production. The RRI is responsible for much of the work that has been done resulting in both the new high-yielding clones and other new knowledge that made technically possible increased yields and the new uses of natural rubber. The work of the RRI was most directly relevant to the estates in these years and certainly was much more directly accessible to the estates than to the smallholders. These tax arrangements, though understandable, added to the difficulties of increasing the relative position of the smallholder of rubber.

Despite all this, it is important to appreciate that land development was, in these early years and later, an important success. Of the several land development programs, FELDA accounted for 30 percent of the land actually developed outside of estates during the years from 1961 to 1965 and 63 percent during the last half of the 1960s, so increasing reliance was placed on FELDA, other programs became less important, and some ceased completely. The cultivated land area increased at about 2 percent a year from independence to 1970, and the rural population grew at an average annual rate of 2.7 percent. Although one cannot say firmly what would have happened in the absence of the land development, it seems likely that a more rapidly falling land-labor ratio would have meant greater difficulties in preventing rural incomes from falling. The increase in the quantity of available land could not have occurred without the government's organized land development projects. The increased availability of cleared land also contributed to the low rate of urbanization in Malaysia, and this lower rate has had a number of favorable side effects. In the same way, the new lands helped to prevent unemployment from rising—although again one must note that it is impossible to say what would have happened had the lands not been cleared.

Perhaps the biggest disappointment has to do with smallholding yields. Data from Snodgrass (1980, p. 1976) show a disturbing picture. From 1950 to 1954 smallholder rubber yield per acre planted was 95 percent of that of estates (365 pounds compared with 389). This percentage declined steadily until 1970. It was 85 percent in the period from 1955 to 1959 (359 and 420), 59 percent in the first half of the 1960s (305 and 516), and 55 percent in the last half (379 and 689). (Young and others 1980, p. 223, show smallholder yields to be 66 percent of yields on estates in 1970. These estimates refer to mature acreage only and are based on data supplied by the Economic Planning Unit.) After 1970 the growth of yields among smallholders increased sharply, but continued to be only slightly more than one-half of the yields on estates until well into the 1970s. The World Bank estimates that value added per worker in smallholding rubber was about one-third of that on estates and value added per acre something over one-half in 1970 (Young and others 1980, p. 224). These data refer to all smallholdings, not just those in FELDA and other land development projects. Presumably those in such projects had higher than average yields, although there are no data to support this presumption. Many of these differences are a result of variations in the use of the high-yielding clones and the range of problems caused by the attempt of one group to catch up with another. Some of it, however, also results from intractable difficulties discussed above, and to the major problems that arise when people who have lived long in a relatively nongrowing, isolated environment try to learn to adapt to new opportunities.

Paddy Policy

The second major component of rural development in these years was intended to improve the lot of paddy farmers, almost all of whom were Malays, and almost all of whom were very poor. Malaysia does not offer the large flat areas that make paddy growing easy. The major rice-growing areas are in specific parts of the northern states that border Thailand and three other small areas in Province Wellesley, Perak, and Selangor farther south on the west coast. There were Chinese paddy farmers in Selangor. Rice is grown here and there in other parts of the country, but not on a large scale. Much of the rice does not enter the market, and rice farmers, more than any other group in Malaysia, are subsistence farmers. This is especially true of those in the northern states. Most of the marketed rice comes from the west coast rice-growing areas. Most of the paddy farmers have other jobs and other sources of income, a fact that seems relevant to the explanation of their acceptance of innovations of seed and fertilizer. Paddy farmers were, at independence, among Malaysia's poorest people and were engaged in an activity where productivity was very much below that of other activities in Malaysia and below that of rice farmers in other countries.

The early policy to help paddy farmers consisted of two major aspects—drainage and irrigation and price supports. A discussion of drainage and irrigation is followed by a review of the price support program in rice. Drainage and irrigation projects were similar in many respects to the land development projects. Actually their main objective, to permit a great increase in double cropping, was a means of increasing the land use. The 1956 to 1960 Plan spent M$38.3 million on drainage and irrigation, about 4 percent of total expenditures. About M$108 million from 1961 to 1965, also about 4 percent of the total, was spent on these things. It was in the last half of the 1960s that the big projects in the catchment of the Muda River and in Kemubu got in full swing, and then expenditures increased by very large amounts. The Drainage and Irrigation Department (DID) was one of the first Malaysian agencies to use formal benefit-cost analysis, and, as Snodgrass (1980, p. 186) notes, DID seemed to follow the dictates of the results rather closely, at least in terms of the order in which projects were undertaken. As with all benefit-cost analyses in those years, those of DID were quite elementary. No shadow prices were used for inputs and the output (mainly rice) was priced at domestic prices, which were much higher than border prices. As far as one can judge, no effort was made to introduce distribution issues into the analysis. Then, of course, there was the usual array of the impossible problems of benefit-cost analysis—estimating costs, projecting output and receipts, and so forth—that can never be solved with great reliability.

World Bank consultants had estimated that the Muda River project would have a benefit-cost ratio of at least three before it was undertaken, but studies done after its completion put the figure at about unity. Again there seems to have been no weight given to distribution issues. The point of all this is to call explicit attention to the care with which DID went about its tasks, and to point the way into the discussion of the equity questions associated with these projects.

The location of drainage and irrigation projects is, of course, affected by the geographic situation. The Muda River catchment provided a good, natural physical environment for development. It happened that the rice farmers in the state of Kedah, where the Muda project was located, were among the poorest in the country. The same observation holds for the Kemubu project in Kalantan. As pressure developed in other areas, however, where physical conditions were less suitable and incomes not so low, large investments were also made. The Muda project was implemented exceptionally efficiently, and the Kemubu quite well. Costs per acre in the latter area were approximately 1.7 times greater than in Muda, and costs will be higher at the other locations that are less suitable physically (Goldman 1975, p. 288). The impact of Muda and Kemubu on production and productivity was not realized until the 1970s and will be reviewed later. By 1970 about two-thirds of the almost 950,000 acres of paddy had been provided with irrigation by DID, of which about 286,000 acres could be double cropped (Snodgrass 1980, p. 186). Much of the later work of DID seems to have been partly a purely political phenomenon—that is, the maintenance of political loyalty demanded that some DID activity be provided in many areas where output and distribution objectives alone would not have indicated that it was appropriate to have them. Along with pressure from local political leaders, those who had sizable land holdings (and hence some political clout) were also urging DID activity in their area. In 1970 the government formally decided not to initiate any new drainage and irrigation projects (Snodgrass 1980, p. 186), but this decision did not prevail very long. During the 1970s approximately $875 million were earmarked for DID in the second and third Malaysia plans. It can be said that these projects did help the very poor rice farmers significantly, although in the process further investments were made that probably were, in some narrow economic and equity sense, not justified. This is not a criticism (or if it is, it applies to every large organization in every country). It does illustrate the advantages (and difficulties) of a government with a great deal of money at its disposal. It is, perhaps, appropriate to think of such politically induced investments (that is, investments that the customary form of benefit-cost analysis would not justify) as an inherent component of the cost of the projects in those areas where they are genuinely intended by the government. Such costs go along with a democratic (that is, elected) government, and obviously lower the measured rates of return.

The very large-scale investments to raise the income and productivity of rice farmers (and to some extent the investment in land development) put into sharp focus the importance of the basic strategy of large-scale in situ development. As already noted, the geography of Malaysia is suitable for neither rice nor many other agricultural products—except tree crops of rubber and oil palm. Rice could always be imported at prices well below the costs of growing it within Malaysia. The market for natural rubber was wavering, and longer-run prospects were especially dim. Besides, the estates could produce rubber and oil palm much more cheaply than could the smallholder. Why then go in so heavily for increased rice and new rubber production? Viewed from the outside, it is possible to conclude that it was a misguided decision, but viewed from the inside, it was surely the correct decision. Part of its correctness is based on what constituted equity in Malaysia at this time. The very low-income Malays were paddy farmers and rubber smallholder operators—activities that themselves were part of the definition of the good life. The objective was to relieve the Malay poverty within this paddy, smallholder environment. To have undone, or tried to undo, this environment at the time of independence and immediately after would have greatly reduced the welfare of the rural Malays, even if it had raised their real income, or their share of GNP. The prevailing social milieu was as much a constraint as the fact that mountains ran down the middle of the peninsula. The strong, efficient estate sector made it feasible to accept this kind of a constraint, while maintaining a growing economy.

The other source of the correctness of the policy rests on the role of custom and practice. "The disregard of custom and decency always betrays a weak and ill-regulated mind" (Gibbon 1909, vol. 3, p. 381). Certainly tradition dictated against a massive government intervention in the economy. In particular it dictated against any risk of inflation. The new government was bolder than the colonial government, but this greater boldness was cautiously exercised (Ness 1967). Another aspect of traditional wisdom was that a regular supply of rice was the basic recognized need. The relatively large amount of rice that had to be imported, therefore, was considered a source of vulnerability, so rice production itself offered an external benefit of considerable magnitude, independent of any effect on poverty relief or employment. Finally, it may be noted that the government was essentially Malay, and, although one cannot document this, the government officials thought much more in terms of the rural and agricultural sector than they did in terms of industry and urbanization. This argument seems especially applicable to the first prime minister.

An additional point that should be made about the drainage and irrigation projects is that the prices charged for water and other associated services were well below operating costs (possibly no more than one-half), and naturally did not include any share of capital costs. This practice was justified mainly because of the poverty of the rice farmers, which called for a subsidy. Insofar as it can be determined, there was little or no distortion on the production side because of the subsidy. This subsidy could also be justified by the externality argument noted above. In terms of the rationale that entered the government decisionmaking process, both of these aspects were relevant, but probably some greater weight was placed on the first.

These considerations help to explain the rejection of a proposal by three foreign advisers to the Malaysian government, Gates, Goering and Keare (1967), to proceed with land reclamation at an even faster rate than in fact was the case. Physical resources to accomplish this were surely available or could have been acquired on sensible terms. Such a higher rate would have upset the life-styles of many rural Malays by, in effect, forcing them into an estate form of economic organization, which the government recognized would be undesirable. It is doubtful whether the government (as an elected government) could have survived had it sought to do this. As just noted, the government was deeply instilled with the colonial attitudes toward fiscal and monetary policies. Such cautious attitudes would reject large-scale borrowing, whether internal or foreign, as an alien concept and would consider inflation a constant and damaging threat. This cautious approach was not shared, and possibly not appreciated, by Gates, Goering, and Keare, who were particularly unconcerned with inflation. It is interesting to note that a later adviser did share the more cautious fiscal and monetary views of the government. Although GDP could have increased more rapidly in Malaysia in the 1960s, equity would have been less well served and the government would have had to violate its own received economic policy practices. It might well have meant that, with free elections, it would not have remained in office.

Another major aspect of the paddy policy package was the guaranteed minimum price (GMP) for rice. The price support program for rice was in effect well before independence. During the boom in rubber prices in the early 1950s, the support price was relatively high (M$17 per picul) to try to prevent a shift from rice into smallholder rubber. The price was lowered to about M$16 by independence at which level it remained throughout the 1960s. The subsidy is financed in a round-about way as follows. The National Paddy and Rice Authority (LPN) purchases a substantial amount of rice at the GMP. (Before the 1970s the program was administered by the Supplies Division of the Ministry of Commerce and Industry.) Importers of rice are required to buy local rice from the LPN in direct proportion to their imports at the "release price" set by the rice authority. This release price is usually higher than the GMP. The LPN then makes a profit that it uses to cover the cost both of the GMP and of maintaining a buffer stock of rice. Because the release price is above the market price, the importer suffers a loss. This loss is equivalent to a tax on imports, because it can be avoided by not importing. Rice imports are then limited, however, so that the domestic price exceeds the c.i.f. (cost, insurance, and freight) price by an amount sufficient to allow the importer to recoup his loss from his government purchase and make a profit. The importer makes his money on the sales of the high-quality imported rice at this higher price. Because rice of similar quality must sell at the same price and because there is considerable substitution among varieties, the price of all rice is pushed up by this process. It is equivalent to a tariff on rice. Because the subsidy was the same for all varieties of rice, the GMP system tended to result in the government's buying the lowest quality rice. It also meant that farmers were able to ignore market signals indicating demand for specific varieties and produce what they wished because the government would buy whatever the market did not absorb.

Rice is, of course, the staple food of most of the low-income people of Malaysia. Consumer expenditure data for the mid-1960s suggest that low-income families spend about 26 percent of their income on rice. Goldman (1975, p. 286) estimates that the implied tariff on rice raised its price by about 19 percent in this period, so that incomes of the poor were reduced by about 5 percent by virtue of these financing arrangements. The subsidy also usually meant higher incomes for someone, although it is not clear for whom. Presumably, landowners' profits became the capitalized value of their land price increases. How this affects rents is unclear because of the widespread practice of renting from relatives and other land-sharing arrangements. The owner who operated his own farm—usually small—clearly gained most from the subsidy. A final point that affected income concerns marketing. The GMP applied to the paddy brought to the mill. The farmer, especially the small farmer, seldom took his paddy directly to the mill, but used a middleman to handle the marketing, so the farmer would generally not get the full GMP. The price the farmer did receive would, of course, be higher with the price support program than without it.

The drainage and irrigation projects affected output most directly by enabling double cropping. The second paddy crop greatly increased the demand for labor and, therefore, tended to increase employment and push up wage rates. This wage effect was especially evident in the Muda area where there is some evidence to suggest that wage rates were more rigid than rent levels (Goldman 1975). For the landless laborer and the farmer with very small holdings, who also worked for wages on other paddy fields, the rise in wages was especially helpful. The increased income, to whomever it accrued, did have some linkage effects in the various regions, and such effects would have some employment and other income-generating consequences.

There were other policies intended to help the rural Malays. Marketing and credit had been problems for years—principally because of the role of the Chinese in marketing and in supplying credit. Fertilizer had been subsidized and some attention had been given to extension services and the development of more suitable need varieties. These matters were not strategic until after 1970: therefore, discussion of them is delayed until the 1970s are reviewed.

Education

The particular characteristics and role of the education system described in the background section explain the reason that the new state would give a great deal of attention to this subject. Indeed, even before full independence, in 1955, a major report was prepared by a committee under the chairmanship of Dato Abdul Razak, the first minister of education and later deputy prime minister and prime minister. This was an influential report at the time (Snodgrass 1980, p. 245), and became even more so after independence and in the early 1960s. The main objective of the committee was to propose an educational system that would result in "a rational system of education acceptable to people of the Federation as a whole which will satisfy their needs to promote their development as a nation, having regard to the intention to make Malay the national language . . . while preserving and sustaining the growth of the language and culture of other communities in the country." The plan called for free primary education to all children beginning in 1962. Instruction was to be offered in English, Malay, Mandarin, and Tamil. English and Malay were to be taught as subjects irrespective of the medium employed in the school, and any school would teach Chinese or Tamil if the parents of fifteen or more children so requested. Secondary education was to be only in Malay and English. The report also made recommendations for the expansion of "secondary trade and technical education to meet the needs of the country for trained personnel" (Malaya 1956).

The general tone and the explicit policy objectives here are different indeed from those of the colonial governments described earlier. In the 1960s over 10 percent of the planned central government's development expenditure was allocated to education, but actual expenditures were markedly less than planned in the last half of the decade. Planned expenditures on education were the third largest, after land development and transport, of the major categories of the plan. Actual expenditure fell to fourth place in the years from 1966 to 1970. Recurrent expenditures on education were also high, amounting to 20 percent or more of total current expenditures in these early years. Education expenditure was the largest single item in the current budget in most years. There is no doubt that the newly independent state was placing significant emphasis on education. Such emphasis emerged as a consequence of several considerations. There was a widespread view that a major factor, perhaps the major factor, that limited opportunities for Malays, especially rural Malays, was the educational system inherited from the colonial times. The source of the difficulty for Malays was not their value system and traditions, as the British insisted, but it was, among other things, the educational system. There is little doubt that both rural and urban Malays believed this and were prepared to sacrifice consumption to obtain more education. Data from Meerman (1979, p. 116) show that about 70 percent of the lowest income quintile paid 18 percent of their income for out-of-pocket costs of education in 1974. This, of course, is a very high figure. It is probably misleadingly high for 1974 and undoubtedly so for the early 1960s. Even so it is a pretty strong signal that the very low-income groups were willing to pay dearly to provide their children with some education. The rationale of such willingness could hardly have been other than the expectation that education was the means to economic and social improvement.

During these years enrollments rose rapidly, especially in primary and secondary schools. From 1956 to 1968 total primary enrollment increased by 60 percent, while the English language instruction more than doubled. Enrollment in Malay-language schools increased by more than 50 percent and in Chinese-language schools by almost 30 percent. By the mid-1960s almost all children of the relevant age group attended primary school. It was in secondary schools that the really big increase took place. Total enrollment between 1956 and 1968 jumped by over a factor of five, but enrollment in Malay-language schools jumped by a factor of 45 and English-language schools by a factor of 5.6.

The prevailing situation included a firm belief on the part of the new government that the colonial educational policy was extremely unfortunate in general, but especially so with respect to its effect on the role of Malays in the society. Evidence also existed that the very poor in the society were keen on significantly improved and increased educational opportunities for themselves. The government in turn allocated relatively large amounts to new school construction, to teacher training, to providing materials, and so forth, as well as to routine recurrent expenses associated with operating the educational establishment. Enrollments increased, and primary school attendance became nearly universal. What were the consequences of all this for growth and equity?

There were many difficulties, three of which merit examination. The first, and in a way the most fundamental, was that the understanding of the role of formal schooling in the growth and equity process was (and, of course, is) quite inadequate. Even had the decisionmakers drawn heavily on professional opinion they would have found considerable confusion and disagreement. It is probably correct to say that the schooling policies followed were generally those that were consistent with what economists were advocating at the time. The second great difficulty was most explicitly that of language, but more generally the difficulty was that of the role of schooling in maintaining and extending the heritage and traditions of the society. This is no small matter in a very homogeneous society, but in a plural society, the problem is truly complex. The language and the heritage and tradition issues were further complicated by the fact that the English language was unambiguously the medium that provided the greatest advantage with respect to GDP growth and personal economic advancement. The third aspect to be examined is the role of noninstitutional or, more accurately, nonacademic, training and its links with formal schooling.

The Role of Schooling in Development

The term schooling is used here because the government's policy was intended mainly to increase school attendance. Attending school does not ensure acquiring an education, but it is an important part of that process. There is a vast literature on schooling and education and development. The task here is to apply to the Malaysian story those aspects of this literature that seem most illuminating and informing. (A recent illuminating review of the issues and data is Psacharopoulos and Woodhall 1985. See also Psacharopoulos 1980 and Metcalf 1985).

RETURNS TO EDUCATION. O. D. Hoerr (1973) calculated the internal rate of return for schooling for peninsula Malaysia as of 1967–68. There are problems with the data, method, and so forth, but still the findings are relevant. Hoerr has estimated total costs of schooling and the increase in wages as the number of years of schooling increase. He compares the two in the usual way to obtain the internal rate of return. These calculations show a sharp difference between the social and private rates of return because many of the costs are not paid by the person who receives the schooling. Net private rates were found to be from one-third greater to more than twice as great for teacher training. Gross private returns (ignoring noneducational determinants of income and the probability of actually achieving the income) were very much larger. Hoerr estimates that noneducational uses of capital would yield a 10 percent internal rate, which is higher than the social rate for all forms of schooling except secondary. All private rates of schooling are above the 10 percent. The attractiveness of school attendance is further illustrated by comparing increases in income from double cropping a paddy farm and from completing a university education. In the early 1970s the latter achievement would result in a salary of about M$9,000 a year. Double cropping would increase annual income from M$1,000–1,500 to M$3,000–4,000. Similarly, the college-educated person could expect fairly constant increases over his working life (Tan 1982, p. 337). The one catch is that the graduate must obtain a job. Thus a typical situation emerges in that there is a strong inducement for individuals to seek that which is profitable to them individually, but not for the society. This evidence led Hoerr to conclude that Malaysia had reached the point where, in these narrow terms, it was overinvesting in school. Other estimates, reported in Psacharopoulas (1980) and Pscharopoulas and Woodhall (1985), show even higher private rates of return (especially in rural areas) than does Hoerr.

There are other terms, of course. One is that a labor force that is literate and trained to reason and follow instructions not only is more productive with given complementary resources, but also is a relevant factor in creating new knowledge and in disseminating it throughout the economy. For example, it is sensible to say that widespread illiteracy was one of the reasons for the slow spread of higher-yielding clones among rubber smallholders. The same applies to those rice farmers whose yields were very much below average. Some of the consequences of such activities might be captured in the higher wages of the educated, but not much. A similar point is shown by Hoerr's data. The more schooling one has the more one gains from job experience, from on-the-job training. Thus, on-the-job experience seems to reinforce the differences in schooling, rather than correct for them. So, individuals tend not to overcome the effects of school deprivation. This is true, although a large percentage of the productivity of older workers may be attributable to experience.

A second point refers to employment. Evidently, if a person who attended school cannot find a job, the rate of return on the schooling is zero. Mention was made earlier of the fairly loose labor market in Malaysia in the 1960s. Demand for labor might have been greater had there been more investment in physical capital and less in schooling. To have done this might have increased the demand for labor, but it might not have. There are two points to note here. One is that additional schooling might have exacerbated the unemployment problem by creating false expectations about what the economy offered in the way of job opportunities. This is the often noted "educated unemployed" problem. It might be expected, or at least hoped, however, that schooling would make an individual more adaptive, more flexible, and more able to adjust so that employment would be found, or even created. Note also that unemployment makes attending school cheaper by reducing the opportunity cost of such attendance to zero, so as the difficulty of finding a job increases the demand for places in the schools, especially secondary and postsecondary schools, increases.

A final point refers to various externalities—wiser voting, greater tolerance of diversity, greater understanding of policy issues. Evidence about such externalities is virtually nonexistent, but it is always comforting to acknowledge that they are at least possible.

These last two points raise the question of the quality of the schooling. Quality in schooling is an elusive concept. In the most obvious way it refers to the capacity of teachers to teach and to the availability of teaching materials. There is little doubt that many teachers were ill-equipped to carry out their assignments, and that teaching materials were often lacking. This deficiency was much more widespread in rural than in urban areas. These considerations might mean that more, not fewer, resources should be allocated to schooling to raise the quality of teaching to the standards required to make the investment in schooling yield acceptable returns. No one can be sure about such things, of course, but in any event it does seem unlikely that more resources could have been allocated to education because of the nature of the decisionmaking process in the government. The rapid growth of the school-age population and the great politically expressed demand for schooling led to a politically determined amount of resources going to schooling, and to its distribution among regions being determined by notions of equity rather than return. In summary it can be said that the low internal social rates of return tell us that the social productivity of schooling is low. This may have resulted from "too much investment in education," but it may also have resulted from its poor quality because of too small an investment in education or to a concentration of the investment in areas where the capacity to profit from schooling was below what it was in other areas. A part of the explanation of the low return is owing to the latter, which means that notions of equity took precedence over output objectives.

TEACHING METHODS. Even if there were an ample number of teachers and all were well trained, there would still be the question of what to teach. This was an especially complex question in Malaysia in these years. Investment in schooling is often like investment in physical infrastructure. It is thought of in terms of creating certain qualifications. A person, through attending school, acquires certain skills, with the presumption that there is a position now (or soon to become) vacant in the economy where these skills can be applied. The implication of this way of thinking is that the student attends school to receive some kind of ready-made answers to a set of specific questions. The student can then be certified as qualified, and entitled to a specific job with salary and social position. In the language of Ronald Dore (1972, p. 492) this is schooling "to be," not "to do." Such an attitude toward schooling is likely to be followed by a similar attitude toward one's eventual job—a job is a means to a salary and status, not an activity that provides its own satisfaction and an opportunity to be of service to society (Dore 1972, p. 501).

How to teach otherwise is a complex question. It is even more complex in the context of development in a plural society, where teaching has long been characterized by going through rote exercises. Ill-equipped teachers often teach in this way simply because they can do nothing else. Poor teaching in almost all countries has always been characterized by requiring memorization and regurgitation. It is also true, however, that the idea of training people, now deemed untrained, for jobs in a new activity or an attempt to tell them something "useful" about increasing productivity in their present activity encourages the rote-exercise approach. Genuine education, however, creates an incentive to act, to seek, and to probe, and it seems evident that in a community long dominated by stagnation and widespread poverty, this sort of attitude must be instilled or created to implement change.

The passive acceptance of ready-made answers does little to create a flexible, adaptable labor force. Indeed, it makes it more difficult to provide appropriate employment opportunities and actually can contribute to the appearance of unemployment. These arguments apply no matter how well the teacher teaches. The better the teacher, one might even argue, the move severe the difficulty. The arguments about employment and unemployment probably are more applicable to secondary and postsecondary schooling than to primary, but the rote learning issue is relevant at all levels of schools.

The preceding discussion distinguished sharply between genuine education and the passive rote learning of pat answers to specific questions. The schools of Malaysia in the period from 1957 to 1960 were not so neatly defined, but the sharp distinction does help to clarify the issue. The schools in rural Malaysia in particular were historically rote-learning institutions; therefore, the task of making these schools effective instruments of change was exceptionally difficult and necessarily slow. Even so, one should recall the very favorable estimates of internal rates of return to schooling for Malaysians in rural areas. The problems were exacerbated by the fact that only modest funds were available for educational purposes, but the basic problems were those deep-seated difficulties discussed above, and the ones that will be addressed.

OBJECTIVES. Schooling, as much as any other activity, reveals the great ambiguity in the objectives of both individual families and the government. As noted above, the generally accepted view was that one major reason for the relative poverty of the Malays was the schooling arrangements under the British. At the same time, there was resistance to introducing new content into the classes and to new teaching methods. This resistance arose in part from the commitment to Islam and its associated traditions and beliefs. In part it is also an illustration of the difficulty of divesting ideas, routines, and positions even when they are recognized as disadvantagous.

VOCATIONAL EDUCATION. An equally complex issue concerns a more specific question about vocational schooling relative to more general educational programs. This question applies most immediately to the postsecondary level, but also affects what kinds of things are emphasized in secondary schools. Several investigators (for example, Meerman 1979) have argued that the strong tendency of Malays to concentrate in liberal arts and social sciences has been a major obstacle to their becoming qualified to perform effectively in modern industry. Meerman argues further that these disciplines are the first to produce an oversupply of inappropriately trained people, which leads to an unemployment problem. Rather, Malays should take programs that equip them for employment in engineering, agricultural extension and research, medicine, and other technical occupations. The two development plans of the 1960s also reflected this view as did a World Bank mission of this period. This approach is compatible with, indeed is part of, the "qualifications" argument described above as well as with manpower projection models that were common in the 1960s. These views prevailed at the same time that there was great political pressure simply to increase the number of Malays in the university system. It appeared that most Malays wanted a university degree of any sort because that was the principal requirement for a government job. This was clearly the case by the late 1960s, when Malay enrollments were reaching 35 to 40 percent of the total university students. Data from Psacharopoulos (1980, p. 129) show that the private rate of return to a university education compared with sixth form in 1978 was almost 40 percent in the public sector and 50 percent in the private sector. Much of this return was doubtless owing to recently graduated Malays acquiring jobs that were not previously available to them.

Training in engineering, medicine, and similar professions is of course important. The major difficulty is that projection of demands for specific slots is very unreliable, and to try to force, by artificial means (for example, exhortation), students into certain programs is almost certain to fail. The other difficulty is even more fundamental. At the early stage of development, it is highly problematical that formal vocational training schools can turn out a product that fills a skill gap in the economy. In a well-known article, P. J. Foster (1966) suggests that, in the initial stages of development, technical and vocational institutions follow growth—they are the cart, rather than the horse—and to put the cart before the horse is to waste resources. Vocational education must be closely related to those points where development is already taking place, or evidently about to occur, and demand for these skills is becoming increasing apparent (Foster 1966). Thus a school such as the Massachusetts Institute of Technology (MIT) in the United States may have a significant role to play in U.S. development, while an equally "good" MIT in Malaysia will simply be a drain on resources, with few compensating benefits. Even an MIT in the United States, one must acknowledge, has only an indirect effect on productivity growth. There are many instances in many countries of vocational schools turning quickly into white elephants. Snodgrass (1980, p. 254) refers to studies that found the vocational schools in Malaysia in the 1960s were attended mainly by people who could not get into other schools, and such schools apparently offered little that was of value in terms of finding a job and advancing in it.

DEMAND. Finally, it is abundantly clear to all that there is an enormous emotional content to schooling. It is equally clear that some schooling creates a demand for more schooling. As more students complete secondary school, more students want additional, more advanced training. This seems inevitable, irrespective of job opportunities. It becomes even more widespread if the private rates of return are believed to be very high.

CONCLUSION. Malaysia, and the Malaysian government specifically, faced then an exceedingly complex situation. Previous education policy had prolonged, possibly exacerbated, the inequality between and within ethnic communities. At the same time, the role that schooling could play in alleviating that inequality, as well as in contributing to the growth of productivity and output, was far from clear. The general approach—more schools at all levels, higher rates of attendance in general, more attendance by Malays in particular, and greater concentration on technical and vocational subjects, especially by Malays—was consistent with conventional wisdom of the day. At the same time, the evidence suggests that not a great deal was accomplished by these efforts, at least through the 1960s. Part of the reason for this modest accomplishment is explained by what was happening in the rest of the economy, especially with respect to the demand for labor. Part lies in the fact that formal schooling can contribute only indirectly and with considerable lag to productivity. Part lies with the difficulty of finding the right teaching techniques, and part lies in the widespread resistance to any educational programs that appeared to be inconsistent with prevailing tradition.

Language

All of these issues were complicated further by the language question. As a part of culture and tradition, language must be preserved. A choice of one language as the national language in a multilingual community will give one community an advantage over the others. In Malaysia it was also true that a command of the English language offered the best prospects for economic gain—for the individual and for the nation as a whole. There is, of course, no "right" solution to this language question.

As noted earlier, primary education was to be offered in all the major languages, and English and Malay were to be used in secondary schools. In 1960 public support was withdrawn for secondary schools in languages other than Malay and English. Most Chinese shifted to English-language schools, while the Malay students remained in the Malay-language schools. The University of Malaya taught in English, with minor exceptions, throughout the 1960s. It was not until 1965 that students from Malay-language secondary schools were admitted to the university, and these students had major problems in finding a comfortable place in the university community, partly because of language difficulties. By the end of the 1960s between 35 and 40 percent of the students at the University of Malaya were Malays, of which 75 to 80 percent were enrolled in the nontechnical faculties. It was in the post-1969 period that the biggest effort was made toward the exclusive use of Malay in all educational institutions.

Documentation is unavailable, but it is undoubtedly correct to conclude that the government policy was based mainly on political considerations and on the genuine belief that in moving increasingly toward the use of Malay in all schools, disparities in income and opportunities would be more quickly eliminated. The political considerations were based on the assumption that for the government to maintain the support of the Malay community, these schooling and language measures were necessary. Presumably the government weighed the effect on the Chinese and Indian communities, and decided that whatever opposition or dissension was created would be minor or at least could be coped with. There may also have been the view, probably implicit, that the Chinese and Indians would respond quickly to the new medium of instruction. The decision that Malay should be the medium, rather than English, rested on short-run political considerations, but also on firmly held views that the Malay language must be maintained as an essential element in the national culture. Even before 1969 it seems, at least in retrospect, that the idea of the Razak Committee to find a system of education that would recognize the "intention to make Malay the national language . . . whilst preserving and sustaining the growth of the language and culture of other communities in the culture" had been found impossible to implement.

The move to Malay, at the expense of English, was similar in many respects to the large-scale investment in paddy and smallholder rubber farming. It (the decision for Malay) reflected, as did the decisions on the other two matters, traditional, historical, and nationalistic views. The effort to "maximize" growth was constrained by these considerations, and there is little doubt that the growth of output was less than it would have been had these constraints not been recognized or had they been dealt with in different ways. On the equity front the issue is more complex, and a more complete discussion is postponed until other matters are examined. The principal point at the moment is to emphasize that to help the Malays in this fashion without, at the same time, penalizing members of the other communities was simply impossible. Thus the decisions that were made did not lead to Pareto improvements, but represented an effort to help one group even though the other groups were penalized. Whether the Malays were actually helped is questionable.

Nonacademic Education

The Hoerr study showed that the more schooling an individual had, the more that person profited from job experience and on-the-job training. In many circumstances, the main question to ask about formal schooling is whether or not it prepares the student to learn on the job. It has already been mentioned that one of the major reasons that the social rate of return on education was surprisingly low in Malaysia was that the labor market remained loose. Unemployment, however, is a consequence of labor's productivity being too low relative to the prevailing wage rate, and the purpose of training is to raise labor's productivity. If labor's productivity were increased, at given wage rates, the demand for labor should increase. Some of the difficulties of education result from its failure to raise labor's productivity, and the main reason for that failure was that the link between production activity and education was often absent. The major attribute of nonformal training is that it, by its very nature, links directly with production. As such it can be of great relevance. There are two types of nonformal education that are of interest. The first are specific training programs to equip participants to perform a particular task. The second is the training and learning that comes from working and accumulating experience.

In Malaysia in the 1960s there did not appear to be much interest or understanding of either category. Schooling was viewed as a means of certification and as a slot-filling exercise, which was the prevailing view in the economics profession at large. There were some training programs, of course. An institute of technology, established by the Council of Trust for Indigenous People (MARA) in the mid-1960s, offered a number of specific training programs in various technological categories and the National Productivity Center offered programs for managers of enterprises. The First Malaysia Plan (p. 171) notes that the government was the nation's largest employer and, as such, was implementing a growing number of training programs. These and other similar programs had some effect. The MARA Institute, though apparently extremely costly, was perhaps the most effective, although it is difficult to convince oneself that the MARA approach was the most suitable that could have been devised. There is little explicit recognition in these plans for the importance of creating an environment in which an essential characteristic of a job was that it resulted in continuing increased learning and rising productivity. If this nonformal, on-the-job learning is a necessary ingredient to rising productivity and rising earnings, then the absence of attention to these aspects of education is of great importance.

The attitude and approach to schooling and education was very similar to that of land development. Certain assets were to be provided to the poor (land with young rubber trees, places in school and universities) and certain policies followed (language, and other similar matters) that were intended to give Malays an advantage relative to the other two major communities. In the context of the 1960s, this approach was understandable from the standpoint of both political evaluations and the understanding of economists. The chief difficulty with the approach was that it was, in large measure, a welfare program instead of a development program, which would provide opportunities to learn, to grow, and to find one's own path to development and increased productivity. The relative slack in the economy contributed to this result. The conventional wisdom held that a more rapid investment and growth rate—and hence a more rapid rate of growth of demand for labor—would exacerbate the distribution difficulties was widely shared. Also at work were the other factors mentioned above, especially the fear of inflation. To the extent that such policies alienated the Chinese and Indians, they inevitably created additional social problems.

Industrial Policy

The major pillars of the growth and equity policies in the 1960s were education and land development. There were also some important industrial policies to which some attention must be devoted. The main immediate rationale for an industrial effort was the weak prospect for natural rubber and the reduced tin supply on the one hand and the employment problems on the other. There was also the recognition of year-to-year instability in rubber even by those who were optimistic about its long-run possibilities. It seemed clear that the rapid expansion of oil palm could not pick up much of the slack created by declining rubber and tin activity.

There was a major change in industrial policy in 1968, and the present discussion is limited to the period before 1968. The two main topics that are considered in this section are the general strategy of industrialization and its rationale and then the more specific aspects of that policy.

The principal industrialization strategy in the 1960s was import substitution. The First Malaysian Plan (Malaysia 1965, p. 9) called special attention to the possibilities for import substitution. Similarly a World Bank Mission Report (1963, p. 28) noted a substantial scope for import substitution in many fields. It added that "it will be neither possible nor desirable to substitute for many of these [presently imported] manufactured products for many years to come." Such a statement is ambiguous and possibly misleading, but does indicate the extent to which an import substitution strategy of industrialization was pushed by economists at this time. Retained imports of chemical products, manufactured foot products, textiles, manufactured tobacco, machinery and transport equipment, and other manufactured products amounted to almost $2,000 million in 1961. Acceleration of the replacement of imports by local production was to be emphasized in the First Malaysian Plan as was the processing of domestic and imported raw materials. The plan states further (p. 9) that "from the assembly of imported components industrialists will move on to the manufacture of some and eventually all of the components in Malaysia." Although the government role would become "increasingly purposeful and coordinated" in "creating and maintaining a favorable investment climate," the manufacturing operations themselves would be in the hands of the private sector. The commitment to import substitution appeared very strong, indeed, with minor reference to encouraging manufactured exports.

The role of import substitution in the 1960s is shown in the data of table 13-1. The percentages for each category of demand have been determined in the usual way following the original formulation of Hollis Chenery. These data show unambiguously that, with the exception of wood, import substitution was a much larger source of demand than was export promotion. For all categories, except wood and nonmetals, import substitution accounted for over one-half of the increase in demand, and only in textiles and nonmetals did export demand play a major role. A more detailed breakdown would show a few

Table 13-1. Sources of Demand for Manufacturing Output Growth, 1959–68

(percent)

Industry group	Domestic demand	Export expansion	Import substitution	Total
Food	33.6	7.9	58.5	100.0
Textiles	7.8	24.8	67.4	100.0
Wood	81.6	10.7	7.7	100.0
Chemicals	37.9	8.0	54.4	100.0
Nonmetals	49.4	20.4	30.2	100.0
Metals	37.9	2.0	60.1	100.0
Machinery	33.2	5.4	61.4	100.0
Consumer goods	38.1	7.3	54.6	100.0
Intermediate goods	33.8	17.1	49.1	100.0
Investment goods	40.3	4.2	55.5	100.0
Manufacturing	39.6	9.5	50.9	100.0

Source: Hoffmann (1973).

higher and lower percentages for import substitution, but in general the detailed picture is similar to that shown by the data in table 13-1. For the manufacturing sector as a whole, half of the new demand was a result of import replacement.

Another important aspect of the industrialization effort was that foreign investors were welcomed in the pre-1969 period. The rationale for this position is difficult to nail down. The obvious textbook reasons—foreigners would bring capital, technology, and marketing skills—were often mentioned, but other factors were also relevant. Industrialization meant creating larger-scale, modern manufacturing establishments similar to those of the West. This idea was also pushed by both foreign advisers and the World Bank in the last half of the 1960s. Meanwhile the government policymakers seemed to recognize that it was impossible for the Malay community to organize and manage these kinds of organizations. Certainly Malays did not have access to the large amounts of capital that were necessary. Members of the Chinese community could have raised the capital, and doubtless could have learned rapidly how to organize and manage a large, modern, Western-type firm. As it was, the Chinese were well established in medium-size units, and left the large-scale operations to foreigners. Data in Tan (1982) show that control was often in the hands of foreigners even when it appeared that ownership was not. The 1968 Census of Manufacturing shows that a mere 6 percent of establishments were controlled by foreigners, but this 6 percent accounted for about one-half of gross sales, of total value added, and "profits" (nonlabor value added). Evidently, foreign control was as important in manufacturing as in estate rubber and palm oil.

The idea of encouraging foreign investors was not popular with all groups in Malaysia. Opposition came from two main sources. The first was the non-Malay—mainly Chinese—business community that argued that foreigners should be kept out so that Malaysians would have a clearer run at establishing and developing the new manufacturing sector. Had the foreign investor been kept out or strongly discouraged, the evidence seems beyond dispute that the Chinese would have done much more in this area than they actually did. The government certainly recognized this possibility, and it was a factor in the decision to encourage foreigners to come in. The other source of opposition to foreign investment were those Malays who were strongly committed to a more independent, nationalistic development policy and who feared that greater foreign participation would undermine the values and traditions of the Islamic society.

Both of these arguments have a great deal of validity. The Chinese were, to a considerable extent, blocked. It can be argued that the manufacturing sector would have expanded more rapidly had full, or almost full, reliance been placed on domestic entrepreneurs. Some evidence suggests that reinvestment of retained earnings was greater from domestically owned and controlled firms than was true of foreign-owned firms. Certainly enterprises would have been smaller and more consistent with Malaysia's own managerial skills. There does not seem to be data available on the labor intensity of domestic manufacturing firms compared with those owned and controlled by foreigners, but bits and pieces of evidence—value added per employee, size of firms, sources of physical capital, managerial background and attitudes, and so forth—suggest that employment per dollar invested was greater in the domestically owned firms. Data calculated by David Lim (1973, p. 160) from census figures show that value added per employee in Malaysian controlled companies ranged from 16 to 82 percent of that in foreign-controlled companies. In one industry—leather and leather products—Malaysian-owned firms showed a higher productivity (higher by 21 percent) than foreign firms. Wages paid by foreign firms were higher than in the economy generally. It is probably correct to argue that the technology employed in the Malaysian firms was more appropriate—more compatible with factor supplies and qualities and social attitudes and organizations—than was true foreign-owned activities. Malaysia's international credit was good, there was ready access to funds in Singapore, and domestic saving rates were impressive, so it is difficult to believe that the supply of investible funds would have been a barrier. With the import substitution policies, there should not be a demand problem, at least during the early stages. Tentatively, then, one can risk the conclusion that the rate of investment would not have suffered. Given these facts, had foreign investment been barred, both output and demand for labor would have increased more rapidly than they actually did.

Consider again the rationale for government policy encouraging private foreign investment. Two points are especially important. The first is that developing the manufacturing sector meant—to Malaysian policymakers, to foreign advisers, and to World Bank missions—building large-scale Western firms, and such enterprises were, almost by definition, available only from Western multinationals. The second point is more relevant to the Malaysian story. The presence of the British in the estates, in trading and financial companies, and then in manufacturing, had given a continuity to the economy that the Malay government found reassuring. The fact that the Malays were economically insecure relative to the Chinese made this continuity extremely appealing; it helped to demonstrate that Malay political control remained intact (Golay 1969). It was evident that the Malays could neither create nor manage modern sector activities, so the foreign firms would then provide sufficient competition to the Chinese to prevent their gaining undue dominance. It is not clear, however, what expectations were for the longer-run consequences of foreign investment. In particular, there is little evidence that there would be a substantial learning effect for the Malays. Thus a rather peculiar situation emerged in which the Malay community was recognized by the government to be ill-suited and ill-equipped to establish and manage the "modern" manufacturing firms deemed to be essential by the policymaker. Yet, the same policymaker resisted giving a clear field to the Chinese, and, therefore, sought foreign investment. The foreign investment, for reasons already stated, offered fewer opportunities for Malay employment and Malay learning than would have been available from a domestically run industrialization effort. This point is especially important when it is noted that there were numerous institutions set up and policy changes made that were intended to facilitate Malay participation in "modern sector" activities. In light of the results that these efforts produced, one may agree with Golay (1969, p. 369) that such institutions and policies appeared well in advance of Malay capabilities to use them. Improving these capabilities was necessary, therefore, before the other changes could have full effect. Again one sees an approach to helping Malays that takes the form of providing assets and other results of development, rather than attacking directly their productivity capacity.

The specific content of the policy package intended to achieve the industrialization objective was similar to that found in many other countries. There was, however, one major exception—the level of protection was, relative to that in most other developing countries, modest, and tariffs were usually reviewed carefully before being imposed. Similarly, other measures aimed at effecting the import replacement strategy had relatively innocuous potential to distort the economy.

The industrialization policy was built around the Pioneer Industries Ordinance adopted in 1958. This legislation authorized the minister of commerce and industry to grant "pioneer status" to a company that convinced him that the domestic industry was not now of a scale sufficient to meet the requirements for continued development in Malaysia, the prospects were favorable for the further development of the industry, and that it was in the public interest to encourage the industry. Evidently all of these criteria are quite subjective, and leave a minister great discretionary power. A firm given pioneer status was entitled to complete relief from the company income tax for a period ranging from two to five years. The number of tax-free years depended on the amount of investment. Losses could be carried over into the years after pioneer status had ended. If there were room for only one new firm in the industry, preference was given to the one with the largest amount of local capital.

Tax holidays were the most common of investment incentives in the 1960s, although even at that time they were generally considered to have little or no effect on the absolute amount of investment. Their most obvious shortcoming was that a firm must make a profit before they had any effect at all, and early years of operations are often years of very low or zero profits. In the case of foreigners, the effect of a tax holiday in Malaysia could well mean that the company would simply pay more taxes to its home government. There are some data that suggest that the tax revenue forgiven was concentrated on a handful of companies, and the largest number of pioneer status firms received essentially no help from the tax relief provisions.

The policy did have some effects other than on total investment. The link between the size of the investment and the length of time taxes were forgiven obviously encouraged as much substitution of capital for labor as was possible. In addition, there were instances where applications for pioneer status were rejected because the machinery that the firm intended to use was not the most sophisticated available. (This practice was not uncommon in development banks and other sources of funds for manufacturing investment.) Until 1971 there was a 2 percent tax levied on a firm's payroll, which hardly encouraged employment. Employment in these firms grew at a surprisingly low rate. After ten years (by 1968) there were slightly more than 22,000 full-time employees in firms with pioneer status. The productivity—value added per worker—was about three times that in the industrial sector as a whole and five times that in the economy as a whole (Snodgrass 1980, p. 208). Pioneer status firms were largely foreign firms, with about 70 percent of the value added produced by foreign firms. Pioneer status did nothing to induce firms to locate in the northern or east coast states where poverty was the greatest. Pioneer firms did have a much larger percentage (42) of Malay employees in 1968 than did nonpioneer firms (24), but over the ten years from 1958 to 1968, all manufacturing firms were hiring more Malays, and it is doubtful whether pioneer status was an important explanation. One must conclude then that pioneer status as such tended to exacerbate inequality both because of its regional effects and because of the evident tendency to a capital intensity that was well above that of the rest of the manufacturing sector. There is little reason to believe that the legislation led to a higher rate of investment.

The other major component of the industrialization policy was protection from imports, afforded almost entirely by tariffs. As already mentioned, the rates of protection were generally low compared with those in most other developing countries. For example, for the six developing countries included in the Balassa study (Power 1971), the average effective rate of protection for the manufacturing sector for Malaysia was 7 percent, compared with 79, 54, 21, 92, and 32 percent for the other five around the 1960s. Malaysia could maintain the lower rates largely because it enjoyed a strong balance of payments position. Unlike many developing countries, Malaysia did not initiate its import substitution strategy in response to a balance of payments crisis. The continued strength of the balance of payments did not depend on reducing total imports relative to GDP. The management of the rubber estates, a significant political force, opposed industrialization behind protection because of its potential for causing wage rates and the price of intermediate goods to be pushed up. The large import houses, also a political force, were opposed because import replacements could well undermine their own position in distribution activities. The earliest directives to the tariff-making authorities reflected this opposition by forbidding the marketing of domestically made goods of poor quality or at prices that were deemed excessive. In the First Malaysia Plan, it was stated that tariff protection would continue no longer than "absolutely necessary." In these respects Malaysia's implementation of import substitution had an unusually favorable starting position.

John H. Power (1971) calculated effective rates of protection in Malaysia for 1963 and 1965, and the Economic Commission for Asia and the Far East calculated rates for 1969. All these rates are low, but there is considerable variation and the familiar escalation from lower to higher stages of processing is evident. Power's estimates for 1965 are the highest for nondurable consumer goods, and there are a number of negative rates, especially on some export activities. Thus there does not appear to have been an established tariff policy that reflected a general appreciation of the possible distorting effects of tariffs. The

First Malaysia Plan did recognize the key role that increased productivity plays in the protected activities, but there was little discussion of the possible sources of that productivity growth.

Another study (Edwards 1975) of effective protection in Malaysia shows markedly higher rates than does Power, but still below most of those for other developing countries. (Estimates by other investigators contain troubling differences.) More important, the calculations in Edwards show sharply rising levels of protection over the 1960s. By his calculations, the 1969 effective rates of protection of Malaysia can no longer be considered low, but, rather, moderate to high. His data also allow him to argue that there is a relationship between rates of growth of output and levels of protection. It seems likely that Power's estimates are too low, but that those of Edwards are too high; therefore, one may still say that through the 1960s, Malaysia's tariff structure was still low by international standards. Protection probably increased somewhat over the 1960s.

Tariffs were probably more important than tax holidays in encouraging investment in both foreign and domestic manufacturing. Tariffs, however, were not a sufficient condition. Of equal, possibly even greater, importance was the exceptional price stability that prevailed during the 1950s and 1960s. General price stability was made possible by a conservative monetary policy and, more important, by fairly constant wage rates. There was no wage push or pull in these years, which contributed mightily to the price stability. This does not mean that prevailing wage rates equaled the "shadow price" of labor. Little and Tipping (1972) estimated the shadow wage of the Malaysian economy to be about one-quarter to one-third of the prevailing wage. These estimates are crude, of course, but the evidence that wage rates were "too high" does seem convincing. There was, however, stability, and price and wage stability meant that the exchange rate was under little pressure during these years. The exchange rate was essentially unchanged (M\$3.05 per US\$1.00) from 1950 to 1970. The balance of payments was protected (with the help of tariffs), but for a wide range of other products, an exchange rate of M\$3.00 per US\$1.00 represented an overvaluation. This mild case of the Dutch disease was a relevant factor in the efforts to diversify exports and to induce investors to search hard for foreign markets. The prevailing (overvalued) rate did help keep the domestic price level stable, and, it should be repeated, the overvaluation did not worsen over the years.

There were several specific efforts to facilitate increased Malay participation in the new manufacturing activities. A National Investment Company was established in 1961 to acquire stock in the new companies for Malays and Malay interests. MARA Unit Trusts also helped to market stock to Malays. The Rural and Industrial Development Authority (RIDA) had been set up before independence to promote

Malay participation in nonagricultural activities. In the 1960s relatively little money was allocated to RIDA, and that which was did not seem to be used in an effective way. Snodgrass (1980, p. 212) notes that by 1969, despite the efforts of RIDA and MARA, more than 90 percent of the chief executives of small-scale industrial activities were Chinese. Therefore, one must conclude that these programs did little to get Malays directly involved in establishing and managing new industrial activities. The one area where industrial activity could have made a noteworthy contribution to Malay development, employment creation, was especially weak.

In summary, manufacturing output grew more rapidly than GDP from 1957 to 1970, and by the latter date around 15 to 16 percent of GDP originated in manufacturing compared with 9 to 10 percent ten years earlier. The range of products produced within the country also increased. In 1959 there were more than twice the value of consumer goods imported relative to domestic production, and in 1968 imports were less than 80 percent of domestic production. Reduction in the relative role of imports was even greater for some specific consumer goods, such as manufactured food, bicycles, soaps, pharmaceuticals, and so forth. In both the intermediate and capital goods sectors there were also reductions in the import–domestic output ratios, but not as sharp as those in the consumer goods categories. Generally, consumer goods accounted for 65 to 70 percent of imports in the mid-1950s and about one-half in the mid-1960s. Capital goods increased from 7 percent in the earlier period to 20 to 25 percent in the later, and intermediate goods from 6–8 to 17–18 percent. So, there was diversification in domestic production, and the usual decline in the ratio of imported consumer goods to total availabilities and the increase in the importance of imported capital goods appears clearly in the data. Exports of manufactured products were less than M$150 million in 1960 and averaged over 9 percent growth over the decade. By the end of the decade they were still a very small proportion of total exports, about 7 percent, up from less than 5 percent in 1960. In general, exports in manufactures did not keep pace with the growth of output.

Employment growth in manufacturing was the major disappointment. New investment seemed to be less labor-intensive than was technologically possible. This was especially true of firms with pioneer status, but for almost all new firms as well. Value added per worker was higher than in other sectors and so, too, were wage rates. Therefore, the manufacturing sector had begun to take on the aspects of an enclave, with productivity and wages well above average, but with a relatively small labor force, and only modest links with the rest of the economy, especially the small, informal manufacturing activities. The difficulties created for smallholder rubber operators by the absence of learning links between them and the much more productive estates have already been shown. The same difficulty seemed to be emerging in the manufacturing sector in the 1960s. The existence of slack in the economy was the main (or most obvious) anomaly in the economic system in these years.

Equity

Inequality increased over the decade. Table 12-1 in chapter 12 shows a 20 percent increase in the Gini coefficient in 1970 relative to 1957–58. The highest decile increased its share by 18 percent and the share of income of the lowest half of the households fell by almost 30 percent. Table 12-2 shows that these changes were similar in all three of the major ethnic groups. The table also shows that Chinese average household income rose more rapidly over the period than did that of the Malays. Some estimates show that the average monthly income of the lowest 40 percent actually fell in real terms between the two years by as much as 10 percent. Given the increase in GDP and the generally favorable paddy prices, an absolute decline seems doubtful, but such estimates do support the position that inequality increased and poverty alleviation made little, if any, headway.

The single most important explanation of this increasing inequality was the failure of employment to increase rapidly at the same time that investment was high and GDP was expanding strongly. The large-scale land development programs generated income for contractors and their employees long before they raised the income of farmers. The result was that the former group, already in the higher income categories, gained, while the farmers did not.

It may be noted that implementing the import substitution strategy did not seem to contribute significantly to the increasing inequality. The strategy was not pursued strongly enough in the 1960s to create many sources of rents that have, in other countries, often contributed to inequality. The industrial policies, as just noted, did not help on the employment front. Malaysia was unable to design and implement a policy that led to new activities that produced growing labor productivity and that allowed a great deal of substitution between labor and nonlabor inputs. These two conditions, the most suitable for increasing employment and relieving poverty, were not readily found in the developing world in the 1960s (Bruton 1976).

The land development programs were supposed to accomplish several objectives, but primarily they were to help relieve rural poverty and to do so in a manner deemed congenial to the prevailing Malay social and cultural milieu. The idea was neither to "modernize" nor to "restructure," but to improve the conditions in which the rural Malays lived. In this sense the idea of development involved of building onto prevailing customs and prevailing social arrangements, which was an appealing approach.

It was, however, during this decade that the tensions and antagonisms evolved that produced the great riots of 1969. The origins of these riots are discussed fully in the next section. It may be noted here that a major source of the racial antagonisms evolved from the increasingly evident inequalities between the Chinese and Malays. The evidence was not only in household income as in table 12-1, but also in education, access to health care, access to interesting jobs, and so forth. As all these differences were generally recognized, tensions mounted, and the Malay community began to think more in terms of changing traditions and life-styles, rather than simply improving the existing arrangements. The tensions created by these changes within the Malay community exacerbated those that were emerging between the races because of the great disparities among them. Meanwhile the development strategy and policies to implement it did little either to create learning opportunities for Malays or to equip them to perform new activities effectively.

14 The 1970s: The Search for Equity

By the end of the 1960s Malaysia was widely considered a success story. The new nation had achieved a high rate of economic growth, relatively high levels of per capita income, a remarkable record of price stability and balance of payments strength, and an ever-widening provision and coverage of basic services, such as education, health, water, transportation, and communication. In addition, it had enjoyed political stability. These achievements were attained against the backdrop of a potentially inflammable political and social structure—a society divided along ethnic lines that spilled over into culture and language difference. Over the 1960s, the nation held together, but the racial riots of May 1969 forced everyone to reevaluate the Malaysian story and to question whether its development was actually truly successful.

Race relations in Malaysia have often served as the criterion of success or failure in development. An outbreak of racial violence has been perceived to reflect a failure of the system, while the absence of racial violence supposedly reflects success. In the aftermath of the May 1969 racial riots, therefore, most Malysians concluded that the political-economic system had failed in a particularly damaging way. The argument was frequently made that the development policies of the 1960s had enriched the wealthy and further impoverished the poor, which had caused the riots. A radically different approach from that of the past was necessary, therefore, if the events of May 1969 were not to be repeated. In 1971 the government announced its New Economic Policy (NEP) in the *Second Malaysia Plan 1971–1975* as its answer to the riots. The NEP marked a reorientation of government policy in a very fundamental way and constituted a major turning point in the history of independent Malaysia.

This chapter will present numerous aspects of the NEP—its background, rationale, achievements, and consequences over the 1970s. The next section will review the 1980–85 period to see what further changes have been introduced into the economy as a result of the experience of the 1970s.

Background to the New Economic Policy

Prelude to the Racial Riots

Any account of the NEP will have to begin with the political events and climate of the late 1960s and the general elections of 1969.

The period from 1964 to 1969 was one of unusual ethnic political militancy, partly the result of the People's Action Party's call for a "Malaysian Malaysia," and partly because one of the pro-Malay parts of the 1957 Bargain came due—the National Language Bill. That bill proposed that Malay become the sole official language by 1967. Malay apprehensions over the fate of the Malay language were heightened by the prime minister's statement in 1965 that it might not be possible to implement completely the use of Malay by 1967. There was strong demand from the more radical Malays to have the Malay language policy fully implemented.

Meanwhile, Chinese groups were pressing for a more liberal stand on the language issue. The pressure from Chinese and, to a lesser extent, Indian groups led to concessions regarding official use of their languages. The National Language Bill, which was passed by Parliament in March 1967, included clauses that provided assurance for the use of languages other than the national language. Many Malays felt betrayed over this bill, and there were mass demonstrations against it. Divisions arose within the United Malay National Organization (UMNO), the ruling party, and the position of the prime minister was weakened.

To the non-Malays, on the one hand, the ruling alliance coalition was becoming sensitive to the demands of the Malay extremists, and the Malaysian Chinese Association (MCA) and Malaysian Indian Congress (MIC) were losing considerable support of the non-Malays. (The alliance coalition was made up of UMNO, MCA, and MIC.) To some Malays, on the other hand, UMNO was acceding to the non-Malays by making further concessions to them, and thereby threatening the dominant role of the Malays. The general election campaign of 1969 was characterized by widespread communalism, which created the spark that set off the postelection events. In the election campaign the alliance paid little attention to the non-Malay voters, but focused its attention instead on the threat posed by the more radical Malay parties. A more communalistic and aggressive approach was adopted by opposition parties. The slogan "Malaysian Malaysia" was used by a number of parties, and was interpreted by the Malays as essentially an attack on the special position of the Malays provided by the constitution. Some parties also urged the adoption of an integrated educational system in which schools using the major languages as media of instruction and examination were recognized as national schools. The content of the educational program was to be oriented around Malaysia and the national language taught as a compulsory second language in all schools. Some parties and individuals went further; for example, there was a proposal to amend the constitution to abolish privileges granted to any particular ethnic group. There were groups, it is important to emphasize, that sought a more noncommunal image and worked for a more moderate approach on a number of difficult issues.

The immediate cause of the racial riots was the result of the general election of May 10, 1969 (Vasil 1971; Ratnam and Milne 1970). The ruling alliance suffered a serious setback as it won less than half of the total votes. In the state elections it lost control of Penang, Perak, and Trengganu, while in Selangor, the most populous state and the seat of the national federal capital, it won only half the seats of the state assembly. This caused a deadlock, as the combined opposition controlled the other half. The UMNO lost to the more extreme pro-Malay party in the predominantly Malay areas. In turn the MCA lost to the more extreme non-Malay parties. The alliance won 66 seats out of the total 104 parliamentry seats in West Malaysia. It, therefore, lost its two-thirds majority in Parliament and its capacity to amend the constitution.

The immediate events leading to the May 13 riots were the victory marches of a number of parties. (For an official account of the racial riots see National Operations Council 1969.) According to official sources, several parties held racially provocative and intimidating victory marches in Kuala Lumpur on May 11 and 12. On the evening of May 13, the UMNO began its procession, and rioting between Malays and non-Malays broke out soon afterward. Officially, 196 people died and 6,000 were classified as "refugees." The racial violence lasted for four days.

Political and Institutional Developments after May 1969

The immediate effect of the racial riots was the declaration of a national emergency, the suspension of the constitution and Parliament, suspension of the election in Sabah and Sarawak, and the establishment of a National Operations Council (NOC). Power was centralized in the NOC headed by the deputy prime minister.

New institutional and political arrangements and a search for an all-embracing ideology were pursued under NOC rule. Particular emphasis was put on the root cause of the deterioration in race relations, problems of integration, and the possible ways and means of building a united society. A Department of National Unity was established and was entrusted with the task of undertaking research and study into various aspects of national unity and into the ways of promoting it. A National Consultative Council (NCC) was also established to provide a forum for the exchange of ideas and to find a "permanent solution." A national ideology was sought to find sources and means of social harmony, and fifteen months after the May riot, *Rukunegara* was promulgated as the national ideology.

Major constitutional changes were introduced in early 1971 at the time that emergency rule was ended, and Parliament reconvened. A white paper entitled "Towards National Harmony," stated that the main purposes of the constitutional changes were "to remove sensitive issues from the realm of public discussions in order to allow the smooth functioning of parliamentry democracy; and to redress the racial imbalance in certain sectors of the nation's life and thereby promote national unity." Certain parts of the constitution would be "entrenched," and the consent of the conference of rulers would be necessary to amend them. The entrenched parts covered subjects on the powers and status of the Malay rulers, citizenship rights, Malay special rights, status of Islam as the official religion, and the status of Malay as the sole national language. The Sedition Ordinance was amended to restrict the freedom of speech and the press by making it seditious "to question any matter, right, status, position, privilege, sovereignty or prerogative established by the provision of Part II of the Federal constitution or Article 152, 153 or 181 of the Federal Constitution." These proposed amendments, which were incorporated in the Constitution (Amendment) Bill following the debate, were duly passed by the Parliament. Some parties opposed the amendments.

Following the restoration of parliamentary rule, the NOC was disbanded and replaced by the National Security Council composed of the same members but with much more limited areas of responsibilities. A National Unity Council replaced the NCC and was to be responsible for discussing issues of national harmony.

Background and Content of the New Economic Policy

The NEP, established in 1971, completed the package of major changes made by the post-1969 government. Almost every aspect of policy and policymaking was influenced by the NEP, and it became the basis and framework for assessing all development policies and programs. This section provides the background to the formulation of the NEP.

Early Views on Growth and Equity

It was widely believed among the Malay leaders in the UMNO, and by many Malays, that the racial riots of 1969 occurred primarily because of the economic grievances of the Malays. Development since independence, the argument went, had not really benefited the Malays. The view was widespread that the non-Malays, especially the Chinese, had profited most from development. This conclusion further implied, therefore, that the economic disparities between the Malays and non-Malays had not been narrowed, and that the government strategy and policies had failed to raise the income of the Malays relative to that of the non-Malays. If racial riots were to be avoided in the future, it was argued, it was imperative that radical measures be implemented to satisfy Malay economic aspirations and to reduce the economic imbalances that still persisted between the races.

The main concern of those involved in the preparatory work of the NEP was the debate on the "growth-equity" tradeoff issue. It was generally assumed that emphasizing equity would mean sacrificing growth. The argument was usually made largely on a priori grounds, and couched in terms of how a strong focus on equity would adversely affect efficiency, productivity, and savings, and would, therefore, lead to a slower growth for the economy as a whole. It is difficult to document the details of the arguments on these issues and the views of the various major actors in the work on the NEP. It appears clear, however, that there was such a strong interest in narrowing the gap between the races that few objected to sacrificing growth to achieve this objective. Evidently, much of the sentiment for this approach toward development was influenced by the conviction that the pro-growth phase of the postindependence period had led to increasing inequality and general dissatisfaction on the part of the Malays. This latter view was widely shared by the bureaucracy and became an important influence in the government. There were, however, those who urged a more cautious approach, and who still argued that faster growth could alleviate poverty and improve the distribution of income as well. This progrowth faction proved influential enough to substantially affect the final content of the NEP and the way it was implemented.

Planning for Equity

In the *Second Malaysia Plan 1971–75*, published in early 1971, the government officially presented the NEP to the nation. A summary of the plan stated that the overriding objective of the NEP was the achievement of national unity and that

> the Plan incorporates a two-pronged New Economic Policy for development. The first prong is to reduce and eventually eradicate poverty, by raising income levels and increasing employment opportunities for all Malaysians, irrespective of race. The second

prong aims at accelerating the process of restructuring Malaysian society to correct economic imbalance, so as to reduce and eventually eliminate the identification of race with economic function. This process involves the modernization of rural life, a rapid and balanced growth of urban activities and the creation of a Malay commercial and industrial community in all categories and at all levels of operation, so that Malays and other indigenous people will become full partners in all aspects of the economic life of the nation (Malaysia, Economic Planning Unit 1970, p. 1).

More specifically the second plan stated that

the government has set a target that within a period of 20 years, Malay and other indigenous people will manage and own at least 30 percent of the total commercial and industrial activities in all categories and scale of operation. The government has also stipulated that the employment pattern at all levels and in all sectors, particularly the Modern Rural and Urban Sectors, must reflect the racial composition of the population (pp. 41–42).

Very early, however, it was appreciated that economic means alone would not solve the many problems of a pluralistic society, but the belief remained strong that such means could make important contributions to the achievement of racial harmony. So the plan stated that "This search for national identity and unity involves the whole range of economic, social and political activities" (p. 3), and would include educational policies that were designed to encourage common values and that cultivated a sense of dedication to the nation. Emphasis was also given to developing a national language, literature, and music. The plan stated in a variety of ways the view that "national unity is unattainable without greater balance among Malaysia's social and ethnic groups in their participation in the development of the country and in the sharing of the benefits from modernization and economic growth" (p. 3). This theme was to be carried through the 1970s.

The remaining parts of the second plan then went on to amplify the "philosophy" of the two prongs of the NEP. Growth was stressed to achieve the objectives because the NEP "can best be undertaken in the context of an expanding economy." It was declared that the government would have to play an important role in helping to achieve all objectives. The plan provided the general basis for the role of the government and the private sector. Both were believed to have "complementary" roles but "government will assume an expanded and more positive role in the economy than in the past" and generally:

The government will participate more directly in the establishment and operation of a wide range of productive enterprises. This will be done through wholly-owned enterprises and joint ventures with the private sector. Direct participation by the government in commercial and industrial undertakings represents a significant departure from past practice. The necessity for such efforts by the government arises particularly from the aims of establishing new industrial activities in selected new growth areas and of creating a Malay commercial and industrial community (p. 7).

As for its role in the creation of a Malay commercial and industrial community, the government would be directly involved in constructing business premises, in investing in productive commercial and industrial enterprises to be controlled and managed by Malays and other indigenous people, and in providing financial and technical services. The equity objective became defined as concern for "economic balance."

The term economic balance obviously is many-sided. Generally it meant that those members of the Malaysian society "who have benefited relatively little from past development must now be assured ample opportunities to gain fairer share of the increased goods and services that development brings." Balance also refers to the different ethnic groups' shares in management and ownership as well as their employment in the various sectors of the economy. Special mention was made of the manufacturing and commercial sectors as two growing sectors that were dominated by the non-Malays and foreigners. The target of 30 percent ownership and management of the commercial and industrial activities in all categories and scales of operation proved to be quite controversial. Similarly, the employment balance target was emphasized and raised questions. Balance also included income equality between rural and urban areas and among the various regions.

In the *Mid-term Review of the Second Malaysia Plan, 1971–1975*, published in 1973, a little more of the content of the NEP was spelled out. Two things in particular may be noted in the *Mid-term Review* (MTR-2). First, data from the *Post-Enumeration Survey* (PES) of the *Population Census 1970* allowed details of the extent of income inequality to be published in a government document for the first time. These data (table 12-1) showed that the top 10 percent of households accounted for about 40 percent of total income, while the bottom 40 percent received about 12 percent of total household income in Peninsular Malaysia. The mean household income (per month) of the Chinese household was M$387 in 1970—more than twice that of the average income of the Malay household, which was M$179. Average Indian income was M$310 (MTR-2, p. 11).

There was also an explicit move to focus more attention on the ownership of share capital in the corporate sector. It was emphasized that "ownership and control of wealth or asset is an important source of household income" and that "an important element in this regard is the ownership of capital in the corporate and noncorporate sectors of the economy" (MTR-2, p. 10). Evidence was then presented of the ownership of share capital of limited companies; that is, the corporate sector, and of fixed assets for the noncorporate sector. In MTR-2 there was the first reference to wealth defined in terms of financial and physical assets, including land. The planners stressed the importance of ownership of one kind of financial asset, equity or share capital, for "as the economy develops and modernizes, however, and as the country's financial structure becomes increasingly sophisticated, the key to the ownership and control of wealth will be through ownership of the equity capital of various enterprises. The government will, therefore, take effective measures to enable Malays and other indigenous people to expand their ownership of share capital" (MTR-2, p. 11).

There were other changes as well. The gradual reinterpretation and evolution of the ownership restructuring aspect of the NEP is clearly seen in the revision of the prospective plan. In the second plan itself, no ownership targets were made for the non-Malays and foreign interests. However, the prospective plan indicated that by 1990 Malaysians would own about 70 percent of the total share capital of limited companies, with Bumiputera (Malays and other indigenous people) owning at least 30 percent, other Malaysians owning 40 percent, and foreign interests owning the remaining 30 percent. It also reassured the other interests that "the attainment of the growth targets of the Prospective Plan will enable non-Malay ownership of share capital to expand by nearly 12 percent per year and to increase its share of the total to over 40 percent by 1990"(MTR-2, p. 85). The growth of Malay ownership was understood to take place at the "expense" of foreign interests; "In relation to total share capital, however, the expansion for Malays and other indigenous people . . . will involve a sizable decline in the share of foreign interests from 61 percent to about 30 percent during the period" (p. 85). The total amount of foreign investment, however, was projected to increase by about 8 percent a year from 1970 to 1990. This elaboration gave official birth to the famous "30:40:30" ownership restructuring target under the NEP. The targets were obviously exceedingly ambitious in all respects.

Numerous specialized agencies were established to provide a variety of support and assistance in creating a Bumiputera commercial community. These agencies either invested on their own or had joint ventures in various industrial and commercial activities, and provided financial and technical assistance, consultancy services, and conducted training courses. They exhibited the clearest manifestation of the burst of public enterprises in industry and commerce following the establishment of the NEP.

Between 1970 and 1974 little progress was made in assessing the poverty situation in the country, principally because of lack of data. By the mid-1970s some data from the PES were made available (Anand 1983), and together with work from the Economic Planning Unit the first poverty estimates were made public in the *Third Malaysia Plan, 1976–80.*

More important, the third plan introduced yet another long-term target, namely that the incidence of poverty would be reduced to about 17 percent by 1990 from its estimated level of 50 percent in 1970. The planners defined a controversial and sensitive target to give more specific content to the NEP. The target actually did generate controversy. The revelation that almost half of the total households in 1970 were classified as officially poor surprised many people, and the incidence of poverty among paddy farmers, fishermen, and rubber smallholders was known to be higher.

Perceptions and Understanding of the NEP

It was quite obvious that the NEP meant different things to different people within the government, and this diversity of views added to the already complex problems of implementation. There were differences as well between the government and the private sector and within the private sector. Questions and discussions on the meaning of the NEP were extensive. For example, was ownership of share capital to be confined to the corporate sector? What is the corporate sector? Should restructuring be measured at the "global" level, or should it apply to the individual companies? Is restructuring to be implemented through growth? Is growth only to be restricted to share capital growth, or growth in other aspects of the enterprise? And on and on. There were also numerous questions about poverty: What is poverty? How should it be defined? What poverty line income level makes sense? How are the various target groups defined?

There was also concern over the relative emphasis to be given to poverty eradication relative to restructuring. Some critics of the government argued that the government was spending far more on programs for the restructuring of society than on poverty eradication programs. It was only in the third plan (1976–80) that an attempt was made to assess the amount of financial resources that were allocated and expended on poverty and restructuring programs. Some 38.2 percent ($47 billion) of the total development expenditure was allocated directly for projects and policies to reduce poverty in the 1976–80 period. Such projects included programs for land development; the replanting and new planting of rubber trees; drainage and irrigation schemes; rehabilitation and consolidation of existing holdings; promotion of intercropping, off-season cropping, and crop diversification; and credit and marketing services. Funds were also allocated to provide extension and advisory services, low-cost housing, rural electrification, water supply, health, and education. About 19 percent ($3.5 billion) were classifed as projects to restructure the economy during the same period.

For the *Fourth Malaysia Plan, 1980–85*, the official figures showed that poverty eradication was still given a higher allocation than was restructuring, $9.3 billion compared with about $4.4 billion. Critics, however, continued to argue that the government was spending far more on the restructuring programs than on the poverty eradication programs. Evidently where one objective ends and the other begins is influenced by one's view about which is more important.

There was little appreciation of the likely quantitative relevance of putting the emphasis on poverty alleviation or on restructuring. One study (Anand 1983) in the early 1970s did introduce evidence for the first time in support of the argument that it did seem to matter to overall inequality which aspect of the NEP was emphasized. Anand analyzed the poverty and inequality position using the PES for 1970. Two of his findings may be noted in the present context. First, he argued on the basis of a decomposition analysis that inequality within a race explained much more of the overall income inequality than did income inequality between the races. On the basis of this study, therefore, it was argued that policies attacking income imbalances within the Malay community, for example, would go farther in reducing overall inequality than policies that focused entirely, or mostly, on the inequality between the Malays and the Chinese. The second of Anand's findings is very much tied in with his first. It was argued that a much better policy option for Malaysia would be to focus more on poverty eradication than on the restructuring aspect of the NEP, because this would do more to reduce overall income inequality than would a policy aimed primarily at restructuring. It was also generally appreciated, however, that these two notions—poverty alleviation and restructuring—were not really independent. To relieve the poverty among Malays would necessarily require that they be moved into more productive activities and, increasingly, into urban areas; that is, it would require restructuring.

That the emphasis should be placed on reducing intraracial inequality rather than interracial inequality was, however, not consistent with the declared objective of the NEP. The NEP did not suggest that the objective was to reduce overall income inequality. In fact, official pronouncements made little distinction between racial and overall income inequality. It is probably correct to suggest that there was a perception, generally implicit, that raising Malay income relative to Chinese income would somehow be good for overall income inequality. One might indeed go farther and argue that the formulators of the NEP were quite prepared to accept a widening of overall income inequality, if that were the necessary outcome of reducing income inequalities between the Chinese and Malays.

Agricultural Development and Rural Poverty

Land Development

In this section the efforts to alleviate poverty that were made over the 1970s are examined in more detail. The focus is on rural poverty and the role of agriculture in alleviating poverty in the rural areas. Table 12-3 has shown that the incidence of poverty fell from about half in 1970 to about 39 percent in 1976. Poverty was, and is, largely a rural phenomenon. As much as 88 percent of the total of poor households were located in the rural areas by the mid-1970s. Three major target groups accounted for the bulk of the poor rubber smallholders, paddy farmers, and estate workers. There was a rapid decline in urban poverty, with the incidence falling from 21.3 percent in 1970 to 17.9 percent in 1976.

Progress in poverty alleviation was more rapid during the first half of the 1970s. The major socioeconomic indicators also pointed to substantial progress in raising the standard of living. Life expectancy at birth "for Malaysia" for males increased, and sharp falls were also recorded for the infant mortality rate. All indicators for basic services tell the same story of progress in coverage and accessibility. By 1980 an estimated 43 percent of the rural population was supplied with potable and piped water, and 48 percent with electricity.

Growth in the agricultural sector over the decade averaged about 4.3 percent a year, and by 1980 agriculture accounted for about 22.2 percent of GDP compared with 30.8 percent in 1970. Agricultural employment also declined (from one-half to 40 percent), but by the end of the decade it was still the largest employer. Employment growth in agriculture of 2.3 percent a year was better during 1971 to 1975 than during 1976 to 1980, when it managed 1.5 percent. The bulk of the employment growth came from land development and from livestock production and forestry. Estate employment declined by about 22 percent, mainly because of the conversion of rubber into the cultivation of oil palm, the technological changes in the rubber industries, and the phasing down of labor use in replanting activities. Oil palm employment contributed about 72 percent of the new jobs generated in agriculture. Productivity growth, measured in terms of value added per worker, in the agricultural sector over the 1970s grew at about 2.4 percent a year, compared with the economywide growth in productivity of 3.6 percent a year. Output per worker in manufacturing, for example, was about 1.9 times that of agriculture in 1970 but by 1980 it increased to almost two-and-half times. (Data in this paragraph are from fourth and fifth plan documents and World Bank, *World Tables*.)

There were numerous distinguishing features of the policies adopted for agriculture and rural development during the 1970s. The "initial conditions" in the Malaysian agricultural sector at the beginning of the 1970s were more favorable than in the preceding decade. A strong foundation for further growth for the major agricultural commodities and the institutional support for the sector were in place and did not seem to be the inhibiting constraint. A great deal of experience had been accumulated in implementing the big land development programs in the 1960s. And there was, by the end of the 1960s, a record of success. Agricultural land and labor were still relatively abundant. So the country entered the 1970s with confidence that further development could be made in agriculture. The NEP essentially did not alter the basic policies of the agricultural sector that had been followed during the 1960s. The broad strategy continued to be one of large-scale land development schemes, which entailed rural migration from the low-productivity and unorganized traditional sectors to the more productive, better-organized modern farms managed by FELDA. The policy measures that were pursued and implemented include land development for the landless laborers, extensive irrigation schemes for rice farmers, and the support programs for replacing old, low-yielding rubber trees with high-yielding varieties.

The approach to the land development by FELDA during the 1970s also remained more or less unchanged. Contractors prepared the land for the settlers who then moved into the settlement schemes. Continuing concern was expressed about the paternalism and anti-self-reliance features of this approach. Yet, even more so than in the previous decade, the mood of rapidly accelerating land development was much more pervasive and these reservations never exercised much influence. A great deal of discussion centered on the capability of FELDA to implement the land development targets for the period of the second plan. The plan had revised the land development target, and had now set it at 1.2 million acres. About 83 percent of the plan's target, more than one million acres of land, was opened up from 1971 to 1975. For the next five years, from 1976 to 1980, about 2.2 million acres of new land were developed, with FELDA responsible for slightly more than two-thirds of the total developed. In this latter period more emphasis was given to the further development of the existing smallholders, than to opening up new lands (Galenson 1980).

While the land development programs were impressive, new policy issues emerged. Many observers were convinced that the land development schemes were becoming too costly to be continued without some modifications to the basic model. A combination of factors had contributed to the rising costs. Apart from the general rise in the cost of inputs that go into land development, FELDA began to face a constraint of the supply of good land and was developing more difficult and relatively inaccessible land. Because land was a state matter—involving power guarded by the state—complications emerged on this score. The other factor, basic to the whole approach, was that FELDA continued to shoulder the entire cost of developing the land for the settlers. Proposals to reduce the costs included the suggestion that the settlers should also share the burden of the costs and should, for example, be brought in earlier to assist in the preparation of the land schemes. The costs incurred include the preparation of the land by private contractors, maintenance costs that were contracted out during the first year, housing, and other amenities. Wage income and, where necessary, a minimum subsistence were provided to the settler before the maturation of the main crop. All this added considerably to the total costs of providing the settler with eight to ten acres of rubber or oil palm per family. Rates of return for the FELDA schemes are relatively high, much higher for the settler than for the government, which implies that the settler was receiving a substantial subsidy (Tan 1982).

The land development policies also raised equity issues. FELDA's substantial expenditures benefited a relatively small number of the landless. Part of the concern had to do with the selection of settlers. Apart from criteria for the selection of the settlers on the basis of age and previous experience in agricultural activities, there was the issue of the source of the settlers. Because land is a state matter, the provision of land for the schemes had to recognize the interests of the state itself. Some preference for settlers from the state supplying the land could not be totally avoided, and some states were reluctant to allow much freedom in recruiting settlers from other states. These were difficult issues, which were usually resolved by a compromise between conflicting interests.

Paddy Farming and the Cultivation of Rubber

Earlier in this study we traced the development of paddy farming and examined the major features of paddy policies. We look now at the changes in policies in this sector. After this, we will examine rubber, mainly its cultivation by the smallholders. In 1970 about 44 percent of the peasants engaged in paddy farming and cultivated rubber; by 1976 that figure had decreased to 29 percent.

RICE. The major measures for paddy farming established during the 1960s were more or less continued in the 1970s; these included the heavy investments in drainage and irrigation and the maintenance of the GMP. Reduction in the high incidence of poverty for paddy farming occurred far more quickly during the latter part of the 1970s and in the early 1980s than in the first half of the 1970s. The incidence declined from 88 percent in 1970 to about 80 percent by 1976, and fell to about 58 percent in 1984 (table 12-3). Why the level remained high by the mid-1970s is not very clear. During the first half of the 1970s about 324,000 acres of paddy land in Peninsular Malaysia were provided with improved irrigation facilities, out of which 272,000 acres were provided with double-cropping facilities. Two major schemes were completed; the Muda Irrigation Scheme was completed in 1974 and the Kemubu Irrigation Scheme in 1975. Both extended the double-cropping acreage in their areas. For the second half of the 1970s, an additional 167,960 acres of land were provided with irrigation facilities for single and double cropping of paddy, in addition to the 143,178 acres of the existing acreage that were already provided with such facilities. A total of 136,800 families benefited from the provision of these irrigation facilities. (Data are from third and fourth plan documents.)

Yields for paddy increased from 50 to 90 percent in the areas where major projects were undertaken. These increases were heavily affected by double cropping. Yields in the nation as a whole for paddy, however, were far below those in these regional schemes. The average yields in Peninsular Malaysia, for example, increased only from 430 *gantangs* (about 5.6 pounds of padi) per acre in 1970 to 470 *gantangs* in 1975. The domestic production of paddy increased from about 1.6 million tons in 1970 to two million tons in 1975 and 1980, representing almost 90 percent of the domestic consumption.

Several paddy farming and poverty issues must be noted because they are relevant in contributing to the poverty story for the 1970s. One obvious point is that understanding of the socioeconomic position of paddy farmers greatly increased during this decade. The reason was simply that more data, information, and studies were made available during this period. The finding that poverty among paddy farmers was as high as it was despite massive drainage and irrigation schemes seemed to surprise and disappoint the government. Several factors were emphasized: the small size of paddy farms, limited double-cropping farming, and tenancy problems were the most frequent. Low yields were a major cause of poverty and better yields were obtained for the well-managed, closely supervised farms that utilized higher-yielding seeds, fertilizers, and pesticides. Availability of credit schemes and extension services were additional favorable factors.

Structural changes in the paddy growing areas, especially the major areas, raised broader policy matters, but these were closely linked to the constraints imposed by the small size of paddy farms. It became increasingly doubtful whether, given the political and economic constraints, paddy farming could continue in the existing form and could be depended upon to alleviate further rural, especially Malay, poverty. Most of the small farms were tenant operated. The growing pressure on the land may be seen from the evidence that in the mid-1960s in the Muda areas about 38 percent of the farms had less than 2.8 acres and were operating about 17 percent of the paddy land, and ten years later the proportion was 47 percent.These trends were accompanied by an increase in the number of paddy farms that were not owner-operated, which suggests that tenants were being displaced by owners who were able to reclaim land that had been previously leased to the tenants. Mechanization also displaced some labor from the major paddy growing areas. Experiments in alternative forms of land ownership and participation by the paddy farmers, however, began to take shape only in the 1980s.

At the same time there was idle land. Shortage of labor was often cited as a reason that land was abandoned; rural-urban migration had been somewhat age-specific; the relatively younger people left the rural for the urban areas. Those that remained behind were in the older age groups. Thus the "aging" of the rural labor force meant that fewer able-bodied men were available to make use of the agricultural land. Sociocultural factors also contributed to the problem of idle land. Islamic inheritance laws impede the transfer of ownership, lead to fragmentation of land, and result in uneconomic-size holdings. Disagreements about land use sometimes led to land being left idle. All of these factors suggest that the real issue was not a shortage of agricultural land in any real sense; rather, it was a matter of getting the proper institutional arrangements to ensure a better allocation of the land to the needy farmers. This process proved much more complex and, therefore, created greater disputes than had simply the opening up of hitherto uncultivated lands.

RUBBER. There are an estimated 2.0 million hectares of land under rubber cultivation in Malaysia, less than one-quarter of which are under estates, and the remainder are run by smallholders (under 100 acres). Production grew at a rate of about 3.0 percent a year over the 1970s. Acreage under the estates has declined consistently in recent years, but there was a rapid increase in the acreage under smallholdings, mainly through the programs of FELDA. (Data are from fifth plan, pp. 300 and following.)

The incidence of poverty of rubber smallholders fell from about 65 percent in 1970 to 58 percent in 1976, but it still accounted for the largest single poverty group, except for the poor classified as engaged in "other agriculture" (table 12-3). By the mid-1980s poverty incidence had fallen to about 43 percent. This decline in the incidence of poverty for the rubber smallholders is impressive. Yet it must be emphasized that the investment made to assist the rubber smallholders was extremely large. So the real question is: why did the incidence remain as large as it did? A number of reasons seem relevant. Rubber prices declined in 1974 and 1975. To meet this decline, the government intervened in the rubber market in the mid-1970s to try to stabilize rubber prices, and a national price stabilization scheme was initiated in November 1974 when the price of rubber fell below M$1.00 per kilo. Measures aimed at curtailing output were implemented by the government to rationalize the supply of rubber. On the international front the government promoted the establishment of the International Rubber Price Stabilization Scheme in cooperation with other members of the Association of Natural Rubber Producing Countries.

But underlying the perennial problem of the instability of rubber prices was the general unattractiveness of the long-term prospects of rubber when compared with other crops. Thus the major policy issue of whether to continue efforts to support rubber became increasingly urgent. It was also at this time that the government undertook a major effort to reexamine the entire agricultural sector and to study strategies and policies for the future. This effort culminated in the formulation of the National Agricultural Policy, which was formally accepted in the early 1980s. Rubber's attractiveness in generating income was being replaced by oil palm. At prices prevailing in the 1970s, oil palm generated much higher revenue than rubber per hectare of land. Oil palm was less labor intensive than rubber and required about half the time to mature. Even the returns to high-technology rubber, on a number of assumptions, were about half that of the return to high-technology oil palm. Returns to low-technology rubber, common on smallholdings, would yield still lower returns when compared with the returns to oil palm. Even so, in the latter half of the 1970s rubber continued to have strong support. The *Third Malaysia Plan, 1976–80* stated that "rubber replanting will continue to be undertaken on a substantial scale" and that "priority will be given to smallholders with holdings of five acres or less." The appeal of rubber was strong indeed.

The government experimented with various forms or models of farm operation for rubber smallholders. The main purpose was to try to get around the constraint imposed by the uneconomic size of holdings of rubber smallholders, a characteristic generally recognized as the main reason for the low yields and low returns to the rubber smallholders. Much emphasis, especially in the latter part of the 1970s, was put on an "integrated approach to agricultural development," which meant providing a package of inputs, including credit, extension services, planting materials, and other subsidies to the smallholders. Much of this effort was directed at trying to support an activity that was declining in a rather unqualified way.

Organizational and Institutional Factors in Alleviating Poverty

Organizations and institutions reflect a combination of complex factors. The basic institutional structure as it evolved in the 1970s spread power and responsibilities. Three central agencies, the Ministry of Agriculture, the Ministry of Lands and Regional Development, and the Ministry of Primary Industries, all played key roles in the agricultural development and poverty alleviation programs. Problems of coordination inevitably emerged. Responsibility for producing rice, for example, was separated from that for its marketing and processing. The Ministry of Agriculture was mainly responsible for the production of rice and other agricultural crops, while primary commodities, such as rubber and palm oil, were the responsibility of the Ministry of Primary Industries. The persistence of such an institutional framework and the dispersal in the sharing of responsibilities meant that the "integrated approach to agricultural development" and to poverty alleviation was difficult, indeed, to implement.

Substantial government intervention and support in agriculture tended to disguise the real costs of the various programs of poverty alleviation. A major proportion of the expenditure by the government in agriculture was for subsidies to assist farmers. The bulk of the subsidies provided by the federal and state governments were for programs that reduce the cost of inputs to the farmer. These subsidies were administered directly through grants of cash or materials, cost-recovery arrangements, or debt forgiveness. They included, for example, the paddy fertilizer subsidy, farm mechanization subsidy, livestock and fisheries subsidy schemes, the storage and milling subsidy for paddy, and the zero rate of interest loans from the Agricultural Bank. Implicit subsidies normally operated through, for example, the absence of cost recovery (drainage and irrigation schemes), abandonment of commercial principles, rescheduling, and debt forgiveness. Data are unavailable to estimate the amount of these subsidies, which undoubtedly were very large during the 1970s. The diffuse institutional arrangements also resulted in administrative inefficiency; for example, in some instances the same household could receive subsidies from different agencies to cover the same thing.

Throughout the 1970s the prevailing official view on the nature of the market mechanism in agriculture ranged from suspicion to outright hostility. This latter view was quite prevalent within the bureaucracy. Marketing and middlemen especially were viewed with suspicion, and it was widely believed that they were exploitive and superfluous to the development of the agricultural sector. There was, however, little accumulated empirical evidence and analysis in Malaysia to either confirm or deny this conventional view of the exploitive middlemen. Several points can be made. First is the simple fact that an impressive network of institutions develops a life of its own and tends to be self-perpetuating. Despite this the institutions apparently did provide visible benefits to some farmers. Whether the benefits were delivered in a way that helped the poorest groups is less clear. Some evidence suggests that the subsidies seemed to have benefited the larger and better-off farmers. Second, the impressive progress made generally in rural and land development apparently convinced the government that other agencies could emulate the efficiency and success of FELDA. FELDA, however, took well over a decade to achieve its position, and had absorbed most of the experienced and dedicated personnel who were available. Third, and most important, the government was persuaded that it had a crucial role in bringing development to the rural areas and that its intervention was necessary to alleviate the poverty of the farmers. Political factors, of course, influenced maintaining the widespread government presence in agricultural development. Disbursing resources to the right constituencies and the patronage system both required an effective institutional network. The development machinery right down to the district level, composed of technocrats and politicians, ensured that the benefits were shared among local politicians who exercised their influence in distributing the benefits of development projects at the district level (Shamsul 1986).

Restructuring of Society

Overview of Progress

We now move on to review the progress that has been made on the second prong of the NEP—the restructuring of society to correct the identification of race with economic function. The two major elements to be considered are employment and ownership of share capital and the associated objective of creating a Bumiputera commercial and industrial community or, more briefly, the development of Bumiputera entrepreneurs. Each of these aspects will be considered in turn.

EMPLOYMENT. The most comprehensive and detailed reporting on the progress in the restructuring of society is contained in the various government five-year development plans and their reviews. Although much has been achieved in this respect, the progress made has not matched the targets. The targets themselves, taking into account all the relevant factors, were, as already noted, exceedingly ambitious. The basic target was that employment in all sectors should reflect the racial composition of the population at all levels. An unusually rapid growth in employment of 4.5 percent each year during the period from 1971 to 1975 provided favorable opportunities for all races and

Table 14-1. Employment by Sector and Ethnic Group in Peninsular Malaysia, 1970, 1975, and 1980
(thousands)

Year and ethnic group	Sector			Total employed	Labor force	Unemployment
	Primary[a]	Secondary[b]	Tertiary[c]			
1970						
Malay	902.3	215.6	359.7	1,477.6	1,608.3	130.7
Chinese	265.4	394.3	383.9	1,043.6	1,122.4	78.8
Indian	154.0	57.1	90.3	301.4	338.7	37.3
Others	12.9	4.7	10.1	27.7	28.6	0.9
Total	1,334.6	671.7	844.0	2,850.3	3,098.0	147.7
1975						
Malay	1,009.2	336.6	509.5	1,855.4	1,975.7	120.3
Chinese	287.3	500.0	515.3	1,302.6	1,397.7	88.1
Indian	167.3	88.6	121.6	377.5	421.8	44.3
Others	12.7	7.5	13.3	34.2	37.2	3.0
Total	1,476.5	932.8	1,157.9	3,567.2	3,823.1	255.9
1980						
Malay	1,020.2	495.4	695.5	2,211.5	2,331.4	119.9
Chinese	306.1	636.0	615.9	1,558.0	1,645.4	87.4
Indian	199.4	105.8	155.5	460.7	498.1	37.4
Others	13.4	7.5	13.3	34.2	37.2	3.0
Total	1,539.1	1,244.7	1,480.6	4,264.4	4,512.1	247.7

a. Argiculture.

b. Mining, manufacturing, construction, and transport.

c. Wholesale and retail trade, banking, public administration, education, health, defense, and utilities.

Source: Malaysia, *Fourth Malaysia Plan, 1981–85.*

for the desired restructuring of employment (table 14-1). Employment grew at about the same average rate for all three ethnic groups. Malays made considerable headway into manufacturing and other nonagricultural sectors, especially mining and trade. Their share of employment in secondary and tertiary activities increased from about 37 percent in 1970 to over 40 percent in 1975. In manufacturing, mining, and trade the Malay share rose from around one-quarter in 1970 to one-third in 1975. The Chinese share declined somewhat.

Indian and Chinese unemployment rates increased slightly while the rate for Malays fell from 8.1 percent to 6.1 percent. Despite these changes Malays still accounted for slightly more than two-thirds of those employed in agriculture. Malays also made a very small advance into the professional and technical occupations—approximately 48 percent of the employed in this category were Malays in 1980 compared with 47 percent in 1970. A large proportion of the Malays were teachers and nurses, however, and the progress made tends to overstate advancements into new activities. Slightly faster restructuring was made in the administrative and managerial category, where the Malays increased their share from almost one-quarter in 1970 to over 30 percent in 1975. Chinese, however, remained dominant in the administrative and managerial occupations and in 1975 still accounted for about 58 percent of the total employed. In the sales and related occupations their share had reached about two-thirds of the total employed. (All data are from the *Fourth Malaysia Plan, 1981–85*)

Employment growth in Malaysia was slower during the second half of the 1970s, 3.7 percent each year compared with 4.5 percent in the first half. The momentum of employment restructuring, however, continued. By 1980 Malays accounted for almost 40 percent of the total employed in the secondary sector. They also continued to increase their share in the tertiary sector. Malays also made some headway into the higher-paying occupations, but remained severely underrepresented in occupations such as engineering, architecture, medicine, and accounting. Thus, there were still imbalances within the major occupational groups, but, unlike in the 1960s, movement was present and evident.

The full achievement of the employment targets would have required massive movements of labor among sectors of the economy. Such massive movements could not occur quickly and painlessly. One implication in particular was essentially impossible. As Malays moved out of agriculture, non-Malays were to move into this sector. In the *Mid-term Review of the Second Malaysia Plan* and in the *Third Malaysia Plan, 1976–80* the target was announced that the Chinese, for example, would account for about 28 or 29 percent of the total employed in the agricultural sector by 1980. This would have meant that approximately 200,000 Chinese would have to move into agriculture. By 1975 the proportion of Chinese was about 19 percent, and remained at that level over the last half of the decade. There was little mention of this performance or target in the fourth plan. The share of Indians did increase from about 11 percent in 1970 to 13 percent in 1980, above the target of about 9 to 10 percent by 1980. The state governments that controlled land were often reluctant to allow a substantial influx of Chinese into the sector, and, therefore, resisted opening up land settlements to Chinese. Also, for most Chinese, returns in nonagricultural activities would have been far more lucrative and attractive. In any event, it was clear that this specific target was quite unrealistic.

Designing and implementing the employment restructuring policies required detailed interpretation of the meaning of employment. This fact was not fully appreciated at the outset of the NEP, but gradually emerged as practical difficulties with implementation became increasingly evident. Such interpretations placed heavy demands on the institutions responsible for implementing the employment policy.

Table 14-2. Ownership of Share Capital (at par value) of Limited Companies, for Selected Years, 1971–85
(millions of Malaysian dollars)

Type of owner	1971 Amount	1971 Share (percent)	1975 Amount	1975 Share (percent)	1980 Amount	1980 Share (percent)	1985 Amount	1985 Share (percent)	Average annual growth rate, 1981–85 (percent)
Malaysian residents Bumiputera	2,512.8	38.3	7,047.2	46.7	18,493.4	57.1	56,701.5	74.5	25.1
Individuals	168.7	2.6	549.8	3.6	1,880.1	5.8	7,679.2	10.1	32.5
Trust agencies	110.9	1.7	844.2	5.6	2,170.4	6.7	5,867.7	7.7	22.0
Total	279.6	4.3	1,394.0	9.2	4,050.5	12.5	13,546.9	17.8	27.3
Other Malaysian residents	2,233.2	34.0	5,653.2	37.5	14,442.9	44.6	43,154.6	56.7	24.5
Foreign residents	4,051.3	61.7	8,037.2	53.3	13,927.0	42.9	19,410.5	25.5	6.9
Share in Malaysian companies	2,159.3	32.9	4,722.8	31.3	7,791.42	24.0	11,259.5	14.8	7.6
Net assets of local branches	1,892.0	28.8	3,314.4	22.0	6,135.8	18.9	8,154.6	10.7	5.9
Total	6,564.1	100.0	15,084.4	100.0	32,420.4	100.0	76,112.0	100.0	18.6

Note: Data are not completely comparable over time.
Source: Malaysia, Fourth Malaysia Plan, 1981–85, and Fifth Malaysia Plan, 1986–90.

For all practical purposes, implementing the policy had to begin with individual enterprises. Problems with rigid enforcement of the employment policy appeared very early in the 1970s. It was clear that some flexibility was needed concerning the location and the nature of the enterprise. An industry or enterprise, for example, located in an overwhelmingly Chinese area would be hard pressed to employ a substantial number of Malays and Indians. Similarly, an enterprise engaged in manufacturing products or providing services not consistent with Islamic teachings would not attract Malays. Thus, flexibility in implementing the employment restructuring policy of the government became a permanent and complex feature, and the targets became more ambiguous and more difficult to achieve.

OWNERSHIP AND ENTREPRENEURSHIP. A wide range of programs and assistance was provided by the government to assist the growth of Bumiputera commercial and industrial enterprises. The belief in the government was widespread that entrepreneurial skills could be taught, and that preferential treatment to fledgling Malay businessmen would facilitate that learning. The programs included training, credit assistance, advisory and extension services, technical assistance, administrative support, and direct government participation in institutions. Training provided by MARA, the National Productivity Center, and PERNAS (National Corporation) for example, benefited approximately 22,170 Bumiputera in 1980 compared with 2,340 in 1973. And Bumiputera increased their share of loan advances from $149.3 million, or 5 percent, in 1971 to $4,780 million, or about one-fifth, in 1980. All other major indicators of support show a similar trend of increasing assistance to Bumiputera businessmen.

As shown in table 14-2, total share capital increased from $6.5 billion in 1971 to $15.0 billion in 1975 and to $32.4 billion in 1980. Thus, between 1971 and 1980 total size of share capital increased almost fivefold. Out of the total net increase of $25.8 billion, about one-third was accounted for during the period from 1971 to 1975. The main message of the table is simply that the share of Bumiputera individuals and trusts increased sharply over the decade, albeit from a very small beginning. Most of this increase was accomplished through trust agencies because individual holdings by Bumiputera increased very slowly. The share of other Malaysians, mainly Chinese, also increased, and, in absolute terms, by a much larger amount ($12 billion compared to less than $4 billion). The share held by foreign residents declined by one-third, but the absolute amount tripled. Again, movement toward the targets was evident, but the share of the Bumiputera failed to reach the announced goal for 1975 and 1980, while that for other Malaysians was exceeded. Clearly, in setting the targets, the decisionmakers had underestimated the difficulties of their achievements. The failure to meet the announced targets added to the frustrations and resentment of many.

Some Details on the Demand and Supply of Bumiputera Labor

We now consider a few specific points on the employment objectives that help to illuminate the complexities of the restructuring process. These points will be briefly stated.

- It was generally assumed, but without much empirical support, that non-Malay employers discriminated against Malays in their employment decisions. A quota system was, therefore, imposed to try to prevent such alleged discrimination. This system had to be enforced with considerable flexibility. The policy led to some tokenism and efforts to meet the quota by hiring Malays for less important positions. Malays were disproportionately represented in the government and military, and non-Malays argued that the quota system should apply to these agencies as well as to private sector activities. Such an arrangement was not acceptable to UMNO or to the Malays in general. The quota idea probably did more harm than good but does illustrate the difficulty of effectively restructuring employment in a short period of time.
- A significant proportion of labor in the estate and mining sectors is recruited by labor contractors. Available evidence suggests that more Chinese and Indians are hired through the contract labor system than are Malays. In these instances it seems clear that the ethnicity of the contractor matters in the choice of the workers.
- Available data suggest that the larger the enterprise, the larger the proportion of Malays employed. Malays in the large firms, however, are usually in nonmanagement positions. The small-scale, family-owned enterprises employ very few workers who are not of the race of the owners. Most of these small-scale operations are run by Chinese. This fact is one of the reasons that the government was concerned about entrepreneurship among Malays.
- Foreign-owned enterprises employed a much larger proportion of Malays than did Chinese-owned firms. During the 1970s, however, all firms were becoming increasingly Malay-intensive. For example, in 1970 there were about seven Malays in each Chinese firm on the average, and by 1979 there were twelve. For foreign firms the number of Malays was much larger, but foreign firms themselves were, of course, much larger.
- The NEP included a major effort to educate more Malays. About 7 percent of the Second Malaysia Plan, 1971–75 outlays were for education and over 16 percent of a much larger third plan went

for education. Enrollment at all education levels increased dramatically, but especially at secondary and university levels. Malay enrollments in Malaysian and foreign universities increased rapidly enough so that by 1980 they were accounting for 40 percent or more of students at these levels. There were, however, three major problems with this education effort.

First, Malays were concentrated in arts and languages, humanities, and Islamic studies programs, and appeared reluctant to pursue science, management, and administration. This changed over the decade, but slowly, so that by 1980 Bumiputera were still concentrated in the former categories. Most people following these programs anticipated government employment upon graduation. The number in government service jumped from 397,000 in 1970 to 710,000 in 1980, an increase of almost 80 percent.

Second, the education problem discussed in the previous chapter—education as a claim to "be something" rather than as a preparation to "do something" continued in evidence. It is also undoubtedly correct to say that the quality of education fell at all levels as enrollments increased, although expenditures rose sharply. Many observers seem to think that, at least at the university level, quality suffered as entrance requirements were lowered and more students were admitted from rural areas, where elementary schools were usually of lower quality. So the best (and wealthiest) students went abroad. All of this meant that the educated product probably deteriorated over the decade, and firms seeking to hire Bumiputera were often disappointed in their capacity.

Third, the economy generated neither the kind nor the number of jobs to satisfy this supply of educated people. The failure of the manufacturing sector to create many new jobs was especially unfortunate, and one reason for the growth in government employment was the slack demand for educated people in the private sector. At the same time, turnover rates among Malays were high, especially for the very good workers, which added to the employer's reluctance to hire and train Bumiputera.

Thus, the record of the 1970s in regard to employment restructuring was somewhat mixed. That there was progress is undisputed, and it is important to emphasize this progress. More Malays than ever before were finding jobs in activities that previously were either closed to them or for which they were ill-prepared. Ever-increasing numbers of Malays were now entering postsecondary schools and graduating with the proper credentials. But the pace of employment—especially occupational—restructuring, seemed slow to the Malays and to the government. The widespread belief—reflected in publications, comments in Parliament, comments by government officials, and so forth—was that employers could and should do far more than they had to increase Malay employment, especially in the higher-paying occupations. Malays, it was believed, still faced barriers to entry and discrimination was still a fact of life. Non-Malay employers, given the variety of constraints they faced, thought that they had done about as much as could have been expected. Additional qualified Malays and more time were required so that employment restructuring could proceed smoothly with minimal dislocations and discontent. All of this occurred during a decade of relatively high growth rates of GDP and of employment. Restructuring the labor force had presented a far more complex task than had been anticipated in 1971.

Some Details on the Restructuring of Ownership

It was abundantly clear in 1970 that foreign interests owned a substantial share of the wealth of Malaysia and that the Malay share was insignificant. Estimates in the *Third Malaysia Plan* place the foreigners' share capital of limited companies at 63 percent, the Chinese at 27.2 percent, Malay and Malay interests at 2.4 percent, and Indians at 1.1 percent. (The rest, 6.90 percent, was allocated to "other.") Table 14-3 gives further evidence of the dominance of foreigners and, to a

Table 14-3. Ownership of Principal Sectors of the Economy, by Ethnic Group

(percent)

	Share owned by				
Sector	Malays	Chinese	Indians	Other	Foreign
Modern agriculture (planted acreage, 1973)					
Rubber and oil palm	21.0	26.3	2.6	7.9	42.2
Coconut and tea	0	19.9	10.8	0.4	68.9
Industry (value of fixed assets, 1972)					
Mining	0.7	35.2	0.1	9.5	54.5
Manufacturing	6.9	32.5	0.8	14.0	45.8
Construction	2.4	85.6	1.4	3.8	6.8
Trade (turnover value, 1972)					
Wholesale	0.8	55.0	2.7	0.6	40.9
Retail	3.6	75.6	6.5	0.2	14.1
Private professional establishments (annual revenue, 1973)	5.3	51.0	11.4	18.4	13.9

Source: Malaysia, *Third Malaysia Plan, 1976–80*, p. 183.

lesser extent, the Chinese. That an important objective of the NEP was to increase the Malay share at the expense of the foreigners is naturally understandable. Accomplishing this, however, was no small task. Several points are relevant to our story.

- Details of the 1990 target of 30–40–30 (Malay, non-Malay, foreign) were difficult to define. Should it apply to all firms, to only new firms; to small, family-owned firms; or only to large ones? Should it apply to Malay-owned firms? If not every company, then which ones? Such questions did not lend themselves to neat answers, and only broad guidelines emerged even as specific questions arose. Although these guidelines were enforced loosely, they caused misgivings among all groups—the Malays, non-Malays, and foreigners. Given the inevitable ambiguity of the targets, they introduced uncertainty into the investment climate, which surely dampened private investment. Given the low level of individual Malay saving and income, and considering their preferences about life-styles, there were many Malays who doubted both the feasibility of the target and its desirability. Others, of course, believed that it was too little and that 1990 was too long to wait for its achievement.
- The government did not wish to frighten away foreign investment, and, after the 1969 riots and the announcement of the NEP, efforts were made to reassure foreign investors of their welcome. Still the rules of the game had changed, and domination by the foreign firm was coming to an end. Foreign investment did begin to decline relative to the 1960s, but the government also had underestimated forms of control, other than ownership, that could be exercised by foreign investors. The government sought to convince everyone that the target would be implemented through growth, and that it was a global one that did not necessarily apply to each firm separately.
- New agencies were established in the early 1970s to encourage and control foreign investments and mergers and takeovers. Firms that wished to avoid Malayization could generally find ways to do so. For example, firms that were directed to restructure sometimes revalued their assets so that the costs to Malay interests were greatly increased, or firms would increase their capital through a special issue for Malays only, and so forth. Foreign firms would often separate their investment interest in Malaysia from their interests in other countries and limit Malay ownership to the company in Malaysia. To seek further control, a new agency with greater power was created by the Industrial Coordination Act of 1975. This act required that manufacturers have a license, and the issuance of the license depended on the firm's meeting

standards of ownership defined by the government. This was a very unpopular act even though it was applied with considerable flexibility. The Chinese business community especially complained, and their complaints increased as the decade wore on.

• Beginning around the mid-1970s, the government policy with respect to foreign firms changed. Takeovers of foreign-owned companies became more common and, indeed, became an integral part of the restructuring strategy. A number of factors contributed to this change in approach. Acquiring established companies was a much faster way of increasing Malay ownership than waiting for new companies to be established, to grow, and then to be restructured. It was apparent as well that the established foreign companies were not restructuring as fast as the government wanted. Acquiring established companies gave the new owners a ready-made and ongoing concern, and the benefits and expertise of the established companies, it was believed, could be transferred fairly quickly to Malays. Finally, the possible threat of competition from the Chinese for the foreign firms probably imparted a new sense of urgency to the new approach.

A number of lessons emerged from a few cases of takeovers of foreign companies. First, while nationalization as such was ruled out, other options were available, if gaining ownership and control are the ultimate objectives. Any such option is, however, costly—economically and politically. The acquisition of a number of major foreign corporations was presented by the government as normal market transactions following the rules of takeover procedures and the relevant legislation. The government was careful not to present these acquisitions as nationalization by a host country, although the foreign interests affected by the takeovers sometimes referred to them as "back door nationalization."

Second, restructuring schemes implemented through takeovers and mergers had implications for the position of the non-Malays—especially the interests of the Chinese. Chinese interests were fairly successful in thwarting the restructuring scheme of some companies that they feared would dilute their own ownership interests. Collaboration between the Chinese and the Malays to acquire foreign-owned companies, although feasible, did not appear, at least on the basis of available examples, to be widely acceptable. There was, rather, competition between both communities to acquire the remaining large foreign-owned companies, and the Chinese were active as well in the corporate takeover game.

Third, though much was achieved by the Malaysians in gaining ownership and control over the economy in the 1970s, no interests seemed satisfied. Foreign interests, although declining in importance, still retained about 43 percent of the share capital of companies in 1980. Each major ethnic group performed differently. Other Malaysians—mainly Chinese—owned about 45 percent, and Malay interests owned only 12.5 percent of the total share capital in 1980. Anomalies had thus appeared well before 1990. The non-Malays had increased their stake above the stipulated 1990 target of 40 percent, the Malays appeared unlikely to attain their 30 percent share, and, on past trends, it appeared likely that the foreign stake would go down below their targeted 30 percent. So by the end of the decade, despite fairly robust growth, the racial imbalances in ownership continued to create misgivings and dissatisfaction.

• A vital part of the NEP was to create an active Malay entrepreneurial class. It was widely believed that part, possibly a large part, of the reason for the failure of the Malays in making much progress in the nonagricultural sectors was their lack of skills, experience, and acumen in business, commerce, and industry. The Chinese, however, were believed to possess an abundance of these characteristics. It was widely argued that the social, religious, and cultural milieu of the Malays was not conducive to equiping them to engage in business, while the reverse was true for the Chinese. It was argued, therefore, that the Malays must catch up with the non-Malays by participating actively in running and managing their own enterprises. Thus, owning and managing their own enterprises would give Malays opportunities to learn how to be entrepreneurs.

At the beginning of the 1970s, the prospects of promoting Bumiputera entrepreneurial development were not bright. The domination of the urban and commercial and industrial life by the Chinese and foreign interests was, as shown above, almost complete. From the beginning of the NEP it was recognized that large-scale support of the government would be necessary if the Malays were to make any headway at all. Government intervention was necessary, therefore, and would have to be sustained. Most of these arguments are also relevant in explaining the rationale for the growth of public enterprises in the 1970s to be considered later.

The government provided support in the form of finance, education and training, consultancy services, and provision of premises and contracts. Several new agencies and banks were established to provide their services. Two aspects of the approach to developing Bumiputera entrepreneurs are especially interesting. It was often argued that the motivation of Malays to succeed in modern business activities was weak. There was optimism that such psychological barriers could be overcome by a heavy dose of government-backed assistance, education, and training. Thus, training programs, apart from the universities, were established with the expectation that they would provide the environment and the training of entrepreneurial skills for the Malays so that they could operate independently in commerce and industry. At the same time there were skeptics who questioned whether entrepreneurs could be produced in the fashion thus described. Entrepreneurship in the Schumpterian sense, this argument emphasized, could not be taught, but emerged from the social and cultural factors of the community. The question was never resolved, but the government remained firmly committed to helping Malay businesses through training.

The other aspect has to do with the performance of the Malay enterprises. There were success stories, but generally the performance of Malay businesses was disappointing. Many failed and many others did not perform well, and seemed to require support indefinitely. The reasons became quite obvious. A large number of the recipients of government assistance were without good managerial or financial skills. The choice of the commercial projects was frequently questionable. Pressures on many of the government agencies to provide assistance to the Malay businesses often led to granting finance to questionable clients. Less than stringent follow-up and professional accounting led to the accumulation of sizable bad debts. In some instances the small Malay businesses even lacked basic accounting knowledge to keep track of the financial position of the business. The granting of patronage and monopolistic positions meant that many Malay businesses were insulated from the pressures of competition.

It is difficult to generalize about the reasons that some of the enterprises were successful. One study suggested that a profile of the successful Malay entrepreneur includes such things as a greater willingness to mix with the other races, an ability to use the English language, and a less strong commitment to Islam (Popone 1980). Some rough data that compare Malay and Chinese businesses show that Malay enterprises earned less income than their Chinese counterparts, started with less capital, and seemed to take more risks than did Chinese businessmen, and that Malay enterprises had more management and financial problems than the Chinese. Agencies entrusted with assisting Malay businessmen were often not adequately staffed with experienced people to provide effective assistance. A study conducted in the mid-1970s showed that almost all these agencies had limited capability in providing relevant advisory assistance to small businesses (Malaysia, Economic Planning Unit 1976). All these problems were compounded by the fact that there was an "anti-small-enterprise" bias in the system of incentives.

So by the end of the 1970s the record of performance by Malay entrepreneurs was mixed. It should be reemphasized that many things were achieved. There were many more Malay businesses in the urban areas; Malays were now engaged in new activities, and in greater numbers in activities where they were once underrepresented. The Malays now had far more visibility in commerce and industry in the urban areas. These achievements had created a small, growing, and influential Malay business class, significantly larger than at the beginning of the NEP in 1971. By the end of the decade, however, there were also major problem areas. To some, in and outside government, the successes seemed modest, indeed, and they were disappointed that, despite the significant support by the government, many Malay businesses had failed. During this period demands and requests for more assistance and protection were increasingly frequent and widespread. Requests came for more finance, easier forms of credit, lengthier grace periods for repayment, more training programs, better business premises, and so forth. Slowly but perceptibly a more critical viewpoint made its presence felt and an alternative approach began to be identified. The view was increasingly expressed that too much protectionism, apart from the other factors, also had to be blamed for the poor performance of the Malay businesses. Malay enterprises lacked self-reliance and they were excessively dependent on the government. The phenomenon of the "Ali-Baba" enterprises began to make its appearance during this period. The term was quite derogatory. The Ali-Baba enterprises essentially involved an inactive Malay partner (Ali), who furnished his name, license, and influence to the enterprise, which was really controlled and managed by a Chinese partner (Baba). These enterprises promoted a rentier Malay class and did nothing to further their business skills and experience. Malay businesses seemed to languish behind a wall of protection and, therefore, did not develop a capacity to learn and to grow. This view gradually became widely expressed toward the end of the 1970s and gathered momentum in the post-1980 period.

So, as with the other objectives of the NEP, the efforts to create a Malay entrepreneur class had a qualified success in accomplishing its target, but simultaneously managed to antagonize a large number of non-Malays, especially as the decade wore on. Although the increasing direct assistance to Malays provided some benefits to some non-Malays, the latter were discontented and claimed discrimination.

Industrialization and the NEP

In late 1968, a few months before the riots of 1969, the Investment Incentive Act was announced. This act represented Malaysia's first serious push toward industrialization. Its two main objectives were to create employment and to diversify the economy. The NEP added a third objective—the participation of Malays in the modern, nonagricultural activities. Because industrialization was so central to the NEP, it is useful to examine its development over the 1970s in some detail.

Incentives and Protection

The Investment Incentive Act of 1968 consisted of the usual array of policies found in many countries at that time—tax holidays for pioneer industries, investment credits for nonpioneer industries, special concessions for export industries, and protection from imports. A free trade zone was established and foreign investment was welcomed. After the riots of 1969, the government also sought ways to convince the investment community that Malaysia was still a politically stable community with solid long-term prospects. In particular the regulations to ensure Malay participation were presented as means to important ends and not as limitations on creating new industrial activity. It was argued that with the NEP in place, manufacturing could be pushed hard without exacerbating the relative differences in wealth and income between the Chinese and Malays.

Protection continued to be modest, but did increase over the decade. As noted earlier, estimates of effective rates of protection for Malaysia in the 1970s are not very satisfactory, but it is fair to say that rates were higher in this period than they were during the previous decade. As Malaysia's balance of payments was generally in good shape, protection could be designed essentially for the purpose of giving domestic industries some time to acquire expertise. There was, however, great variation in the rates of protection among activities, and some negative rates were also present. The idea of import substitution continued to be the major underlying strategy. The bias against exports, inherent in this strategy, was offset somewhat by the free trade zone, and indeed the growth of exports during the 1970s was dominated by those from the zone. Exports from "inland" companies grew much more slowly, and doubtlessly were penalized by the tariff and other import substitution policies.

It is relevant to note that the exchange rate was not used as an instrument of industrialization policy. The Malaysian ringgit appreciated steadily in nominal terms with respect to the U.S. dollar over the decade. The Malaysian wholesale price level rose at an average annual rate of about 6 percent, so the appreciation of the ringgit in real terms was on the order of 8 percent each year. The exchange rate policy was a major factor in accounting for a number of difficulties that appeared as the industrialization policy evolved. Evidently, this development of the exchange rate was inconsistent with the other efforts to protect industry and to encourage exports. The package of policies also did little to encourage employment growth, although all the plans emphasized that labor intensity was a key feature of the industrial strategy.

Some Results of the Industrialization Policy

Manufacturing output grew at an average annual rate of well over 11 percent during the 1970s. GDP averaged almost 8 percent. By the end of the decade, manufacturing made up almost 20 per cent of GDP compared with 13.4 in 1970. The 1980 figure was still low by international standards for a country of Malaysia's level of GDP. Data for employment in manufacturing are suspect, and those that are available for different points over time are hardly comparable. Still, it does seem clear that employment in manufacturing grew rapidly over the decade, probably averaging more than 6 percent a year with some estimates placing the rate at over 7 percent. Available evidence also supports the view that employment growth in manufacturing was higher in the first half of the decade than in the second half.

Manufactured exports increased tenfold in value terms, representing a rate of growth of over 25 percent a year. The export sector probably accounted for at least one-half of the employment growth in the manufacturing sector. The performance is impressive, but illuminates an important issue. The exports originated principally from firms, mainly foreign owned, in the free trade zones. Electronics and textiles were the major items in this boom. The foreign firms in the free trade zones had very few linkages, forward or backward, with the rest of the economy. Not only did they not create a demand for other Malaysian manufactured goods, they also failed to provide an opportunity for learning and technology transfer to local industries. They were also extremely import intensive, and the value-added that they created was almost entirely through employment. This meant that the Malaysian manufacturing activity was largely an appendage, not indigenous, to the "real" economy. It neither induced complementary investments nor helped to create a network of activities related to manufacturing. It was then, as was rubber, vulnerable to world trade fluctuations, so diversification was not very well served.

The industrialization program was considered an important ingredient in restructuring the economy. Tables 12-5 and 14-1 summarize data for the 1970s. Both tables show that the Bumiputera position improved with respect to participation in the nonagricultural, urban sectors. The data do not bring out the fact that the jobs held by Malays were usually in the unskilled category. For example, a survey of manufacturing for 1979 showed that 15 percent of the full-time managerial and professional occupations were held by Malays compared with 71 percent by Chinese. Similarly, Malay-owned firms accounted for about 2 percent of value added in manufacturing in 1981. They also had much lower assets per worker and paid lower wages than did either Chinese- or foreign-owned firms. Given the inherent inertia of an economy, especially with regard to changing basic characteristics such as composition of output, employment, wealth ownership, and so forth, the changes shown in the tables are to be looked upon as "large." As already emphasized, many Malays were disappointed that the changes were not greater, and many non-Malays resented the fact that so many of the government's resources were being used to help one ethnic group.

An unexpected result also appeared by the end of the 1970s. This was the appearance of a strong Malay group that profited enormously from the government program and exercised considerable influence on government policy. Rent seeking became common and complaints of favoritism and overt corruption were frequently heard. Such a development made policy modifications and adjustments more difficult than they had been early in the decade.

The Role of Government

The preceding review has made it evident that the NEP resulted in the government's taking a much more active role in the economy than it had in the years from 1957 to 1970. This increased role covered its conventional activities—land development, education and training programs, building infrastructure, and so forth—and added new activities in industry and commerce. The idea of the government as a "trustee" for Malay interests emerged early in the NEP period. The government would remain the trustee until the individual Malays could take over. This meant that the government began to be heavily and directly involved in establishing and operating productive enterprises. This involvement was made explicit in the *Second Malaysia Plan*. Plan allocations for "commerce" and "industry" amounted to 16 and 14 percent in the second and third plans, respectively. The share of agriculture and rural development came to about 20 percent in both plans. Major problems quickly appeared, three of which may be briefly noted.

- Public enterprises did not perform as well as expected, and substantial losses were incurred. The explanations are well known—ambiguous objectives, political interests affecting choice of managers, considerable monopolistic power, and so forth.
- The direct participation by the government in industrial and commercial activities had some unexpected effects on Malay businessmen. There were frequent complaints that public enterprises were encroaching into areas where Malays already were operating or could easily move into. Instead of complementing Malay efforts, it was argued, the new public companies were competing, and rather unfairly so, with them.
- At the same time no one doubted that the government should

play an active role and that a major portion of the growth in Malay ownership and control of the economy must be through the trust agencies. Tables 14-2 and 14-4 show how the trust and individual Malay holdings developed over the 1970s. The point here is to note that frequently Malay individuals who had been allocated shares by the government or private companies were selling them, mainly through the stock exchange and mainly to non-Malays. Companies then resisted efforts by the government to force them to restructure again to maintain Malay representation.

The Chinese

The NEP was explicitly designed to help the Malay community become more involved in modern, urban activities and to raise its income relative to that of the Chinese and Indian communities. The latter two communities were, of course, affected, sometimes adversely, by the various policies followed during the 1970s. We now consider briefly some of the consequences and reactions of the Chinese, and, to a lesser extent, the Indians.

The data shown in the several tables of this chapter suggest that the Chinese were not heavily penalized by the NEP. Their employment grew as rapidly as did that of Malays, their ownership of share capital increased sixfold, and doubtless their investment in small-scale, individually owned activities grew as rapidly. Ownership of small commercial establishments—retail shops, laundries, photographic studios, travel agencies, beauty salons, and so forth—were as heavily Chinese in 1981 as in 1971 (*Fifth Malaysia Plan*, p. 114). Larger firms—wholesale houses, hotels, cinemas, shipping companies—were, in 1981, as Chinese dominated as in 1971. In many cases it seems clear that the Chinese, rather than the Bumiputera, replaced the foreigners. The new legislation about education and language imposed an inconvenience, but did not appear to impose serious obstacles, to the Chinese continuing their strong economic performance. The Chinese in 1980 still were overwhelmingly dominant among registered professionals (architects, accountants, engineers, doctors, and similar professions). The *Fifth Malaysia Plan* shows that in 1980 over 63 percent of such people were Chinese, 17 percent Indian, and 15 percent Bumiputera. The rate of increase in the number of Bumiputera in these occupations over the 1970s greatly exceeded that of the Chinese and Indians, but in both of the latter communities the growth rate of professionals was well above that of their population. Finally, as was noted earlier, Chinese household income grew strongly in the 1970s, although at a rate somewhat below that of the Malays. Indian household income was a weak third.

Table 14-4. Ownership of Share Capital in Limited Companies in the Manufacturing Sector, 1971, 1975, 1981
(thousands of Malaysian dollars)

Type of owner	1971		1975		1981		Average annual growth rate (percent)		
	Amount	Share (percent)	Amount	Share (percent)	Amount	Share (percent)	1972–75	1976–81	1972–81
Malaysian residents Bumiputera	729.3	43.7	1,808.6	48.7	4,507.5	56.3	25.5	16.4	20.0
Individuals	68.7	4.1	182.9	4.9	486.5	6.1	27.7	17.7	47.9
Trust agencies	—	—	157.3	4.3	493.9	6.2	—	21.0	—
Total	68.7	4.1	340.3	9.2	980.4	12.3	49.2	19.3	30.5
Other Malaysian residents	660.6	39.6	1,468.3	39.5	3,527.0	44.0	22.1	15.7	18.2
Foreign residents Share in	938.6	56.3	1,906.2	51.3	3,449.6	43.7	19.4	10.7	14.1
Malaysian companies	778.4	46.7	1,719.6	46.3	3,231.6	40.4	21.9	11.1	15.3
Net assets of local branches	160.2	9.6	186.7	5.0	268.0	3.3	3.9	6.2	5.3
Total	1,667.9	100.0	3,714.9	100.0	8,007.2	100.0	22.2	13.7	17.0

— Not available.
Source: Malaysia, Department of Statistics (1985).

The evidence, therefore, does not suggest that the NEP either seriously harmed or constrained the Chinese. The reason is partly that the more restrictive aspects of the NEP were enforced with considerable flexibility. Another factor was that the Chinese were so well-established in key sectors of the economy that they were able to adapt quickly and effectively to the new policies and new regulations.

There was another important factor at work. As was argued earlier, the Malaysian government tolerated considerable slack in the economy for fear that a more rapid growth would exacerbate the ethnic imbalances. In the 1970s, with new policies and new regulations in place, the government pushed the economy harder, thereby creating a wider range of opportunities in the economy available for all groups. The Chinese then responded readily and the Indians much less so.

In an important way it was (and continues to be) the Chinese who make the economy go, who make the market work so well in Malaysia. They were effective at all levels—large- and small-scale, production and service activities, financial and trade undertakings. They were especially good middlemen and organizers. They could keep transaction costs low and find ways to take advantage of opportunities and to search out opportunities. These characteristics and capacities were the consequence of history and social arrangements and not of formal training programs. The role of the Chinese was, therefore, crucial to the operation of the NEP, and to the efforts to create opportunities from which the Bumiputera could learn and change. Far from the Chinese being an obstacle to the NEP, they were essential to it. Unfortunately, this contribution was not clearly seen and appreciated, so frequently the Chinese were considered an obstacle and thereby caused antagonism.

It is not surprising, therefore, that there is much evidence that the NEP created considerable ill-will and misgivings among Chinese and Indians. After the riots of May 1969, all groups agreed that some action was necessary—that changes were necessary. The NEP itself and its implementation were generally accepted. As the decade wore on and some of the policies were considered increasingly discriminatory, the early acceptance began to fade, and resentment among non-Malays became more apparent. The resentment was heightened by the evidence, already examined, that the policies failed to produce a Bumiputera group that could manage in the modern sectors without continued large-scale government support. Along with this development was the more nebulous, but perhaps more important, one of the effect on the general atmosphere of the society. The existence of rules and practices that explicitly discriminated against many members of society created, almost inevitably, widespread resentment and antagonisms. At the end of the 1970s the Chinese, and the Indians to a lesser extent, were, therefore, less committed to the basic idea of the NEP.

Both groups began to oppose with greater frequency and greater openness specific policies and regulations that came along in the late 1970s. In this sense, then, the NEP did not contribute to an increasing unification of the society.

Meanwhile the impressive economic performance of the Chinese was essential to the continued strong growth of the economy. Indeed the fact that the Chinese (rather than the Bumiputera as intended) often replaced the foreigner is an important part of the explanation for continued growth through the 1970s. The Chinese were thus essential to the NEP, although its strategy sought to impede them so that the Bumiputera could catch up.

The economic difficulties of the 1980s—discussed in the next chapter—added to these problems as the Chinese became less able to maintain their 1970s growth record. Complex and unpleasant problems were sure to emerge.

Conclusion

This chapter has concentrated on the efforts to "restructure" the economy in such a way that the Bumiputera would become increasingly engaged in modern sector activities. Equity was defined in terms of this increased participation, and it has been demonstrated that restructuring did in fact take place, albeit more slowly and painfully than was originally anticipated. There are three points to make by way of conclusion.

Growth

The discussions surrounding the NEP emphasized equity and implied that some growth might have to be sacrificed. As it turned out, the average growth rate of the 1970s exceeded that of the 1960s by a significant margin—7.9 to 6.5 percent. Both public and private investment rates were higher. Exports in constant and current prices grew faster in the 1970s than in the previous decade. National savings and the balance of payments remained as strong as in the 1960s. Prices rose faster, but there were no dangerous inflationary tendencies evident. Employment grew much better. In short, the economy boomed. This boom occurred despite the fact that the implementation of the NEP introduced considerable inefficiency and "waste." The boom was driven by the high investment rates applied in a fairly undistorted, noninflationary economy. The development of oil and the strong demand for rubber and oil palm not only relieved the balance of payments constraint, but also helped to create a favorable investment climate. So the economy could respond well to the investment. This boom lends support to the view, examined elsewhere, that in the

1960s the government hesitated to push growth for fear it would exacerbate the economic differences between the Chinese and Malays. With the new institutions and policies of the NEP, the government pushed the economy to reduce these disparities.

Equality

Increased equality in the distribution of measured GDP was not an important objective of the NEP. Table 13-1 in chapter 13 shows that income shares of decile groups changed insignificantly between 1970 and 1979. The Gini coefficient also remained essentially unchanged. It is clear, however, that the incidence of poverty was reduced by a significant degree.

There are no firm data to show the change in the average income of Malays relative to that of Chinese. There are data in the third and fifth Malaysia plans that allow such comparisons, but they are of doubtful comparability. These data show that the "disparity ratio" fell from 2.29 to 1.90 over the period. Other bits and pieces of data support the view that there was some catching up by the Malays. Certainly the reduction of the incidence of poverty would have been concentrated on Malays. Available data also suggest that the rural-urban income ratio rose over the period and this lends modest support to the view that the Malay-Chinese income ratio rose. It is possible then to conclude that there was a reduction in the disparity ratio, but not that income was more equally distributed in general.

The General Situation

We have shown many instances of tension and doubts arising from and about the NEP. In loose terms, the NEP did not really seem to "take." There was an artificiality about the NEP because it was imposed from the outside instead of emerging from within the system. The effort to change Malays quickly and drastically proved to be a far more complex process than expected. It often violated deeply held views of the idea of the good life as well as of values and meanings. There were established institutions in place that were, in many ways, incompatible with the objectives and methods of the NEP. History had not prepared either ethnic group very well for the new experience. The productivity of Malays did not increase very rapidly, and the learning process appeared tortuous. The basic approach of the NEP was probably not very effective and, as is discussed later, illustrated many of the inadequacies of development economics at that time.

So, by 1980, there were misgivings and doubts, despite the considerable success. A quick look at the years from 1980 to 1985 will identify more specifically these problems.

15 *1980 to 1985:*
Growth and Equity

Problems were beginning to appear at the end of the 1970s. At the same time, there was little to suggest that in the first half of the 1980s there would be major policy changes and a movement away from the full commitment to the NEP. Yet both of these happened. The UMNO-led coalition (now called Barisan Nasional, National Front, rather than Alliance) continued in power, but there were significant changes in the leadership. The new leadership, unlike the old, was neither associated with the royalty nor had it been educated in Britain. Both the prime minister, who took office July 1, 1981, and the deputy prime minister had been expelled from UMNO in the wake of the riots of 1969 for criticizing the then prime minister. The new leaders were less committed to the NEP and to the prevailing development strategy than had been the previous leaders. As the world recession of the early 1980s began to bite, it was consequently easier for the government to move in new directions. The strong showing of the government in the 1982 elections gave a clear mandate to the policies of the new regime.

The development strategy was increasingly complicated by the appearance of a strong Islamic fundamentalist movement beginning with the 1979 elections. Members of this movement pressured the government to change the constitution to make it more compatible with Islamic law—to create an explicit Islamic state.

This chapter opens with a review of developments from 1980 to 1985, and then discusses the origin and nature of some of the major policy shifts.

Economic Conditions

The period can be conveniently divided into two phases—1980 to 1982 and 1982 to 1985.

Economic Recession, 1980–82

The world recession began in 1980, principally as an immediate consequence of the 1979 increase in oil prices. The growth rate (in constant
prices) of the OECD countries was 2.3 percent in 1981, -0.8 percent in
1982, and 1.3 percent in 1983. The GNP of the United States, again in
constant prices, declined in both 1980 and 1982, and in 1983 was only
2.7 percent higher than it had been in 1979. This slack world market
had an immediate effect on Malaysia's exports. Export earnings had
boomed during the last half of the 1970s, and had continued to grow
at 6 percent in 1980. In 1981 they fell by almost 4 percent and had
barely recouped to 1980 levels by 1982. Prices of all major export items
declined sharply over these years. Imports, however, continued
strongly, especially of capital goods. During these two years, Malaysia
experienced an import surplus on the merchandise trade account,
which had rarely happened since independence. Service payments
also continued high, so the current account turned modestly negative
in 1980 and extremely negative in 1981 and 1982. Foreign exchange
reserves, though still ample by usual standards, began to fall sharply.
For the first time, a balance of payments problem of the conventional
sort appeared in Malaysia. Clearly, the effort to become less dependent on foreign trade—particularly, on a few export items—had not
yet succeeded.

Accompanying the fall in export earnings was an equally sharp fall
in private investment. Table 15-1 shows the strong performance of
this variable in the 1970s and the abrupt fall in the growth rate as the
1980s began. Much of this fall may be associated with the weak export
market. The *Fifth Malaysia Plan* (p. 44) states that oil investment declined by 11.1 percent each year (over the 1980 to 1985 period) while
nonoil private investment grew at 4.4 percent. The plan also attributes
the abrupt slow-down in private investment to "rigidities in the implementation of industrial development strategies, the noncompeti-
tiveness of domestic industries as well as the lack of investment opportunities" (p. 44). There are no data on total foreign investment for
these years, but it does seem likely that it declined as inland investment in the major export commodities became less attractive.

There was thus evident slack in the economy, and the government
responded by a 41.5 percent increase (50 percent in current prices) in
public investment in 1981 and 20.7 percent in 1982. These increases
had the desired effect of preventing declines in the general level of
activity. Much of the public investment was in construction and con-
struction-related activities, so that that sector emerged as a leading
sector in these years and, indeed, over the entire five years. The results, however, of this big push on public investment (coupled with
the fall in commodity export taxes) was a large increase in the public

Table 15-1. Economic Indicators in the 1970s, Fourth Plan Targets, and 1980–85

Indicator	1970s	Fourth plan target	1980–85	1981	1982	1983	1984	1985
Growth rates (percent)								
GDP	7.9	6.4	5.8	6.9	5.6	6.3	7.6	2.8
Agriculture	5.1	4.2	3.4	4.9	6.5	0.6	2.8	3.6
Manufacturing	11.4	6.0	4.9	4.6	3.8	8.2	11.6	-3.0
Construction	9.8	11.6	8.1	14.6	9.8	10.4	4.2	2.0
Private investment	10.6	10.7	1.8	4.1	-2.3	5.8	10.6	-8.0
Public investment	10.6	3.7	12.5	41.5	20.7	10.2	-4.4	0.2
Private consumption	7.4	5.4	3.6	5.1	3.3	3.2	6.5	0.3
Exports and net factor services	—	8.2	8.0	-0.8	10.7	12.3	14.1	4.4
Imports and net factor services	—	7.8	5.5	5.6	13.8	9.0	6.4	-6.1
Commodity exports value	16.7	8.5	6.2	-3.8	3.7	16.6	17.9	-1.4
Commodity imports value	14.9	—	5.6	13.4	9.1	6.1	6.9	-6.7
Balance of payments (millions of ringgets)								
Merchandise	2,224	1,978	2,926	-243	-1,758	1,098	6,913	8.628
Service	—	-7,849	-8,456	-5,312	-6,576	-9,098	-10,566	-10,728
Current account	—	—	—	-5,633	-8,049	-8,026	-3,743	-2,230
Government finance (millions of ringgits)								
Current account	239	—	376	120	19	234	999	508
Overall account	-486	—	-8,888	-11,015	-11,170	-9,182	-7,075	-5,998
As share of GDP								
(percent)	0.04	—	14.00	19.70	18.70	14.00	9.50	8.20
Consumer price index	5.9	4.5	4.6	9.7	5.8	3.7	3.9	0.3
GDP deflator	7.0	—	2.0	0.1	2.8	4.8	5.9	-4.2

— Not available.

Source: Compiled from Malaysia, Department of Statistics (1986).

sector deficit, another new phenomenon for Malaysia. The deficit reached almost 20 percent of GDP in 1981 and 1982, which led to a sharp curtailment of the growth of government outlays in later years.

Note that the growth rate of real GDP remained respectable throughout these years. It fell compared with the 1970s, but was still right behind the growth rates of Korea, Singapore, and Hong Kong and above all other countries in Malaysia's income category. The fall from 7.9 percent in the 1970s to 5.8 percent in the first half of the 1980s did, of course, constitute a sizable decline. The rate of growth of consumption over the five-year period fell by about one-half, mainly because its 1985 growth was negligible. So, although the growth rate remained respectable, it was also noticeably smaller than in the 1970s. Government's quick action in 1981 did much to keep the economy moving. It was, therefore, the balance of payments deficits, private investment decline, and government budget deficits, not slow growth, that created the view that there was something fundamentally wrong in the system. Before considering what, if anything, was wrong, a brief look at the period from 1983 to 1985 is helpful.

More Recession, 1983–85

With exceptions here and there (for example, agriculture) things picked up in 1983 and 1984. Private investment came back, especially in 1984, as did foreign exchange earnings and the current account of both the balance of payments and the government budget. The following year, 1985, however, proved to be the worst of all. Per capita GDP declined in 1985 relative to 1984, and other variables—private investment, manufacturing, exports, and so forth—all turned abruptly and sharply down. The balance of payments remained reasonably safe, but only because commodity imports declined by almost 7 percent and the inflow of foreign capital continued. The short recovery in 1983 and 1984 and the sharp fall in 1985 seemed to convince a wide spectrum of people that something was basically wrong with the Malaysian economy.

Structuralism

It was in 1980 that the question of structural problems in the Malaysian economy began to appear. The basic issue was whether there were entrenched characteristics of the economy that placed hitherto unrecognized constraints on growth and development. These characteristics are distinct from those that produced the cyclical movements that had long plagued the economy. Overcoming these latter problems had led to the efforts to diversify, especially with respect to exports. Structural difficulties, however, referred instead to those characteristics that are inherent in a society. If such characteristics are to be changed, then the society must be changed, which is no small undertaking.

The evidence offered to support this view took many forms. Private investment had not shown much sustained dynamism. The public sector had had to carry much too large a share of the investment, and had had to act in a much too paternalistic fashion. Growth in productivity and yields in smallholder agriculture, especially rubber and paddy, seemed slow to take off. The available supply of good land was diminishing, even while idle land appeared. Manufacturing was heavily concentrated on a few industries, and the export of manufactures was concentrated on even fewer industries in the free trade zones. Labor shortages in agriculture and unemployment among the educated in urban areas were becoming familiar to observers. These developments and the available data suggested that the economy was being pushed into directions in which most of society could not, or did not wish to, go. The transformation problem became increasingly evident—that is, the capacity of economic agents to respond quickly and effectively to new opportunities, to perceive new opportunities, to create new opportunites, to appreciate the advantages of adjusting to a new environment, and so forth did not seem adequate to meet the challenge. Entrepreneurship is also part of this transformation notion. The government, especially the prime minister, began to urge a change in attitudes and in work habits and the development of "progressive values" in an effort to achieve higher rates of growth of productivity and a more competitive system. At the same time, the *Fifth Malaysia Plan* stressed the importance of "harmony between the material and spiritual aspects of development." Values such as trustworthiness, responsibility, diligence, discipline, and cooperation are used in the plan in a way that clearly indicates that they are not simply political rhetoric. As these basic changes were pushed, possibly because they were pushed, a formidable Islamic fundamentalism began to appear as well. Consequently, an enormously complex process seemed to have been set in motion, which created many management problems that were different from those experienced in either of the two preceding decades.

Changes in Policy and Strategy

The early 1980s was a favorable time for a rather fundamental review of development. Economic events just described convinced many that new policies were essential. Both the political leadership and the political and social milieu were such that changes seemed not only possible, but, indeed, necessary if political and social stability and continued growth were to be maintained. This section examines some of these changes and their underlying rationale.

The Change in Emphasis from Equity to Growth

The single most important policy change was a reduction in the weight the government placed on equity and the increased attention given to growth. Prior to 1980 such a shift in emphasis would have been quite unthinkable, but with the ascendancy of Prime Minister Mahathir in 1981, a more critical review of the NEP became possible. Dr. Mahathir's views on development were fairly well established before the recession began, but the economic difficulties gave him a much stronger and more convincing reason to give renewed attention to growth.

The *Mid-term Review of the Fourth Plan* stated in 1983 that "the Government will continue to put emphasis on raising the rate of growth of the economy as growth is a necessary condition for making further progress on the objectives of the NEP." The *Fifth Malaysia Plan*, published in early 1986, states that "The emphasis of development for the second half of the 1980s will be based on growth with stability. At the same time, in view of resource constraints, increased efforts will be made to mobilize resources and improve efficiency" (p. 20). It was further emphasized that the government would not borrow as it had in the early 1980s, because such borrowing was incompatible with financial stability. Financial stability includes balance of payments strength as well as the government budget position and the price level. This is very different from the language of the second and third plans of the 1970s. In particular, the emphasis on financial stability harks back to the 1960s.

Partly as a consequence of the weight given to "financial stability" and partly for other reasons, questions were increasingly raised about the large role that government had played in the growth of the 1970s. The "other reasons" were concerned with the social dangers of paternalism and the great advantages of personal independence, responsibility, and hard work. There were also complaints about the bureaucracy and an increased willingness to publicize its shortcomings. Public enterprises came under closer scrutiny, some of those that chronically lost money were closed, and others were pressured to earn their own way or be closed. Growth was to be emphasized and it was to be driven by the private sector. All of these views, again, were very different from those of the 1970s.

There is no evidence that anyone argued that growth itself would serve equity. The arguments for growth were not that growth and equity went hand in hand, but rather that growth must come first and distribution later. This view became entrenched in late 1986 when revised estimates made it evident that GDP in real terms had actually

Table 15-2. Consolidated Public Sector Expenditure and Financing, 1980–85

(millions of ringgits)

Item	1980	1981	1982	1983	1984	1985	Cumulative 1981–85
Total federal revenue	13,926	15,806	16,690	18,608	20,805	21,861	93,770
− Federal current expenditure	13,617	15,686	16,671	18,374	19,806	21,353	91,890
− Federal current surplus	309	120	19	234	999	508	1,880
+ States' current surplus	999	909	1,512	1,432	1,237	957	6,047
+ NFPES current development expenditure	2,504	2,826	3,423	4,306	5,005	5,955	21,515
− Public sector current surplus	3,812	3,855	4,954	5,972	7,241	7,420	29,442
− Net public sector development expenditure	10,022	15,284	16,315	17,048	17,172	14,512	80,331
− Overall deficit	6,210	11,429	11,361	11,076	9,931	7,092	50,889
Percentage of GNP	12.0	20.5	19.0	16.8	13.3	9.7	16.3
Sources of financing							
Net foreign borrowing	1,590	4,235	6,580	7,131	5,351	2,866	26,163
Net domestic borrowing	3,650	4,259	6,497	5,198	4,314	3,955	26,163
Assets and special receipts	+970	+2,935	−1,716	−1,253	+266	+468	n.a.

n.a. Not applicable.

Note: + indicates drawdown from reserves; − indicates buildup in reserves.

Source: Malaysia, Ministry of Finance, various documents.

declined in 1985. Given these views and the state of the economy, attention became focused on the specific policies themselves.

Structural Adjustment

As it became evident in 1982 and 1983 that the recession was more severe than first thought and the economy less able to ride it through, the government began to cut back on development outlays. Although the World Bank and International Monetary Fund pushed their conventional restructuring package, Malaysia did not formally accept that package and the conditions that its acceptance would impose. It did, however, proceed with its own version of adjustment. As table 15-2 shows, public sector development expenditure (in current prices) increased slightly in 1983, remained constant in 1984, and fell 15 percent in 1985. Consequently, the overall deficit of the government was less than 10 percent of GDP in 1985 compared with 20 percent three years earlier. The pruning was severe and abrupt. These cutbacks began at a time when inflationary pressure was essentially absent, exports were resuming their strong growth, and foreign exchange reserves were rising. The concern, therefore, seemed to have been with the idea of a government deficit, as well as its presumed effect on the values and the personal characteristics of the members of the community rather than with the economic consequences of the deficits.

Most of these reductions fell on the federal government, and the expenditures of the large state-owned and -controlled enterprises continued very much as in the past. The operation of some of these units actually yielded a surplus that helped to reduce the government deficit. The government's operating budget was also difficult to reduce because so many expenditures—salaries, debt service, pensions, and so forth—were more or less inflexible in the short run. The adjustment burden, therefore, fell primarily on direct development expenditure by the government.

Finally, there was a relaxation of the NEP conditions that had accompanied approvals from new industrial activities, especially those that applied to foreign investment. The government apparently was convinced that foreign investment was necessary if growth were to be maintained without large-scale government help. This view was supported by the fact that by 1985 estimates showed that foreign interests controlled only about one-quarter of share capital—well below the 1990 target of 30 percent. The new policies essentially granted complete ownership to foreign manufacturing enterprises on condition that they were "sufficiently" export oriented. Also the "exemption threshold" above which NEP requirements concerning ownership, work force, and so forth had to be met was raised from $250,000 or more than twenty-five workers to $2.5 million or seventy-five workers. This naturally freed a large number of firms from any pretense of complying with the NEP objectives. Similarly, there was a relaxation of efforts on takeovers, mergers, and so forth. In the manufacturing sphere, therefore, there was an explicit backing away from the NEP in an effort to get private investment moving.

National Agricultural Policy

In the *Mid-term Review of the Fourth Plan* (Malaysia 1984), the argument was made that the government role in agriculture had been excessive and that the private sector must contribute more in this sector. Commercialization of agriculture and the need to increase yield in traditional crops and develop new crops for export were stressed. Specific emphasis was placed on cooperative farming. These cooperative farms were to be organized on an estate basis and supported by modern plantation management. Indeed modern management was seen as an important factor in the success of cooperative farming. The government (Malaysia 1984, p. 14) stressed that:

> Large scale, organized and commercialized farming through the creation of a co-operative system of farming will be adopted as a key element of the agricultural development strategy.

> The emphasis on a system of co-operative farming will be an important element in the new strategy for agricultural and rural development in the coming years. In view of the structural changes, there is a need to promote co-operative farming by consolidating farm holdings and managing them on an estate basis. The major structural changes include the emergence of a shortage of labour in certain areas, idle land, ageing of the labour force in agricultural occupations, constraints imposed by the small size of agricultural holdings and the shortage of agricultural land.

Another new element was also added to rural development, the idea to "amalgamate scattered villages to form organized settlements to enable it to provide services and facilities." This approach, it was argued, would reduce the costs of providing basic services to rural communities and to exploiting idle land on a cooperative basis. Meanwhile the importance of nonfarm income was recognized, and rural industries and other activities were to be promoted to supplement the farmers' income. These new approaches to agriculture and rural development were a response to some of the traditionally intractable problems—land size and low productivity in smallholdings—and to newly appearing problems in agriculture such as idle land, shortage of labor, and the aging agricultural labor force. These new approaches are similar in form and content to the FELDA model and to estate agriculture. The idea obviously was to try to create the advantages of the large-scale operations in an environment of small-scale farmers through cooperatives.

There were problems, however. The costs of land development were rising and labor problems were becoming increasingly complex. Special difficulties arose because educated youth were increasingly unwilling to work on farms or even to remain in rural areas. There had been, for some years, various forms of cooperative schemes and a mixture of incentive and payment schemes that had met with mixed success. The problems of organization, land fragmentations, and the reluctance to give up ownership of land remained strong and made cooperatives extremely difficult to arrange. The government, although committed to private sector agriculture, was reluctant to go all out to induce search for productivity growth and for new rural activities through policies that made such efforts profitable. The strength of a traditional approach to the land remained powerful, indeed.

Industrial Development

Both the fourth and fifth plans emphasized a rapid expansion of manufacturing as a leading sector to provide an overall dynamism to the economy and to create a major source of employment. In the plan documents and associated other material, there is evidence that policy formulation was based increasingly on an "outward-looking" strategy. Manufacturing output growth over the years from 1981 to 1985 averaged 4.9 percent a year, which was short of the *Fourth Malaysia Plan* target of 6 percent, but the failure was largely a consequence of a 3 percent decline in output in 1985. A modest 3 percent growth in that year would have enabled the target to be reached. Exports of manufactured products doubled in value between 1980 and 1985, and their share of total exports increased from 22 percent in 1980 to 32 percent in 1985. The 14.3 percent growth rate still fell short of the *Fourth Malaysia Plan* target of 19.1 percent. Employment growth averaged 1.9 percent a year—hardly a figure that would contribute much to solving the employment problem. As noted earlier, most of the exports were from free trade zone companies and were dominated by textiles and electronics. Bits and pieces of evidence on productivity growth suggest that productivity growth remained low while wage rates were rising in most inland manufactures. Clearly this sector was not doing what was expected of it.

A review of industrial policies was completed in 1982. This review confirmed that the incentives—tax holidays, investment tax credit, and similar arrangements—were having only modest effects and that protection of domestic industrial activities was higher than was generally recognized. Data for the five years from 1981 to 1985 show that about 36 percent of manufacturing investment projects that were approved received incentives, but this 36 percent accounted for over 70 percent of the proposed total investment, so the relatively small-scale projects were rarely included within the incentive schemes. An Industrial Master Plan, completed in 1985 (UNIDO 1985), urged greater emphasis on natural resource-based activities—wood, petroleum, and so forth.

The exact source of the difficulties in manufacturing is hard to pinpoint. The bureaucracy was often accused of being sluggish in implementing new policies. By the 1980s a variety of protected and subsidized activities had become established, and these activities could be penalized if changes were made. The emergence of a small Bumiputera industrial group with great political power made it especially difficult to change the policies—for example, to restructure tariffs or to remove financial support—that had permitted them to come into existence. The government was no longer as free to act as it had been in 1970 after the trauma of the race riots.

The main difficulty was surely something else. The small-scale activities were not helped by the incentives package; yet, it is these very activities that were the most consistent, and the most compatible, with Malaysia's own resources, skills, and social and cultural environment. Foreign investors and large-scale, government-supported industrial projects sought to impose on both the economy and the society production processes and organizations that could not be readily adapted to the Malaysian environment. This is the basic reason that the firms in the free trade zones had so few links with the inland economy, and the large government-supported firms had and continued to have such low productivity. These are again the transformation capacity, entrepreneurial, life-style issues. New industries needed to adapt to the environment that these characteristics created (Cernea 1985).

The single most important policy instrument for the encouragement of manufacturing was the exchange rate. As already shown, the Malaysian ringgit appreciated over these years, thereby reducing protection and incentives to search for export opportunities. A policy package dominated by an "undervalued exchange rate," common tariff rates, and little foreign investment would, it is argued, lead to the emergence of a truly indigenous manufacturing sector. This point has been made before, and further elaboration will be postponed until later. Here it may be noted that, as in agriculture, the government, though explicitly committed to a more market-oriented strategy, found it difficult to move aggressively in that direction.

Privatization

The NEP called for a far greater government role in the economy than it had previously played. As the NEP was downplayed and growth was emphasized, the government began to dispose of some of its investments. Privatization was expected to accomplish a number of objectives, from reducing the financial burden on the government to increasing competition, efficiency, and productivity growth. Some even argued that privatization would contribute to the NEP objective of restructuring the economy.

In the middle of the 1980s, privatization was just beginning. The container terminal of Port Klang had been sold to private interests. The Telecommunications Department, the national airline, and the Malaysian International Shipping Corporation all had been partially privatized by the middle of the decade, as had the overhaul and maintenance activities of the Ministry of Defense. Other government organizations have been identified for sale to the private sector in the immediate future.

There is as yet little evidence of the actual impact of these efforts at privatization. Problems with implementing the broad policy have, of course, appeared (Soenarno and Yusof 1985). Opposition has come from those directly affected employees and the labor unions, both of whom fear that privatization might result in reduced advantages of one kind or another. Constraints were, therefore, placed on the companies that took over. The two most important constraints were that employees were to be allowed to choose either the government wage and tenure plan or that offered by the new company, and that company was forbidden to discharge workers. Others worried that competition would not be adequate to keep product prices from rising, and hence the position of the low-income groups would be further jeopardized. Talk of privatizing health, water and electricity, even education added to the fears that social welfare was being penalized merely to cater to private interests. The outcome of all this was not clear in the mid-1980s, but it appeared likely that the government would remain sufficiently involved in the economy that few wholesale changes in existing practices would occur.

Malaysia, Inc., and the Look-East Policy

Bureaucracy is often described as a major hindrance to the rapid development of the private sector. The purpose of "Malaysia, Inc.," inspired by the Japanese experience, was to create a milieu of cooperation between the public and private sectors to replace the traditional confrontation and suspicion. The view was advanced of the nation as a company with government, business, and labor all holding shares and all committed to the success of the company. In many ways Malaysia, Inc., became a buzz term to encourage the change of attitudes and work habits and to encourage cooperation.

The business community used the notion to urge the government to respond the way business wished and, in particular, to deregulate in various ways. Actual changes have been few because, as in all governments, bureaucratic habits and routine usually change slowly, and exhortation can play only a limited role in effecting such change. Similarly, as noted in other connections, there existed in the early 1980s a new rich and powerful group that had achieved status through the regulations and, therefore, opposed their removal. Marked change would be slow.

Along with Malaysia, Inc., there was a similar notion—Look East—and its implied corollary—Stop Looking West. This notion was pushed hard by the prime minister himself in various situations (Mahathir 1984). Mahathir has been strongly critical of Western domination of the East, as well as of the aping of various aspects of Western culture by Malaysians. Instead, he has urged that Malaysians look East, where "values, work ethics, and management practices that stress hard work, loyalty to the enterprise, dedication and the need to be self reliant through the individual's own hard work, determination and initiative prevail" (Mahathir 1984, p. 31). Organization and discipline were stressed often.

On the surface such an approach seemed to be saying that all that is necessary for development is hard work. There is, however, a more convincing and fundamental point. Values, culture, and heritage matter and are deep-seated and resistant to change. Growth and modernization require changes, however, and the economic success of Japan and Korea, achieved at the same time that they have maintained a commitment to their really basic values, seemed to be a reliable guide to follow, or at least to try to follow.

Islamic Resurgence and Development

In the latter part of the 1970s there appeared unmistakable evidence of a strong resurgence of Islam, and, in particular, the more extreme forms of Islam usually identified as Islamic fundamentalism. Many reasons for this development could be cited, but a full, unambiguous understanding is impossible. Two arguments, however, are important to our story. In the first place, the strong push toward "modernization," including the pressures to change values, life-styles, and sources of meaning, caused many Malays to claim that the entire idea of "development" was un-Islamic and, therefore, to be rejected. In the second place the rise of Islamic fundamentalism led the government to do a number things that it surely would not have done in the absence of such a resurgence. These included establishing an Islamic Development Bank and an Islamic Insurance Scheme and giving considerable attention to the dissemination and absorption of Islamic values. In 1982 the president of the Moslem Youth Movement of Malaysia, an important Islamic organization, joined UMNO. He was subsequently appointed a deputy minister in charge of the Islamic Affairs Section and, still later, became the minister of education. The *Fifth Malaysia Plan* contains a strong statement to the effect that "Material development alone at the expense of spiritual needs of man will be detrimental to the well being of the Malaysian society" (p. 44). The same paragraph also states that "religious extremism in any form cannot be tolerated at all." (There is a fine literature on this general subject: Kua 1983; Saravanamuttu 1983; Roff 1967; Nagata 1979, 1980, and 1984; and Muzaffar 1987 are especially illuminating.)

The full impact of this resurgence was not clear at the end of our period. In part it is responsible for the emphasis on exhortation on the one hand and the hesitancy in taking strong action on the policy front on the other. As noted earlier, it has affected the continued attention to land development, and some analysts suggest that the emphasis on free trade zones was, in some part, an effort to separate these modern, alien activities from the genuine Malay society. More generally, it makes more urgent the task of finding ways to fit the development process to the institutional, cultural, and social environment, as well as to the factor endowment. Such a fitting will not only help maintain harmony and thereby add to social welfare, but also contribute to the more narrow economic objective of raising productivity (Cernea 1985).

Equity and the Changed Strategy

The reduced play given to the NEP of course did not mean that its objectives were completely neglected. It was noted at the outset of this chapter that the new emphasis on growth did not arise from any notion that growth itself would lead to restructuring and a more equal distribution of income and wealth. Rather the notion was that growth was necessary before these objectives could be achieved. The final task is to examine briefly what did happen over these years to poverty, distribution of income, and to equity more generally. The main conclusion is a simple one, but of considerable interest: the various measures and criteria of equity show little difference in their pattern of change over these years relative to earlier years.

Poverty

Table 15-3 shows the incidence of poverty for 1970, 1976, and 1984. The years are not completely comparable, but the direction and general orders of magnitude are surely correct. The reduction between 1976 and 1984 is larger than seems likely, given the growth rate over these years (7.0 percent) compared with that over the years from 1970

Table 15-3. Incidence of Poverty in Rural and Urban Areas in Peninsular Malaysia, 1970, 1976, 1984 (thousands of households)

Area and sector	1970 Total households	1970 Total poor households	1970 Incidence of poverty (percent)	1976 Total households	1976 Total poor households	1976 Incidence of poverty (percent)	1984 Total households	1984 Total poor households	1984 Incidence of poverty (percent)
Rural	1,203.4	705.9	58.7	1,400.8	669.6	47.8	1,629.4	402.0	24.7
Rubber smallholders	350.0	226.4	64.7	126.7	73.8	58.2	155.2	67.3	43.4
Paddy farmers	140.0	123.4	88.1	187.9	150.9	80.3	116.6	67.3	57.7
Estate workers	148.4	59.4	40.0	28.0	—	—	81.3	16.0	19.7
Fishermen	38.4	28.1	73.2	28.0	17.6	62.7	34.3	9.5	27.7
Coconut smallholders	32.0	16.9	52.8	19.3	12.4	64.0	14.2	6.6	46.9
Other agriculture	144.1	128.2	89.0	528.4	275.4	52.1	464.2	158.8	34.2
Other industries	350.5	123.5	35.2	510.5	139.5	27.3	763.6	76.5	10.0
Urban									
Agriculture	—	—	—	24.8	10.0	40.2	37.5	8.9	23.0
Mining	5.4	1.8	33.3	4.5	0.5	10.1	7.8	0.3	3.4
Manufacturing	84.0	19.7	23.5	55.3	9.5	17.1	132.3	11.3	8.5
Construction	19.5	5.9	30.2	34.7	6.1	17.7	86.6	5.3	6.1
Transport and utilities	42.4	13.1	30.9	53.2	9.1	17.1	73.9	2.7	3.6
Trade and services	251.3	45.4	18.1	242.2	33.7	13.9	472.7	21.9	4.6
Activities not adequately defined	—	—	—	116.1	26.0	22.4	180.9	30.9	17.1
Total	1,606.0	791.8	49.3	1,931.4	764.4	39.6	2,621.1	483.3	18.4

— Not available.

Source: Malaysia, Department of Statistics (1970, 1977); and *Household Income Survey, 1984.*

to 1976 years (7.9 percent). The most important results of the table
are the estimates for 1984 of poverty among the rubber and coconut
smallholders and the paddy farmers. While the incidence of poverty
was more than halving in the urban areas and in the economy as a
whole, it declined by about one-quarter in these traditional sectors.
Investment was naturally very large in the sectors, yet they responded
only moderately. These activities continued to be difficult areas to
change.

Income Distribution

Table 15-4 compares income growth of the various ethnic groups in
1979 and 1984. The Bumiputera continued to catch up with the
Chinese and to greatly outdistance the Indians. Rural incomes grew
more slowly than did urban incomes. Because in those years most
rural people were Malays and urban people non-Malay, it is a bit

**Table 15-4. Monthly Household Income by Ethnic Group,
for Peninsular Malaysia, 1979 and 1984**

(ringgits)

Category	Constant 1970 prices			Current prices		
	1979	1984	Average annual growth rate, 1980–84 (percent)	1979	1984	Average annual growth rate, 1980–84 (percent)
Bumiputera						
Mean	296	384	5.3	492	852	11.6
Median	197	262	5.9	237	581	19.6
Chinese						
Mean	565	678	3.7	938	1,052	9.8
Median	373	462	4.4	620	1,024	10.6
Indian						
Mean	455	494	1.7	756	1,094	7.7
Median	314	347	2.0	521	770	8.1
All ethnic groups						
Mean	417	494	3.4	693	1,095	9.6
Median	263	326	4.4	493	723	8.0
Urban						
Mean	587	695	3.4	975	1,541	9.6
Median	361	463	5.1	600	1,027	11.3
Rural						
Mean	331	372	2.4	550	824	8.4
Median	222	269	3.9	369	596	10.1

Source: Malaysia, Department of Statistics (1980a) and *Household Income Survey 1980
1984.*

Table 15-5. Employment by Sector and Ethnic Group, 1980 and 1985

Sector	1980					1985				
	Bumiputera	Chinese	Indian	Other	Total	Bumiputera	Chinese	Indian	Other	Total
Agriculture[a]										
Thousands	1,396	313	185	15	1,910	1,428	318	188	17	1,953
Percent	73.1	16.4	9.7	0.8	100.0	73.2	16.3	9.6	0.9	100.0
Mining and quarrying										
Thousands	27.2	43.8	8.5	0.6	80.1	21.3	32.5	6.0	0.7	60.5
Percent	33.9	54.7	10.6	0.8	100.0	35.2	53.7	9.9	1.2	100.0
Manufacturing										
Thousands	308.8	380.8	60.7	4.8	755.1	352.7	394.1	75.4	5.8	828.0
Percent	40.9	50.4	8.0	0.6	100.0	42.6	47.6	9.1	0.7	100.0
Construction										
Thousands	105.6	144.3	17.3	3.0	270.2	147.7	206.4	20.8	3.8	378.7
Percent	39.1	53.4	6.4	1.1	100.0	39.0	54.5	5.5	1.0	100.0
Electricity, gas, and water										
Thousands	20.8	3.0	7.0	0.2	31.0	27.1	3.5	9.1	0.2	39.9
Percent	67.1	9.7	22.6	0.6	100.0	67.9	8.8	22.8	0.5	100.0
Transport, storage, and communication										
Thousands	110.2	73.3	24.9	1.1	109.5	147.3	88.5	28.3	0.8	264.9
Percent	52.6	35.0	11.9	0.5	100.0	55.6	33.4	10.7	0.3	100.0
Wholesale and retail trade[b]										
Thousands	249.5	373.9	50.1	2.7	676.2	323.3	460.4	60.1	2.5	846.3
Percent	36.9	55.3	7.4	0.4	100.0	38.2	54.4	7.1	0.3	100.0

	1980					1985				
Sector	Bumiputera	Chinese	Indian	Other	Total	Bumiputera	Chinese	Indian	Other	Total
Finance^c										
Thousands	28.9	43.3	5.8	0.3	78.3	38.8	55.0	7.4	0.4	101.6
Percent	36.9	55.3	7.4	0.4	100.0	38.2	54.1	7.3	0.4	100.0
Government services										
Thousands	389.2	195.8	64.2	9.0	658.2	506.0	221.6	81.8	10.1	819.5
Percent	59.1	29.7	9.8	1.4	100.0	61.7	27.1	10.0	1.2	100.0
Other services										
Thousands	87.9	42.3	15.3	1.9	147.4	108.7	46.3	18.8	2.1	175.9
Percent	59.6	28.7	10.4	1.3	100.0	61.8	26.3	10.7	1.2	100.0
Total employment										
Thousands	2,275.0	1,613.9	439.1	38.9	4,816.9	3,101.7	1,826.6	496.2	44.0	5,468.5
Percent	56.6	33.5	9.1	0.8	100.0	56.7	33.4	9.1	0.8	100.0
Labor force										
Thousands	2,921.3	1,679.4	468.1	40.1	5,108.9	3,397.3	1,931.9	541.6	46.3	5,917.1
Percent	57.2	32.9	9.1	0.8	100.0	57.4	32.6	9.2	0.8	100.0
Unemployment										
Thousands	196.3	65.5	29.0	1.2	292.0	295.6	105.3	45.4	2.3	448.6
Percent	67.2	22.4	10.0	0.4	100.0	65.9	23.5	10.1	0.5	100.0
Unemployment rate (percent)	6.7	3.9	6.2	3.0	5.7	8.7	5.5	8.4	5.0	7.6

a. Includes forestry, livestock, and fishing.

b. Includes hotels and restaurants.

c. Includes insurance, real estate, and business services.

Source: Malaysia, Department of Statistics (1980a, 1980b).

puzzling that Malay income grew faster than did non-Malay. If these estimates are about right, Malay urban income grew much more rapidly than Malay rural income. The catching up by the Malays was slight, however, and the Chinese incomes remained about 75 percent higher on the average than those of Malays.

Median incomes grew more rapidly than mean income for all ethnic groups and in both rural and urban areas. This result is consistent with the conclusion that income became more equally distributed over these years. There was a slight fall in the calculated Gini coefficient between 1979 and 1984. Any change in distribution probably was toward a more equal distribution, but the change was slight. It is important to our story that the income of all ethnic groups increased, although the growth rate fell. It can be argued that this was at least partly a result of the policies and practices implemented as part of the NEP.

Employment

Employment growth slowed markedly from 1980 to 1985, which further dampened efforts to raise the participation of Bumiputera in modern sector activities. As table 15-5 shows, the overall unemployment rate increased sharply—by about one-third. Although the unemployment rate of the Malays rose by a smaller percentage than that of other ethnic groups, the Malay rate was still higher than the rates for the Chinese and Indians. Underemployment surely increased more rapidly than did unemployment. The distribution over occupations of the various ethnic groups changed hardly at all during the period. Falling growth rates, therefore, appeared to penalize the employment restructuring of employment.

Ownership of Share Capital

Columns 5 and 8 of table 14-2 show that, despite the fairly depressed economy, total share capital more than doubled during the years from 1980 to 1985, which was a surprising development. The foreign share fell to one-quarter, well below the 30 percent NEP target. Bumiputera share increased from 12 to 17 percent, but did not approach the NEP target. The non-Malay absolute increase was almost three times that of the Malays. This was progress, but, as in the 1970s, slower than expected.

Social Welfare: The Larger Equity Question

In 1985 per capita GDP was about 2.7 times higher than in 1960. Some restructuring of ethnic groups had occurred and was continuing.

Malay income had risen a bit compared with non-Malay income. The riots were less painful to recall and less often recalled. Malaysia had achieved a good quarter century. At the same time, many expectations had not been realized. Racial tensions persisted. The economy was still vulnerable to international events. New activities had certainly developed, but manufacturing had not really taken hold, except in free trade zones. The small-scale rubber, coconut, and paddy farmers remained poor despite huge expenditures on them and in the rural areas in general. High rates of investment, and outward-looking policies, which were truly sensible policies generally, had not had a full effect. Numerous Islamic groups were raising important questions about the development process and its consequences. The call to change values and to work harder to promote growth was not convincing to many. Change was proving more painful than anyone had anticipated. For some reason the economy and the society appeared to be in trouble, although admittedly major things had been accomplished.

In the last chapter, an attempt is made to discuss what went wrong—what really went wrong—as the Sri Lankan and Malaysian stories are compared.

IV The End of the Stories

16 Conclusions and Final Questions

Development and Equity

The general view of development and equity underlying the Malaysian and Sri Lankan stories that are told in the preceding chapters may be briefly summarized. At independence, each country had a labor force with a set of characteristics—skills, experience, commitment—and a capital stock of a particular age distribution that embodied technical knowledge and other qualities. In each country there was a body of knowledge not embodied in the existing capital that was distributed among the economic agents, which helped to determine the productivity of the capital and labor. These productive resources were set in an institutional and social environment that directly affected their productivity. In this environment were also found sources of meaning and, hence, of welfare and equity. Such institutions and social arrangements imposed constraints or limits on what the individual economic agents and the government deemed appropriate and acceptable, as well as on their capacities to perceive and understand arguments and ideas about alternative modes of economic endeavor and economic policy. These institutions and perceptions are largely the consequence of each country's history and the path that it had followed before its independence.

Growth of measured GDP occurs as resources increase in quantity and in productivity. Continued growth of factor productivity is necessary for continued growth of output. Productivity growth in turn depends somewhat on investment, but primarily on other things, especially searching and learning. The growing economy is one with strong and evident inducements to search and to learn, and in which there are relatively few bottlenecks. Freedom from the latter is necessary to prevent the stop-go syndrome that is so damaging to productivity growth. The principal role of relative prices is to help prevent the emergence of bottlenecks that force the economy to stop or slow down in an attempt to eliminate the bottlenecks. With this kind of

economy, productivity growth is much more likely to induce investment than is investment to carry productivity growth. This is especially so in Malaysia and Sri Lanka where availability of investable
resources did not seem to be a constraint, except in a few specific
periods.

The growth takes place in a social and institutional environment,
and is limited and directed by this environment. Equity requires
—among other things—that this environment be respected; the
search takes place within the constraints created by the environment,
and in this sense it is respected. The kinds of inducements that are
appropriate and possible also depend on the extent to which these
social institutions, practices, and perceptions produce entrepreneurial
activity and generate a genuine interest in "more" among the population. Investment that is inappropriate for the society will be less equitable—and will, therefore, fail to increase either welfare or physical
output—than is investment that is compatible with these basic and
entrenched social characteristics. In particular, bottlenecks in the form
of social unrest and tensions are to be avoided, because they can
impede productivity growth. These, then, are the risks of large-scale
imports of foreign capital—private or otherwise—that impose the
alien, the suspect, and the incomprehensible on the community.

Equality of the distribution of measured GDP is another component
of equity, but in Sri Lanka and Malaysia it was a less important part
than were other considerations that affected equity. The same observation holds, although much less emphatically, for poverty reduction
and elimination.

Policymaking enters into this approach in several ways. As noted
earlier, the way in which economic actors perceive reality affects their
actions. This is true of government officials as well, whose perceptions
are also affected by history and experience. They, too, are subject to
bounded rationality, to lack of information, to various pressures, and
to internal disagreements. Great difficulty in designing and implementing specific policies, therefore, exists. To establish a coherent,
effective policy in these circumstances is all but impossible. The Sri
Lankan and Malaysian stories also demonstrate that governments are
frequently so bound by circumstances that some severe and overt
event is necessary to create the freedom to move in new directions.
Effective governments may tend, then, to be forever trying to adjust—to change a policy here today, there tomorrow. Governments
must also search and learn. Both are difficult.

This final chapter uses the general approach to development and
equity just described to compare the postindependence experiences
of Sri Lanka and Malaysia. It seeks to uncover some generalizations
about these phenomena—development, equity, and decisionmaking—that appear applicable to both countries, and that suggest modi-

fications or ways to increase our understanding of how development occurs and equity is enhanced.

The Historical and Institutional Context

Sri Lanka and Malaysia have much in common. Some of the similarities arise from British rule over an extended period. The colonial experience was, as such experiences go, reasonably amicable, and the independence movements were equally harmonious and smoothly implemented. In both countries the nationals had been involved in governing for several years prior to actual independence. Thus, the British approach toward handling government and economic activities was well known and appreciated. In particular, the generally cautious economic policies that the British supported and followed in their possessions were continued. This was more evident in the case of Malaysia than in Sri Lanka, but in both countries the fear of inflation, the essential reliance on the private sector, and the acceptance of foreign investment all were inherited from the British. After independence in each country, the government accepted a more active role in promoting economic development. Development as such was not an agenda item for the British in either country. The British policies, however, did result in substantial growth in the two countries, and were responsible for the evolution of strong, largely foreign-owned, agricultural sectors. As has been noted, the existence of these strong sectors enabled certain development and other policies that would not have been possible without them.

The British also left behind a governmental and legal system that was basically democratic. Elections were generally open and free, and the legal system in each country was orderly and fair. There is no evidence of widespread abuse of human rights or of the legal system's being throttled or misused. The Indian Tamils, who worked on the estates in Sri Lanka, were denied influence in the political processes until the 1980s and were certainly mistreated and suffered an exceptional poverty. They were not, however, directly penalized by the legal system nor by the methods of its enforcement. With the exception of the periods of explicit riots and conflict, "law and order" were maintained and due process observed to an extent that made both countries relatively satisfactory places in which to live. Evidently during actual disturbances (the Emergency, the 1969 race riot in Malaysia, the several ethnic conflicts, and the 1971 upheaval in Sri Lanka) law and order collapsed. It is, however, useful to separate these unhappy events from the routine operation of the legal system.

Property rights were established and recognized. In rural areas in both countries land titles were occasionally vague and often recognized more by traditions and history than by the formal deeds and properly processed documents. There is, however, no evidence of widespread confiscations or of overt violations of legitimate (that is, legally or traditionally recognized) property claims.

Both countries were, then, in these categories, well managed, and the governments were disciplined and restrained by convention and by recognized and generally accepted legal arrangements. The specific disturbances were naturally important exceptions to all this. Each country entered its independence with the considerable advantage of a stable government operating in a society that accepted that government and its position. The long and peaceful British rule was principally responsible for this, but part of the explanation is that the societies were fairly well established. The Sinhalese in Sri Lanka and the Malays in Malaysia were societies with great traditions. The Chinese in Malaysia, while not so much a traditional society, were well organized and established. The Sri Lankan Tamils, although not so firmly established as the Chinese nor nearly so large a proportion of the population, did have roots and legitimate claims. There was, then, social and political stability on the one hand, and ethnic divisions that constituted a tinder box on the other. It is development and equity in these environments that will now be examined.

The Process of Growth

The process or mechanism that produced the growth in Malaysia and Sri Lanka is not very clear. It seems reasonably clear that a simple capital formation model is not satisfactory, although investment was, of course, a necessary accompaniment of growth. The conventional model that has the developing country exporting primary products and importing physical capital that was then employed to build new activities, mainly manufacturing, behind protection does not seem especially helpful, at least until 1980 and afterward. Even in this latter period such a picture is not very convincing. Certainly the use of a constant incremental capital output ratio as a growth parameter would not be justified by the available data and by other evidence. Efforts to calculate incremental capital output ratios (ICORs) did not seem to illuminate anything. One may repeat that such a finding does not mean that capital formation was not a crucial means of growth, but, rather, that it was not the prime mover—the generator of growth. Similarly, the rate of growth output (GDP) did not seem to be closely linked to the rate of capital formation, at least on an economywide basis. We also concluded that, for most years, neither saving capacity nor foreign exchange constituted a significant constraint on the rate of growth of output.

Investment in Agriculture

Land development was a major form of investment in both countries throughout most of the period. The two categories of land investment included the building of irrigation and other infrastructure facilities, and the provision of physical assets—land, buildings, seed and plants, and so forth—to specific individuals at heavily subsidized prices. A third category of investment common to both countries was an agricultural price support program—primarily for rice. The rationale of identifying this policy as an investment is examined later. Consider briefly each of these categories of agriculture investment, beginning with the provision of physical assets.

- The provision of an asset at subsidized prices implies that the person to whom the asset is provided is capable or can become capable of using that asset in a sufficiently productive manner to warrant the transfer. If this is not true, then the transfer is essentially that of a consumption good. If it is the latter, the justification would be that ownership itself—rather than production—was a source of welfare. Evidently the general idea was that both production and ownership were relevant. At the same time, the policy approach in Malaysia implied that the heavier weight was given to ownership. The role played by FELDA was, as has been emphasized, so extensive that it doubtless had adverse effects on the capacity of the new land settlers to accumulate the experience and knowledge necessary to become efficient farmers. The justification for this policy was in terms of the importance of effecting the transfers as rapidly as possible. The consequence was that the yields of newly settled farmers were low and increased slowly. Yields remained well below those on the estates throughout the period, but were generally higher than yields on non-FELDA smallholdings.

In Sri Lanka the paternalism of the land settlement programs was somewhat less pronounced than in Malaysia, but there also less attention was given to providing inducements to farmers to seek ways to increase yields than to the objective of providing lands to the landless and to those whose plots were extremely small. The government did not provide as extensive a range of services as in Malaysia, but neither was it able to create an effective incentive scheme for achieving steadily increasing yields, except possibly for rice. In both countries extension services were provided, but these, as in many other countries, at best were only modestly effective. Norman Uphoff (in Cernea 1985, p. 378) states that the agreement between Sri Lanka and the United States Agency for International Aid (which helped with the financing) called for farmer participation in water management, but the Irrigation Department, the implementing agency, regarded farmer "participation as simply doing what they [the farmers] were told" to do. This one-sided arrangement apparently changed somewhat later on.

The notion that land ownership itself was a source of welfare, that a society composed of small-scale landowners was a good, stable society, was especially strong in Sri Lanka. Some observers believed that this objective outweighed even the employment objective. It surely reflects the widespread view that the large, foreign-owned estates had usurped lands that rightly belonged to the Sinhalese. In Malaysia, too, land development had major attractions other than output, employment, and distribution effects. The rural political base of UMNO was especially relevant as was the fact that land development was assumed not to upset the existing economic power structure of foreign and Chinese interests in the modern sectors.

- The big irrigation project was a common feature of investment in agriculture in both countries. As has been noted, such projects are attractive from many points of view, not the least of which is that they lend themselves to foreign financing. The Muda project in Malaysia and the Mahaweli Ganga Project in Sri Lanka were the two largest, but there were other projects in each country. These projects were intended to make more land available for cultivation, which they did. As we have seen, there were some administrative and political problems in implementing these giant projects, but they were generally done well. The Muda project in Malaysia especially was carried out well, and the Mahaweli Project in Sri Lanka has been cited by several observers (Cernea 1985) as having done especially well in helping the new settlers to become acclimated to their new environment.

There are also, however, difficulties with the big irrigation and settlement projects. Joseph Stern (1984, p. 26) cites data that suggest that almost as much new land could have been brought into cultivation in Sri Lanka by repairing approximately 7,000 tanks as the completed Mahaweli Project would make available. This estimate is perhaps unduly optimistic about the tanks, but it does remind us that full use had not been made of an important indigenous technology. On the one hand, the Mahaweli Project excited the imagination and enthusiasm of the population and also attracted foreign financing. A rehabilitation program for tanks, on the other hand, would have imposed less strain on domestic resources, would have enabled Sri Lanka to proceed somewhat more independently of foreign influences, and, most important, would have enabled the community to have worked more closely together, to have exploited the links with its past, and to have learned a great deal. In Malaysia an approach to land settlement and irrigation other than FELDA was less evident, but it is widely believed that that approach created dependence and a dependent attitude. The yield story supports the view that the big projects might have been premature.

In both countries, there are reasons and arguments for proceeding with the large land development and settlement schemes, but there are also reasons that other approaches might have produced a more rapid growth of social welfare and simultaneously helped to establish a firmer basis for an adaptable, flexible economy.

• Each country had some kind of a price support program for rice. The rationale for these arrangements was largely that of helping the poor and supporting the objective of self-sufficiency in rice. To consider such a policy an investment, the effect must be that it induced some increased capacity, some increased yields. The evidence cited in previous chapters supports the view that this in fact happened to some extent. In general, however, the forms that these subsidies took were not especially conducive to increased search for ways to increase yields, but they could have been easily modified to do this. It will be suggested below that had such a modification been in place, additional policies may well have been unneccessary.

Much of the growth in agriculture originated from the introduction of higher-yielding varieties of seeds and clones in the rubber, tea, and oil palm sectors, especially on the plantations. The availability of these new varieties induced replanting, which was a form of investment. The increased output, however, was owing to the new seeds. The large-scale land development programs in both countries were also a major form of investment, and especially in the 1970s accounted for a significant proportion of total investment. The relationship between investment in the form of land development and increased output depended heavily on numerous factors—the experience, skill, and commitment of the people who worked the new lands; the availability of credit and produced inputs, especially fertilizer and water; marketing arrangements and facilities, and various other factors that acted directly on the output from the new lands. In both countries, the major land development programs were intended to achieve objectives other than, or in addition to, increased output of agricultural products. Among these objectives were those of helping specific ethnic or regional groups and the corollary of this objective—the support of specific types of investment, smallholder rubber in Malaysia, and small-scale rice production in both countries. These considerations, arising from notions of equity (especially ideas of what constituted a desirable life-style for the several groups) and political stability, were of major importance in investment decisions. They meant not only that investment may well have gone into less productive (measured, for example, by the ICOR) activities than were available but also that such productivity would vary widely over time and among regions. Land development schemes often have a long gestation period and generate relatively modest employment opportunities per unit of investment. Because each country faced an employment problem over almost the entire period considered, it seems reasonably clear that the investment that did occur did not make as much of a contribution to job creation as other possible investment allocations might have. Neither did these investments make as much of a contribution to learning and productivity and yield growth as would appear to have been possible with other policies aimed directly at these objectives.

Investment in Education

For reasons elaborated in some detail in earlier chapters, education was of great interest in both countries. The education that took place was intended to make people more productive and more able to identify and respond to new opportunities. There were great difficulties in accomplishing this task, given the form of education that was pursued and the other developments taking place in the economy. Education did have another effect: it made the younger people less willing to work as rice and smallholder rubber farmers and to live in isolated rural areas. Of course, education is another investment component with a long gestation period, and if that investment produces a product that cannot be (or is not) used (for example, there is unemployment or underemployment or college graduates perform tasks that require only elementary school education), then little is added to output. In these instances, education creates tension and resentment in the society that did not exist before education was widespread. More important is the fact that education, as such, does not create jobs. The economy must generate demand for people who have acquired the education, and this demand comes from investment in activities that the educated consider suitable sources of employment. Neither country accomplished this meshing very well. As just noted, the big land development investments did not create a demand for the labor that the educational programs were turning out. One consequence of this failure was the continued existence of unemployed young people along with increasing employment in the public sector. Although most of the "educated unemployed" were young people who eventually found jobs, their existence is important because it influenced political decisions and investment allocations in both countries.

The evidence provided by the two countries helps to clarify the role of investment in education in the search for growth and equity. The rationale of much of the investment in education was based on considerations relating to the broad issues of equity—a rationale based principally on history and historical interpretations. From this historical and social environment came the decision to push education as such. In view of this history and its interpretation, it is arguable that both governments proceeded in a reasonable manner and—to a large extent—in a manner consistent with prevailing economic beliefs. Alternative views on education were, therefore, difficult to appreciate and would have been even more difficult to put into practice. One alternative policy, consistent with the development approach outlined above, would have been to push investment in activities that directly and immediately increased the demand for labor. The first task would be to get the demand for labor growing strongly, thereby creating inducements for labor to find ways to qualify for the available jobs. This alternative is discussed in more detail later.

The education issue is more complex and more controversial in Malaysia than in Sri Lanka. This is principally a result of the difference in the ethnic composition of the two countries. The Chinese are such a significant part of the Malaysian society that their linguistic and educational needs cannot be dismissed. The Indians of Sri Lanka, however, are a much smaller minority and are concentrated in specific geographic areas. In brief, in Malaysia the complexity of the education issue is further compounded by linguistic and ethnic considerations, while in Sri Lanka the latter two sources of difficulty were less pronounced.

Investment in Manufacturing

One of the more interesting aspects of the Malaysian and Sri Lankan stories is that neither country aggressively pursued import substitution despite the fact that considerable evidence and argument would have supported such a strategy. There were policies designed to protect and encourage domestic industry, but these policy packages were mild compared with those found in many other developing countries. The explanation of this "failure" seems to rest on several considerations. In Malaysia the general strength of the balance of payments, absence of inflation, prevailing support of a market economy (until 1970), and the generally favorable growth rates made any change in policy difficult to justify. Even after 1970, although the role of government greatly increased and the evidence of rising protection appeared, the move toward import substitution was surprisingly modest. After 1980 this move was accelerated. In Sri Lanka the general difficulties associated with policy changes were principally political, and there was widespread approval of taxing the plantations to support the welfare program. Yet, some new leading sector clearly was necessary to sustain the system over an extended period. Still, manufacturing investment was not strongly encouraged.

Consider the following argument. Traditional activities in a country show signs of long-term weakness on either the demand or supply side, which is reflected most clearly in declining terms of trade. Traditional activities, however, continue to be the most productive sectors, and are important in maintaining a healthy balance of payments. The country then faces a definite choice—it can continue to rely on its traditional activities and suffer a decline in the growth rate or possibly even of the income level, or it can increase protection and create new activities that are presently less productive than the traditional ones. Current output might decline more because of the latter policy, but the real cost might be relatively brief. The cost of the shift depends principally on two things—transformation capacity and the productivity of the growth rate. The former notion determines the cost differential between the traditional and the new activities. The greater the transformation capacity, the less the differential. Productivity growth, of course, determines how long the differential will last. Protection results in a reduction in the current level of output available to the society, and so may be viewed as an investment. The returns on this investment, as on all investments, are realized in the future and here in the form of a more flexible, versatile economy (that is, one in which the transformation capacity is high) and one where productivity growth is generally strong.

Transformation capacity is not independent of the areas into which the economy seeks to move. To seek to jump from, for example, smallholder rubber or coconut into modern steel milling is almost sure to mean that costs will be very high—that is, low transformation capacity and modest productivity growth. The point here is that the strong plantation economies had made it difficult for new activities to appear.

The main difficulty with this approach is that of finding ways to provide protection in a manner that does not distort the economy and to ensure that productivity growth actually occurs regularly. We have noted that an unusually effective form of nondistorting protection is a significant undervaluation of domestic currency. A good criterion of an undervaluation is whether or not the country is accumulating foreign exchange over time from its export earnings. It should. The most convincing evidence from productivity growth studies suggests that such growth is best encouraged by a strong and continuing demand pressing against sharply rising marginal cost curves. It then becomes very lucrative to the producer to find ways to increase output to exploit the strong demand. If output can be increased simply by adding to physical capital (for example, by importing capital from GDP rich countries), there will be little inducement to search and experiment. If, however, no new capital can be imported, then there is great inducement to find ways to increase output from existing capacity—that is, to increase productivity. Malaysia and Sri Lanka had great trouble accomplishing these objectives.

It has been argued that in Sri Lanka especially there appeared to be a considerable transformation problem—that is, the shift into new activities appeared very costly, and the tea and rubber plantations made it possible to continue primary reliance on these sectors until the economic difficulties were so severe that change was forced on the community in 1977. In Malaysia, the reluctance to encourage new industries for fear that the ethnic inequalities would be exacerbated was a factor in the 1960s explaining the hesitation to pursue a more active industrialization strategy that involved protection. In the 1970s the regulations of the NEP offered the prospect of a more rapid industrialization with the Bumiputera enjoying full participation. Protection was increased, therefore, and the role of government was expanded. In both countries, the process began a bit late and was not implemented in a completely satisfactory way.

Both countries then experienced a mild case of Dutch Disease through most of the interval studied. The balance of payments was, to a considerable degree, protected by the strength of traditional exports. The exchange rate that resulted meant that imports were "too cheap" to support in the long run, but domestic production was discouraged by these imports. The argument here is that neither country provided import substitution, in the nondistorting form just described, sufficiently early or sufficiently strongly to facilitate the emergence of a manufacturing (or other new) sector that could help to resolve the existing unemployment and poverty problems and that could provide a new source of dynamism to the economy. It should be repeated that this argument also requires the assumption that there be no aggregate saving problem, and this, as noted in several places in previous chapters, seems to have been the case.

Constraints on Investment

The argument has been made that neither country was confronted with any of the constraints conventionally identified by economists—domestic saving, foreign exchange, labor or specific skills, and so forth. There was then slack, possibly considerable slack, most (not all) of the time with respect to these variables. An explanation has been offered for the existence of this "slack." (To repeat, slack existed with respect to these conventional variables. "Something" constrained the rate of investment, or it would have increased until it hit one of the conventional constraints. Further elaboration of this point is found in Bruton 1985). The task now is to examine two consequences of its existence.

The most obvious consequences were that potential investable capacity was not fully exploited, so demand for labor was less than it could have been, which was probably true of the growth of GDP. In terms of poverty reduction or elimination, the continuing weak demand for labor is, of course, extremely important. There are enormous difficulties in raising the incomes of the poor despite a weak demand for labor. The fact that such weak demand and widespread poverty existed at the same time that investable resources were underutilized exacerbated the situation and created the potential for even more social unrest.

The objective now is to examine the notion of a tradeoff between growth and equity in this kind of situation. The simplest tradeoff argument is along the following lines. The two basic assumptions are that capital formation is the strategic source of development and that inequality of income distribution is necessary to achieve sufficient savings to support an investment target. The Harrod growth model, popular in the 1950s and 1960s, was built on this notion. If the inequality were corrected, saving would decline, capital formation would fall, and so then would growth. A tradeoff was clearly possible.

This conventional argument must be modified by the evidence that productivity growth is more crucial to growth than is capital formation as such. The focus must then shift to the effect of the growth of productivity of both capital and labor. Conventional wisdom on this issue is less well established, and we will have to proceed with caution later when this topic is discussed a bit more. Similarly, the evidence that inequality of any sort is necessary for an acceptable saving rate is far from convincing. It is, of course, clear that in all countries it is the higher-income groups who do most of the saving, but this is not the same thing as saying that inequality is necessary to achieve a high rate of saving. The Arthur Lewis argument that it is capitalists who save, not simply any rich group, is relevant to both countries. The fact that a substantial amount of profits accrued to foreigners, whose savings, if not reinvested in their own activities, were taken out of the country, further complicated the situation.

There is another tradeoff that may be far more important. This refers to the necessity, or alleged necessity, that sharp and disrupting structural, social, and cultural changes occur to allow the growth process to continue. The tradeoff is then between growth on the one hand and the continued existence of familiar and accepted institutions and practices that are important sources of welfare and meaning on the other. This tradeoff arises largely in the context of "modernization," which involves importing into the developing country the physical artifacts of development from the world's rich countries. For these artifacts to be as productive in the importing country as in their country of origin requires changes in the more basic features and characteristics of the society. Rapid changes of the latter almost always result in a degree of tension and unrest, which potentially leads to chaos and upheaval. Such difficulties, of course, reduce welfare and can well offset possible welfare gains that follow from increased output.

It is the contention here that this last sort of tradeoff did actually confront both Malaysia and Sri Lanka, and that both sacrificed growth—that is, traded growth for what was generally perceived to be a stable and welfare-yielding status quo of political and social arrangements. (It is, perhaps, misleading to speak of a tradeoff in this present context. Governments simply chose the set of policies that they believed would yield the greatest welfare.)

The preceding argument seems most directly applicable to Malaysia in the years prior to the 1969 racial conflicts. Then, after the NEP was in effect, investable resources were used explicitly to seek to change some of the basic institutions of the society. Growth of GDP was surely sacrificed in the 1970s in an attempt to effect changes in the economic and social structure, rather than to preserve it. Some of the difficulties of the 1980s, however, undoubtedly have arisen because of an attempt to impose truly fundamental changes on the society—changes that required more rapid adjustments than the society seemed able to accommodate. The result, therefore, was the structural unemployment, the immigration of Indonesians and Filipinos, the rise of Moslem fundamentalist groups, the balance of payments difficulties, the increased intraethnic group inequality, the apparent corruption, and so forth, all generally absent in the 1960s and most of the 1970s. These have been accompanied by increasing ethnic tensions as well. It is useful to recall that the actual growth rate was higher in Malaysia during the 1970s than during the 1960s, but this resulted, as frequently noted, from the policy of allowing considerable underutilization of resources in the earlier decade.

Sri Lanka, however, traded output growth not only for increasingly greater welfare payments, but for the continuation of a very active role by the electorate to which each government had to respond, and to the established routine of relying on the tea and rubber estates to carry the economy. These policies reflect both the difficulties of decisionmaking in the government and the associated problems of designing and implementing a new economic strategy. Added to this was an apparently severe transformation problem and an assumed shortage of entrepreneurs, both of which made all the governments hesitate to modify significantly the prevailing strategy. Growth was sacrificed, but so was the establishment of a learning process that would at some point produce a more flexible and responsive economy that Sri Lanka so greatly needed. It was not until 1977, when the state of the economy became so precarious, that some sharp modifications in strategy appeared feasible. That these changes were then made so rapidly and sweepingly is again, in Sri Lanka's case, part of the explanation of the difficulties that have been encountered there during the 1980s. Tradeoffs were made, but they proved to be very complex and troublesome.

The second consequence of the presence of slack that must be examined is its impact on productivity growth or, more accurately, its impact on the search and other efforts to find ways to increase productivity. As noted earlier, productivity growth seems best encouraged by a strong and recognized demand for output in the face of sharply rising marginal cost curves. This situation induces search for ways to increase output at acceptable costs—ways to raise productivity. It was further argued that nondistorting protection was an important means of accomplishing this, and that a marked undervaluation of domestic currency was such a means of protection.

The presence of slack in the economies made this approach difficult. With the economy not pressing against a conventional resource constraint, the effective incentives were principally to find ways to get more inputs, rather than ways to increase productivity. Tea and rubber faced a weak world demand relative to their supply capacity (at least in the 1960s) and tin faced a supply problem that new technology was not at all likely to resolve. Yet, the slack made it easy, more so in Malaysia than in Sri Lanka, not to search for productivity growth, but to enlarge and use more inputs of intermediate and final goods. The slack—vis-à-vis conventional resources—did more than cause output to be less than what was actually technically possible. It contributed to a situation where search and experimentation and trial and error were deemed unnecessary. With the development of oil in Malaysia and its high price in the late 1970s and early 1980s, and the great flood of aid to Sri Lanka after 1977, these problems were exacerbated, not resolved.

The conclusion, then, is that the tradeoff that resulted in the slack economy dampened the inducements to search for productivity growth. This dampening, in turn, not only affected the rate of growth of output, but also impeded the evolution of new activities to replace the traditional ones. Such an impediment also tended to exacerbate the social tensions. Finally, the slack, by dampening search and learning efforts, also dampened the development of the kind of flexibility and responsiveness that characterizes a strong, dynamic economy with good transformation capacity.

Further Notes on Productivity Growth

In addition to the argument just completed about productivity growth, a few more points can be made. Efforts to develop an index or measure of productivity growth for the two countries did not yield usable results. We must proceed, therefore, in an empirical vacuum, so caution, always advised, is now necessary.

The clearest success story is that of rubber in Malaysia. The Rubber Research Institute was unusually effective in developing new uses for natural rubber and new means to increase yields and labor productivity. These results were especially important for the rubber estates. In Sri Lanka growth of rice yields was impressive during much of the period. This yield growth was largely a matter of new seeds, better water use, and increased supplies of fertilizer. In the land development projects in general, as has been noted, both the pressure to proceed rapidly and the generally paternalistic approach tended to dampen the growth of productivity that results when labor undertakes new tasks and assumes new responsibilities. The very large-scale projects—Muda in Malaysia and Mahaweli in Sri Lanka—certainly created opportunities for significant increases in yields and in labor productivity. As the effects of these great projects are further realized, it may be that major further increases in productivity will occur.

In manufacturing even less can be said. There is no evidence of sustained increases in either labor or total factor productivity in this sector. Activities in the free trade zones showed considerable evidence of being competitive, but there is little firm evidence that productivity increased over time. In some inland manufacturing activities—for example, automobile manufacturing in Malaysia—productivity was low and apparently declining.

It does seem that in neither country was the general environment conducive to productivity growth. The Dutch Disease and the resulting overvaluation of the exchange rates; the frequent slack in the economies; the difficulties on the education and training side; the absence of links among the modern estate sectors, the free trade zones, and the indigenous economy; and the concerns of the government for internal political matters—all created an environment in which search and innovation and increased effort were weak. Even in the absence of concrete empirical evidence, it seems safe to conclude that productivity growth over most of the economy did not become an integral feature of either economy during the years under review. Perhaps the major difficulty in achieving the objectives of the NEP in Malaysia was that of expanding the productivity of the Malay community. Similar difficulties were evident in the nonrice sectors of Sri Lanka.

Policymaking and Implementation

Policymaking in both countries was difficult. The difficulties arose from numerous considerations. The ethnic heterogeneity with its several further implications (language, history, religion, and so forth), the fact that governments in both countries were responsive to the electorate and eschewed coercion, and the international vulnerability of the countries all contributed to the inherent complexities of public policymaking. As noted previously, there did not seem to be a small, powerful, vested-interest group that dominated policies in either country—at least not until later in the period. There were, of course, pressure groups in both countries that had some influence. Foreign companies were the most obvious examples. In Malaysia, for example, the foreign companies probably had some effect on the labor policies that were followed. Even so, the point remains that the policies followed by the two countries cannot be explained generally by reference simply to rent seekers. To understand the reason that certain policies were followed and others were not requires some examination of this policymaking process.

The Policymaking Environment

To help appreciate these various issues, consider three cases. One case is a very small city-state—a Singapore or Hong Kong. The options for broad strategy or the specific policies to implement that strategy are severely limited. An outward-looking, trade-oriented strategy is virtually the only option available, and the policymaker has an easy choice. Little opposition to this policy is expected.

Another case is a large country with abundant natural resources for which a strong world market exists. Policy options have multiplied. Revenues from the export of the minerals can be used to support numerous policies. Then, of course, choice becomes difficult and political matters begin to play an important role, and the policies that emerge may be very ill-suited to the economy. A strong export sector also often makes it possible for the policymaker to live with "wrong" policies—that is, corrective action is not forced by balance of payments deterioration, inflation, or anything else. Aid and capital inflows can perform the same role as abundant natural resources, although they are not likely to yield as large a fund as do many mineral deposits. In such a context, policymaking is much more difficult than in the city-state case simply because there are so many options for the policymaker to consider and debate.

A third case is a relatively large country with very few natural resources. It does, however, have people. The general strategy is clear. Ways must be found to utilize this one resource—people. In this case, the country must live—and develop—by its wits. Its people must learn—must learn first how to learn and then continue learning. This is the only option, but there are numerous ways to seek this objective. If the country is able to find a way that accomplishes this objective—that establishes this learning process—then growth will occur, and equality—and possibly equity as well—can be expected to be well served. This case is important because it clarifies the roles of learning, adapting, and searching. It has been argued that these are the real heart of development, no matter what the resource endowment happens to be. Countries described by this third case are forced into this direction, and they either succeed or they fail. The economies of the Republic of Korea and especially Taiwan have succeeded, while the Arab Republic of Egypt and Bangladesh have not. The question then is why some countries find their way while others fail. The answer is surely to be found—or at least to be sought—in the organizational and institutional characteristics of the societies. It is, perhaps, helpful in this context to refer to a hypothesis about the source of the success of Italy, Japan, and the Federal Republic of Germany in the postwar years. Ronald Rogowski (1983) argues that these countries succeeded economically after the war because "losses of territory, of empire, or of the hope of empire left them with factor endowments that indisputably forced them to trade" (p. 728). This, in turn, forced them to realize that they had to find ways to increase productivity and to respond to trade opportunities, otherwise they would fall by the wayside in the world economy. They responded.

The argument now is that the policymaking environment of both Malaysia and Sri Lanka was such that it made it difficult to identify the appropriate strategy. Neither country was in the position of any of the three cases just defined, and both countries could, in the 1950s and 1960s, "continue," and continuing is always simpler than designing and implementing a specific new policy. Yet, as emphasized earlier, continuing was not possible for either country for the indefinite future. In this sense, the initial conditions of the two countries and their policymaking process made explicit action to modify the economy difficult and risky, and, hence, easily postponable.

The Decisionmaking Process

One can imagine a decisionmaking process of the following sort. A government, with access to a great array of empirical knowledge and analytical skill, wishes to determine the preferences of the individuals who compose the society. Then it seeks somehow to aggregate these preferences into a social welfare function, and, finally, to design and implement the policies that maximize this function. This "rational choice" model of public decisionmaking has a certain esthetic appeal, and also helps to organize, or begin to organize, thoughts about the way in which policy decisions are made. The approach, however, omits or at least hides many, perhaps most, of the considerations that actually affect decisionmaking. In particular, the rational choice approach does not facilitate the study of how power, history, and culture enter into the decisionmaking process. An effort has been made throughout this study to demonstrate that these latter factors are essential to understanding the policies chosen by Malaysia and Sri Lanka.

Of greater importance, perhaps, is that in countries that are undergoing change, individual preferences, far from being established, are actually in a state of flux and ambiguity. The tension between old and new makes the very notion of individual preference difficult, and any sort of aggregating of individual preferences doubly so. Similar difficulty arises in any effort to establish a social welfare function that is more than an empty box. In a society where ethnic issues are endemic, this aggregation faces further conceptual and empirical difficulties. These notions differ from the more prosaic one of the unavailability of necessary data. Indeed, all of these considerations lead to the conclusion that the decisionmaking in the two countries was, indeed had to be, much more of a trial and error, tentative nature. There was, therefore, a great temptation to continue a strategy that was widely accepted and congenial to large segments of the society. This conclusion should not be a great shock to the reader, because the story has repeatedly identified specific factors that rendered economic policy decisions halting and uncertain.

Some of the more specific issues in decisionmaking that have emerged in each country will now be examined.

Decisionmaking in Sri Lanka

The effective democracy in Sri Lanka, combined with the fact that the two main coalitions were so evenly matched, made all governments extremely responsive to wishes of the voters, or, more accurately, to the wishes of the voters as those wishes were perceived by government officials. For any government to avoid myopia, to make "hard decisions," and to move determinedly in one direction, was extremely difficult. For example, no government could simply abandon food subsidies and hope to survive. The change in government that followed each election (until 1983) suggests further that the "preferences" of the society were far from settled. The "right" policy package was, for reasons already examined, not sufficiently clearly determined to prevent dispute. The electorate removed whatever government was in power at each election partly because it did not know what it wanted from government policy.

The comparison of policy changes in the late 1960s, and in 1977 and the years following helps to identify the existing difficulties. The UNP was returned to power in 1965, and by the late 1960s economic policy had begun to move slowly and cautiously in the direction of a more open and more market-oriented system. There was some response to these changes, and in the last couple of years of the 1960s the economy appeared to have improved considerably. Yet, the UNP was decisively defeated in the 1970 election. In 1977, on the other hand, the UNP was returned to power and immediately made the kinds of sweeping policy changes that it had attempted in the late 1960s. These were welcomed by the electorate. The UNP was retained in office in the 1983 election and its reforms continued.

What accounted for the difference between the two periods? Clearly, it was not the role of aid donors. Aid in substantial amounts rolled in after 1977, but there is little reason to believe that the policy changes of 1977 were made because of pressure from aid donors. There had been smaller amounts of aid in the years from 1965 to 1970 period, but again there is little evidence to support the view that had aid come earlier or in greater amounts, the UNP would have been able to push harder on its reforms or to have won the election of 1970. Aid, especially that from the World Bank, seemed to follow rather than lead policy change, and it was rarely considered a means to facilitate policy change. More often it appeared, or was interpreted, as a reward for already accomplished policy changes. It is easy to see that such an interpretation would lead many to resent both the aid and the policy changes that won it.

The general content of the policy package supported by most donors, most explicitly by the Bank, was well known. This package had its supporters in Sri Lanka, mainly among the UNP, but there were also many in both coalitions who objected to it. The difficulties of achieving the reform in the late 1960s were real. In particular, strengthening the balance of payments was a task that required a great deal more than the conventional liberalization and devaluation package. More than any other interval perhaps, the period from 1965 to 1970 illuminated the great transformation problems that faced Sri Lanka as she sought to remodel her economy. The fact that the UNP was defeated in 1970 also demonstrates the strong appeal of the traditional policy to Sri Lankans. It seems likely that, even had the UNP retained power in 1970, their efforts to change policy would have proceeded much more slowly than was the case in the late 1970s. To be more accurate, perhaps, had the UNP moved more slowly in the period from 1965 to 1969, it might have remained in power.

The World Bank explicitly stopped all of its new lending in 1970 because it did not approve the policies of the new government, and thereby not only lost any influence that it might have had in helping Sri Lanka modify its policies, but also supplied evidence to those in Sri Lanka who resented the Bank as an outside influence trying to force its will on the country. This only added to the difficulties of changing policy. Mason and Asher (1973) note that in 1970 the "conditions attached to a Bank loan became an issue in a bitterly fought election campaign."

The role of the Bank in the late 1960s made it an issue in the 1970 election, and illustrates the difficulty of convincing a government or a society of the appropriateness or inappropriateness of a development strategy or of the details of implementing that strategy. Aside from the merits of the various arguments, it seems evident that Sri Lanka was not "ready" in the late 1960s to make significant changes. Mason and Asher (1973) conclude their discussion by noting that the Bank's experience with Sri Lanka at this time "seems to show that loan conditions that may be perfectly acceptable in one country can become the source of political turmoil in another; that these political reactions can be seriously exacerbated if the Bank works with one political party to the exclusion of its oppositions, and that there is probably a trade-off between conditions thought necessary to the viability of a project and conditions that permit satisfactory relations between the Bank and its borrowers" (p. 441). In other words, in 1970 Sri Lanka was not convinced that its traditional strategy was wrong and that if it changed its policy, its economic performance would improve.

By 1977, of course, the economy was in an exceptionally unfortunate position. It was not only, or primarily, that the country sorely needed help, that it changed its government, and that the government made sweeping changes in strategy. Rather, it was that both the society in general and the government policymakers could now genuinely appreciate that the old approach could not really work. They therefore accepted the notion that a major change was necessary, but, despite any change, new policies would have to recognize history and acknowledge the established roots that Sri Lankans cherished. This education was painful; both the government and the economy in general were poorly prepared to manage such sweeping changes, despite the large amounts of suddenly available aid. The results of the changed policy were discussed earlier, and many of the problems examined in that discussion suggest that the new policy strategy imposed tasks on the government that were exceedingly difficult to implement and manage.

All of this meant that the government in 1977 did not have a well-studied position or package of policies that it could begin to apply slowly and with a great deal of careful monitoring. The sharp line between the policy approach that had been followed and the one pushed by the Bank, the International Monetary Fund, and many bilateral donors did not facilitate a continuing discussion of the exact content of a suitable new policy. The position of the major donors was clear in broad outline, but a broad outline is not a policy package that is immediately useful to the policymaker. In this sense the aid group did not help as much as it might have in preparing appropriate means of changing from an old to a new strategy. The most overt consequence of this situation was the acceleration of the Mahaweli Ganga project, which occupied so much attention, required such large outlays, and was of dubious appropriateness at this time. Although the policy changes that began in 1977 had important consequences, it should be emphasized that this, or any other, policy change would require a great deal of preparation and thought. Such study was not available in the early 1970s, and when large-scale aid began to flow after 1977, there were numerous difficulties that the government was not very well prepared to meet—the composition of investment, a policy for the tree sector, the means of getting new sectors underway, the stimulation of nontraditional exports, a way to increase saving, controlling the government deficit, and so forth. As was shown in the several figures in the chapter on growth and equity in Sri Lanka, a number of series began to appear out of control in the late 1970s as the government began to encounter a new set of problems. Policy change was inevitable, but much had to be learned about what to do and how to do it, and learning takes time. It should be emphasized that a change in policy creates new problems, and a government must be prepared to meet them. Change that takes place slowly and continuously places modest new burdens on a government while it facilitates learning. Aid donors must recognize this as well. Sri Lanka needed help to ease into the new strategy. Instead, it received huge (relative to the past) amounts of money for projects that in fact made the shift to a new strategy even more difficult.

Opposition to policy changes that are aimed at establishing a more open, more liberalized regime frequently comes from those who enjoy the rents present in a closely controlled system. This opposition did not seem especially important in Sri Lanka in 1977 nor, indeed, at other times. The population did want the welfare system and the subsidies, but there did not seem to be any pressure to maintain the status quo because particular interests profited from it. This situation made policy change more complex as the opposition to change was more widely based and grounded in more fundamental features of the system than is the case when opposition is concentrated among specific, identifiable groups.

Decisionmaking in Malaysia

The decisionmaking process in Malaysia is similar in some respects to that in Sri Lanka, but there are also important differences. The most obvious difference is that Malaysia has been governed, since its independence, by a single coalition originally called the Alliance Party and now known as the National Front. Its main constituent member is the UMNO, but there are a dozen or so other parties included. The government, therefore, did not have to worry about losing an election, and in that sense was different from Sri Lanka's successive governments. At the same time, the coalition was extensive enough that decisive action on controversial questions was quite difficult. In Malaysia, too, a major event, the racial conflicts of 1969, was necessary before significant changes in strategy could be made. In addition, as in Sri Lanka, the difficulties were so entrenched and extensive that any new policy was almost sure to run into opposition within the party itself. The fact that a single party had a firm hold on government did not simplify implementing major changes in policy. Finally, when significant change was forced on the Malaysian society, the appropriate policy was not available and a great deal of improvisation was necessary. The events of the 1980s are partly a consequence of the difficulties of finding a workable policy in a context of great urgency. Indeed, the policy changes that appeared necessary as the NEP approach ran into problems in the late 1970s and early 1980s illustrate again the argument that some specific event is often required to permit a government to act. In this case it was the world recession that forced that forced attention directly on the need for policy change.

Policymaking in Malaysia was a more formal process and the government was able to proceed on the basis of argument and accumulated evidence more frequently than was the case in Sri Lanka. The complications associated with a substantial rate of change—in GDP, urbanization, employment, and other aspects—in addition to the ethnic divisions, made it difficult to define individual preference functions. It was virtually impossible for the government to aggregate such functions to find a "social welfare function" or, more important, even to think in such terms. Rather, the strategy was to try to maintain a situation that was recognized to be extremely unstable by dampening discontent whenever it appeared. This strategy may well have been the only feasible one in the 1960s, given the complexity and volatility of the situation and the heterogeneity of the ruling coalition. The political difficulties were exacerbated by the fact that in Malaysia, unlike Sri Lanka, state governments had considerable power, especially over matters such as land issues, and extremely diverse interests and ideas prevailed among the state governments. Decisive action was, therefore, impossible, although the Alliance Party was in no danger of losing an election, and high-ranking government officials recognized (by 1966–67) that the existing arrangements in the society were not sustainable. The strength of rubber, palm oil, tin, and (in the late 1970s) oil made this a feasible strategy in economic terms. The fact that the UMNO, a Malay party, dominated the Alliance coalition made it a feasible political strategy. The weaker economic community had its party in control of the government, which in turn had the effect of dampening most of the overt pressures from Malays to strengthen their economic position. The plans were intended to achieve important objectives, and occasionally they succeeded, but they did not significantly overhaul the way in which the economy was organized and performed.

The racial conflicts of 1969 showed, however, that the strategy was not working, and the horror of that conflict convinced virtually everyone that explicit action was necessary, that continuing was not sufficient. The government then became much freer to act, and, equally important, saw that it was freer to act. Meanwhile, the very fact that a crisis had produced this recognized freedom made it difficult to produce a carefully designed and implemented policy, even for a government that was unusually well organized and managed and that functioned in a generally strong economy. The NEP was a significant effort to "redress the structural imbalances" in the country, but, as chapter 14 has documented, it left many issues unresolved and actually created various new problems. In particular it was not able to create some of the basic sources of productivity growth among the Malay community (or in the country at large), and contributed little to achieving a more effective plural society. In Malaysia's case, as in that of Sri Lanka, the decisionmaking problem did not appear (until the late 1970s) to be one of rent seekers and rent recipients—those who profit from the existing situation—impeding policy changes. Rather, the difficulty was one of organization and control that could produce new policies in a fairly buoyant economic environment. This situation, combined with the previously noted factors that made the "right" policy so elusive, produced essentially a holding action, until an event occurred that forced more specific policy review.

Summary

This discussion of policy and decisionmaking in the two countries suggests two major points. On the one hand, sharp, abrupt changes in broad strategy or in the detailed components of a given strategy require considerable support and understanding by the population. This is not primarily because of the power of those who profit from possible rents, but rather because the community's history, institutions, and organizations create a milieu in which change that affects deeply rooted views and practices cannot be seen as either appropriate or necessary. It then takes an event of some magnitude to convince the population and the government that new directions are necessary and possible—that, in some real sense, the government is free to move in sharply new directions.

On the other hand, abrupt changes in strategy and approach often create new problems with which a government may be unable to cope. Our stories of Sri Lanka and Malaysia after the late 1970s illustrate this clearly. It is also reflected in the way the several series in our figures move. Both economies were going along in a traditional fashion, along traditional routes. The figures appear very unexciting—the economies performed reasonably well. Then, as great changes are imposed, for various reasons, many of which are quite valid, the economy seems to be out of control and the figures show an array of problems appearing that are difficult indeed to manage.

These considerations suggest that policy changes should always be under way. A government should always be responding, nudging, identifying areas where policy change is needed and is possible and act accordingly. Such changes have many advantages, which will be discussed further in the last section of this chapter.

Growth with Equity

In both countries equity was certainly a live issue. In Sri Lanka the notion was dominated by the relief of the effects of poverty in the society. Thus the widespread subsidies of food, education, health care, and so forth certainly reflected a deep-seated and generally accepted idea of what an equitable society was all about. The other important component of equity in Sri Lanka was the commitment to the rice culture on the part of the Sinhalese. There were, of course, many aspects of the rice culture, some more fundamental than others, some contributing more to welfare than others. Yet "rice culture" is a meaningful concept and was an important source of welfare. The general strategy of development in Sri Lanka was aimed primarily at defending this culture. It also seems correct to emphasize that growth for the sake of growth was given a modest weight, at least among many Sinhalese, in what was conceived as the good life. It is then correct to say that equity considerations mattered in designing strategy and in making policy.

In this way of looking at equity, income inequality played a relatively modest role. As the data reviewed in early pages showed, income inequality was marked and showed little change over the years after independence. The reduction in the most severe consequences of poverty by subsidies seemed to meet the nutritional and health related problems of the poor, which were considered to be the main costs of inequality.

In Malaysia, as well, income distribution as such was not an essential element of the government's view of equity. In the NEP discussions it was especially clear that equality within ethnic groups was of little concern to the government. It is also probably correct to say, although documentation is less clear, that in the society as a whole intraethnic group income equality was of less concern than outside observers would expect. This seems to be the case because the Malay community was primarily interested in restructuring and the Chinese (and Indians to some extent) seemed less interested in equality than in the freedom to pursue economic gain. The primacy of the restructuring notion led to two important difficulties. We have noted that the NEP originally called for some Chinese to move from urban activities into agriculture. This move did not materialize, and indeed represented an idea that was quite incompatible with Chinese preferences. Clearly, it could have been accomplished only by force, which no one was prepared to use. The main issue here is that the restructuring notion sometimes led to ideas that strongly violated preferences, and hence were looked upon as violating valid notions of equity.

There was a more fundamental difficulty created by the emphasis on restructuring. In the late 1970s and 1980s there emerged in Malaysia a strong group of Bumiputera who had gained considerable wealth and power, and whose position was a result of the many subsidies and advantages created for them by the NEP. This consequence of the NEP contributed to the creation of increasing inequality within the Malay community. More important, it created a potent group of individuals who, having become rich and powerful largely from rents, were important defenders of a policy that was generating problems that could not be tolerated indefinitely. The flexibility and freedom for policymaking that the 1969 riots created was, therefore, eroded by the appearance of rent seeking and the political clout of those who gained. Earlier it was argued that the policymaker in Malaysia (and in Sri Lanka) was not hamstrung by rent seeking. That situation had changed by the beginning of the 1980s in Malaysia. And, it is argued here, this result was a consequence of the fact that the equity objective was defined as restructuring rather than primarily as poverty reduction in a strongly growing system. In the 1980s it was harder to change policy and to adjust to new circumstances (for example, the fall in the price of oil) because those who had gained from the NEP were now in a position to protect those gains.

There are two other issues of equity that are even more important, although more nebulous and elusive. One refers to a search for a plural society and the other has to do with wants and want creation.

The Search for an Equitable Plural Society

Throughout our story, we have given considerable attention to the existence of distinct ethnic communities in both countries. The existence of these communities had consequences for the policies that were followed, for the manner of decisionmaking, for the process of development, and for the ideas of equity that seemed to prevail within the governments and within the societies in general. The character of the various groups was so distinct that it seemed apparent to everyone that creating a homogeneous, thoroughly integrated society was neither an appropriate nor a feasible objective. Rather, the objective was, indeed had to be, the creation of a plural society. This last term was used often from the beginning in Malaysia. It was less explicitly used in Sri Lanka, but the notion seems to prevail generally. Pluralism places heavy demands on achieving equity.

A plural society can be defined as one in which different perspectives exist about various fundamental matters that affect ideas about appropriate life-style, social objectives and organizations, attitudes toward the role of government, and notions of a nation's independence and place in the world. The ancient and appealing phrase found in the Rig Veda, "Truth/Being is One: the wise speak of it in multiple ways" reflects pluralism in its most profound sense. Pluralness in Malaysia and Sri Lanka is perhaps most apparent with respect to religion, but it so permeates all aspects of a community's life that there is rarely an area where the notion is not relevant either in understanding events or in policymaking. The problems created by the existence of pluralism were made even more intractable by the absence of significant social and economic categories that cut across ethnic boundaries. Perhaps the single most important gap in the policies of both countries was that of the failure to create some sort of cross-ethnic grouping or identification. This gap made the existing diversity more stark, unrelenting, and potent.

In Malaysia, especially, the evidence suggests that policies followed to effect the "restructuring" made achieving an equitable plural society more difficult. The numerous policies designed to encourage and enable Malays to move into new activities and new positions also created the notion of a favored group. So too, of course, did the emphasis on the notion of special rights or a special position for Malays. The "special rights" for Malays were, in their earliest form, intended to ensure that the Malays were able to maintain their traditional ways and social structure. It was well after independence that the notion was used to justify policies that helped Malays to move into new activities, and hence to change their traditional ways. Earlier chapters discussed ways in which the colonial policies and experiences produced the various distinctions among ethnic groups in Malaysia and Sri Lanka. It can even be argued that at some early stage the particular patterns that the British created were actually consistent with an equitable plural society. The categories that the British sought for the bureaucracies, however, created an image, a target, for other groups. It defined what people, especially young people and their parents, perceived as the way out of their poverty, hopelessness, and ennui. It also meant that the bureaucracies were hardly neutral or apolitical, because their members would be affected by almost any new strategy or new approach. After independence the British approach and assumptions governing the pluralness were unambiguously inappropriate, and changes had to come. The effort to restructure in Malaysia and the effort to establish even more firmly a Sinhalese society in Sri Lanka led to policies that appeared to penalize some groups while favoring others. While such an approach was hardly compatible with the notion of equitable pluralism, one may argue that it was a necessary way to begin.

The social contract accepted at Malaysia's independence, the "Bargain of 1957," was no longer acceptable after 1969. In effect, equity became defined in terms of a different arrangement, a new "contract," that would have the effects sought by the NEP. The design of such a contract acceptable to all ethnic groups became increasingly difficult as the 1970s wore on and the economic difficulties of the 1980s became increasingly severe.

It seems more or less clear that the sharpest forms of discriminatory policies were initially intended to be temporary, to be in effect until they were no longer necessary—that is, until the Malays had caught up, in some sense. Two things, however, seemed to happen. In the first place, the catching up was much more complex and time consuming than originally anticipated. Pressure remained heavy, therefore, to maintain the discriminatory policies longer than was originally expected. The second development was more political in nature. Special Malay rights were interpreted by many to mean that the Malays would remain essentially in control of the government, and, to ensure this, the special position would have to be maintained, presumably indefinitely. Thus the favored position for Malays was viewed from one side as remedial and temporary and from the other as permanent and inalienable (Gordon P. Means in Nevitte and Kennedy 1986). Such contrasting views were obviously not conducive to the emergence of a harmonious pluralism.

In Sri Lanka the ethnic issue of the country was less overpowering, but no less basic, in the search for growth and equity. The Sinhalese, made up of the Low-Country and Kandyan groups, and Sri Lanka Tamils were the most explicit components of the society. The latter group, however, accounts for approximately 11 to 15 percent of the population over the period, and is concentrated in specific geographical regions. The Indian Tamils in the tea plantation added to the heterogeneity. The small number of Christians (most of whom are Sinhalese) constitute a strong, well-organized group. The major source of difficulties in Sri Lanka, as in Malaysia, was that a significant group, the Sinhalese (especially the Kandyans), believed that their interests had been neglected, possibly violated, by the colonial governments and even during the early years of independence. The evidence supporting this view has been examined in the early chapters. On the other side the great emphasis on education had created among many

Sinhalese the expectations of prestigious occupations, which were simply not forthcoming in any acceptable time period. Pluralism and equity actually seemed to be completely incompatible.

By the time of the 1977 election the various policies since independence had solidified the Sinhalese position, and policies were in place that made compliance by the minority groups with Sinhalese policies mandatory. The new government had little choice but to continue this state of affairs. It seems clear that many members of the ethnic minority groups were convinced that the dominance of the majority was unjustified and unacceptable and that they (minorities) were being forced into a situation that they believed violated their notions of an equitable plural society. The various racial conflicts of the 1980s were the result. The election of 1977 gave the UNP a new opportunity to act over a wide front, but, as just noted, it found it essentially impossible to move in the direction of allowing greater participation by the Tamils. In this context the big surge in investment, mainly public investment in construction and infrastructure, did little to ease the tensions. Job creation was modest, and in particular the kinds of jobs that the youth "wanted" were generally unavailable. The inflation undermined, to some extent, the poverty relieving effects of the food stamps.

The ethnic diversity had similarities, but there were also differences that affected policymaking, the impact of the policies followed, and the content of the notion of equity. In Malaysia the ethnic differences were more inherent than in Sri Lanka. In the former country there were no movements for an "independent" state by either major group, and the task was to find a way for two basically different groups to live peacefully side by side, but meanwhile remain distinct groups. In Sri Lanka there has been great pressure for a political separation that would allow the Sri Lankan Tamils some political independence. That possibility was based in part on the fact that the Tamils were heavily concentrated in the Jaffna Peninsula area and in an adjoining district. Similarly, the sources of conflict have not been primarily the differences in per capita income or economic status between the Sinhalese and the Tamils.

The explicit approach to removing economic differences between the Malays and Chinese in Malaysia increasingly emphasized the ethnic divisions. In particular the widespread use of quotas for education, for landholding, for access to loans, and so forth made ethnicity a major item. The fact that the government bureaucracy was, throughout most of the period, overwhelmingly Malay made difficult its achievement of neutrality, and doubtless had considerable negative effect on efficiency. The same was true in the universities, where after the mid-1970s Malays were given preference for appointments and promotions. That such a policy might be acceptable over a short period is quite possible. That it would create major sources of tension and unease if continued over a longer period seems inevitable. The basic problem with the NEP was that it did not effect a widespread increase in the productivity of Malays within the short period that its discriminatory content would be accepted by the non-Malay Malaysians. Inevitably, the problems became even more evident when the economy began to run into difficulties in the 1980s.

Earlier, attention was called to the failure of any cross-ethnic organizations or institutions to emerge or to be encouraged by the government. An illustration of the kind of institution that could have helped in this respect is the labor movement. The Malaysian government exercised considerable restraint on such a movement and on the appearance of labor unions of significant strength. Such a position may have helped with respect to keeping wage rates from a growth that would penalize employment and contribute to a wage inflation. The policy may also have prevented the emergence of a cross-ethnic organization of some strength. A tradeoff may then have been present here. One cannot be sure of such things, but the general point is surely relevant. (See E. Lee 1984 for discussions of the labor policy in both Sri Lanka and Malaysia.)

In Sri Lanka the story is somewhat different. Several observers (such as Robert Oberst in Nevitte and Kennedy 1986) argue that although Sri Lanka has been a competitive democracy for many years, its "democratic structure is majoritarian in nature" (Oberst in Nevitte and Kennedy 1986, p. 152). The large majority were Sinhalese, policies followed by both coalitions reflected this fact, and such policies were often at the expense of the Sri Lankan Tamils. Oberst argues that early on the Sinhalese majority had allowed the Tamils a role in the government and in policymaking. Over the years, however, a change had taken place. The change had been one of an "open system stressing reciprocal exchange obligations between the leaders of the ethnic groups to a system marked by strengthened central control exercised by one ethnic group with limited consideration of the other group's demand" (Oberst in Nevitte and Kennedy 1986, p. 135). Although the UNP government was generally more sympathetic to the original intent of recognizing reciprocity between the main ethnic groups, it could do little to exercise this sympathy. Even after its great victory in the 1977 elections, the UNP could not take explicit action because the status quo was so firmly entrenched.

The capacity of the government to act was, therefore, limited. A history and commitment to a culture and tradition and the idea of past injustices on the part of the majority made cooperation extremely difficult between a large majority and a relatively small minority. Any sort of NEP for Sri Lanka, therefore, does not seem to be in the works. Just as the economy had to fail in an especially painful and evident way before a fundamental redirection of economic strategy could occur, so one can argue that further trauma is necessary before a more satisfactory relationship can be established between the majority and the minority. In this sense, equity is indeed elusive.

Wants and Their Creation

The notion of equity cannot be separated from that of wants. Conventionally, of course, economists have assumed that everyone has a well-established preference function, and this function is taken as given. This convention has been questioned by numerous economists over the years, and is now being discussed even more fully. This issue is especially relevant with respect to the search for growth with equity in Sri Lanka and Malaysia. Its importance arises in part from the ethnic diversity of the two nations and, more important, from the entrenched and cherished traditions followed by many in both populations. The tensions that arose from commitments to the past existing alongside the strong appeal of the new and presumably better have been noted at several points in our story. The task now is to comment briefly on the ways in which the ambiguity of wants affected the growth with equity search.

"Better" wants may be considered an essential component of development. Frank H. Knight especially examined this issue. For example, in *The Ethics of Competition and Other Essays*, he wrote, "We propose to suggest that these wants which are the common starting point of economic reasoning are from a more critical point of view the most obstinately unknown of all unknowns in the whole system of variables with which economic science deals" (Knight 1935, p. 20). Knight says explicitly that wants are variables with which economics deals. One cannot hand the task over to another discipline. Michael S. McPherson (1983) has made a stronger statement:

> When we recognize that preferences have analyzable structures—as means to deeper ends, in the conflict between an ideal that is striven for and actual conduct that falls short, or in other ways—it becomes especially important to move beyond observations of overt behavior to understand these phenomena. For precisely the meanings that activities and choices have for people, the underlying reasons for their actions, are embedded in these structures. It is just perverse to try to tease these meanings out under the self-imposed discipline of refusing to look at any evidence but "revealed preferences"—a bit like playing charades.

We have emphasized in several places in the preceding chapters that it is the cultural and social setting that gives goods and services their meaning. It is also this setting that provides opportunities and insights that are necessary for personal development, for changing wants, for finding new, more rewarding wants (McPherson 1983, pp. 110 and following). Poverty is demoralizing, not only because it may deprive people of basic physical needs, but also because it deprives them of the opportunity to expand their wants, to find these new and better wants, of which Knight and McPherson speak.

Such wants are learned. They are neither "given" nor are they obtained by psychological reflection or introspection on the part of the individual. Learning, we know, is difficult and painful. The failure of the traditional approach in Sri Lanka—a rice culture, substantial food subsidies, "free" education and health services, and so forth, financed from taxes levied mainly on plantations that were frequently foreign owned—created the necessity not only of asking what could be afforded in the usual sense, but what, in a rapidly and necessarily changing environment, it made sense to "want." The disruptions of 1971, not related to race, reflected not just the difficulties of finding a job, but also finding a set of circumstances that provided some meaning for the educated young people. The spread of information about other products, other activities, and other societies created prospective alternatives that were immediately appealing, but that often proved unsatisfying and disappointing as they were experienced.

In Malaysia, also, the search for new wants was complex and painful. The notion underlying the NEP was that the Bumiputera wanted what the Chinese had. It seems clear that the Bumiputera wanted something that they did not have, but it is also clear that most were still not convinced that simply imitating the Chinese (or the British, or anyone else) made much sense. Earlier in this study we discussed many of the complexities that resulted in the NEP producing less than, and other than, the effects expected, and indeed sought, by the new approach. Emphasis was given to difficulties created by lack of skills, entrepreneurship, access to credit, experience, and so forth. All of these are indeed important parts of the story. The point here, however, is that the strategy to restructure the economy and society forced Bumiputera into activities that, in a very fundamental sense, they resisted, that they did not "want." The existence of educated unemployed illustrates this point in both Malaysia and Sri Lanka. The new recruits did not "want" jobs that were available and, therefore, they demanded something else that they hoped would be more satisfying. The recent importation of labor from Indonesia and the Philippines into Malaysia reflects the same kind of thing, as does the increasing interest in Islamic fundamentalism.

The literature on development (and the economics literature in general) has not explored this issue in much detail, and few hypotheses, empirical or otherwise, have been proposed and even fewer examined. (Some of the work of Scitovsky, Hirschman, Amartya Sen, Mc-

Pherson, Arrow, and several others offer important insights, explore arguments, and suggest hypotheses.) Only one point can be made in the present context. This point, at its simplest, is that rapid changes make the task of want creation more complex than do slower, more cautious changes. It can be said that the opening of an economy, certainly its abrupt opening, adds to this complexity. Both Malaysia and Sri Lanka were forced, by economic and other circumstances, to act rapidly, to seek to change things rapidly; therefore the community's task of learning what was actually wanted was further complicated.

The historical development had created a culture in both countries that had become well established. Our story has emphasized how it became impossible for all, or even most, of the aspects of the two cultures to be maintained as their economic bases faltered. To change quickly, however, implied that new wants were known, but this was surely not the case. Preferences then did not have "time" to develop. As "personal autonomy" became increasingly possible—increasingly visible in the two countries—it became ever more important to allow time for the learning of new wants. This greater autonomy created a more favorable environment for choice, and individuals of the societies had the prospect of more control over the way in which they developed. As incomes increased, people were less constrained by resource problems and less subject to outside forces that impede the capacity to find one's own way (McPherson 1983). That capacity, however, must be learned; it does not merely exist. This is one of the important senses in which the rewards of independence, political and economic, must be learned. Again, rapid change in a plural society imposes demands on preference formation that can hardly be expected to be realized immediately.

Why Growth Rates Differed

Policymaking Again

Development economics, like most of economics, has experienced significant changes in approach and emphasis over the years since the late 1940s. In the first couple of decades attention was given to the physical characteristics and needs of the developing country—capital and savings, entrepreneurship, labor skills, foreign trade, and so forth. There was relatively little discussion of policy as such except from staunch defenders of free trade. For example, the term "import substitution" does not seem to have appeared until the middle of the 1960s. From about 1970 attention seemed to turn to policy. Implicitly, in most cases, it appeared that observers had accepted the view that there were reasons to believe that these physical characteristics either were never really the problem or had been overcome. Any failure to overcome them was a result of policy mistakes; in other words, any failure could be overcome with the correct policy. The correct policy has recently, with great frequency, been framed in terms of greater reliance on the market, a reduced role for government and for direct controls of any kind, a heavy emphasis on the value of exports, and a generally favorable attitude toward foreign investment. It is not unkind to development economists to say that these policy views seemed to emerge after the success of the economies of Taiwan and the Republic of Korea became apparent.

Then, of course, one can question the reason that countries follow the "wrong" policies. The favored answer to this question is that those who gain from the rents created by wrong policy prevent change. Certainly this is often a relevant point. Another potential answer is that the "right" policy is simply not known or not recognized by the policymaker. It is understood in this context that an expert's simply telling the policymaker what the right policy is rarely has much of an effect. And, of course, the expert might well be wrong.

There is then a last position. All policy change must begin from a status quo, and must take place within a set of institutions and social arrangements, a history, and a political climate. What the "right" policy is, then, depends as heavily on these considerations as it does on the behavior of conventional economic variables. We have tried to document that this was true in both countries over the period examined. That changes in the economic variables can force modification of policy (as in Sri Lanka) is clear, but so also can changes in social arrangements and community relationships (as in Malaysia) force modification in the way the economy functions. Thus policymaking is far more complex than simply designing the correct policy and having the skills and resources to implement it.

Policies and Economic Performance

Tables 16-1 and 16-2 summarize the changes in the major economic variables in the two countries. The table for Malaysia shows an impressive performance, and that for Sri Lanka is certainly adequate. Our basic task now is to try to account for the differences summarized in the two tables. Within this broad question, there are several specific questions that will occupy most attention, the most general of which is: To what extent can the differences in performance between the countries be explained by different policies? A similar question is: To what extent would different policies have produced different development and equity stories? Equally relevant but more difficult to pin down is a third question: To what extent is it possible to identify the

Table 16-1. Summary Data for Sri Lanka

Growth rate (percent)	1950–60	1960–70	1970–77	1977–85	1950–85
GDP (1980 prices)	3.4	4.8	2.9	5.5	4.7
Population	2.5	2.3	1.6	1.6	2.1
Exports (U.S. dollars)	2.1	3.2	4.4	7.0	4.4
Consumer price index	0.6	2.8	5.7	13.6	5.2
Economic indicator (percent)	1950	1960	1970	1980	1985
Agriculture/GDP	38.9	37.7	28.3	27.5	27.5
Manufacturing/GDP	10.6	15.4	16.7	18.0	14.6
Tea and rubber exports/ total exports	74.0	80.5	76.6	49.8	40.2
Gini coefficient[a]	0.46	0.45	0.35	0.44	0.45
Share of highest decile[a]	40.6	36.7	28.0	35.8	37.3
Share of lowest decile[a]	1.9	1.5	2.8	2.1	2.2
Proportion of population 14–64	40.6[b]	54.3	54.5	59.6	62.0
Foreign currency debt/ exports	4.7	11.1	45.0	103.9	160.2
Foreign exchange reserves[c]	9	3	2	2	3
Government deficit or surplus/government revenue	−2.2	−32.8	−33.2	−105.0	−48.1
Investment/GDP	11.2	13.8	17.3	25.3	25.1
Social indicator	1950	1960	1970	1980	1985
Life expectancy at birth (years)	62	64	64	68	70
Crude birth rate (per thousand)	36	33	29	28	25
Crude death rate (per thousand)	9	8	7	6	6
Infant mortality rate (per thousand)	71	63	58	44	36
Child death rate (per thousand)	7	6	5	3	2
School enrollment[d]					
Primary	95	93	99	100	104
Secondary	27	35	47	51	61
Urbanization[e]	18	20	22	27	21

a. Estimates are for 1953, 1963, 1973, 1978–79, and 1981–82. The estimates for 1973 are quite misleading.

b. Estimate is for 1946.

c. Equivalency in months' worth of imports.

d. Number enrolled in school as a percentage of age group.

e. Urban population as a percentage of total.

Source: Statistical appendix and text tables.

Table 16-2. Summary Data for Malaysia

Growth rate (percent)	1960–70	1970–80	1980–85	1960–85
GDP (1970 prices)	6.5	7.9	5.7	6.9
Population	2.5	2.8	2.5	2.6
Exports (U.S. dollars)	5.1	23.0	3.2	11.5
Consumer price index	0.9	5.9	4.7	3.6

Economic indicator (percent)	1960	1970	1980	1985
Agriculture/GDP	40.0	30.8	24.1	20.3
Manufacturing/GDP	8.6	13.4	21.8	19.1
Rubber, tin, and oil exports/ total exports	73.1	56.9	49.0	34.8
Gini coefficient	.42[a]	.50	.51[b]	.48[c]
Share of highest decile	34.8	41.1	39.3	36.6
Share of lowest decile	2.2	1.2	1.3	1.4
Proportion of population 14–64	53.3	51.5	55.6	59.0
Foreign currency debt/ exports	9.9	14.4	17.2	55.5
Foreign exchange reserves[d]	5	5	5	4
Government deficit or surplus/government revenue	12.3	−18.9	−50.4	−27.4
Investment/GDP	14.7	20.2	31.8	29.2

Social indicator	1950	1960	1970	1980	1985
Life expectancy at birth (years)	53	55	59	64	68
Crude birth rate (per thousand)	45	42	36	31	30
Crude death rate (per thousand)	16	13	10	7	6
Infant mortality rate (per thousand)	72	57	45	31	28
Child death rate (per thousand)	7	5	3	2	2
School enrollment[e]					
Primary	96	90	87	92	97
Secondary	19	28	34	51	53
Urbanization[f]	25	26	27	29	38

a. Estimate is for 1957–58.
b. Estimate is for 1979.
c. Estimate is for 1984.
d. Equivalency in months' worth of imports.
e. Number enrolled in school as a percentage of age group.
f. Urban population as a percentage of total.
Source: Statistical appendix and text tables.

reason that the policies were followed? The discussion in this section and the following one is built around these questions.

As of 1950 or so both economies were in good shape. This strength was primarily a consequence of an impressive export sector, largely owned and managed by the British. The Sri Lankans taxed this sector to finance their rice (and other) subsidies and to enable the Sinhalese to sustain their rice culture satisfactorily. The Malaysians used their export sector to maintain an exceptionally strong balance of payments and a zero inflation position, as well as to help finance the land development schemes. Very early on, however, there were convincing signals that such an approach could not be maintained very much longer. The world market for natural rubber was declining, tea was in some trouble for various reasons, and tin (in Malaysia) was facing major supply problems. The conversion from rubber to oil palm went well in Malaysia, but oil palm could not be expected to take up all the slack of a failing rubber. By the early 1960s, at the latest, the evidence seemed convincing that both countries had to find a new source of support and dynamism if they were not to suffer a decline. Finding and establishing this new source of dynamism became the basic economic question in both countries, and of course had to be considered in the context of the great ethnic diversity and other social problems.

We can also identify a major difference between the two countries in this context. Policies followed in Sri Lanka hurried the relative decline of the estate sector, and, therefore, exacerbated the difficulties inherent in the failure of new, dynamic sectors to appear. In Malaysia the policies followed penalized the estates hardly at all, and, therefore, enabled the economy to be supported better during the search for new sectors. In addition, the Rubber Research Institute in Malaysia, as previously noted, enjoyed unusual success. There was less success in these areas for tea. A major decision frequently exists as to how many new resources should be applied to an important sector to slow down an inevitable long-run decline. Malaysia resolved this issue more satisfactorily than did Sri Lanka. Malaysia's situation was also eased by the development of significant amounts of oil and the great rise in oil prices in the late 1970s.

The difficulties in developing new activities to supplement traditional ones were the principal reasons for the employment problems and other problems associated with a somewhat slack economy. Earlier sections briefly discussed intergenerational inequality. It is helpful to note this argument now a bit more completely. Throughout most of the period, the concentration on traditional activities in both countries resulted in greater available supplies of goods and services than would have been possible with another output composition. The communities, therefore, enjoyed a higher income than would have been possible had trade restrictions been more severe. Comparative advantage was served. At the same time this approach led to an increasingly rigid economy—an economy in which it became increasingly difficult to move into new activities and to either respond to or create new opportunities. More briefly, the approach contributed to weak transformation capacity. Thus, when the traditional activities began to fail, both economies found it difficult to pick up the slack. Had the economy sacrificed its advantage when the traditional activities were still powerful, however, and thereby built up its capacity to adjust and respond—built up its transformation capacity—the later generation would have been less penalized. The earlier generation would have had less; the next generation would have enjoyed more. Intergeneration equity would have been served. The movement would have been eased from dependence on the traditional activities to new activities. Some protection would have been necessary. Such protection would then constitute a form of investment—investment in the creation of a more flexible, responsive economy (Bruton 1989). The trick, of course, is to protect without imposing severe distortions on the system and to ensure that during the protection, capacity in new activities emerges. It is no small trick, and our basic criticism of the policies in both countries is that they failed to achieve it. The economics profession, be it noted, did not offer much help.

The mild Dutch Disease that each country suffered made designing and implementaing this kind of strategy difficult and less than urgent. The argument is clearer for Malaysia than for Sri Lanka because Malaysia had the stronger economy throughout most of the period. The development of oil in the latter half of the 1970s was particularly important in clearly defining the issues for Malaysia. In Sri Lanka the argument is reasonably clear for the 1950s and 1960s, but the years from 1970 to 1977 were so precarious that nothing much was clear. After 1977 the large inflow of foreign aid created the problem all over again.

The most convincing form of protection without distortion is, as noted in earlier chapters, an "undervalued" exchange rate. The term "undervaluation" is in quotes because it is hardly unambiguous in the best of circumstances. In any circumstance, it would mean that foreign exchange is accumulated, not for the purpose of adding to foreign exchange reserves, but because the undervaluation helps to create opportunities that induce efforts to increase productivity and output. These inducements are provided without eliminating competition and without distorting internal signals, except to give extra encouragement to tradables relative to nontradables. The inducements, by encouraging search for ways to increase productivity, act directly on this strategic source of growth. Evidently there are many aspects of this approach to protection that have to be considered, but only five that are directly relevant to Malaysia and Sri Lanka can be discussed here.

- Such an instrument creates inducements throughout the system, not just in specific sectors. In this way the transformation problem is also addressed. The undervaluation operates well in those activities where indigenous entrepreneurs are effective. It was noted earlier that both transformation capacity and entrepreneurial ability may be appraised only with respect to the demands placed on them. The protection provided by an undervalued exchange rate helps to promote consistency between the demands for such capacity and its availability. This is an especially relevant point in both of our countries.
- This approach would help to relieve the intergenerational inequality to which reference was made earlier.
- The approach could help to effect the transition from the export enclave economy to the more diversified, flexible system. As our figures have shown, both economies experienced an increasing array of problems—inflation, budget deficits, balance of payments problems—as the period wore on. This we have explained by the breakdown of the old system before the new was in place. Had the transition begun earlier and proceeded more slowly, it (the transition) would surely have been less difficult.
- This particular policy instrument must be seen in the context of other policies, especially the land development and general agriculture policies. Implicit in the argument, however, is the notion that these large-scale projects with their substantial subsidies should have proceeded more slowly and only after other, smaller projects had been completed. The economy then would have been better equipped to absorb and to utilize them more effectively.
- The economy (and society) is protected in a very fundamental way by undervaluation. Imports are made expensive in domestic currency, and the economy is given time to learn new technologies, new ways of approaching problems, and new ways of building onto what is already there. Protection in this form also helps to slow down the influx of materials (periodicals, books, television shows, and so forth) below a rate that would create wants that could violate, with undue abruptness, existing patterns of consumption and behavior. Tourism would be encouraged by undervaluation, and additional forms of protection (for example, high hotel tax or visa requirements) would be necessary if this activity were to be discouraged.

A final general policy issue refers to aggregate demand and supply constraints. It has been argued that neither country was lodged regularly against conventionally identified constraints—saving, balance of payments, labor, and so forth This statement is more directly valid for Malaysia than it is for Sri Lanka, but is applicable to Sri Lanka in most intervals. Thus, neither country seemed successful in fully utilizing its available resources. In Sri Lanka a conventional distortion explanation is partly responsible, which was also true of Malaysia in the 1980s. In general, however, other explanations are more important. Especially in Malaysia it is clear that constraints were imposed in the 1960s because of concern for differences in the income and position of the Bumiputera and Chinese. The higher growth of the 1970s was possible because, with the NEP in place, the government deemed it appropriate to push harder on utilization. Even then there was underutilization and the economy was not really pressed hard. Malaysians were also very inflation conscious, which made them far more cautious than Sri Lankans about fiscal and monetary policy. In Sri Lanka the evidence is less direct. There was always considerable unemployment for reasons studied earlier. The big land development and irrigation projects did not offer as much employment as other projects would have, nor did they capitalize on the potential savings of small-scale producing units that face profitable investment opportunities. More than in Malaysia, the observed slack in Sri Lanka was a consequence of a particular investment allocation policy.

Productive growth is encouraged by good, evident opportunities facing potentially manageable constraints, which the undervalued exchange rate policy helps to accomplish. Another necessity is for the economy to resist acceptable constraints, which was not achieved effectively in either country, and, therefore, dampened productivity growth and growth of output.

All of this leads to a counterexample that may be briefly summarized. An exchange rate that resulted in a steady accumulation of foreign exchange would have afforded nondistorting protection for each country. This kind of protection, accompanied by very few other impediments to trade, would create a major inducement to find ways to capitalize on the profitability of exporting, and of import substitution. New activities would, therefore, have been expected to appear that would supplement the traditional ones which, as emphasized, were experiencing long-run difficulties in both countries. Each economy would, in this counterexample, also be pushed hard enough for labor bottlenecks to begin to appear. If the undervaluation alone did not accomplish this objective (by increased and very evident investment opportunities), additional government outlays would be warranted. Reducing unemployment to the maximum extent consistent with controllable inflationary pressure would add further inducements to search for ways to increase productivity. It would also help to alleviate poverty and, with the protection, to create employment opportunities in nontraditional activities. Ample job opportunities would have made school attendance in secondary and advanced institutions more expensive, thereby helping to reduce the demand for places in these programs.

In this counterexample there would be very little foreign capital or foreign aid coming into either country. This would be justified because there was little evidence of a major saving problem in the two countries. There would be no free trade zones.

Such a strategy, it is argued, would have created opportunities, investment, and employment in activities where transformation and entrepreneurial obstacles were modest. The profitability of increasing output combined with the rising cost of labor and imported capital would have induced search for ways to increase productivity. Increased productivity is, we all agree, the heart of the growth process. The counterexample about equity will be discussed later.

The Differences in Economic Performance

The data show Malaysia's performance to be markedly superior to that of Sri Lanka. The growth rates of GDP are the most explicit measure of this superiority, but there are other indicators as well. Unemployment was never as severe in Malaysia as in Sri Lanka. The structure of GDP changed in a more satisfactory way, and the dependence on a few export items was relieved more satisfactorily in Malaysia. The investment rate was higher, the balance of payments stronger, and inflation and the government budget under better control. There is no single explanation for these differences. Many factors were at work to account for the observed differences. In other words, the explanation is found in our story.

The most frequently discussed explanation of the apparent better showing of Malaysia is in terms of foreign trade policy. Although neither country pushed as hard for import substitution in the 1950s and 1960s as did many developing countries, Malaysia was the much more open economy of the two. Protection was modest and the exceptional price stability over these years allowed the exchange rate to remain fairly stable without a constantly increasing overvaluation of the domestic currency. The absence of any inflation made it easier to keep wage rates from rising, and Malaysia continued to be considered a low-wage, abundant labor economy with little labor union activity. The sharp distinction often found between import substitution and export promotion does not seem as relevant for Malaysia as for other countries (H. Osman-Rani in Fisk and Osman-Rani 1982, p. 263). Policy toward foreign investment was generally open and encouraging. In addition there were relatively few direct controls and government interventions into the economy. The absence of such interventions in Malaysia contributed to its flexibility and adaptiveness.

After 1970 this open, market-oriented approach began to be modified. Tariffs were increased, tax concessions were offered for investment, export promotion became a common term, and free trade zones
were established. In addition, all the various regulations designed to
implement the NEP became increasingly important and impinged more
and more frequently on private economic decisions. Growth continued strong in the 1970s, but the economy became less flexible and
little headway was made toward replacing the traditional activities
with alternative sources of dynamism. When the slowdown in world
trade began in 1980, Malaysia was not well prepared, and the various
difficulties, previously reviewed, became evident.

Sri Lanka, however, was always less open and outward looking,
and, probably more important, was never able to establish a clear-
cut, long-run development strategy. The latter difficulty resulted from
frequent changes in government combined with the marked difference in outlook between the two dominant coalitions. Import controls
were more prevalent than in Malaysia, and the move toward nationalization of plantations far stronger. The scope of public sector industrial
activities was also greater and the array of direct controls, especially
with respect to foreign trade, tended to discourage all private investment—domestic and foreign. Export incentives were much weaker
than in Malaysia and, as previously noted, Sri Lanka's management
of the phasing out of foreign ownership and control of the estates was
especially costly.

The industrial sector's performance may be compared with that of
the rice sector, and of the rural sectors in general. The rural sector,
agriculture in particular, was indeed favored by both coalitions in a
variety of ways, rather than squeezed as in many developing countries. The various food subsidy arrangements were tilted toward the
rural resident. There were the institutional supports as well that contained a large subsidy component. Rice production, as has been emphasized, responded well to all this, and self-sufficiency in rice, an
especially important target, was more or less achieved. These developments in the rural sectors, however, could not compensate for the
difficulties in the plantation and industrial sectors.

The argument here is *not* that Sri Lanka pursued an inward-looking
policy and, therefore, was unable to exploit export opportunities,
while Malaysia was more open and, therefore, did enjoy sustained
export growth, thereby achieving the flexibility and adaptiveness that
characterizes a strong economy. Indeed, as the 1980s have shown,
Malaysia did not accomplish this. Rather, it was Sri Lanka's inability to
establish a long-run strategy to create an environment that facilitated
productivity growth that caused problems. The various distortions in
Sri Lanka seemed to force on it a stop-go sequence that always defeats
productivity growth. Malaysia avoided this particular stop-go diffi-

culty. The greater degree of outward lookingness (in addition to oil) is one reason, but not the basic reason, for Malaysia's apparently better showing.

In addition to the inward-looking, outward-looking explanation, considerable attention has also been given to the role that subsidies may have played in accounting for differences in the performance of the two economies. The food subsidies in Sri Lanka have long been evident to all observers. It is obvious that if most of the resources that were allocated to subsidies had been used for capital formation, the Sri Lanka story would be different. Undoubtedly, the food subsidies in Sri Lanka were unnecessarily extensive before 1977—the poor could have been adequately helped with smaller outlays. We have, however, attempted to demonstrate that the food subsidy programs were not an especially important factor in accounting for Sri Lanka's less impressive growth story. Malaysia, too, provided large-scale subsidies in the form of education, land and crop development, health care, and so forth. These subsidies were less evident than the food subsidies of Sri Lanka, but may have been as large a proportion of GDP or government expenditure as in Sri Lanka. Direct comparisons were not possible, but general evidence supports the preceding statement. Although Malaysia was better able to sustain its large subsidies than was Sri Lanka, the growth of the latter country was rarely constrained primarily by the availability of investable resources. In other words, if Sri Lanka had done nothing different except abolish food subsidies, the consequence would have been that a large share of the population would have been hungry, not that the economy would have grown faster.

A more nebulous difference in policy matters between the two countries is the independence, the "degrees of freedom," each country had in choosing its specific policy and broad strategy. We have argued from the beginning that policymaking is necessarily constrained in any country. No country has complete freedom to do what the economist says is correct. This argument is especially clear with respect to Sri Lanka at its independence in 1950. It is frequently asserted that because Sri Lanka is a small, island country, it should have been evident to everyone that foreign trade was its best hope for an engine of growth. Sri Lanka's experience with trade over the period from 1920 to 1950 was not a happy one; indeed, it had suffered severely as a consequence of the dislocations and costs created by the sluggish 1920s, the Great Depression, and World War II. Virtually no one projected that world trade would grow at rates never previously experienced in history. Most projections were the opposite—a return to the unfortunate state of affairs that prevailed in the 1930s. It is, therefore, virtually inconceivable that, in 1950, a Sri Lankan government would have gone all out for an open, trade-dominated economy.

By the time of Malaysia's independence, the big trade boom was evident, and it could proceed—confident that the world market was growing strongly. Differences in perceived options were surely important, and greatly favored Malaysia throughout the years studied.

Part of the explanation for the differences in perceived options as well as actual performance is attributable to the fact that management (as distinct from policies) was better in Malaysia than in Sri Lanka. The previous decisionmaking discussion bears on this issue as well. The difference in management is partly a result of the greater stability of the Malaysian government and its capacity to think in longer-range terms than were the various governments of Sri Lanka. The nonestate, private sector was also stronger and better managed in Malaysia mainly because of the particular dynamism of the relatively large Chinese sector. If it were possible to compare the nonestate Bumiputera sector of Malaysia with the nonestate Sinhalese sector of Sri Lanka, we would surely find these differences much less pronounced. The Sri Lankan Tamils may have been better managers over these years than were the Sinhalese, but were not numerous enough to affect the entire economy as were the Chinese in Malaysia. The fact that the private sector Bumiputera and Sinhalese were less experienced and less effective is accounted for by the historical and social factors reviewed in previous chapters.

The resource base of Malaysia was certainly larger and richer than that of Sri Lanka. The rubber and tin activities in the 1950s and 1960s, the capacity of the estates to shift into oil palm with its strong market, and, finally, the discovery of oil at an opportune time meant that Malaysia has, throughout its independence (and indeed since 1950), been functioning from an unusually strong resource base. Petroleum, in particular, came along at a helpful time to keep the economy moving as the other major sectors were failing to some degree. Sri Lanka's resource base was much less impressive, and no new activity appeared—such as oil palm or oil—to take up the slack created by sluggish tea and rubber sectors. It bears repeating that Sri Lanka's policy toward the tea estates in particular had adverse effects on that sector. Still, it seems indisputable that Malaysia's natural resource base was much stronger than that of Sri Lanka, and that this is an important part of the explanation for the differing growth rates.

A final explanation may well be the most fundamental. It seems to have been true that the Sri Lankans attached lesser importance to growth of GDP than did the Malaysians. In other words, Sri Lanka accepted a variety of constraints on growth because these "constraints" were features of their society to which they attached great value. It is even clearer that the Sinhalese placed less importance on growth than did the Malaysian Chinese. Hard evidence to support such a view is naturally unavailable. The most convincing evidence is simply the fact of the frequent changes in government (until the post-1977 years) in Sri Lanka, and the evidence that no government could be elected or remain in power that did not pursue a variety of policies that protected, or sought to protect, the traditional Sinhalese approach to economic matters. The land development schemes, the hesitancy with respect to foreign investment, the subsidies, and the appeal of the Transfer State idea, all suggest a casual attitude toward growth as such in Sri Lanka. The explanation for this attitude also can only be found in the long history of the two nations and how that history evolved over time.

It could be argued that, although GDP growth rates for Malaysia were markedly higher than those for Sri Lanka, growth rates of social welfare may have been more nearly equal, or even reversed. This is conjecture, of course, but the general evidence seems to support it—Sri Lanka grew more slowly because it wanted to. It is obviously an important conclusion. The failures of the years from 1970 to 1977 were not only economic failures, but also convinced many that a tradition, which had always constituted a major source of welfare and meaning, was no longer viable.

Why the GDP in constant prices grows more rapidly in one country than in another can rarely be answered in specific, categorical terms. The stories of Sri Lanka and Malaysia illustrate how dangerous it is to identify one or two or characteristics and attribute the different growth rates to them. Meanwhile, as one studies and reflects on the two stories, it becomes understandable that measured GDP would grow more rapidly in Malaysia than in Sri Lanka. The fact that the explanations for different growth rates are to be found in the general features of the countries' economic, political, and social evolution contributes to the complexity of implementing a new approach toward addressing deep-seated economic questions to raise the growth rate. It also should make us hesitate to condemn or praise the approach that a given country actually followed. Perhaps, as someone observed, Malaysia grew faster because it was Malaysia and Sri Lanka grew more slowly because it was Sri Lanka.

Policy and Equity

Neither country had much success in achieving equity as it is defined here. Overall income distribution changed only modestly over the period. In Malaysia the data show an impressive reduction in the incidence of poverty, especially after 1976. Similarly, the average rate of growth of the incomes of Malays exceeded that of Chinese, so the Malays did catch up a little relative to the Chinese. The Malaysian Indians, however, were generally ignored, and their position worsened. Targets of the NEP were generally not reached, although it was recognized by the mid-1970s that the targets were unrealistic. As the difficulties of the 1980s emerged, the NEP faded into the background, and other aspects of equity also began to receive less attention. Increased tension surfaced between the Chinese and Malays, the most explicit evidence of which was the emergence of a significant Islamic fundamentalist movement.

In Sri Lanka ethnic conflicts continued. Measured income equality changed little, and it seems clear that the real costs of poverty became more severe after 1977. The Indian Tamils on the estates rarely shared in any improved economic performance. By the mid-1980s it was evident that the new policy approach was not providing the employment and income that would compensate for the reduction in subsidies. In both countries there continued an employment problem among the younger age groups.

Numerous difficulties in establishing an equitable plural society were discussed previously, and another point or two can be added. Consider the equity implications of the counterexample that was presented earlier. That story, it was claimed, would have produced sufficiently strong demand for labor to reduce unemployment significantly. It is argued that a strong demand for labor is necessary to achieve equity. Powerful economic incentives can contribute to breaking down barriers that might be tolerated when the cost of doing so is low. Ample job opportunities with rising wage rates make it costly for youth to stand idle on the street corner. Similarly, the protection via undervaluation would help to create a range of opportunities that could be exploited by small-scale, indigenous economic agents. This, too, promotes equity—and learning. The push on education, on Malay employment quotas, and so forth in Malaysia was less effective, and caused greater irritation among non-Malays because of the continued slack in the system. In Sri Lanka the creation of widespread employment opportunities was probably the single most important means to a more equitable society available to the nation. One can then conclude that growth and increased equity would both have been served by the approach outlined earlier.

The other point is that changes in characteristics as cherished and as historically and culturally determined as those that produce ethnic difficulties must be expected to change slowly. In part, they change slowly because they are an inherent part of the social framework, which, in other respects, is a source of strength. It is important to be impatient about the correction of an acknowledged inequity. It is also important to recognize that what appears to be a slow rectification is often, in fact, the most secure one, and hence the most rapid.

In both countries, had purposeful policy changes occurred slowly and regularly from the time of independence, social and economic development might have proceeded more smoothly and might have had a stronger base than they actually experienced. This means, as mentioned in the beginning, that policymaking and changes should be continuous—move where it is possible to move, adjust where it is possible to adjust, and thereby avoid having to make decisions that impose abrupt, severe, and deep-seated changes in the country's social and economic functions. A government should be searching, experimenting, learning, constantly moving as it seeks to respond to issues before they become crises. A strategic role that the analyst can play is to identify such issues and suggest ways to respond to them that do not require drastic and disruptive action. Such a role is much more productive than one built around major readjustments and attempts at permanent change. Indeed there are no truly permanent changes, because the situation itself is fluid.

The same notion applies to equity. There is no final definition of equity. There is, however, the search for equity, and it is the search that is its own reward.

Statistical
Appendix

Table A-1. Sri Lanka: National Product, 1950–85

Year	GDP (millions of rupees)		Population (millions)	GDP per capita, 1980 prices (rupees)
	Current prices	1980 prices		
1950	4,169	17,156	7.68	2,234
1951	4,817	18,599	7.88	2,360
1952	4,538	19,287	8.07	2,390
1953	4,717	19,091	8.29	2,302
1954	4,997	19,654	8.52	2,307
1955	5,608	20,870	8.72	2,393
1956	5,384	19,719	8.93	2,208
1957	5,607	20,997	9.16	2,292
1958	5,935	21,987	9.39	2,341
1959	6,362	22,635	9.62	2,353
1960	6,684	23,885	9.90	2,413
1961	6,687	24,303	10.14	2,397
1962	7,006	24,878	10.38	2,397
1963	7,382	26,461	10.65	2,484
1964	7,793	28,100	10.90	2,578
1965	8,084	28,782	11.16	2,579
1966	8,337	30,261	11.44	2,645
1967	9,037	32,094	11.70	2,743
1968	10,718	33,492	11.99	2,793
1969	11,695	36,231	12.25	2,958
1970	13,664	41,963	12.52	3,352
1971	14,050	41,937	12.61	3,326
1972	15,247	45,222	12.86	3,516
1973	18,404	46,816	13.09	3,576
1974	23,771	48,667	13.28	3,665
1975	26,577	50,950	13.50	3,774
1976	30,203	53,211	13.72	3,884
1977	36,407	55,244	13.94	3,963
1978	42,665	59,098	14.19	4,165
1979	52,387	62,880	14.47	4,345
1980	66,527	66,527	14.74	4,513
1981	85,005	70,386	14.99	4,695
1982	99,238	73,975	15.19	4,870
1983	121,601	77,645	15.42	5,035
1984	153,746	80,800	15.60	5,179
1985	162,375	84,805	15.84	5,354

Source: For GDP in 1950–81, IMF (annual for 1979 and 1986); in 1981–84 IMF *International Financial Statistics* (March 1988); in 1985, Central Bank of Sri Lanka (annual for 1985).

Table A-2. Sri Lanka: Components of GDP, 1950–85
(ratio of indicated component to GDP; percent)

Year	Investment	Private consumption	Government consumption	Exports	Imports	Saving
1950	9.5	71.7	10.5	39.1	30.9	17.7
1951	10.4	73.9	10.4	40.5	35.3	15.6
1952	13.3	80.5	12.6	34.4	40.9	6.8
1953	10.6	77.8	13.1	36.0	37.6	9.0
1954	9.4	71.1	12.0	38.3	30.8	16.9
1955	10.7	70.7	11.2	36.9	29.5	18.1
1956	14.6	69.5	12.3	36.5	33.0	18.1
1957	15.6	72.8	13.3	33.4	35.3	13.7
1958	14.1	72.8	14.6	31.1	32.5	12.7
1959	14.8	73.4	14.2	31.7	34.2	12.3
1960	14.1	74.5	14.4	30.1	33.0	11.2
1961	13.7	72.7	14.6	28.5	29.5	12.7
1962	14.5	72.8	14.2	28.1	29.6	13.0
1963	15.7	72.3	13.7	25.8	27.5	14.0
1964	14.3	73.8	14.0	24.8	27.0	12.1
1965	12.5	72.7	14.4	25.9	25.5	12.9
1966	14.3	75.2	13.9	22.4	26.7	10.0
1967	15.2	73.9	13.7	20.5	23.3	12.4
1968	15.9	74.0	13.1	20.6	23.6	12.9
1969	19.3	74.4	12.6	18.4	24.6	13.1
1970	18.9	72.3	11.9	25.4	28.6	15.7
1971	17.1	72.4	12.5	24.6	26.6	15.1
1972	17.3	71.8	12.5	22.3	23.9	15.7
1973	13.7	76.5	11.0	24.3	25.6	12.3
1974	15.7	80.2	11.6	26.4	33.9	8.2
1975	15.6	82.6	9.3	27.5	35.0	8.1
1976	16.2	76.1	10.0	29.0	31.4	13.8
1977	14.4	73.3	8.6	33.8	30.1	18.1
1978	20.0	75.2	9.5	34.8	39.5	15.3
1979	25.8	77.1	9.1	33.7	45.7	13.8
1980	33.8	80.3	8.5	32.2	54.8	11.2
1981	27.8	80.1	8.2	30.4	46.5	11.7
1982	30.7	80.0	8.2	27.4	46.3	11.8
1983	28.9	78.1	8.1	26.3	41.4	13.8
1984	25.3	72.9	7.8	29.0	35.0	19.3
1985	23.8	77.9	10.2	26.0	38.0	11.8

Note: The saving ratio is given by the sum of the investment and export ratios minus the import ratio. All ratios are calculated from the current price series. Constant price series would give slightly different values.

Source: Calculated from data in IMF, *International Financial Statistics* (various issues).

Table A-3. Sri Lanka: Components of Production, for Selected Years, 1950–85

(ratio of indicated component to GDP; percent)

Year	Agri-culture	Manu-facture	Trade and finance	Transport and communi-cation	Con-struction	Other
1950	38.2	10.4	17.7	6.2	2.9	24.6
1955	35.1	15.6	14.9	7.0	3.7	23.7
1960	31.5	15.3	19.2	8.9	3.9	21.2
1965	27.8	16.5	20.7	9.9	3.3	21.8
1970	27.3	16.1	19.6	9.2	5.4	22.4
1975	29.3	19.4	19.9	7.8	3.8	19.8
1980	25.7	16.6	19.0	7.9	8.3	22.5
1985	23.8	14.6	24.1	11.1	7.8	18.6
1950–60	34.8	14.3	17.5	7.6	3.6	22.2
1960–70	30.0	15.8	19.9	9.5	4.3	20.5
1970–80	27.4	17.6	19.5	8.3	5.8	21.4

Source: Calculated from data in World Bank, *World Tables* (1984) and Central Bank of Sri Lanka (annual for 1985). Ratios are calculated from current price series.

Table A-4. Sri Lanka: Commodity Trade, 1950–85

(millions of rupees)

Year	Exports	Imports	Trade balance	Current account	Trade index (1980 = 100)		
					Terms of trade	Export volume	Import volume
1950	1,563	1,167	396	137	333	80	44
1951	1,904	1,559	345	89	316	81	50
1952	1,502	1,702	−200	−446	246	81	50
1953	1,568	1,608	−40	−158	249	83	50
1954	1,809	1,397	412	306	310	86	46
1955	1,840	1,460	480	323	368	92	53
1956	1,735	1,629	106	82	349	86	59
1957	1,682	1,805	−123	−195	293	84	63
1958	1,711	1,717	−6	−153	329	89	64
1959	1,754	2,075	−321	−208	329	87	74
1960	1,831	1,966	−135	−220	329	93	72
1961	1,808	1,703	105	−94	309	96	58
1962	1,809	1,660	149	−140	309	103	59
1963	1,731	1,490	241	−168	276	99	50
1964	1,876	1,975	−99	−160	231	108	61
1965	1,949	1,474	475	59	249	112	46
1966	1,700	1,907	−207	−290	233	102	64
1967	1,690	1,773	−83	−288	217	106	54
1968	2,035	2,139	−104	−357	208	109	55
1969	1,916	2,499	−583	−797	195	104	59
1970	2,033	2,295	−262	−350	182	108	55
1971	2,039	2,100	−61	−216	173	105	49
1972	2,016	2,199	−183	−196	163	103	48
1973	2,630	2,763	−133	−161	143	104	43
1974	3,503	4,770	−1,267	−907	127	90	30
1975	3,969	5,196	−1,227	−772	102	108	37
1976	4,840	4,902	−62	−50	133	103	41
1977	6,570	6,061	509	−1,266	175	95	52
1978	13,193	15,100	−1,907	−1,032	172	101	71
1979	15,282	22,603	−7,321	−3,556	124	102	88
1980	17,595	33,942	−16,347	−10,912	100	100	100
1981	21,043	36,583	−15,540	−8,498	95	111	104
1982	21,454	41,946	−20,492	−11,844	87	117	107
1983	25,096	45,558	−17,776	−11,122	108	116	129
1984	37,347	47,541	−10,194	−1,400	131	133	132
1985	36,207	54,049	−17,842	−11,532	101	140	105

Source: Export and import data, Central Bank of Ceylon (1984, 1985). Volume index, IMF (annual for 1979 and 1986). Current account data for 1950–59, Snodgrass (1966), table A-57; for 1960–85, Central Bank of Sri Lanka (annual for various years). Data before 1960 are not strictly comparable with those after that date. Terms of trade estimates have been calculated from the unit export and import value series in IMF, *International Financial Statistics* (1979 and 1986 *Yearbooks* and March 1988 issue).

Table A-5. Sri Lanka: Foreign Exchange Developments, 1950–85
(millions of U.S. dollars)

Year	Current account	Unrequited transfers[a]	Capital account[b]	Reserves[c]	External debt[d]	Rupees per U.S. dollar
1950	29	—	—	191	16	4.762
1951	19	—	—	217	15	—
1952	−94	—	—	163	15	—
1953	−33	—	—	114	14	—
1954	64	—	—	170	26	—
1955	68	—	—	211	30	—
1956	17	—	—	234	30	—
1957	−40	—	—	183	33	—
1958	−32	−5	7	172	37	—
1959	−44	−2	19	132	43	—
1960	−46	4	2	90	47	—
1961	−20	2	10	90	49	—
1962	−29	1	6	85	56	—
1963	−35	3	25	75	70	—
1964	−33	8	39	52	80	—
1965	12	9	−2	73	94	—
1966	−61	8	14	43	121	—
1967	−59	4	59	55	180	4.861
1968	−60	3	32	52	187	5.952
1969	−134	7	114	40	235	—
1970	−59	12	64	43	263	—
1971	−36	14	34	50	317	5.952
1972	−33	12	32	46	444	5.970
1973	−25	13	53	70	429	6.403
1974	−136	42	102	60	439	6.651
1975	−110	75	86	45	529	7.007
1976	−6	65	43	78	591	8.412
1977	142	72	−10	269	1,194	8.873
1978	−66	79	137	363	949	15.611
1979	−226	192	224	488	1,017	15.572
1980	−655	274	357	246	1,347	16.534
1981	−446	363	383	304	1,516	19.246
1982	−549	426	500	338	1,662	20.812
1983	−466	445	445	278	1,956	23.529
1984	1	479	350	505	2,110	25.438
1985	−412	412	356	445	2,491	27.163

— Not available.

a. Estimates are the sum of public and private transfers. They are included in the net current account.

b. Estimates are the sum of direct investment, "other long-term" investment and "other short-term" investment (see IMF, various years).

c. Estimates are foreign exchange reserves (net of gold and IMF SDRS, both of which are negligible over the entire period) as of the end of the year.

d. Government debt converted from rupees to U.S. dollars at the exchange rate prevailing at the time.

Source: IMF, International Financial Statistics (various issues).

Table A-6. Sri Lanka: Composition of Exports, for Selected Years, 1950–85

(millions of rupees)

Commodity	1950	1960	1970	1980	1985
Agricultural produce	1,401	1,658	1,914	10,873	19,027
Tea	752	1,096	1,120	6,170	12,003
Rubber	401	378	440	2,590	2,566
Coconut	248	184	291	1,234	3,093
Other	*	*	63	879	1,365
Industrial products	*	*	36	5,814	13,980
Textiles and garments	*	*	8	1,826	7,899
Petroleum products	*	*	19	3,123	3,873
Other	*	*	9	865	2,204
Minerals	*	*	17	805	1,177
Gems	*	*	4	664	873
Other	*	*	13	141	303
Unclassified	162	174	66	103	2,024
Total	1,563	1,832	2,033	17,595	36,208

* Included in "unclassified."

Source: For 1950, Central Bank of Ceylon, Statistics Department (1955); for 1960, 1970, and 1980, Central Bank of Sri Lanka (annual for various years).

Table A-7. Sri Lanka: Composition of Imports, for Selected Years, 1960–85

(millions of rupees)

Category	1960	1970	1980	1985
Consumer goods	1,195	1,294	10,158	14,261
Food and drink	752	1,069	6,408	5,908
Rice	242	318	882	1,082
Flour	65	260	1,825	206
Sugar	65	170	2,026	1,985
Intermediate goods	397	451	15,522	25,532
Fertilizers	58	81	1,339	1,579
Chemicals	40	66	748	2,765
Petroleum	124	59	8,090	10,986
Investment goods	355	546	8,144	10,387
Unclassified	13	22	942	3,869
Total	1,960	2,313	33,942	54,049

Source: Central Bank of Sri Lanka (annual for various years).

Table A-8. Sri Lanka: Agricultural Output, 1950–85

Year	Paddy Product index (1980 = 100)	Paddy Bushels per acre	Rubber Product index (1980 = 100)	Rubber Pounds per acre	Tea Product index (1980 = 100)	Tea Pounds per acre	Index of agricultural output (1980 = 100)
1950	22	—	86	—	72	—	38
1951	22	26	80	—	77	—	39
1952	29	31	73	—	75	—	41
1953	20	27	75	—	81	—	40
1954	30	30	71	—	87	—	44
1955	36	32	71	—	90	—	49
1956	26	30	72	—	89	—	44
1957	30	27	74	—	90	—	46
1958	36	34	76	—	98	—	47
1959	36	35	69	—	98	—	48
1960	42	36	74	326	103	747	51
1961	42	36	69	320	108	775	52
1962	47	38	74	340	111	790	55
1963	48	38	73	342	115	825	57
1964	49	39	78	368	114	814	60
1965	36	34	79	459	119	848	58
1966	45	36	91	508	116	823	60
1967	54	41	99	555	115	813	64
1968	63	46	105	576	117	830	66
1969	69	50	112	618	115	810	66
1970	76	51	119	617	111	784	68
1971	65	46	105	—	111	—	66
1972	61	47	107	—	110	—	65
1973	61	45	115	—	107	—	64
1974	75	46	98	634	112	875	67
1975	54	44	111	691	112	912	70
1976	58	45	113	705	103	839	69
1977	79	49	109	690	109	897	75
1978	89	51	116	754	104	855	77
1979	90	54	114	732	108	886	93
1980	100	57	100	641	100	823	100
1981	104	59	92	629	110	765	93
1982	101	64	93	650	98	882	87
1983	116	70	104	730	94	—	92
1984	106	60	106	749	109	—	92
1985	117	—	103	747	112	—	—

— Not available.

Source: Output data for paddy, tea, and rubber for 1950–79, Peebles (1982), pp. 122, 123, 127; for 1980–85, Central Bank of Sri Lanka (annual). Paddy yield estimates for 1951–60, Snodgrass (1966), p. 331. Yield estimates for all three crops for years after 1960, Central Bank of Sri Lanka, *Monthly Bulletin* and *Annual Report* (various years). Index of agricultural output for 1950–60, Snodgrass (1966), p. 339; for later years, FAO (annual for various years).

Table A-9. Sri Lanka: Money and Prices, 1950–85
(millions of rupees)

Year	Money[a]	Liquidity[b]	Government deficit or surplus	Government rupees debt	Annual change In consumer price index (percent)	Annual change In GDP deflator (percent)	Deficit or surplus as share of GDP (percent)
1950	897	965	−14	359	5.4	—	..
1951	991	1,075	−56	516	4.1	6.5	−1.2
1952	884	984	−276	729	−0.8	−9.2	−6.0
1953	817	916	−241	926	1.6	5.0	−5.1
1954	947	1,081	32	826	−0.4	2.9	..
1955	1,061	1,211	124	753	−0.6	5.6	2.2
1956	1,118	1,304	−36	799	−0.4	1.5	..
1957	1,032	1,246	−240	964	2.6	2.3	−4.3
1958	1,067	1,320	−236	1,083	2.1	1.1	−4.0
1959	1,169	1,463	−470	1,490	0.2	4.1	−7.4
1960	1,197	1,554	−453	1,881	−1.6	−0.4	−6.8
1961	1,275	1,622	−385	2,176	1.3	−1.7	−5.7
1962	1,333	1,729	−452	2,535	1.4	2.3	−6.4
1963	1,494	2,183	−423	2,831	2.4	−0.9	−5.7
1964	1,610	2,230	−466	3,162	3.1	−0.6	−6.0
1965	1,704	2,312	−492	3,408	0.3	1.3	−6.1
1966	1,644	2,264	−518	3,839	−0.2	−1.9	−6.2
1967	1,790	2,517	−616	4,120	2.2	2.2	−6.8
1968	1,895	2,741	−702	4,709	5.8	13.6	−6.5
1969	1,868	2,886	−825	4,922	7.4	0.9	−7.0
1970	1,949	3,128	−898	5,808	5.9	0.9	−6.6
1971	2,128	3,461	−1,153	6,444	2.7	2.9	−8.2
1972	2,461	4,002	−1,168	7,096	6.3	0.6	−7.7
1973	2,755	4,116	−978	7,531	9.7	16.6	−5.3
1974	2,923	4,608	−1,038	8,143	12.3	24.3	−4.4
1975	3,064	4,770	−2,106	9,254	6.7	6.8	−7.9
1976	4,133	6,319	−2,917	10,652	1.2	8.8	−9.7
1977	5,332	8,824	−2,130	11,840	1.2	16.1	−5.8
1978	5,895	11,593	−6,003	12,935	12.1	9.5	−14.1
1979	7,643	16,551	−7,609	15,671	10.8	15.4	−14.5
1980	9,333	21,303	−14,772	24,502	26.2	20.0	−22.2
1981	9,949	25,536	−13,258	29,487	17.9	20.8	−15.6
1982	11,672	32,014	−17,479	36,653	10.8	11.0	−17.6
1983	14,589	37,712	−16,580	40,399	14.0	16.8	−13.6
1984	16,647	44,833	−13,632	42,060	16.6	20.6	−9.9
1985	18,663	50,657	−18,778	56,047	1.5	—	−11.5

— Not available.
.. Negligible.
a. Currently outside banks plus private demand deposits at end of year.
b. Money plus time and saving deposits at end of year.
Source: IMF, *International Financial Statistics* (various issues).

Table A-10. Sri Lanka: Personal Income Distribution, for Selected Years, 1953–82

(percent)

Decile	Share of income receivers in total income				
	1953	*1963*	*1973*	*1978–79*	*1981–82*
Lowest	1.31	1.17	1.80	1.20	1.21
Second	3.56	2.70	3.17	2.56	2.49
Third	3.56	3.56	4.38	3.60	3.47
Fourth	4.37	4.57	5.70	4.76	4.61
Fifth	5.71	5.55	7.10	5.93	5.57
Sixth	6.31	6.82	8.75	7.29	6.93
Seventh	7.94	8.98	10.56	9.12	8.56
Eighth	10.39	11.46	12.65	11.23	10.64
Ninth	14.16	16.01	15.91	15.26	14.82
Highest	42.29	29.24	29.98	39.05	41.70

Source: Reports on consumer finance surveys, conducted by the Central Bank of Sri Lanka in the years indicated.

Table A-11. Sri Lanka: Personal Income Distribution, for Selected Years, 1953–82

(percent)

Decile	Share of spending units in total income				
	1953	*1963*	*1973*	*1978–79*	*1981–82*
Lowest	1.90	1.50	2.79	2.12	2.18
Second	3.30	3.95	4.38	3.61	3.55
Third	4.10	4.00	5.60	4.65	4.35
Fourth	5.20	5.21	6.52	5.68	5.24
Fifth	6.40	6.27	7.45	6.59	6.35
Sixth	6.90	7.54	8.75	7.69	7.02
Seventh	8.30	9.00	9.91	8.57	8.69
Eighth	10.10	11.22	11.65	11.22	10.71
Ninth	13.20	15.54	14.92	14.03	14.52
Highest	40.60	36.77	28.03	35.84	37.29

Source: Reports on consumer finance surveys, conducted by the Central Bank of Sri Lanka in the years indicated.

Table A-12. Sri Lanka: Income Distribution by Sector, 1973, 1978–79, and 1981–82

(percent)

Sector and period	Share of income receivers in total monthly income					Median monthly income (rupees)
	Lowest quintile	Second quintile	Third quintile	Fourth quintile	Highest quintile	
Urban						
1973	5.39	10.74	16.13	22.42	45.32	255
1978–79	3.34	8.49	13.24	19.26	55.67	539
1981–82	3.57	7.66	11.63	18.15	58.99	977
Rural						
1973	5.35	11.60	16.95	23.39	42.71	197
1978–79	3.49	8.60	14.11	20.82	52.98	429
1981–82	3.71	8.78	13.50	19.90	54.11	781
Estate						
1973	7.51	11.73	14.90	20.65	45.21	88
1978–79	7.73	13.21	16.76	22.22	40.08	252
1981–82	8.24	12.63	16.51	21.65	40.97	376
All island						
1973	4.97	10.08	15.85	23.21	45.89	180
1978–79	3.76	8.36	13.22	20.35	54.31	408
1981–82	3.70	8.08	12.50	19.20	56.52	612

Source: Central Bank of Ceylon, Statistics Department (1984).

Table A-13. Sri Lanka: Gini Coefficient by Level of Education, 1973, 1978–79, and 1981–82

Level of education	Gini coefficient[a]		
	1973	1978–79	1981–82
No schooling (illiterate)	0.37	0.46	0.44
No schooling (literate)	0.37	0.38	0.39
Primary	0.37	0.47	0.48
Secondary	0.37	0.48	0.51
Passed GCE O level	0.48	0.58	0.58
Passed GCE A level	0.48	0.58	0.58
Undergraduate	—	0.34	0.19
Passed degree	0.34	0.47	0.38

— Not available.

a. Based on one month's income.

Source: Central Bank of Ceylon, Statistics Department (1984).

Table A-14. Sri Lanka: Central Government Current Revenue, for Selected Years, 1950–85

| Category | Millions of rupees | | | | | | Percentage of GDP | | | | | |
	1950	1960	1970	1980	1985		1950	1960	1970	1980	1985
Direct taxes[a]	132.1	226.7	496.0	2,344.2	6,342.8		3.2	3.4	3.6	3.5	3.9
Indirect taxes[b]	377.2	814.7	1,643.2	10,162.6	24,401.8		9.0	12.2	12.0	15.3	15.0
Other sources of revenue[c]	182.1	362.4	597.2	1,561.5	8,265.0		4.4	5.4	4.4	2.3	5.1
Total revenue	691.14	1,403.8	2,736.4	14,068.3	39,009.6		16.6	21.0	20.0	21.1	24.0

a. Includes income tax, wealth tax, property transfer tax, and so on.
b. Includes turnover tax, selective sales tax, external trade tax and license fees, FEECS, and so on.
c. Nontax revenue.
Source: Central Bank of Sri Lanka.

Table A-15. Sri Lanka: Spending on Social Services, for Selected Years, 1955–84

(percentage of GDP)

Year	Education	Health	Food subsidies	Other	Total
1955	2.7	1.8	0.8	0.4	5.7
1960	3.8	2.2	3.1	0.6	9.7
1965	4.9	2.1	3.6	0.6	11.2
1968	4.1	2.0	3.0	0.5	9.6
1969	4.3	2.1	3.1	0.4	9.9
1970	4.6	2.1	2.8	0.4	9.9
1972	4.4	2.6	4.1	0.5	11.6
1973	3.5	1.5	3.8	0.3	9.1
1974	2.8	1.3	4.0	1.2	9.3
1975	2.8	1.4	4.8	0.4	9.4
1976	3.1	1.6	3.4	0.8	8.9
1977	2.7	1.4	4.1	0.5	8.7
1978	2.7	1.5	5.3	0.3	9.8
1979	2.7	1.5	5.7	0.1	10.0
1980	2.9	1.4	3.1	0.3	7.7
1981	2.7	1.2	2.1	0.2	6.2
1982	2.9	1.3	1.8	0.4	6.4
1983	2.6	1.8	1.3	0.6	5.7
1984	2.5	1.4	1.2	—	5.1

— Not available.
Source: Central Bank of Sri Lanka (annual for various years).

Table A-16. Sri Lanka: Urban and Rural Population, for Selected Years, 1946–85

Sector	1946	1953	1963	1971	1981	1985
Urban						
Thousands	1,023	1,339	2,016	2,848	3,195	3,326
Percentage of total	15.4	16.1	19.0	22.4	21.5	21.0
Rural						
Thousands	5,634	6,959	8,566	9,842	11,655	12,514
Percentage of total	84.6	83.9	81.0	77.6	78.5	79.0
Total (thousands)	6,657	8,298	10,582	12,690	14,850	15,840

Source: Sri Lanka, Department of Census and Statistics.

Table A-17. Sri Lanka: Social Indicators, for Selected Years, 1950–85

Indicator	1950	1960	1970	1980	1985
Crude birth rate (per thousand)					
Sri Lanka	40	36	29	28	25
Average[a]	—	48	—	31	29
Crude death rate (per thousand)					
Sri Lanka	12	9	7	6	6
Average[a]	—	26	—	12	10
Life expectancy at birth (years)					
Sri Lanka	58[b]	62	64	68	70
Average[a]	—	38	—	57	61
Infant mortality rate (per thousand)					
Sri Lanka	82	71	58	44	36
Average[a]	—	142	—	94	72
Child (age 1–4) death rate (per thousand)					
Sri Lanka	—	7	5	3	2
Average[a]	—	29	—	12	9

— Not available.

a. Average of all low-income countries.

b. Estimate is for 1952.

Source: For 1950, Peebles (1982), pp. 45–48; for 1960–85 and for low-income country averages, World Bank (annual for 1978 and 1985).

Table A-18. Malaysia: National Product, 1960–85

| Year | GDP (millions of ringgits) | | Population (millions) | GDP per capita, 1980 prices (ringgits) |
	Current prices	1980 prices		
1960	6,837	13,236	8.1	1,634
1961	6,696	14,214	8.3	1,712
1962	7,056	15,130	8.6	1,759
1963	7,515	16,213	8.8	1,842
1964	8,056	16,993	9.0	1,888
1965	8,837	18,459	9.2	2,006
1966	9,394	19,902	9.5	2,095
1967	9,774	20,668	9.7	2,130
1968	10,160	22,319	9.9	2,254
1969	11,629	23,410	10.1	2,318
1970	12,155	24,811	10.4	2,386
1971	12,955	26,569	10.7	2,483
1972	14,220	29,063	11.0	2,642
1973	18,723	32,464	11.3	2,873
1974	22,858	35,165	11.6	3,031
1975	22,332	35,446	11.9	2,979
1976	28,085	39,545	12.3	3,215
1977	32,340	42,611	12.6	3,382
1978	37,886	45,446	12.9	3,523
1979	46,424	49,610	13.4	3,702
1980	53,538	53,538	13.8	3,880
1981	57,613	57,009	14.1	4,043
1982	62,579	60,395	14.5	4,165
1983	69,565	64,170	14.8	4,336
1984	79,550	69,151	15.2	4,549
1985	77,547	68,443	15.7	4,359

Source: For population and GDP in current prices, IMF, *International Financial Statistics* (1986 *Yearbook* and March 1988 issue). For constant price series in 1960–70, World Bank, *World Tables*; in 1970–85, IMF, *International Financial Statistics* (1986 *Yearbook* and March 1988 issue).

Table A-19. Malaysia: Components of GDP, 1960–85

(ratio of indicated component to GDP; percent)

Year	Investment	Private consumption	Government consumption	Exports	Imports	Saving
1960	12.6	62.0	12.9	56.2	43.7	25.1
1961	14.3	67.0	13.2	51.7	46.1	19.9
1962	16.7	67.5	13.5	49.4	47.1	19.0
1963	16.2	67.4	14.7	47.9	46.3	17.8
1964	15.9	66.5	16.0	46.7	45.1	17.1
1965	15.7	63.6	16.3	47.5	43.2	20.0
1966	15.7	63.0	17.4	45.8	41.9	19.6
1967	16.1	64.2	17.1	42.5	39.9	18.7
1968	15.8	64.1	16.8	45.1	41.9	19.0
1969	14.6	59.8	15.6	47.3	37.4	24.5
1970	20.3	61.6	16.4	46.1	44.4	22.0
1971	20.8	61.1	16.7	40.2	38.9	22.1
1972	21.3	61.1	19.2	35.8	36.9	20.2
1973	23.6	55.0	15.7	41.3	35.7	29.2
1974	29.6	55.9	15.4	48.1	49.0	28.7
1975	25.5	58.6	17.5	45.4	47.1	23.8
1976	22.8	52.4	15.3	51.5	42.3	32.0
1977	23.8	52.0	16.6	50.1	42.6	31.3
1978	26.6	51.7	16.1	49.0	43.5	32.1
1979	28.9	48.3	13.9	56.0	47.1	37.8
1980	30.7	50.3	16.4	57.3	54.8	33.2
1981	35.0	53.1	18.1	52.3	58.5	28.8
1982	37.2	53.0	18.3	50.9	59.6	28.5
1983	36.0	51.7	17.5	52.2	57.5	30.7
1984	33.6	50.0	14.7	54.3	52.4	35.5
1985	27.5	52.0	15.3	54.9	49.8	32.6

Note: The saving ratio is given by the sum of the investment and export ratios minus the import ratio.

Source: Calculated from current price estimates in IMF, *International Financial Statistics* (1986 *Yearbook* and March 1988 issue).

Table A-20. Malaysia: Components of Production, for Selected Years, 1955–85

(ratio of indicated component to GDP; percent)

Year	Agriculture	Manufacture	Trade and finance	Transport and communication	Construction	Other
1955	36.0	8.7	26.1	4.1	3.0	22.1
1960	36.0	8.7	26.0	4.1	3.0	22.2
1965	30.1	10.1	25.5	5.0	4.1	25.2
1970	30.8	13.4	25.4	4.7	3.9	21.8
1975	28.0	17.5	22.5	5.8	3.6	22.6
1980	24.1	21.9	20.8	5.8	4.9	22.5
1985	20.3	19.1	21.5	6.4	5.1	27.6

Note: Estimates for 1955–80 are in current prices; estimates for 1985 are in 1978 prices.
Source: Estimates for 1955–80 from data in World Bank, World Tables. Estimates for 1985 are from Malaysia (1986).

Table A-21. Malaysia: Commodity Trade Data, 1960–85
(millions of ringgits)

Year	Exports	Imports	Trade balance	Current account	Terms of trade	Export volume	Import volume
					Trade index (1980 = 100)		
1960	3,633	2,786	847	433	117	32	27
1961	3,238	2,816	422	9	97	32	28
1962	3,260	3,056	204	−153	97	33	30
1963	3,330	3,193	137	−238	92	36	30
1964	3,382	3,205	177	−153	97	35	29
1965	3,782	3,356	426	119	103	37	32
1966	3,846	3,380	466	37	97	39	33
1967	3,724	3,325	399	12	89	41	33
1968	4,123	3,552	571	98	81	49	35
1969	5,055	3,605	1,450	732	95	54	36
1970	5,163	4,288	875	25	92	55	40
1971	5,017	4,416	601	−330	77	58	40
1972	4,854	4,543	311	−699	69	58	39
1973	7,372	5,934	1,438	257	75	68	45
1974	10,195	9,891	304	−1,307	83	65	62
1975	9,231	8,530	701	−1,187	67	64	51
1976	13,442	9,713	3,729	1,474	78	83	56
1977	14,959	11,165	3,794	1,073	84	86	65
1978	17,074	13,646	3,428	250	83	93	73
1979	24,222	17,161	7,061	2,033	102	103	90
1980	28,172	23,451	4,721	−620	100	100	100
1981	27,109	26,604	505	−5,728	85	97	104
1982	28,108	29,023	−915	−8,410	80	103	116
1983	32,771	30,795	1,976	−8,118	80	114	123
1984	38,647	32,926	5,721	−3,890	86	116	126
1985	38,328	30,558	774	−2,230	78	122	119

Source: Export and import data: Malaysia, Department of Statistics (annual c). Current account: IMF (annual for 1986); data are in U.S. dollars and have been converted to ringgits by the end-of-year exchange rate. Terms of trade: computed from unit value series in IMF (annual for 1986). Volume indexes: export series from IMF (annual for 1986); import series is an index of imports in constant prices from World Bank, *World Tables* (1976, 1980, and 1983).

Table A-22. Malaysia: Foreign Exchange Developments, 1960–85
(millions of U.S. dollars)

Year	Current account	Unrequited transfers[a]	Capital account[b]	Reserves	External debt[c]	Ringgits per U.S. dollar
1960	141	—	—	356	118	3.0612
1961	3	−64	149	349	122	—
1962	−50	−64	107	373	129	—
1963	−78	−59	125	379	145	—
1964	−50	−25	62	410	143	—
1965	39	−19	88	454	167	—
1966	12	−35	68	473	165	—
1967	−4	−47	80	394	173	—
1968	32	−46	88	417	193	—
1969	239	−59	96	512	244	—
1970	8	−59	90	542	243	—
1971	−108	−45	254	665	357	3.0523
1972	−248	−55	292	796	495	2.8196
1973	105	−62	337	1,146	530	2.4433
1974	−543	−43	819	1,411	622	2.4071
1975	−496	−33	656	1,321	1,013	2.3938
1976	580	−40	510	2,266	1,104	2.5416
1977	436	−32	256	2,688	1,362	2.4613
1978	108	−45	627	3,123	1,666	2.3160
1979	929	−8	202	3,711	2,076	2.1884
1980	−285	−20	1,435	4,114	2,233	2.1769
1981	−2,486	−34	2,616	3,816	3,371	2.3041
1982	−3,601	−32	3,745	3,509	5,634	2.3354
1983	−3,497	−11	3,853	3,509	7,637	2.3213
1984	−1,660	−39	2,954	3,470	8,895	2.3436
1985	−669	−30	2,217	4,621	9,291	2.4829

— Not available.

a. The sum of public and private transfers. They are part of the current account figure.

b. The sum of direct investment, "other long-term" investment, and "other short-term" investment.

c. Government debt converted from ringgits to U.S. dollars at the year-end exchange rate.

Source: IMF, *International Financial Statistics* (1986 *Yearbook* and March 1988 issue).

Table A-23. Malaysia: Exports, for Selected Years, 1960–85

(millions of ringgits)

Commodity	1960	1965	1970	1975	1980	1985
Rubber						
Value	2,001	1,462	1,724	2,026	4,618	2,864
Percentage of total	55	39	34	22	16	8
Sawlogs						
Value	119	87	644	1,111	2,616	2,667
Percentage of total	3	2	12	12	9	7
Sawn timber						
Value	75	—	206	—	1,178	1,020
Percentage of total	2	—	4	—	4	3
Palm oil						
Value	61	107	264	264	2,515	3,944
Percentage of total	2	3	5	3	9	10
Petroleum						
Value	147	87	203	853	6,709	8,970
Percentage of total	4	2	4	9	24	23
Tin						
Value	508	872	1,054	1,206	2,505	1,595
Percentage of total	14	23	20	13	9	4
Manufactures						
Value	—	227	612	1,661	6,270	12,229
Percentage of total	—	6	12	18	22	32
Other						
Value	722	941	456	2,110	1,761	5,038
Percentage of total	20	25	9	23	6	13
Total	3,633	3,783	5,163	9,231	28,172	38,327

Note: All data are not exactly comparable across all years.
Source: For 1960, 1970, 1980, and 1985, Malaysia, Department of Statistics (annual c).
For 1965 and 1975, World Bank (annual for 1978 and 1986).

Table A-24. Malaysia: Composition of Imports, for Selected Years, 1960–85

(millions of ringgits)

Category	1960	1965	1970	1976	1980	1985
Food						
Value	808	839	—	1,651	2,814	3,361
Percentage of total	29	25	—	17	12	11
Fuels						
Value	446	403	—	1,360	3,518	3,056
Percentage of total	16	12	—	14	15	10
Other primary commodities						
Value	362	336	—	680	1,407	1,528
Percentage of total	13	10	—	7	6	5
Machine and transport equipment						
Value	390	738	—	3,205	9,146	14,057
Percentage of total	14	22	—	33	39	46
Other manufactures						
Value	780	1,040	—	2,817	6,566	8,556
Percentage of total	28	31	—	29	28	28
Total	2,786	3,356	4,288	9,713	23,451	30,558

— Not available.

Source: World Bank (annual for various years).

Table A-25. Malaysia: Agricultural Output, 1960–85

(thousands of metric tons)

Year	Index of agricultural production (1980 = 100)	Rice Production	Rice Kilograms per hectare	Rubber production	Palm oil production
1960	37	—	—	696	92
1961	38	843	2,611	746	94
1962	40	946	2,405	761	108
1963	42	1,012	2,541	799	126
1964	42	925	2,405	804	122
1965	46	1,058	2,567	852	149
1966	48	1,041	2,560	915	186
1967	50	1,029	2,620	938	216
1968	55	1,218	2,650	1,060	264
1969	61	1,354	2,710	1,199	325
1970	63	1,429	2,723	1,215	402
1971	68	1,549	2,906	1,276	550
1972	69	1,654	2,902	1,279	660
1973	79	1,728	2,979	1,465	739
1974	84	1,819	3,142	1,485	942
1975	84	1,718	2,937	1,417	1,135
1976	89	1,610	2,835	1,520	1,250
1977	91	1,922	2,633	1,613	1,614
1978	88	1,498	2,569	1,607	1,788
1979	99	2,098	2,761	1,617	2,189
1980	100	2,129	2,698	1,600	2,575
1981	106	2,095	2,898	1,510	2,822
1982	110	1,832	2,674	1,517	3,510
1983	105	1,818	2,674	1,562	3,018
1984	112	1,755	2,659	1,497	3,717
1985	117	1,953	2,977	1,469	4,130

Note: Data were not always consistent. The most recently published data have been used unless there were obvious mistakes.

Source: FAO (various issues).

Table A-26. Malaysia: Money and Prices, 1960–85

(millions of ringgits)

Year	Money	Liquidity[a]	Government deficit or surplus	Government ringgits debt	Annual change In consumer price index (percent)	Annual change In GDP deflator (percent)	Deficit or surplus as share of GDP (percent)
1960	1,171	1,655	132	1,106	—	—	1.9
1961	1,201	1,767	−30	1,232	−0.3	−8.8	−0.4
1962	1,257	1,875	−217	1,377	0.2	−1.1	−3.0
1963	1,345	2,054	−333	1,587	3.1	−0.7	−4.4
1964	1,421	2,222	−362	1,779	−0.5	2.4	−4.5
1965	1,517	2,444	−482	2,183	—	0.8	−5.4
1966	1,681	2,756	−518	2,511	0.9	−1.3	−5.5
1967	1,529	2,818	−524	2,997	4.5	—	−5.3
1968	1,717	3,260	−478	3,490	−0.1	−3.7	−4.7
1969	1,913	3,719	−414	3,906	−0.4	9.0	−3.6
1970	2,017	4,213	−458	4,272	1.9	−1.4	−3.8
1971	2,172	4,661	−1,010	5,000	1.6	−0.5	−7.8
1972	2,715	5,763	−1,305	5,835	3.2	0.3	−9.2
1973	3,735	7,552	−1,040	6,712	10.5	17.9	−5.6
1974	4,055	8,714	−1,371	7,544	17.4	12.7	−6.0
1975	4,349	10,001	−1,892	8,755	4.5	−3.1	−8.5
1976	5,247	12,771	−1,996	10,391	2.6	12.7	−7.1
1977	6,127	14,861	−2,766	12,277	4.8	6.9	−8.5
1978	7,243	17,521	−2,896	13,442	4.9	9.8	−7.6
1979	8,487	21,739	−3,683	15,949	3.6	12.2	−7.9
1980	9,757	27,436	−7,022	18,286	6.7	7.0	−13.1
1981	11,015	32,339	−11,015	22,376	9.7	0.8	−19.1
1982	12,477	37,618	−11,171	28,711	5.8	2.6	−17.8
1983	13,432	41,163	−9,183	33,955	3.7	5.2	−13.2
1984	13,357	45,858	−7,075	37,075	3.9	5.9	−8.9
1985	13,579	48,366	−5,999	41,982	0.3	−1.5	−7.7

— Not available.

Source: IMF, *International Financial Statistics* (1978 and 1986 *Yearbooks* and March 1988 issue).

Table A-27. Malaysia: Income Distribution, for Selected Years, 1957–84

(percentage share of households in total income)

Decile of households	1957-58			1970			1976			1979			1984		
	Total	Urban	Rural	Total	Urban	Rural	Total	Urban	Rural	Total	Urban	Rural	Total	Urban	Rural
Lowest	2.2	2.7	2.8	1.2	1.5	1.2	1.2	1.4	2.2	1.3	1.5	1.4	1.4	1.6	1.5
Second	3.5	4.4	4.3	2.8	2.8	3.5	2.1	2.8	2.2	2.4	2.7	2.6	2.8	3.0	3.0
Third	4.6	5.3	5.6	3.2	3.8	3.7	3.2	3.5	2.7	3.6	3.6	3.9	3.8	3.9	4.2
Fourth	5.4	6.3	6.6	4.5	4.7	5.1	4.6	4.2	4.7	4.6	4.5	4.5	4.8	4.9	5.4
Fifth	6.5	7.4	7.2	5.5	5.7	6.1	5.1	5.3	6.2	5.5	5.5	6.3	6.0	6.0	6.6
Sixth	7.7	8.6	8.7	6.8	6.5	7.7	6.7	6.8	7.0	7.0	6.9	7.3	7.2	7.3	7.9
Seventh	9.2	10.3	10.1	9.1	8.3	9.5	8.4	8.3	8.7	8.6	8.5	9.2	9.3	9.3	9.6
Eighth	11.1	12.5	12.6	10.7	10.9	12.3	11.4	11.7	11.8	11.2	11.2	11.6	11.5	11.9	12.3
Ninth	15.0	16.4	15.3	15.1	16.4	15.6	15.7	16.5	16.0	16.5	15.8	16.5	16.6	16.3	16.1
Highest	34.8	26.1	26.8	41.1	39.4	35.3	41.9	39.4	38.5	39.3	39.8	36.7	36.6	35.8	33.4
Household income (dollars a month)															
Mean	220	262	156	275	441	204	513	829	392	693	975	550	1,095	1,541	824
Median	156	209	124	170	269	141	313	495	262	436	600	369	723	1,027	596
Gini coefficient	0.421	0.347	0.342	0.499	0.485	0.451	0.529	0.512	0.500	0.508	0.501	0.482	0.480	0.466	0.444

Source: Malaysia, Department of Statistics (1970, 1977, annual a for 1957–58, annual b for 1980 and 1984).

Table A-28. Poverty Incidence by State, 1976 and 1984

(thousands)

State or area	1976			1984		
	Total households	Total poor households	Incidence of poverty (percent)	Total households	Total poor households	Incidence of poverty (percent)
Federal Territory of Kuala Lumpur	139.4	12.5	9.0	242.1	11.8	4.9
Johor	268.1	77.8	29.0	365.8	44.5	12.2
Kedah	216.3	131.9	61.0	253.9	93.0	36.6
Kelantan	167.8	112.7	67.1	206.7	81.0	39.2
Melaka	85.8	27.8	32.4	95.1	15.1	15.8
Negeri Sembilan	106.0	35.0	33.0	132.8	17.3	13.0
Pahang	113.4	44.9	38.9	190.9	30.0	15.7
Peninsular Malaysia	1,931.4	764.4	39.6	2,621.1	483.3	18.4
Perak	340.7	146.4	43.0	400.2	81.1	20.3
Perlis	29.7	17.8	59.8	40.1	13.5	33.7
Pulau Pinang	150.1	48.6	32.4	204.2	27.4	13.4
Sabah	163.9	95.5	58.3	229.8	76.0	33.1
Sarawak	205.1	115.9	56.5	282.2	90.1	31.9
Selangor	211.4	48.3	22.9	359.2	31.0	8.6
Terengganu	100.6	60.7	60.3	129.9	37.6	28.9

Source: Malaysia, Economic Planning Unit (1986).

Table A-29. Malaysia: Poverty Incidence by Location and Occupation, 1970, 1976, and 1984

(percentage of households in poverty)

Category	1970	1976	1984
Rural	58.7	47.8	24.7
Rubber smallholders	64.7	58.2	43.4
Paddy farmers	88.1	80.3	57.7
Estate workers	40.0	—	19.7
Fishermen	73.2	62.7	27.7
Coconut smallholders	52.8	64.0	46.9
Other agriculture	89.0	52.1	34.2
Other industries	35.2	27.3	10.0
Urban	21.3	17.9	8.2
Agriculture	—	40.2	23.8
Mining	33.3	10.1	3.4
Manufacturing	23.5	17.1	8.5
Construction	30.2	17.7	6.1
Transport and utilities	30.9	17.1	3.6
Trade and services	18.1	13.9	4.6
Other	—	22.4	17.1
Total	49.3	39.6	18.4

— Not available.
Source: Malaysia, Economic Planning Unit (1986), p. 86.

Table A-30. Malaysia: Federal Government Revenue, for Selected Years, 1960–85

(millions of U.S. dollars)

Category	1960	1970	1980	1985
Direct taxes	191	701	5,664	9,777
Income tax	186	657	5,240	8,863
Company	—	489	2,521	3,990
Individual	—	168	983	1,743
Petroleum	—	—	1,736	3,130
Royalties on petroleum and gas	—	—	345	619
Other direct taxes	5	44	79	295
Indirect taxes	692	1,299	7,131	8,887
Export duties	260	258	2,567	1,839
Petroleum	—	—	677	1,639
Rubber	196	80	1,098	3
Palm oil	—	18	166	93
Tin	55	130	575	38
Other	9	30	51	66
Import duty and surtax	361	557	2,061	2,516
Excise duty	—	249	973	1,375
Sales tax	—	—	696	1,233
Road tax	—	169	390	630
Service tax	58	40	231	107
Stamp duty	—	—	—	290
Other indirect taxes	13	26	213	897
Total taxes	883	2,000	12,795	18,664
Nontax revenue	186	400	1,131	2,805
Petroleum dividend	—	—	—	930
Other nontax revenue	186	400	1,131	1,875
Nonrevenue receipts	—	—	—	392
Total revenue	1,069	2,400	13,926	21,861
GDP at current prices	5,628	9,951	26,228	35,869
Revenue as percentage of GDP	19.0	24.1	53.1	60.9

— Not available.

Source: Malaysia, Ministry of Finance (annual for 1980–81 and 1985–86).

Table A-31. Malaysia: Federal Government Development Expenditure, for Selected Years, 1960–85

(percentage of total outlay)

Category	1960	1970	1980	1985
Economic services	73	62	65	63
Agriculture and rural development	35	27	15	18
Public utilities	9	3	9	13
Commerce and industry	1	14	21	6
Transport	19	11	14	17
Communications	5	7	6	7
Other	4	—	—	3
Social services	15	11	16	26
Education	10	6	7	12
Health	3	3	1	2
Housing	—	—	4	9
Other	2	2	4	3
Security	7	24	16	9
General administration	4	3	3	2
Total	100	100	100	100
Total expenditure (millions of M$)	147	725	7,463	8,010

— Not available.

Source: Malaysia, Ministry of Finance (annual for 1980–81 and 1985–86).

Table A-32. Malaysia: Federal Government Operating Expenditure, for Selected Years, 1960–85

(percentage of total outlay)

Category	1960	1970	1980	1985
Economic services	13	10	6	9
Agriculture and rural development	4	2	1	4
Commerce and industry	9	8	2	2
Transport and commerce	—	—	2	3
Other	—	—	1	—
Social services	31	31	24	25
Education	21	22	16	17
Health	9	7	5	5
Other	1	2	3	3
Security	21	23	16	17
General administration	10	11	9	12
Transfer payments	10	9	34	12
Debt servicing	6	11	11	25
Other	9	5	—	—
Total	100	100	100	100
Total expenditure (millions of M$)	796	2,161	13,617	21,895

— Not available.

Source: Malaysia, Ministry of Finance (annual for 1980–81 and 1985–86.

Table A-33. Malaysia: Enrollment in Educational Institutions by Ethnic Group, 1970, 1980, and 1985

(percentage of total enrollment)

Level	1970 Bumiputera	Chinese	Indian	Other	1980 Bumiputera	Chinese	Indian	Other	1985 Bumiputera	Chinese	Indian	Other
Primary	53.4	36.0	10.0	0.6	58.4	32.2	7.7	1.7	61.0	29.7	7.6	1.7
Lower secondary	51.0	38.8	9.6	0.6	60.3	30.0	8.5	1.2	65.2	27.3	5.7	1.8
Upper secondary	48.8	43.4	7.0	0.8	66.3	27.0	6.0	0.7	68.1	25.2	6.0	0.7
Postsecondary	43.4	49.6	6.0	1.0	61.4	32.9	4.7	1.0	56.9	36.4	5.8	0.9
Diploma and certificate	82.9	15.5	1.0	0.6	87.8	10.6	1.3	0.3	88.3	10.4	1.0	0.3
Degree courses	39.7	49.2	7.3	3.8	62.0	31.2	5.7	1.1	63.0	29.7	6.5	0.8

Note: Comparability across years is not exact because of different coverage.
Source: Malaysia, Economic Planning Unit (1976, 1986)

Table A-34. Malaysia: Urbanization, for Selected Years, 1960–85
(thousands)

Area	1960	1965	1970	1980	1985
Urban					
Population	1,862	2,412	2,805	4,045	5,958
Percentage of total	25.2	26.1	27.0	29.4	38.0
Rural					
Population	5,528	6,828	7,585	9,715	9,722
Percentage of total	74.8	73.9	73.0	70.6	62.0
Total	7,390	9,240	10,390	13,760	15,680

Source: Percentages taken from World Bank (annual for various years). Population estimates are from table A-18.

Table A-35. Malaysia: Social Indicators, for Selected Years, 1960–85

Indicator	1960	1970	1975	1980	1985
Crude birth rate (per thousand)					
Malaysia	44	36	31	31	30
Average[a]	40	—	40	35	28
Crude death rate (per thousand)					
Malaysia	15	10	7	7	6
Average[a]	13	—	12	11	8
Life expectancy at birth (years)					
Malaysia	53	59	59	64	66
Average[a]	55	—	46	60	64
Infant mortality rate (per thousand)					
Malaysia	72	46	35	31	28
Average[a]	101	—	46	80	52
Child (age 1–4) death rate (per thousand)					
Malaysia	8	3	4	2	2
Average[a]	15	—	5	11	4

— Not available.
a. Average of all middle-income and upper-middle-income countries.
Source: World Bank (annual for various years).

Bibliography

Amerasinghe, Nihal. 1976. "An Overview of Settlement Schemes in Sri Lanka." *Asian Survey*, 16(7):620–36.

Anand, Sudhir. 1977. "Aspects of Poverty in Malaysia." *Review of Income and Wealth* 23(1):1–16.

———. 1983. *Inequality and Poverty in Malaysia*. New York: Oxford University Press.

Andaya, B. W., and L. Y. Andaya. 1985. *A History of Malaysia*. London: Macmillan.

Bailey, Conner. 1983. *The Sociology of Production in Rural Malay Society*. Kuala Lumpur: Oxford University Press.

Bandara, C. M. M. 1984. "Green Revolution and Water Demand: Irrigation and Ground Water in Sri Lanka and Tamil Nadu." In Tim Bayliss-Smith and Sudhir Wanmali, eds., *Understanding Green Revolutions*. Cambridge, U.K.: Cambridge University Press.

Bank Negara Malaysia. 1986. *Annual Report 1985*. Petaling Jaya: Percetakan Kum Sdn. Bhd.

Baumol, W. J. 1968. "Entrepreneurship in Economic Theory." *American Economic Review (Papers and Proceedings)* 58(2):64–71.

Bhalla, S. S., and Glewwe, P. 1986. "Growth and Equity in Developing Countries: A Reinterpretation of Sri Lankan Experience." *The World Bank Economic Review* 1(1):35–63.

Bruton, Henry J. 1970. "The Import Substitution Strategy of Economic Development: A Survey." *The Pakistan Development Review* 90(2):123–46.

———. 1980. "Labour Migration and Shadow Wages." *The Pakistan Development Review* 19(1):66–74.

———. 1985 "The Search for a Development Economics." *World Development* 13(10/11):1099–1124.

———. 1989. "Import Substitution as a Development Strategy." In H. B. Chenery and T. N. Srinivasan, eds., *Handbook of Development Economics*. Amsterdam: North-Holland.

Bruton, H. J., and P. G. Clark. 1987. "An Approach to Development Policy Analysis." In Paul G. Clark, ed., *Development Policies and Economic Training*. Williamstown, Mass: Center for Development Economics.

Casson, Mark. 1982. *The Entrepreneur: An Economic Theory*. Totowa, N.J.: Barnes and Noble.

Central Bank of Ceylon. 1955. *Statistical Abstract of Ceylon, 1955*. Colombo.

————. Annual. *Report on Consumer Finances and Socio-Economic Survey*. Colombo.

————. Annual. *Review of the Economy*. Colombo.

————. Annual. *Annual Report*. Colombo.

Central Bank of Sri Lanka. Annual. *Annual Report*. Colombo.

————. Annual *Economic and Social Statistics of Sri Lanka*. Colombo.

Cernea, M. M., ed. 1985. *Putting People First*. Oxford: Oxford University Press.

Cernea, M. M., and P. B. Hammond, eds. 1980. *Projects for Rural Development: The Human Dimension*. Baltimore: Johns Hopkins University Press.

Chee, T. S. 1983. *Malays and Modernization*. Singapore University Press.

Collier, Paul, and Deepak Lal. 1986. *Labor and Poverty in Keyna, 1900–80*. Oxford: Clarendon Press.

Corbo, Vittorio, and Jaime de Melo. 1985. "Liberalization with Stabilization in the Southern Cone of Latin America: Overview and Summary." *World Development* 13(8):p 863–66.

Corea, Gamani. 1965. "Ceylon." In Cranley Oslow, ed., *Asian Economic Development*. New York: Praeger.

DeSilva, K. M., ed. 1977. *Sri Lanka: A Survey*. Honolulu: University of Hawaii Press.

Dore, R. P. 1972. "The Importance of Educational Traditions: Japan and Elsewhere." *Pacific Affairs* 45(4):491–507.

Economic Bulletin of Asia and the Far East. 1972.

Economic Commission for Asia and the Far East. 1957. *Survey of Asia and the Far East*. Bangkok.

Edwards, E. B. 1975. *Protection, Profits, and Policy: An Analysis of Industrialization in Malaysia*. Norwich: University of East Anglia Press.

Ellsworth, P. T. 1953. "Factors in the Economic Development of Ceylon." *American Economic Review* 43(1):115–25.

FAO (Food and Agriculture Organization). Annual a. *Agricultural Yearbook*. Rome.

————. Annual b. *Statistical Yearbook*. Rome.

————. Various issues. *Statistical Bulletin*.

Farmer, D. H. 1957. *Pioneer Peasant Colonization in Ceylon*. London: Oxford University Press.

Fernando, N. A. 1980a. "*Continuity and Change in Plantation Agriculture: A Study of Sri Lanka's Land Reform Program on Tea Plantations*." University of Wisconsin, Madison. Processed.

————. 1980b. "A Study of the Impact of the Land Reform Laws of 1972 and 1975 on Tea Production in Sri Lanka." *Staff Studies* 10(1):54–84. Central Bank of Ceylon.

Fisk, E. K., and H. Osman-Rani. 1982. *The Political Economy of Malaysia*. Kuala Lumpur: Oxford University Press.

Foster, P. J. 1966. "The Vocational School Fallacy in Development Planning." In C. A. Anderson and M. S. Bowman, eds., *Education and Economic Development*. Chicago: Aldine.

Galenson, Alice. 1980. "Agriculture and Rural Poverty." In Kevin Young, Willem Bussink, and Parvez Hassan, eds., *Malaysia: Growth and Equity in a Multiracial Society*. Baltimore: Johns Hopkins University Press.

Gates, W. B., T. J. Goering, and D. H. Keare. 1967. "The Role of Land in the Economic Development of West Malaysia." Processed.

Gavan, J. D., and I. S. Chandrasekera. 1979. *The Impact of Public Foodgrain Distribution on Food Consumption and Welfare in Sri Lanka*. Research Report 13. Washington, D.C.: International Food Policy Research Institute.

Gibbon, Edward. 1909. *The Decline and Fall of the Roman Empire*. London: Methuen.

Gibbons, D. S. 1985. "Rural Development and the Political Process in Peninsular Malaysia Since Merdeka: An Overview." Center for Policy Research, University Sains Malaysia. Processed.

Glewwe, Paul, and Surjit Bhalla. 1987. "A Response to Comments by Graham Pyatt and Paul Isenman." *The World Bank Economic Review* 1(3):533–36.

Golay, F. H. 1969. "Malaya." In F. H. Golay, R. Anspach, M. R. P. Fanner, and E. B. Ayal, eds., *Underdevelopment and Economic Nationalism in Southeast Asia*. Ithaca: Cornell University Press.

Goldman, Richard. 1975. "Staple Food Self-Sufficiency and the Distributive Impact of Malaysian Rice Policy." *Food Research Institute Studies* 14(3):251–93.

Hanson, A. H. 1959. *Public Enterprise and Economic Development*. London: Routledge and Kegan Paul.

Harriss, J. C. 1984. "Social Organization and Irrigation: Ideology, Planning, and Practice in Sri Lanka's Settlement Schemes." In Tim Bayliss-Smith and Sudhir Wanmali, eds., *Understanding Green Revolutions*. Cambridge, U.K.: Cambridge University Press.

Al-Hassan, Ahmad, and Donald R. Hill. 1986. *Islamic Technology*. Cambridge, U.K.: Cambridge University Press.

Hewavitharana, B. 1980. "New Patterns and Strategies of Development for Sri Lanka." *Economic Bulletin for Asia and the Pacific* 31(1):20–45.

Hicks, J. R. 1979. *Causality in Economics*. Oxford: Blackwells.

Hirschman, A. O. 1958. *The Strategy of Economic Development*. New Haven: Yale University Press.

Hoerr, O. D. 1973. "Education, Income, and Equity in Malaysia." *Economic Development and Cultural Change* 21(2):247–73.

Hoffmann, Lutz. 1973. "Import Substitution–Export Expansion and Growth in an Open Developing Economy: The Case of West Malaysia." *Weltwirtschaftliches Archiv* 109(3):452–75.

Hoffmann, Lutz, and T. N. Tan. 1973. "Patterns of Growth and Structural Change in West Malaysia's Manufacturing Industry, 1959–1986." In D. Lim, ed., *Readings on Malaysian Economic Development*. Kuala Lumpur: Oxford University Press.

Ikemoto, Yukio. 1985. "Income Distribution in Malaysia: 1957–1980." *Developing Economies* 23(4):347–67.

International Labour Office. 1971. *Programme of Action for Ceylon: Matching Employment Opportunities and Expectations.* Report and Technical Papers. Geneva.

International Bank for Reconstruction and Development (IBRD). 1953. *The Economic Development of Ceylon.* Baltimore, Md: Johns Hopkins University Press.

IMF (International Monetary Fund). Various issues. *International Financial Statistics.* Washington, D.C.

———. Annual. *International Financial Statistics Yearbook.* Washington, D.C.

Isenmam, Paul. 1980. "Basic Needs: The Case of Sri Lanka." *World Development* 8(3):237–58.

———. 1987. "A Comment on 'Growth and Equity in Developing Countries: A Reinterpretation of Sri Lankan Experience,' by Bhalla and Glewwe." *The World Bank Economic Review* 1(3):521–31.

Jain, Shail. 1975. *Size Distribution of Income: A Compilation of Data.* Washington, D.C.: World Bank.

Jayawardena, Lal. 1974. "Some Country Experience: Sri Lanka." In H. Chenery, M. Ahluwalia, C. Bell, J. Dulay, and R. Jolly, eds., *Redistribution with Growth.* London and New York: Oxford University Press.

Karunatilake, H. N. S. 1975. "The Impact of Welfare Services in Sri Lanka on the Economy." *Staff Studies* 5(1):1–16. Central Bank of Ceylon.

Kearney, R. N. 1967. *Communalism and Languages in the Politics of Ceylon.* Durham, N.C.: Duke University Press.

Kelman, Steven. 1981. *What Price Incentives?* Boston: Auburn House.

Kindleberger, C. P. 1984. *Multinational Excursion.* Cambridge, Mass.: MIT Press.

Kirzner, I. M. 1973. *Competition and Entrepreneurship.* Chicago: University of Chicago Press.

———. 1979. *Perception, Opportunity and Profit.* Chicago: University of Chicago Press.

Knight, F. H. 1935. *The Ethics of Competition and Other Essays.* Chicago: University of Chicago Press.

Kravis, I. B., Alan Heston, and Robert Summers. 1982. *World Product and Income: International Comparisons of Real GDP.* Baltimore and London: Johns Hopkins University Press.

Kua Kia Soong. 1983. "Why Look East?" In Y. Jomo, ed., *The Sun Also Sets: Lessons in Looking East.* Petaling Jaya: Institute for Social Analysis.

Lal, Deepak. 1987. "The Political Economy of Economic Liberalization." *The World Bank Economic Review* 1(2):273–99.

Lee, Eddy, ed. 1984. *Export Processing Zones and Industrial Employment in Asia.* Bangkok: International Labour Organization.

Leibenstein, Harvey. 1968. "Entrepreneurship and Development." *American Economic Review (Papers and Proceedings)* 58(2):72–83.

Levy, Brian. 1985. "Foreign Aid in the Making of Economic Policy in Sri Lanka." Williams College, Williamstown, Mass. Processed.

Lewis, W. A. 1955. *The Theory of Economic Growth.* London: Allen and Unwin.

Lim, David. 1973. *Economic Growth and Development in West Malaysia.* Kuala Lumpur: Oxford University Press.

Lim, Y. 1968. "Trade and Growth: The Case of Ceylon." *Economic Development and Cultural Change* 16:245–60.

Little, I. M. D. 1957. *A Critique of Welfare Economics,* 2nd ed. Oxford: Clarendon Press.

Little, I. M. D., and D. G. Tipping. 1972. *A Social Cost Benefit Analysis of the Kuali Oil Palm Estate: West Malaysia.* Paris: Organisation of Economic Co-operation and Development.

Mahathir bin Mohamad. 1984. "Mid-Term Review of the Fourth Malaysia Plan 1981–85." Speech on the Mid-Term Review of the Fourth Malaysia Plan in the Dewan Rakyat, March 29, Kuala Lumpur.

———. 1984. *The Challenge.* Kuala Lumpur: Pelanduk.

Mair, L. 1984. *Anthropology and Development.* London: Macmillan.

Malaya. 1956. *Report of the Education Committee.* Kuala Lumpur: Government Press.

Malaysia, Government of. Department of Statistics. 1960. *1957 Population Census of the Federation of Malaysia.* Report 14. Kuala Lumpur: Government Press.

———. 1963. *National Accounts of the States of Malaya, 1955–61.* Kuala Lumpur: Government Press.

———. 1970. *Post-Enumeration Survey.* Kuala Lumpur: Government Press.

———. 1977. *Agricultural Census.* Kuala Lumpur: Government Press.

———. 1980a. *Labor Force Survey.* Kuala Lumpur: Government Press.

———. 1980b. *Population and Housing Census.* Kuala Lumpur: Government Press.

———. 1985. *Ownership Survey of Limited Companies.* Kuala Lumpur: Government Press.

———. Annual a. *Household Budget Survey.* Kuala Lumpur: Government Press.

———. Annual b. *Household Income Survey.* Kuala Lumpur: Government Press.

———. Annual c. *Preliminary Figures of External Trade.* Kuala Lumpur. Government Press.

Malaysia, Government of. Economic Planning Unit. 1965. *The First Malaysia Plan.* Kuala Lumpur: Government Press.

———. 1970. *Second Malaysia Plan, 1971–75.* Kuala Lumpur: Government Press.

———. 1973. *Mid-term Review of the Second Malaysia Plan.* Kuala Lumpur: Government Press.

———. 1975. *Guidelines on Privatization.* Kuala Lumpur: Jabatan Percetakan Negara.

————. 1976. *The Third Malaysia Plan, 1976–80.* Kuala Lumpur: Government Press.

————. 1979. *Mid-term Review of the Third Malaysia Plan 1976–80.* Kuala Lumpur: Government Press.

————. 1980. *The Fourth Malaysia Plan, 1981–85.* Kuala Lumpur: Government Press.

————. 1984. *Mid-term Review of the Fourth Malaysia Plan, 1981–85.* Kuala Lumpur: Government Press.

————. 1986. *Fifth Malaysia Plan, 1986–90.* Kuala Lumpur: Government Press.

Malaysia, Government of. Ministry of Finance. Annual. *Economic Report.* Kuala Lumpur: Government Press.

Malaysia Industrial Development Authority. 1987. *Malaysia Investment in the Manufacturing Sector: Policies Incentives and Procedures.* Kuala Lumpur: Inventra Print Sdn. Bhd.

Mason, E. S., and R. E. Asher. 1973. *The World Bank since Bretton Woods.* Washington, D.C.: Brookings Institution.

McPherson, M. S. 1983. "Want Formation, Morality, and Some Interpretive Aspects of Economic Inquiry." In N. Hann, R. N. Belleh, P. Rabinow, and W. M. Sullivan, eds., *Social Science as Moral Inquiry.* New York: Columbia University Press.

Meermen, Jacob. 1979. *Public Expenditure in Malaysia.* New York: Oxford University Press.

Metcalf, D. H. 1985. *The Economics of Vocational Training: Past Evidence and Future Evaluations.* World Bank Staff Working Paper 713. Washington, D.C.

Morris, Morris David. 1979. *Measuring the Condition of the World's Poor: The Physical Quality of Life Index.* Oxford: Pergamon.

Muzaffar, Chandra. 1987. *Islamic Resurgence in Malaysia.* Petaling Jaya: Penerbit Fajar Bakti Sdn. Bhd.

Myint, Hla. 1971. *Economic Theory and the Underdeveloped Countries.* London: Oxford University Press.

————. 1972. *Southeast Asia's Economy.* New York: Praeger.

Nagata, Judith. 1979. *Malaysian Mosaic.* Vancouver: University of British Columbia Press.

————. 1980. "Religious Ideology and Social Change: The Islamic Revival in Malaysia." *Pacific Affairs* 53(3):405–39.

————. 1984. *The Reflowering of Malaysia Islam.* Vancouver: University of British Columbia Press.

Naipul, V. S. 1977. *India: A Wounded Civilization.* New York: Knopf.

National Operations Council. 1969. *The May Tragedy: A Report.* Kuala Lumpur: Government Press.

National Planning Council. 1959a. *Papers by Visiting Economists.* Colombo: Government Press.

————. 1959b. *The Ten-Year Plan.* Colombo: Government Press.

Ness, G. D. 1967. *Bureaucracy and Rural Development in Malaysia.* Berkeley: University of California Press.

Nevitte, Neil, and Charles H. Kennedy, eds. 1986. *Ethnic Preference and Public Policy in Developing States.* Boulder, Colo.: Lynne Rienner.

Oliver, H. M., Jr. 1957. *Economic Opinion and Policy in Ceylon.* Durham, N.C.: Duke University Press.

Peebles, Patrick. 1982. *Sri Lanka: A Handbook of Historical Statistics.* Boston: G. K. Hall.

Peiris, G. H. 1978. "Land Reform and Agrarian Change in Sri Lanka." *Modern Asian Studies* 12(4):611–28.

Popone, Oliver. 1980. "Malay Entrepreneurs: An Analysis of the Social Background, Careers and Attitudes of Leading Malay Businessmen." Ph.D. thesis, London School of Economics.

Power, J. H. 1971. "The Structure of Protection in West Malaysia." In Bela Balassa, ed., *The Structure of Protection in Developing Countries.* Baltimore: Johns Hopkins University Press.

Psacharopoulos, George. 1980. *Higher Education in Developing Countries: A Cost-Benefit Analysis.* Washington, D.C.: World Bank.

Psacharopoulos, George, and Maureen Woodhall. 1985. *Education for Development: An Analysis of Investment Choices.* New York and Oxford: Oxford University Press.

Pyatt, Graham. 1987. "A Comment on 'Growth and Equity in Developing Countries: A Reinterpretation of Sri Lankan Experience,' by Bhalla and Glewwe." *The World Bank Economic Review* 1(3):515–20.

Pyatt, Graham, and Alan Roe. 1977. *Social Accounting for Development Planning with Special Reference to Sri Lanka.* Cambridge, U.K.: Cambridge University Press.

Ratnam, K. J., and R. S. Milne. 1970. "The 1969 Parliamentary Election in West Malaysia." *Pacific Affairs* 43(2):203–26.

Richards, P. J. 1971. *Employment and Unemployment in Ceylon.* Paris: Organisation for Economic Co-operation and Development.

Richards, P. J., and Wilbert Gooneratne. 1980. *Basic Needs, Poverty and Government Policies in Sri Lanka.* Geneva: International Labour Office.

Roe, Alan R. 1982. "High Interest Rates: A New Conventional Wisdom for Development Policy? Some Conclusions from Sri Lanka Experience." *World Development* 10(3):211–22.

Roff, William A. 1967. *Malay Nationalism.* Singapore: University of Malaya Press.

Rogowski, Ronald J. 1983. "Structure, Growth and Power: Three Rationalist Accounts." *International Organization* 37(4):713–38.

Salmen, L. F. 1987. *Listen to the People: Participant-Observer Evaluation of Development Projects.* New York: Oxford University Press.

Samaraweera, Vijaya. 1981. "Land, Labour, Capital, and Sectional Interest in the National Politics of Sri Lanka." *Modern Asian Studies* 15(1):127–62.

Sanderatne, Nimal. 1974. "Agricultural Productivity Considerations of the Land Reform Law of 1972." *Staff Studies* 4(2):75–86. Central Bank of Ceylon.

———. 1980. "Institutionalizing Small Farm Credit: Performance and Problems for Sri Lanka." *Staff Studies* 10(2):85–103. Central Bank of Ceylon.

————. 1981. "A Profile of the Informal Rural Credit Market in the Mid-Seventies." *Staff Studies* 11(1):1–18. Central Bank of Ceylon.

Saravanamuttu, Jayaratnam. 1983. "The Look East Policy and Japanese Economic Penetration in Malaysia." In K. S. Jones, ed., *The Sun Also Sets: Lessons in Looking East.* Petaling Jaya: Institute for Social Analysis.

Scudder, Theyer. 1975. *The Ecology of the Gwembe Tonga.* Manchester University Press.

Sen, Amartya. 1981. "Public Action and the Quality of Life in Developing Countries." *Oxford Bulletin of Economics and Statistics* 43(4):287–320.

Shamsul, A. B. 1986. "The Politics of Poverty Eradication: The Implementation of Development Projects in a Malaysian Context." In Bruce Gale, ed., *Readings in Malaysian Politics.* Kuala Lumpur: Pelanduk.

Silcock, T. H., and U. A. Aziz. 1953. "Nationalism in Malaya." In W. L. Holland, ed., *Asian Nationalism and the West.* New York: Macmillan.

Snodgrass, D. R. 1966. *Ceylon: An Export Economy in Transition.* Homewood, Ill.: Richard D. Irwin.

————. 1980. *Inequality and Economic Development in Malaysia.* Kuala Lumpur: Oxford University Press.

Soenarno, D. S. R., and Z. A. Yusof. 1985. "The Experience of Malaysia Privatization Policies, Methods and Procedures." Papers presented and a summary of the proceedings, Asian Development Bank Conference, Manila.

Solow, R. M. 1984. "Mr. Hicks and the Classics." *Oxford Economics Papers* 36: 13–25.

Sri Lanka. 1971. *The Five-Year Plan, 1972–76.* Colombo.

Sri Lanka, Government of. Ministry of Finance. 1969. *Economic and Social Progress, 1965–69.* Colombo.

————. Ministry of Finance. 1986. *Economic Report, 1986–87.* Kuala Lumpur: National Printing Department.

————. Ministry of Industries and Scientific Affairs. 1971a. *Industrial Policy Statement.* Colombo.

————. Ministry of Industries and Scientific Affairs. 1971b. *A New Industrial Policy.* Colombo.

————. Ministry of Planning and Economic Affairs. 1965. *The Development Programme, 1966–77.* Colombo.

————. Ministry of Planning and Economic Affairs. 1966. *Government Policy on Private Foreign Investment.* Colombo.

————. Planning Secretariat. 1955. *Six-Year Development Programme of Investment 1954/55 to 1959/60.* Colombo.

Staniland, Martin. 1985. *What Is Political Economy: A Study of Social Theory and Underdevelopment.* New Haven: Yale University Press.

Stern, J. J. 1984. "Liberalization in Sri Lanka: A Preliminary Assessment." Processed.

Summers, Robert, and Alan Heston. 1984. "Improved International Comparisons of Real Product and Its Composition, 1950–80." *The Review of Income and Wealth* 30(June):207–62.

Tan, Tat Wai. 1982. *Income Distribution and Determination in West Malaysia.* Kuala Lumpur: Oxford University Press.

Thompson, D. L., and D. Ronen, eds. 1986. *Ethnicity, Politics, and Development.* Boulder, Colo.: Lynne Rienner.

Thorbecke, Erik, and Jan Svejnar. 1987. *Economic Policies and Agricultural Performance in Sri Lanka 1960–84.* Paris: Organisation for Economic Co-operation and Development.

Tocqueville, Alexis de. 1856. *The Old Regime and the Revolution.* New York: Harper.

UNICEF-Colombo. 1958. *Sri Lanka: The Social Impact of Economic Policies during the Last Decade.* Colombo.

UNIDO (United Nations Industrial Development Organisation). 1985. "Overview of the Industrial Master Plan." *Medium- and Long-Term Industrial Master Plan 1986–1995.* Vol.1, part 1. Kuala Lumpur.

United Nations. 1976. *Population of Sri Lanka.* Bangkok: United Nations.

Vasil, R. K. 1971. *Politics in a Plural Society: A Study of Non-communal Political Parties in West Malaysia.* London: Oxford University Press.

Weerawardana, I. D. S., and M. I. Weerawardana. 1956. *Ceylon and Her Citizens.* Madras: Oxford University Press.

Wijesinghe, M. E. 1981. *Sri Lanka's Development Thrust.* Colombo: Atkin Spence.

Wilson, A. J. 1972. "Ceylon: The People's Liberation Front and the 'Revolution' that Failed." From *Pacific Communities.* Center for Developing Area Studies. Reprint series. McGill University, Montreal.

———. 1974. *Politics in Sri Lanka, 1947–1973.* New York: St. Martin's Press.

Winston, G. C. 1974. "The Theory of Capital Utilization and Idleness." *Journal of Economic Literature* 12(4):1301–20.

World Bank. 1963. "*Report on the Economic Aspects of Malaysia.*" Washington, D.C. Processed.

———. 1980, 1983, 1987. *World Tables.* Baltimore: Johns Hopkins University Press.

———. Annual. *World Development Report.* New York: Oxford University Press.

Wriggins, W. H. 1960. *Ceylon: Dilemmas of a New Nation.* Princeton, N.J.: Princeton University Press.

Young, Kevin, Willem Bussink, and Parvez Hasan. 1980. *Malaysia: Growth and Equity in a Multiracial Society.* Baltimore: Johns Hopkins University Press.

Index

(Page numbers in italics indicate material in figures or tables; years are in italics to distinguish them from page numbers.)

Advisors: limitations of outside, 12, 137–38; rice rationing program (Sri Lanka) and outside, 113

Agricultural extension programs, 84

Agriculture in Malaysia, 276–83; in *1960*, 189–90; in the *1980*s, 209, 312–13

Agriculture in Sri Lanka, 57, *58–59*, 60–62, 103–08; difficulties in (*1970–77*), 120–26; *1977–85*, 155–57; slow growth of nonpaddy field crops and, 106. *See also names of specific crops*

Aid, shift from program to project (Sri Lanka), 137–38

Balance of payments in Malaysia, 305

Balance of payments in Sri Lanka: between *1977–85*, 153–55; precarious (in *1970*s), 120; problem with (in *1960*s), 98, 99, 112; strength of (in *1950*s), 31

Bandaranaike, Mrs. S. W. R. D., 73, 119

Bandaranaike, S. W. R. D., 72; formation of SLFP by, 77

Benefit-cost analysis, Malaysian drainage and irrigation projects and, 240–41

British: domination of commerce in Sri Lanka, 22; granting of self-government to Sri Lanka (*1931*), 27; influence on education in Malaysia, 183; influence on Sri Lankan political leaders, 28; legacy of, 329; in Malaysia, 175–82; primary concern of (in Malaysia), 233

Buddism in Sri Lanka, 23, 24, 42, 86; commitment to social welfare and, 26; entrepreneurship and, 132; student insurrection of *1971* in Sri Lanka and, 140

Budget deficit in Sri Lanka, 55

Buffalos as agricultural power (Sri Lanka), 105

Bumiputera: competencies of, 289; defined, 225; demand and supply of labor of, 288–90; education and, 288–89; entrepreneurship and ownership of businesses and, *286*, 287; equity and, 302; preferential treatment for, 286; wealth ownership and NEP and, 225, 271, 273. *See also* Malays

Bureaucracies, social roles of, 352

Capital: expenditures in Sri Lanka for education and health services, 167, 168; formation, 135, 338; imports of (Sri Lanka), 56, 135; -labor and capital-output ratios (Sri Lanka), 63

Cardamon crop, 122

Caste systems (Sri Lanka), 24

Ceylon, 4

Chinese in Malaysia, 299–302; in agriculture, 180; below poverty line, 197; comparative income of, 194; education of, 183; employment of, 284–86; family system among, 185; in industry, 177, 257–58; ownership of shares of companies by, 225, 290–94; relocated from rural villages to urban areas, 182; as traders, 209

The complete backlist of publications from the World Bank is shown
in the annual *Index of Publications*, which contains an alphabetical title
list and indexes of subjects, authors, and countries and regions. The
latest edition is available free of charge from Publications Distribution
Unit, Office of the Publisher, The World Bank, 1818 H Street, N.W.,
Washington, D.C. 20433, U.S.A., or from Publications, The World
Bank, 66, avenue d'Iéna, 75116 Paris, France.